THE OTHER SIDES OF REALITY

Myths, Visions and Fantasies

Walter M. Cummins
Martin Green
Fairleigh Dickinson University

Margaret Verhulst
Mars Hill College

BOYD & FRASER PUBLISHING COMPANY

308 Locust Street, San Francisco, California 94118

Walter M. Cummins, Martin Green and Margaret Verhulst: THE OTHER SIDES OF REALITY Copyright © 1972 by Boyd & Fraser Publishing Company. All rights reserved.

Library of Congress Catalog Card Number: 75–182677

ISBN:0–87835–038–1

Grateful acknowledgement is made to the following publishers and individuals for permission to reprint material which is in copyright, or of which they are the authorized publishers:

MARGARET WALKER ALEXANDER: For "October Journey" by Margaret Walker. By permission of the author.

ALFRED A. KNOPF, INC.: For "Dream Variation." Copyright 1926 by Alfred A. Knopf, Inc. and renewed 1954 by Langston Hughes. Reprinted from SELECTED POEMS, by Langston Hughes, by permission of the publisher.

AMERICAN FOLKLORE SOCIETY: For "Tailypo." Reprinted with permission of the American Folklore Society from: John Harrington Cox, "Negro Tales from West Virginia," *Journal of American Folklore* Number 47 (1934), pp. 341-342.

THE BELOIT POETRY JOURNAL: For "German," by William Zander. Reprinted with permission from *The Beloit Poetry Journal,* Volume 18, Number 3, Spring, 1968.

THE CONDÉ NAST PUBLICATIONS, INC.: For "They Bite" by Anthony Boucher. Reprinted from UNKNOWN WORLDS; Copyright © 1943, 1971 by William A. P. White.

THOMAS Y. CROWELL COMPANY, INC.: For "How Death Came Into the World," a Modoc Indian legend told to Alice Marriott by Mary Chiloquin. From *American Indian Mythology,* by Alice Marriott and Carol K. Rachlin. Copyright © 1968 by Alice K. Marriott and Carol K. Rachlin. Thomas Y. Crowell Company, publishers.

CROWN PUBLISHERS, INC.: For "Lacandon Creation Myth" by Howard Cline and for "A Story of the Underworld," a Tzeltal Indian story recorded by Anne Chapman in Chiapas. Taken from A TREASURY OF MEXICAN FOLKWAYS by Frances Toor. Copyright, 1947, by Crown Publishers, Inc. Used by permission of Crown Publishers, Inc.

DOUBLEDAY & COMPANY, INC.: For "Night-Sea Journey" by John Barth. Copyright © 1966 by John Barth. From the book LOST IN THE FUNHOUSE by John Barth. Reprinted by permission of Doubleday & Company, Inc.

FARRAR, STRAUS & GIROUX, INC.: For "Paraguay" by Donald Barthelme. Reprinted with the permission of Farrar, Straus & Giroux, Inc. from CITY LIFE by Donald Barthelme, copyright © 1969, 1970 by Donald Barthelme. Also, for "Judgment Day" by Flannery O'Connor, copyright © 1956, 1957, 1958, 1960, 1961, 1962, 1964, 1965 by the Estate of Mary Flannery O'Connor.

HARCOURT BRACE JOVANOVICH, INC.: For "Blood, Sea" by Italo Calvo. From T ZERO by Italo Calvino, copyright © 1967 by Giulio Einaudi editore s.p.a., Torino; English translation copyright © 1969 by Harcourt Brace Jovanovich, Inc. and reprinted with their permission.

HOUGHTON MIFFLIN COMPANY: For "The End of the World" by Archibald MacLeish. From COLLECTED POEMS 1917–1952 by Archibald MacLeish. Published by Houghton Mifflin and used with their permission.

JOHN C. HURSTON: For "Anatol Pierre" copyright by Zora Neale Hurston, 1935. Reprinted by permission of John C. Hurston.

CONTENTS

Part I: Creation

Part II: Transformation

Part III: Bewitchment and Enchantment

Part IV: The Other

Part V: Strange Journeys

Part VI: Death and Resurrection

Part VII: Apocalypse

PREFACE

ONE OF THE MOST significant influences of the cultural upheaval which began in the mid 1960's is the attempt to transcend the limitations of our traditional definition of reality. In fiction, film, music, and the visual arts, many important recent works have abandoned previous expectations about form and content in their search for imaginative liberation. Historically, psychologically, and anthropologically, civilizations based on values totally different from our own are being studied with new interest and enthusiasm. The subject of myth itself is pursued with a new seriousness.

This collection contains works which offer a variety of understandings of reality and which directly or implicitly challenge the perspective of material realism which has dominated in Western society for several centuries.

Rather than to develop an exclusive focus on contemporary statements, a deliberate attempt was made to choose material from periods throughout history, going back to the literature of the ancient world. Not only is this material valuable for its own merit, but it also demonstrates a broad perspective in which to place our current assumptions about reality. It allows for cultural and historical comparison as well.

Works from many civilizations are included in the collection: American Indian myths; Japanese legend; seventeenth century, romantic, and modern English and American stories and poems as well as Mexican legends and voodoo tales. A variety of genres is represented, including poems, short stories, myths, fairy tales, and journals. The authors include the anonymous creators of antiquity, the little-known, and the major writers of Western literature, such as Blake, Andersen, Hawthorne, Poe, Whitman, and Yeats. The works themselves are a mixture of the famous and the unfamiliar, the old and the new. Among the recent or contemporary writers included are Barth, Barthelme, and O'Connor. It is hoped that the unfamiliar works will demonstrate their own value, and that the famous selections will yield fresh meanings through this new context.

The collection is organized thematically instead of by genre or chronology because it was felt that these themes are more fundamental to an exploration of the other sides of reality. They are the subjects basic to myth, religion, psychology, and the creative imagination. Creation, Transformation, Bewitchment and Enchantment, The Other, Strange Journeys, Death and Resurrection, and Apocalypse.

INTRODUCTION

IN ONE SENSE, this book is a collection of and about fantasy. That key term—"fantasy"—is at the heart of its conception and is also the source of its problem—yours too as readers.

In our time, until recently, the word has suffered from pejorative overtones, and he who uses it is apologetic because it refers to a realm inferior to reality. We tend to associate fantasy with a bizarre makebelieve, escape, delusion, an instability of the imagination. Its opposite, reality, is substantially here and now. We can know it and touch it and see it in clear outlines; it has a solid ring, like the slamming of a car door.

Cars are reality. Fantasy is a fiery chariot vaulting through the heavens. Houses are reality. Fantasy is an enchanted castle sparkling at the bottom of the sea. People are reality. Fantasy is elves and demons and gliding wraiths of the dead.

In another sense, the actions, emotions, and ideas contained in this book are true, as true as the alarm clock that wakes us every morning. But just where this truth lies is a dilemma. Perhaps it is physical or philosophical or spiritual or psychological.

One man's fantasy is another man's reality.

This generalization most likely has a limited validity for you and the people around you on this day. Probably, all agree that airplanes fly because they fulfill the technical requirements of the complex laws of aerodynamics, not because invisible fairies are holding onto the wings. Yet between you and humans of other ages and other cultures this generalization cannot be denied: much of what you will read as mere fantasy has been and is being accepted by others as literal reality. It is all a matter of belief.

Americans and other contemporary inhabitants of the western world tend to be quite skeptical about anything they cannot hold, measure, and analyze, anything they cannot break down into component parts and whose laws of functioning they cannot calculate. We have no patience with magic.

2

We live in the most secular age mankind has ever known, focusing on the temporal here and now, ignoring the spiritual again and forever.

To satisfy our rational wants, we even have the statistics to prove this is so. Sociologists and sociological theologians have polled and charted. The evidence is not so much in the decline of church attendance as in what those attending believe. For example, not many accept the notion of hell; few spend much time thinking about heaven.

Of course, it might be argued that historical and anthropological information shows that other peoples supposedly noted for their religious consciousness also devoted a great deal of time and effort to the immediate things surrounding them. They spent long hours contriving clothing and shelter to protect them and sowing seeds and tending animals to sustain them. But they also believed in another realm, a supernatural realm existing simultaneously with the natural, which gave purpose and meaning to a life in time and nature.

On the other hand, we tend to seek our gratifications in the reward of things, and we glory in the triumph of our enlightenment over the past ages of superstition. A two-car garage has become much more tangible than an eternity of bliss, pro football on color television much more thrilling than the prospect of an angelic visitation.

3

How did we get this way, so different in values and desires from mankind before us? How did the scope of our reality come to be circumscribed by the limits of rational and scientific knowledge?

The answers would obviously require a full study of the development of western civilization, beginning with an investigation of the special attributes of the classical Greek mind, which was so vital in determining the special inclinations of our intelligence, the kinds of problems we consider important and how we go about solving them.

But some quick speculations can be made. For one thing, western man since the Renaissance has succeeded in dealing with *things* far more than any other peoples. Not only has he been able to explore and observe and understand things, he has been able to manipulate them and make them work for him. And things beget other things until we have become surrounded and obsessed by things.

Clearly, one major fact of western civilization since the Renaissance has been the steady decline of the social, political, and psychological importance of religion and the rise of science and technology in its place.

Perhaps the shift happened because we were so very successful with things and could find satisfaction and security in the verifiable stability of facts. We developed a mentality of "show me" and "prove it to me." And while we could actually observe the stars through telescopes and chart their course with mathematical precision, no man had ever visited heaven or hell, unless he was like Dante—a visitor in his imagination. But the imagination itself was becoming suspect, thought unreliable, frivilously subjective rather than objective.

In its conflicts with science, religion—the supernatural—lost confrontation after confrontation to the natural. The earth was not the center of the universe, surrounded by the moon, the planets, the sun, the hierarchies of angels, and ultimately God in heaven. The earth turned out to be—proof certified—just one small planet in one small solar system overwhelmed by infinity. The earth was not created in 4004 B.C. as one Anglican bishop had claimed, citing the evidence of the Bible. In the early 19th century geologists proved it was many million years old. Man was not created as a rational creature just like us on the sixth day; Charles Darwin demonstrated a long and gradual evolutionary process.

Religion promised ill-fed, ill-housed, miserable man bliss in another existence. But technology was providing comforts for the millions, so much so that the average middleclass American of today enjoys much more ease and convenience than the greatest monarchs of a few centuries ago; we have flush toilets, central heating, airconditioning, and much more. Religion asks us to accept an afterlife on faith. Technology got us to the moon; we saw it on television.

By the late 19th century Friedrich Nietzsche could make his famous declaration: "God is dead." By this he meant not a literal corpse, but that religious values and religious expectations were defunct; man was in charge to shape his own destiny in the natural realm. No other realm mattered.

Theology and metaphysics and other speculations into the unseen became mocked if taken seriously, tolerated if taken as diverting entertainments: that is, as fantasies.

4

Literature, as a reflection of culture, followed the same pattern. Except for an occasional dissident movement like Romanticism, its dominant tendency became the pursuit of realism. The titillation of makebelieve was permitted under the name of "romance" and denied true relationship to real life.

Most of us tend to accept the term "realism" at face value and assume that writers, having acquired more worldly sophistication, were finally becoming able to present authentic reality. Perhaps a more valid observation is not that writers had grown more sensible and perceptive, but that the conception of what constituted reality was changing and that literature was sensitive to the process. The view of reality assumed by the Christian Middle Ages—the starting point of this process—is totally different from that of modern realism.

Erich Auerbach, author of *Mimesis: The Representation of Reality in Western Literature,* defines the characteristics of the Medieval view:

In this conception, an occurrence on earth signified not only itself but at the same time another, which it predicts or confirms, without prejudice to the power of its concrete reality here and now. The connection between occurrences is not regarded as primarily a chronological or causal development but as a oneness within the divine plan, of which all occurrences are parts and reflections. Their direct earthly connection is of secondary importance, and often their interpretation can altogether dispense with any knowledge of it.

This conception of mutual and simultaneous, yet integral, reality, both seen and unseen, in its broadest sense applies to more than just Medieval Christianity, but to all outlooks which have created works we now dismiss as myth and fantasy.

Probably no literary form is more indicative of the modern view of reality than the novel. Significantly, it originated in the early eighteenth century with the social rise of the bourgeoisie and developed with the industrial revolution, which in itself has been a triumph of middle class ingenuity. Not surprisingly, the early novelists, unhappy with the very notion of fiction as untruth, tried to pretend their stories were factual; for example, the publication of a real diary or a discovered packet of letters.

The critic George Steiner says that the novel is "the mirror which the imagination, in its vein of reason, held up to empirical reality." The novel, particularly the European novel of the 18th and 19th centuries, was "secular in outlook, rational in method, and social in context." In fact, Steiner's description of the characteristics of the novel can stand as a description of the total view of reality prevalent in modern Western Civilization:

> The main current of the Western novel is prosaic, in the exact rather than the pejorative sense. In it neither Milton's Satan winging through the immensities of chaos nor the Weird Sisters, from *Macbeth,* sailing to Aleppo in their sieve, are really at home. Windmills are no longer giants, but windmills. In exchange, fiction will tell us how windmills are built, what they earn, and precisely how they sound on a gusty night. For it is the genius of the novel to describe, analyze, explore, and accumulate the data of actuality and introspection.
>
> In rejecting the mythical and the preternatural . . . the modern novel had broken with the essential world view of epic and tragedy. It had claimed for its own what we might call

THE OTHER SIDES OF REALITY

the kingdom of this world. It is the vast kingdom of human psychology perceived through reason and of human behavior in a social context.

Paradoxically, while man's material control has increased, the image of man in the literature of modern realism has diminished. No longer do we have heroic themes—man in saintly, kingly, or tragic grandeur, a creature of great significance in the universal scheme. Rather the stress has been on man limited and oppressed by the petty details and trivial dilemmas surrounding his life. Instead of heroes, we have antiheroes. Instead of magnificence, we have nagging cares. In terms of the products of the literary imagination, knowledge has not meant power.

Even more than in serious literature, the assumptions of modern realism have overwhelmed our popular fictions—bestsellers, movies, television. Crises in love and marriage, comic and dramatic, and variations of cops-and-robbers dominate. Aside from occasional supernatural horror shows, the fantasy is usually a gimmick—unbottled genies, flying nuns, and bewitched housewives. Yet despite their unusual attributes, these characters all want desperately to enjoy middleclass normality like the rest of us.

The most extreme fantasy is reserved for commercials, which are filled with the magic of fairy tale transformations. White knights dazzle our clothes clean with the point of a phallic lance; tornadoes swirl out of bottles; cartoon dwarfs are exposed as the source of our stomach cramps. And we are constantly told that—miracle of miracles!—magic is for sale to all of us at our nearest supermarket. We have only to buy and all powers are ours. But what powers? Note that the rewards of such magic are more sex appeal, cleaner woodwork, and better gas mileage.

5

Although dominant, the prosaic conception of modern realism has not gone unchallenged. In fact, we are now living in one of the most serious periods of challenge, one which many observers believe will ultimately emerge in a new vision of reality much closer to the outlook which has traditionally obtained in human civilizations. Throughout poetry, religion, films, music, psychology, and anthropology, a call has gone out to return a sense of the magical and the mysterious and the holy to physical nature. For many, the smugness of modern man is gone; they confess that we did not know as much as we thought we did.

Albert Camus, for one, expresses this realization that scientific knowledge has not actually penetrated the truths of the universe. Instead, more than ever before, 20th century man feels himself a stranger alienated and terrified and ignorant in a world he cannot comprehend:

Yet all the knowledge on earth will give me nothing to assure me that this world is mine. You describe it to me and
you teach me to classify it. You enumerate its laws and in
my thirst for knowledge I admit that they are true. You take
apart its mechanism and my hope increases. At the final
stage you teach me that this wondrous and multi-colored
universe can be reduced to the electron. . . . You explain this
world to me with an image. I realize then that you have been
reduced to poetry; I shall never know. . . . So that science that
was to teach me everything ends up in a hypothesis, that
lucidity flounders in metaphor, that uncertainty is resolved
in a work of art. What need had I of so many efforts? The soft
lines of these hills and the hand of evening on this troubled
heart teach me much more. I have returned to my beginning.

Camus' denial of modern realism leaves him in despair that truth can
ever be known; he reacts as a man betrayed by a false hope and condemned never to know his place in the universal scheme. More recent
critics hold more hope that poetry and myth can tell us who we are and
where we belong.

An earlier reaction to prosaic reality is equally illuminating. It began in the late 18th century with the movement we call Romanticism,
significantly at a time when cities and industrialization were expand-
ing rapidly throughout Western Europe. From a more intellectual
viewpoint, the reaction was a protest against the mechanistic clock-
work universe resulting from the laws of Newtonian physics.

The thrust of this protest is stated succinctly in a stanza by William
Blake:

The Atoms of Democritus
And Newton's Particles of light
Are sands upon the Red Sea shore,
Where Israel's tents do shine so bright.

That is, reality is not only matter. Vision illuminates matter; nature
abstracted is nature without meaning. Another Blakean stanza celebrates the imagination:

To see a World in a Grain of Sand
And a Heaven in a Wild Flower,
Hold Infinity in the palm of your hand
And Eternity in an hour.

Writing of William Wordsworth in *Science and the Modern World*,
mathematician–philosopher Alfred North Whitehead probes the cause

xiv   THE OTHER SIDES OF REALITY

of the poet's allegation that the scientific method is eluded by the vital qualities of nature:

> His theme is nature *insolido,* that is to say, he dwells on that mysterious presence of surrounding things, which imposes itself on any separate element that we set up as individual for its own sake. He always grasps the whole of nature as involved in the tonality of the particular instance. . . . [He bears] witness that nature cannot be divorced from its aesthetic values, and that these values arise from the culmination, in some sense, of the brooding presence of the whole on to its various parts.

For Wordsworth and the other Romantics this whole was much more than the totality of material substance. Communion with nature was not, as is commonly thought, an end in itself, but part of the larger goal of penetrating to an unseen realm behind nature, the source of the true magic of existence. One of Wordsworth's phrases for this quest is "to see into the heart of things."

Romanticism triumphed only artistically; it had little influence upon events, probably because it was a tendency counter to the dominant movement of Western Civilization. The fate of the current protest against the material conception of reality is less certain. Few of us expect the future to resemble the present. The question is whether the new impulse to myth and fantasy is a harbinger of times to come, a rudimentary expression of a new spirituality, or the last gasp of a romantic sentimentality before new mechanisms and new materials sweep us off.

6

As indicated above, fantasy has negative connotations for most of us and the linking of myth and fantasy tends to debase myth even more, suggesting that fantasy is just an intended fictional lie while myths were widespread delusions actually believed in the ignorance of primitive man. More thought indicates that myth, and therefore fantasy, cannot be dismissed so easily.

Here are two examples of myths:

> Zeus, the supreme god of Greek mythology, transformed into the shape of a swan, raped the human maiden Leda. One of the twin daughters of this union, Helen, the most beautiful of women, by leaving her husband Menelaus for the Trojan Paris, brought about a ten-year war which resulted in the destruction of the city of Troy.

* * *

Through divine conception, a human woman named Mary gave birth to a son whom men consider to be the Son of God and, at the same time, God Himself. Crucified for his teaching, He sacrificed Himself to redeem a mankind fallen in sin and brought to humanity hope of eternal salvation.

The first myth has not been believed for more than two thousand years; the second is still believed today, so much so that many people will take offense that the story has been called a myth. Yet the fact remains that the first is rejected only because few if any believe it ever happened, while the second is accepted because millions of people believe it did occur. In terms of rational criticism, they are equally farfetched. How could a god be transformed into a swan and mate with a mortal? How could one being logically save all mankind?

Both stories have in common at least three characteristics. They elevate a single event to a role of overwhelming importance and they offer an explanation for a long and complex sequence of events. More significantly, they supply a meaningful perspective to events by revealing a design behind human existence, a design worthy of the attentions of the greatest forces in the universe, and they make these forces tangible and comprehensible.

Clearly, the mythic perspective is quite different from the empirical one which dominates us. What are the values of myth? And what is the relationship of myth and fantasy?

7

Analytical thought fosters division and categorization; it distinguishes and groups to reveal structural and functional relationships. In addition to fragmenting the physical world, it makes man a being different in kind from the rest of substantial existence because man alone has the ability to control objects, either through literal force or through the power of speculation.

Albert Camus, in the passage quoted above, saw man as divorced from the rest of creation. The philosopher-psychologist Carl G. Jung, agreeing, assigns the goddess Reason—"our greatest and most tragic illusion"—the role of corespondent in this divorce:

Modern man does not understand how much his "rationalism" (which has destroyed his capacity to respond to numinous symbols and ideas) has put him at the mercy of the psychic "underworld." He has freed himself from "superstition" (or so he believes), but in the process he has lost his spiritual values to a positively dangerous degree. His moral and spiritual tradition has disintegrated, and he is now paying the price for this break-up in world-wide disorientation and dissociation.

Myth, on the other hand, relates and associates. It marries all creation and makes it one flesh and one mind and one soul. The primary partners in such a marriage, from the human outlook, are man and nature.

We call man whose perspective was mythic "primitive," and through the context of that word denigrate him as an inferior lacking adequate mental development to achieve analytical thought. A very different sort of evaluation is becoming prevalent today. Jung saw modern man as inferior in mentality, not superior. Many contemporary anthropologists, avoiding such an extreme comparison, believe that mythic man was a very sophisticated being who was not unable to grasp the empirical differences between things, but lived by a totally different conception of life and nature, one which stresses intensity of feeling, not logic, and dismisses differences of single forms as trivial against the fundamental unity and solidarity of all creation.

Mythic man did not separate the realm of nature and the realm of man. He did not regard all things outside himself as empty and inanimate objects to be measured, related, and calculated, but individual beings with life and will to be engaged in a reciprocal relationship as equals. The relationship of modern man to nature has been called one of I-It, while that of mythic man to nature is one of I-Thou.

The philosopher Ernst Cassirer, in *An Essay on Man,* stresses the emotionality which charges the natural world in the mythic view:

> The mythical world is, as it were, at a much more fluid and fluctuating stage than our theoretical world of things and properties, of substances and accidents. In order to grasp and to describe this difference we may say that what myth primarily perceives are not objective but *physiognomic* characters. Nature, in its empirical or scientific sense, may be defined as "the existence of things as far as it is determined by general laws." Such a "nature" does not exist for myths. The world of myth is a dramatic world—a world of actions, of forces, of conflicting powers. In every phenomenon of nature it sees the collision of these powers. Mythical perception is always impregnated with these emotional qualities. Whatever is seen or felt is surrounded by a special atmosphere—an atmosphere of joy or grief, of anguish, of excitement, of exultation and depression.

These powerful feeling-qualities in mythical perception must be regarded as basic elements of reality. Myth, for this point of view, restores drama and meaning and significance to all parts of the universe,
including the role of man. Events and beings depend upon one another
not merely in terms of mechanistic causes, but in vital living interac-
tions. Here the sacrifice of one being for the salvation of all others is
possible.

8

Fantasy is a second cousin to myth. The products of fantasy are conscious fictions in an age which can no longer believe in the myths
literally. Yet, in ignoring and transcending the limitations of the
material view of reality, its logic and its standards of normality, fantasy may offer a partial fulfillment of our human needs for myths.
However tentatively, however ironically, it may restore a sense of
magic and mystery to our existences.

Fantasy is a broad term. At one extreme it can refer to our entire
process of imagination, all the creations of our minds, all that is not
verified by concrete physical happenings. At the other extreme it
defines a limited subcategory of fictions populated by ghosts, demons,
time machines, talking plants and animals, and other distortions used
mainly to provide escapist excitement.

Of course, all the poems and stories in this book come under the first
extreme, a few of them under the second. But, more importantly, there
is a meaning of fantasy which includes works of spiritual, moral, and
psychological penetration which are able to suggest more about ultimate reality because they do not confine themselves within the narrow
standards of material reality. In this sense, they are fabrications only
according to these narrow standards. Essential to their fascination and
their meaning is the possibility that they may embody much more
truth than fiction.

9

Perhaps the relationship of myth and fantasy can be clarified by considering an intermediary creation—dreams. Obviously, much that is
dreamlike pervades both myth and fantasy, as made clear by Jung's
statements of the general characteristics of dreams:

> . . . a dream is quite unlike a story told by the conscious mind.
> . . . . Images that seem contradictory and ridiculous crowd in
> on the dreamer, the normal sense of time is lost, and com-

monplace things can assume a fascinating and threatening
aspect.... The images produced in dreams are much more
picturesque and vivid than the concepts and experiences
that are their waking counterparts.

Jung goes so far as to make dreams more important and more fundamental than myth and fantasy because he considers dreams to be the
source of both:

One cannot afford to be naïve in dealing with dreams. They
originate in a spirit that is not quite human, but is rather a
breath of nature—a spirit of the beautiful and generous as
well as of the cruel goddess. If we want to characterize this
spirit, we shall certainly get closer to it in the sphere of
ancient mythologies, of fables of the primeval forest, than in
the consciousness of modern man.

Central to Jung's entire theory of man is the assumption that waking
consciousness is a very narrow expression of the individual's being and
that the unconscious is a much larger realm. Dreams are therefore
symbolic communications of basic truths from the unconscious to the
consciousness. What dreams mean privately to individuals, myths and
fantasies—born of dreams—mean to mankind. They are fundamental
expressions of the human condition, more authentic and more profound than the calculated products of conscious reason.

10

At the beginning of this essay it was stated that the contents of this
book may be true and that the exact nature of such truth—physical,
philosophical, spiritual, or psychological—must be determined.

To begin this process the most important consideration is to overcome the tendency to reject the unfamiliar out of hand. The reader who
will not even question the assumptions of material reality can gain
nothing but diversion. To profit he should open himself to the possibility that reality does have many sides and that the myths, poems, stories, and visions in this collection can be documents of discovery.

I
Creation

CREATION

"Where shall I begin," said Alice.
"Begin at the beginning. ..."

IT IS INEVITABLE to begin at the beginning. All stories do, and signify this by conventional formulas ("Once upon a time ..."). Our life has a clear beginning, a specific biological process whereby a single sperm cell generated by the male quickens a single ovum produced by the female. But both stories and human lives imply antecedants; things happened before the arbitrary opening of fairy tales, and our parents were alive before they produced us, as were their parents before they produced them.

Is there any real beginning, then? If we work on the basis of analogy, it is hard indeed to posit one. Spontaneous generation is exceedingly rare in nature, and if we trace back our ancestry, or the ancestry of any living thing, we could do so *ad infinitum.* One of the most hoary riddles is the one about the chicken and the egg. It is indeed a difficult question to answer. Scientific theory has offered several explanations of how life began but even these always imply something anterior.

Primitive man was no less bothered by ultimate origins than we are. He did not have scientific models and molecular formulas to explain the workings of the cosmos. But he had myths which for him were scientific theory and through which he confronted the phenomena of nature in terms of vivid symbols and images which had validity for thousands of years.

Most mythological cycles begin with an account of creation. These visions of cosmogony are primitive man's attempts to find the ultimate answers to the question of origins. Where did the world come from? How did it come into being? A modern reader confronting many of these myths for the first time may be struck by the wildness of much of the imagery and the complexity of the thought behind the myth. In comparison, the cosmogony we are most familiar with—the account of creation in the Book of Genesis—is a model of coherence and simplicity.

But as complex as these cosmogonic myths are, there are several themes running through them all which show the workings of human intelligence on difficult thought. And in their own way, the myths are essentially rational explanations of external phenomena as primitive man saw them.

One of the chief features of all cosmogonic myths is the image of order coming out of chaos. The order is a result, most usually, of the personal action of a deity who shapes matter out of primeval chaos. In other instances, the deity, to create order, must overcome in battle the personified forces of chaos. Later in this anthology (Part VII) we will notice myths in which the reverse process—the lapsing of order back into chaos—is present.

The image of order coming out of chaos may have a deep-seated psychological appeal, judging from the numerous myths from far-flung societies in which it is present. A leading scholar of myth, Joseph Campbell, expresses the psychological effectiveness of this image in this way:

> As the consciousness of the individual rests on a sea of night into which it descends in slumber and out of which it mysteriously wakes, so, in the imagery of myth, the universe is precipitated out of, and reposes upon, a timelessness back into which it again dissolves. And as the mental health of the individual depends upon an orderly flow of vital forces into the field of waking day from the unconscious dark, so again in myth, the continuance of cosmic order is assured only by the controlled flow of power from the source.

This suggests that the way man conceives of the operation of the external cosmos is in some way related to his consciousness of his own human processes and activities.

Imposing a human image on the forces of the cosmos is frequent in cosmogonies—the world is seen being formed through a process like that of human generation. In Greek mythology, the physical world comes into being partly through the sexual intercourse of the primeval sky and the primeval earth (Ouranous and Gaia); in Babylonian mythology, the gods spring from the similar union of Ti'amat and Apsu; in an Egyptian myth, a god gives rise to the world by masturbation (an image hinted at in the castration of Cronos in Greek mythology); finally, in some myths, the world is hatched from a primeval egg.

The imagery of generation is followed in frequency in primitive cosmologies by the imagery of water. Most of the myths conceive of the world emerging, or being shaped, out of a primeval watery chaos. In Jungian terms, the water is a symbol for the human consciousness, as the remarks of Campbell, cited above, make clear. But there are other relevant associations as well. Water has traditionally been a symbol for the life force itself: it is a symbol of unity and totality since the vast ocean is both the source of all living things and the encloser of the world. In early conceptions of the world, it was believed that the Ocean girded the land-mass. And the ancient mythologists were not far from scientific theory, for recent discoveries have indicated that higher forms of vertebrate life may have at one time in primeval history been aquatic organisms. The biological basis of the symbolism of water—the ocean as a vast womb out of which life emerges—should not be over-looked in this connection.

One final pattern which is present in numerous cosmologies is the means by which man was created. The story in Genesis of God shaping man out of the dust or the earth is again the most familiar to us. The Hebrew word for earth (*adahm*) is the same word by which man is called. The creation of man from earth, dust, clay, rocks is found in such scattered mythologies as those of the Greeks, the Hebrews, the Maoris of New Zealand, and the Blackfoot Indians of North America. Such parallels suggest to scholars of mythology some universal human nature which tends to conceptualize in similar patterns. Jung calls this predisposition the "collective unconscious" and he talks about certain basic patterns ("archetypes") which the collective unconscious ex-presses. A reading of many myths from various sources seems to confirm the Jungian idea of archetype, but it is not necessary to see the myths solely in these terms. Rather, it is sufficient for the purposes of this book to recognize the complexity and often the power of these early attempts to grapple with the unknown and the ways in which the kinds of thinking they represent may still have a powerful hold on our imagi-nations, even though we may think of ourselves as more sophisticated and worldly than primitive man.

The selections in the first half of this first section present a variety of cosmogonic myths. The remarks above may serve as a general intro-duction to the group as a whole but by no means are the final word on a vastly complex subject. Some further remarks on the selections are in order here, although the reader can well make his own observations by a close study of the texts.

The story of Creation in Genesis (Chapters 1-3) is generally held to be two different traditions brought together in one place. The tradition represented in the first chapter of Genesis is considered to be later than the tradition represented in the second chapter. In the first chapter creation takes place by divine fiat. God calls into being the things of the earth by the mere exercise of His will ("Let there be light . . ."). In the second chapter, God is seen as a more personal and immanant deity, shaping man, as an artisan shapes his materials, into being from primeval matter. Both traditions raise inevitable questions about what preceded creation but provide only one certain answer—God. The whole account with its stately and measured style expresses the essen-tial faith of the Judeo-Christian tradition that God is the source of all life, the encloser, shaper, and motive force of the cosmos.

The selection from *The Bhagavadgita,* the Hindu religious work, is not strictly speaking a cosmogony. *The Bhagavadgita* concerns the hero Arjuna, who, finding himself in a difficult situation (he must do battle against his own kin), turns to Krishna for advice and solace. The rest of the work is a dialogue in which Krishna instructs Arjuna in the ways of the universe. In chapter IX, excerpted here, Krishna describes himself as the source of all creation yet not a part of creation itself. The passage also points to a cyclical conception of the cosmos in which all things are seen emanating and returning to the One, the source of all things, endlessly through time.

The cosmogonic tales of the American Indians are more etiological in nature than the other creation myths presented here—that is, they try to explain the presence of various natural phenomena as the work of a mythical being (The Old Man in the Blackfoot tale and the Raven in the tale from the Tlingit tribe). The Raven is a familiar figure in folk-tale known as the Trickster, a charming, often malicious fellow, who gets his way by devious means but who is still regarded as a culture hero. The appearances of the Trickster in literature and folk-culture are numerous, from the wily Odysseus to the madcap Marx Brothers.

The rest of the selections in this section illustrate various aspects of the myths of creation in the modern world.

Two seventeenth century poems, Marvell's "The Garden," and the Earl of Rochester's "On Nothing," respond differently to the myth of Genesis. Marvell's poem recalls to us the image of Eden, that place at the beginning of the world where man and nature were one, where there was no conflict or strife, no guilt or shame, where all was total innocence and happiness. The problem for the speaker of the poem is one of confronting a strife-torn world and of having to decide whether to live in it, pursuing the symbols of worldly success and achievement, or to turn his back on it and live in solitude. The resolution of the speaker's dilemma turns on his recognition of the human inability to recapture the Edenic innocence of man before the Fall. And it is also part of the speaker's dilemma to confront the problem of human desire and sexuality, for the Eden he envisages is the Eden before the creation of Eve, the "Two paradises . . . in one."

The Earl of Rochester's poem has a double focus. On the one hand it is a meditation on the Nothingness which preceded creation, and on the other it is a satiric comment on the vanity of human striving since all resolves into the Supreme Negative. The poem is marked by the wit characteristic of seventeenth century poetry which took delight in elaborate verbal games and paradoxes, as the various senses of the word "nothing" indicate.

The rest of the selections are grouped around a common theme which is associated with creation—the relation of the work of the artist to the work of God the creator. From the earliest recorded statements on literary activity there has been a reciprocal relationship between the artist and God. In Genesis, God is seen anthropmorphically working like a master craftsman molding creation out of primal stuff. Conversely, the artist has often been compared to God the creator. The Greek word for poet, *poetis,* 'maker,' implies that art is a creation—a second creation if you will, which imitates the primary creation. In many ways, the writer of fantasy fulfills this definition of maker perhaps more than the realist for he (to quote Marvell) "creates . . . far other worlds, far other seas"—worlds with their own self-consistent laws and principles. Donald Barthelme's story "Paraguay," which appears elsewhere in this volume, is an example of these other worlds the artist calls into being, as are the Middle Earth of J. R. R. Tolkien's Hobbit stories and the Wonderland and Looking-glass world of Lewis Carroll's Alice books.

For the eighteenth century visionary poet William Blake the imaginative act is *the* prime act of creation and the imaginative man is *the* creator—a man of god-like power and majesty. The man who sees imaginatively—who sees as Blake saw the heavenly host in the sun— is the creator of the world. Looked at in this way, the question raised in Blake's deceptively simple poem "The Tyger" has two answers. To the conventional thinker, the obvious answer to the question of who framed the tiger's "fearful symmetry" is God. But to Blake, the real answer, perhaps, is that the tiger's power and terror are the result of the perception of the imaginative seer who not only 'creates' the tiger but also the lamb.

The two Tiger pieces by the Argentinian writer Jose Luis Borges raise some paradoxical questions about the power of the artist to call a whole new world into being. Although Borges is perfectly capable of creating a world (and many of his fictions are just that—new worlds) here he expresses frustration at not being able to capture his dream tiger completely. The paradox is that the tiger he longs for is one of his imagination, yet the attempt to render it in art makes it but a fiction, "a ghost of a tiger, a symbol,/ a series of literary tropes." Yet he feels compelled to continue his imaginative search—the ancient search and quest of the artist to render life in art, although the result may be less than the world itself. But a further paradox may be observed in that Borges' frustration is at the same time his success. In the imaginative realm of art he does succeed in capturing the real tiger, "the real thing, with its warm blood,/ That decimates the tribe of buffaloes." For us, as a result of Borges' poem, the tiger lives and has its solidity and reality, its grace and its terror.

The conflict between reality and art is the focus of Hans Christian Andersen's "The Nightingale." Although a writer of fantasy and fairy tale, Andersen is aware of the primacy of nature over art. The artificial nightingale seems superior to the real nightingale until its delicate mechanism breaks and it loses its power. But again there is a paradox here, for like Borges' Tiger, it is the power of Andersen's art which transforms the real nightingale into a fictive one, one which is in many ways superior to the real nightingale; for it is only in the realm of art and fantasy that nightingales cure emperors and thwart death.

Archetypal patterns and common beliefs can be seen easily in creation myths from the widely-separated cultures of Afro-American and Mexican Indian authors. James Weldon Johnson, one of the poets of the Harlem Renaissance of the 1920's, recreates the tone and feeling of an old preacher as he interprets the myth of Genesis in human terms. The Lacandon myth bears some resemblance to the myths of Genesis and the other Indian tales, but its differences should be noted.

GENESIS

Chapter 1

IN THE BEGINNING God created the heaven and the earth.

2 And the earth was without form, and void; and darkness was upon the face of the deep. And the Spirit of God moved upon the face of the waters.

3 And God said, Let there be light: and there was light.

4 And God saw the light, that it was good: and God divided the light from the darkness.

5 And God called the light Day, and the darkness he called Night. And the evening and the morning were the first day.

6 ¶ And God said, Let there be a firmament in the midst of the waters, and let it divide the waters from the waters.

7 And God made the firmament, and divided the waters which were under the firmament from the waters which were above the firmament: and it was so.

8 And God called the firmament Heaven. And the evening and the morning were the second day.

9 ¶ And God said, Let the waters under the heaven be gathered together unto one place, and let the dry land appear: and it was so.

10 And God called the dry land Earth; and the gathering together of the waters called he Seas: and God saw that it was good.

11 And God said, Let the earth bring forth grass, the herb yielding seed, and the fruit tree yielding fruit after his kind, whose seed is in itself, upon the earth: and it was so.

12 And the earth brought forth grass, and herb yielding seed after his kind, and the tree yielding fruit, whose seed was in itself, after his kind: and God saw that it was good.

13 And the evening and the morning were the third day.

14 ¶ And God said, Let there be lights in the firmament of the heaven to divide the day from the night; and let them be for signs, and for seasons, and for days, and years:

15 And let them be for lights in the firmament of the heaven to give light upon the earth: and it was so.

16 And God made two great lights; the greater light to rule the day, and the lesser light to rule the night: he made the stars also.

17 And God set them in the firmament of the heaven to give light upon the earth.

18 And to rule over the day and over the night, and to divide the light from the darkness: and God saw that it was good.

19 And the evening and the morning were the fourth day.

20 And God said, Let the waters bring forth abundantly the moving creature that hath life, and fowl that may fly above the earth in the open firmament of heaven.

21 And God created great whales, and every living creature that moveth, which the waters brought forth abundantly, after their kind, and every winged fowl after his kind: and God saw that it was good.

22 And God blessed them, saying, Be fruitful, and multiply, and fill the waters in the seas, and let fowl multiply in the earth.

23 And the evening and the morning were the fifth day.

24 ¶ And God said, Let the earth bring forth the living creature after his kind, cattle, and creeping thing, and beast of the earth after his kind: and it was so.

25 And God made the beast of the earth after his kind, and cattle after their kind, and every thing that creepeth upon the earth after his kind: and God saw that it was good.

26 ¶ And God said, Let us make man in our image, after our likeness: and let them have dominion over the fish of the sea, and over the fowl of the air, and over the cattle, and over all the earth, and over every creeping thing that creepeth upon the earth.

27 So God created man in his own image, in the image of God created he him; male and female created he them.

28 And God blessed them, and God said unto them, Be fruitful, and multiply, and replenish the earth, and subdue it: and have dominion over the fish of the sea, and over the fowl of the air, and over every living thing that moveth upon the earth.

29 ¶ And God said, Behold, I have given you every herb bearing seed, which is upon the face of all the earth, and every tree, in the which is the fruit of a tree yielding seed; to you it shall be for meat.

30 And to every beast of the earth, and to every fowl of the air, and to every thing that creepeth upon the earth, wherein there is life, I have given every green herb for meat: and it was so.

31 And God saw every thing that he had made, and, behold, it was very good. And the evening and the morning were the sixth day.

Chapter 2

Thus the heavens and the earth were finished, and all the host of them.

2 And on the seventh day God ended his work which he had made; and he rested on the seventh day from all his work which he had made.

3 And God blessed the seventh day, and sanctified it: because that in it he had rested from all his work which God created and made.

4 ¶ These are the generations of the heavens and of the earth when they were created, in the day that the LORD God made the earth and the heavens,

5 And every plant of the field before it was in the earth, and every herb of the field before it grew: for the LORD God had not caused it to rain upon the earth, and there was not a man to till the ground.

6 But there went up a mist from the earth, and watered the whole face of the ground.

7 And the LORD God formed man of the dust of the ground, and breathed into his nostrils the breath of life; and man became a living soul.

8 ¶ And the LORD God planted a garden eastward in Eden; and there he put the man whom he had formed.

9 And out of the ground made the LORD God to grow every tree that is pleasant to the sight, and good for food; the tree of life also in the midst of the garden, and the tree of knowledge of good and evil.

10 And a river went out of Eden to water the garden; and from thence it was parted, and became into four heads.

11 The name of the first is Pison: that is it which compasseth the whole land of Havilah, where there is gold;

12 And the gold of that land is good: there is bdellium and the onyx stone.

13 And the name of the second river is Gihon: the same is it that compasseth the whole land of Ethiopia.

14 And the name of the third river is Hiddekel: that is it which goeth toward the east of Assyria. And the fourth river is Euphrates.

15 And the LORD God took the man, and put him into the garden of Eden to dress it and to keep it.

16 And the LORD God commanded the man, saying, Of every tree of the garden thou mayest freely eat:

17 But of the tree of the knowledge of good and evil, thou shalt not eat of it: for in the day that thou eatest thereof thou shalt surely die.

18 ¶ And the LORD God said, It is not good that the man should be alone; I will make him an help meet for him.

19 And out of the ground the LORD God formed every beast of the field, and every fowl of the air; and brought them unto Adam to see what he would call them: and whatsoever Adam called every living creature, that was the name thereof.

20 And Adam gave names to all cattle, and to the fowl of the air, and to every beast of the field; but for Adam there was not found an help meet for him.

21 And the LORD God caused a deep sleep to fall upon Adam, and he slept: and he took one of his ribs, and closed up the flesh instead thereof;

22 And the rib, which the LORD God had taken from man, made he a woman, and brought her unto the man.

23 And Adam said, This is now bone of my bones, and flesh of my flesh: she shall be called Woman, because she was taken out of Man.

24 Therefore shall a man leave his father and his mother, and shall cleave unto his wife: and they shall be one flesh.

25 And they were both naked, the man and his wife, and were not ashamed.

Chapter 3

Now the serpent was more subtil than any beast of the field which the LORD God had made. And he said unto the woman, Yea, hath God said, Ye shall not eat of every tree of the garden?

2 And the woman said unto the serpent, We may eat of the fruit of the trees of the garden:

3 But of the fruit of the tree which is in the midst of the garden, God hath said, Ye shall not eat of it, neither shall ye touch it, lest ye die.

4 And the serpent said unto the woman, Ye shall not surely die:

5 For God doth know that in the day ye eat thereof, then your eyes shall be opened, and ye shall be as gods, knowing good and evil.

6 And when the woman saw that the tree was good for food, and that it was pleasant to the eyes, and a tree to be desired to make one wise, she took of the fruit thereof, and did eat, and gave also unto her husband with her; and he did eat.

7 And the eyes of them both were opened, and they knew that they were naked; and they sewed fig leaves together, and made themselves aprons.

8 And they heard the voice of the LORD God walking in the garden in the cool of the day: and Adam and his wife hid themselves from the presence of the LORD God amongst the trees of the garden.

9 And the LORD God called unto Adam, and said unto him, Where art thou?

10 And he said, I heard thy voice in the garden, and I was afraid, because I was naked; and I hid myself.

11 And he said, Who told thee that thou wast naked? Has thou eaten of the tree, whereof I commanded thee that thou shouldest not eat?

12 And the man said, The woman whom thou gavest to be with me, she gave me of the tree, and I did eat.

13 And the LORD God said unto the woman, What is this that thou hast done? And the woman said, The serpent beguiled me, and I did eat.

14 And the LORD God said unto the serpent, Because thou hast done this, thou art cursed above all cattle, and above every beast of the field; upon thy belly shalt thou go, and dust shalt thou eat all the days of thy life:

15 And I will put enmity between thee and the woman, and between

thy seed and her seed; it shall bruise thy head, and thou shalt bruise his heel.

16 Unto the woman he said, I will greatly multiply thy sorrow and thy conception; in sorrow thou shalt bring forth children; and thy desire shall be to thy husband, and he shall rule over thee.

17 And unto Adam he said, Because thou hast hearkened unto the voice of thy wife, and hast eaten of the tree, of which I commanded thee, saying, Thou shalt not eat of it: cursed is the ground for thy sake; in sorrow shalt thou eat of it all the days of thy life;

18 Thorns also and thistles shall it bring forth to thee; and thou shalt eat the herb of the field;

19 In the sweat of thy face shalt thou eat bread, till thou return unto the ground; for out of it wast thou taken: for dust thou art, and unto dust shalt thou return.

20 And Adam called his wife's name Eve; because she was the mother of all living.

21 Unto Adam also and to his wife did the LORD God make coats of skins, and clothed them.

22 ¶ And the LORD God said, Behold, the man is become as one of us, to know good and evil: and now, lest he put forth his hand, and take also of the tree of life, and eat, and live for ever:

23 Therefore the LORD God sent him forth from the garden of Eden, to till the ground from whence he was taken.

24 So he drove out the man; and he placed at the east of the garden of Eden Cherubims, and a flaming sword which turned every way, to keep the way of the tree of life.

BHAGAVADGITA IX

KRISHNA:

Now will I open unto thee—whose heart
Rejects not—that last lore, deepest-concealed,
That farthest secret of My Heavens and Earths,
Which but to know shall set thee free from ills,—
A Royal lore! a Kingly mystery!
Yea! for the soul such light as purgeth it
From every sin; a light of holiness
With inmost splendor shining; plain to see;
Easy to walk by, inexhaustible!

They that receive not this, failing in faith
To grasp the greater wisdom, reach not Me,
Destroyer of thy foes! They sink anew
Into the realm of Flesh, where all things change!

By Me the whole vast Universe of things
Is spread abroad;—by Me, the Unmanifest!
In Me are all existences contained;
Not I in them!

Yet they are not contained,
Those visible things! Receive and strive to embrace
The mystery majestical! My Being—
Creating all, sustaining all—still dwells
Outside of all!

See! as the shoreless airs
Move in the measureless space, but are not space,
[And space were space without the moving airs];
So all things are in Me, but are not I.

At closing of each Kalpa, Indian Prince!
All things which be back to My Being come:
At the beginning of each Kalpa, all
Issue newborn from Me.

By Energy
And help of Prakriti, my outer Self,
Again, and yet again, I make go forth
The realms of visible things—without their will—
All of them—by the power of Prakriti.

Yet these great makings, Prince! involve Me not,
Enchain Me not! I sit apart from them,
Other, and Higher, and Free; nowise attached!

Thus doth the stuff of worlds, moulded by Me,
Bring forth all that which is, moving or still,
Living or lifeless! Thus the worlds go on!

The minds untaught mistake Me, veiled in form;—
Naught see they of My secret Presence, nought
Of My hid Nature, ruling all which lives.
Vain hopes pursuing, vain deeds doing; fed
On vainest knowledge, senselessly they seek
An evil way, the way of brutes and fiends.
But My Mahatmas, those of noble soul
Who tread the path celestial, worship Me
With hearts unwandering,—knowing Me the Source,
Th' Eternal Source, of Life. Unendingly
They glorify Me; seek Me; keep their vows
Of reverence and love, with changeless faith
Adoring Me. Yea, and those too adore,
Who, offering sacrifice of wakened hearts,
Have sense of one pervading Spirit's stress,
One Force in every place, though manifold!
I am the Sacrifice! I am the Prayer!
I am the Funeral-Cake set for the dead!
I am the healing herb! I am the ghee,
The Mantra, and the flame, and that which burns!
I am—of all this boundless Universe—
The Father, Mother, Ancestor, and Guard!
The end of Learning! That which purifies
In lustral water! I am OM! I am
Rig-Veda, Sama-Veda, Yajur-Ved;
The Way, the Fosterer, the Lord, the Judge,
The Witness; the Abode, the Refuge-House,
The Friend, the Fountain and the Sea of Life
Which sends, and swallows up; Treasure of Worlds
And Treasure-Chamber! Seed and Seed-Sower,
Whence endless harvests spring! Sun's heat is mine;
Heaven's rain is mine to grant or to withhold;
Death am I, and Immortal Life I am,
Arjuna! SAT and ASAT, Visible Life,
And Life Invisible!

Yea! those who learn
The threefold Veds, who drink the Soma-wine,

Purge sins, pay sacrifice—from Me they earn
   Passage to Swarga; where the meats divine

Of great gods feed them in high Indra's heaven.
   Yet they, when that prodigious joy is o'er,
Paradise spent, and wage for merits given,
   Come to the world of death and change once more.

They had their recompense! they stored their treasure,
   Following the threefold Scripture and its writ;
Who seeketh such gaineth the fleeting pleasure
   Of joy which comes and goes! I grant them it!

   But to those blessed ones who worship Me,
Turning not otherwise, with minds set fast,
I bring assurance of full bliss beyond.

   Nay, and of hearts which follow other gods
In simple faith, their prayers arise to me,
O Kunti's Son! though they pray wrongfully:
For I am the Receiver and the Lord
Of every sacrifice, which these know not
Rightfully; so they fall to earth again!
Who follow gods go to their gods; who vow
Their souls to Pitris go to Pitris; minds
To evil Bhûts given o'er sink to the Bhûts;
And whoso loveth Me cometh to Me.
Whoso shall offer Me in faith and love
A leaf, a flower, a fruit, water poured forth,
That offering I accept, lovingly made
With pious will. Whate'er thou doest, Prince!
Eating or sacrificing, giving gifts,
Praying or fasting, let it all be done
For Me, as Mine. So shalt thou free thyself
From *Karmabandh,* the chain which holdeth men
To good and evil issue, so shalt come
Safe unto Me—when thou art quit of flesh—
By faith and abdication joined to Me!

   I am alike for all! I know not hate,
I know not favor! What is made is Mine!
But them that worship Me with love, I love;
They are in me, and I in them!

                          Nay, Prince!
If one of evil life turn in his thought
Straightly to Me, count him amidst the good;
He hath the highway chosen; he shall grow

Righteous ere long; he shall attain that peace
Which changes not. Thou Prince of India!
Be certain none can perish, trusting Me!
O Prithâ's Son! whoso will turn to Me,
Though they be born from the very womb of Sin,
Woman or man; sprung of the Vaisya caste
Or lowly disregarded Sudra,—all
Plant foot upon the highest path; how then
The holy Brahmans and My Royal Saints?
Ah! ye who into this ill world are come—
Fleeting and false—set your faith fast on Me!
Fix heart and thought on Me! Adore Me! Bring
Offerings to Me! Make Me prostrations! Make
Me your supremest joy! and, undivided,
Unto My rest your spirits shall be guided.

Here ends Chapter IX. of the Bhagavad-Gîtâ, entitled
"Râjavidyârajaguhyayôg," or "The Book of
Religion by the Kingly Knowledge and
the Kingly Mystery"

THE BLACKFOOT GENESIS

A Legend of the Blackfoot Indians

ALL ANIMALS of the Plains at one time heard and knew him, and all birds of the air heard and knew him. All things that he had made understood him when he spoke to them—the birds, the animals, and the people.

Old Man[1] was traveling about, south of here, making the people. He came from the south, traveling north, making animals and birds as he passed along. He made the mountains, prairies, timber, and brush first. So he went along, traveling northward, making things as he went, putting rivers here and there, and falls on them, putting red paints here and there in the ground—fixing up the world as we see it today. He made the Milk River [the Teton] and crossed it, and, being tired, went up on a little hill and lay down to rest. As he lay on his back, stretched out on the ground, with arms extended, he marked himself out with stones—the shape of his body, head, legs, arms, and everything. There you can see those rocks today. After he had rested, he went on northward, and stumbled over a knoll and fell down on his knees. Then he said, "You are a bad thing to be stumbling against"; so he raised up two large buttes there, and named them the Knees, and they are called so to this day. He went on farther north, and with some of the rocks he carried with him he built the Sweet Grass Hills.

Old Man covered the plains with grass for the animals to feed on. He marked off a piece of ground, and in it he made to grow all kinds of roots and berries—camas, wild carrots, wild turnips, sweetroot, bitterroot, sarvis berries, bull berries, cherries, plums, and rosebuds. He put trees in the ground. He put all kinds of animals on the ground. When he made the bighorn with its big head and horns, he made it out on the prairie. It did not seem to travel easily on the prairie; it was awkward and could not go fast. So he took it by one of its horns, and led it up into the mountains, and turned it loose; and it skipped about among the

---

[1]The personage usually called Old Man is known to the Blackfeet and Arapaho, the western Algonquians as well as the Siouan and Salish tribes. The Crow (Siouan) name for the creator, "Old Man Coyote," is an interesting identification of this character with Coyote. Sometimes a personification of the Great Spirit, Old Man, belongs to trickster-transformer family. In Arapaho myth Old Man is the hero of raft story and diving animals.

rocks and went up fearful places with ease. So he said, "This is the place that suits you; this is what you are fitted for, the rocks, and the mountains." While he was in the mountains, he made the antelope out of dirt, and turned it loose, to see how it would go. It ran so fast that it fell over some rocks and hurt itself. He saw that this would not do, and took the antelope down on the prairie, and turned it loose; and it ran away fast and gracefully, and he said, "This is what you are suited to."

One day Old Man determined that he would make a woman and a child; so he formed them both—the woman and the child, her son—of clay. After he had moulded the clay in human shape, he said to the clay, "You must be people," and then he covered it up and left it, and went away. The next morning he went to the place and took the covering off, and saw that the clay shapes had changed a little. The second morning there was still more change, and the third still more. The fourth morning he went to the place, took the covering off, looked at the images, and told them to rise and walk; and they did so. They walked down to the river with their Maker, and then he told them that his name was Na'pi [Old Man].

As they were standing by the river, the woman said to him, "How is it? will we always live, will there be no end to it?" He said: "I have never thought of that. We will have to decide it. I will take this buffalo chip and throw it in the river. If it floats, when people die, in four days they will become alive again; they will die for only four days. But if it sinks, there will be an end to them." He threw the chip into the river, and it floated. The woman turned and picked up a stone, and said: "No, I will throw this stone in the river; if it floats we will always live, if it sinks people must die, that they may always be sorry for each other." The woman threw the stone into the water, and it sank. "There," said Old Man, "you have chosen. There will be an end to them."

It was not many nights after that the woman's child died, and she cried a great deal for it. She said to Old Man: "Let us change this. The law that you first made, let that be a law." He said: "Not so. What is made law must be law. We will undo nothing that we have done. The child is dead, but it cannot be changed. People will have to die."

That is how we came to be people. It is he who made us.

The first people were poor and naked, and did not know how to get a living. Old Man showed them the roots and berries, and told them that they could peel the bark off some trees and eat it, that it was good. He told the people that the animals should be their food, and gave them to the people, saying, "These are your herds." He said: "All these little animals that live in the ground—rats, squirrels, skunks, beavers—are good to eat. You need not fear to eat of their flesh." He made all the birds that fly, and told the people that there was no harm in their flesh, that it could be eaten. The first people that he created he used to take about through the timber and swamps and over the prairies, and show them the different plants. Of a certain plant he would say, "The root of this plant, if gathered in a certain month of the year, is good for certain sickness." So they learned the power of all herbs.

In those days there were buffalo. Now the people had no arms, but those black animals with long beards were armed; and once, as the people were moving about, the buffalo saw them, and ran after them, and hooked them, and killed and ate them. One day, as the Maker of the people was traveling over the country, he saw some of his children, that he had made, lying dead, torn to pieces and partly eaten by the buffalo. When he saw this he was very sad. He said: "This will not do. I will change this. The people shall eat the buffalo."

He went to some of the people who were left, and said to them, "How is it that you people do nothing to these animals that are killing you?" The people said: "What can we do? We have no way to kill these animals, while they are armed and can kill us." Then said the Maker: "That is not hard. I will make you a weapon that will kill those animals." So he went out, and cut some sarvis berry shoots, and brought them in, and peeled the bark off them. He took a larger piece of wood, and flattened it, and tied a string to it, and made a bow. Now, as he was the master of all birds and could do with them as he wished, he went out and caught one, and took feathers from its wing, and split them, and tied them to the shaft of wood. He tied four feathers along the shaft, and tried the arrow at a mark, and found that it did not fly well. He took these feathers off, and put on three; and when he tried it again, he found that it was good. He went out and began to break sharp pieces of the stones. He tried them, and found that the black flint stones made the best arrow points, and some white flints. Then he taught the people how to use these things.

Then he said: "The next time you go out, take these things with you, and use them as I tell you, and do not run from these animals. When they run at you, as soon as they get pretty close, shoot the arrows at them, as I have taught you; and you will see that they will run from you or will run in a circle around you."

Now, as people became plenty, one day three men went out on to the plain to see the buffalo, but they had no arms. They saw the animals, but when the buffalo saw the men, they ran after them and killed two of them, but one got away. One day after this, the people went on a little hill to look about, and the buffalo saw them, and said, "Saiyah, there is some more of our food," and they rushed on them. This time the people did not run. They began to shoot at the buffalo with the bows and arrows Na'pi had given them, and the buffalo began to fall; but in the fight a person was killed.

At this time these people had flint knives given them, and they cut up the bodies of the dead buffalo. It is not healthful to eat the meat raw, so Old Man gathered soft, dry, rotten driftwood and made punk of it, and then got a piece of hard wood, and drilled a hole in it with an arrow point, and gave them a pointed piece of hard wood, and taught them how to make a fire with fire sticks, and to cook the flesh of these animals and eat it.

They got a kind of stone that was in the land, and then took another harder stone and worked one upon the other, and hollowed out the softer one, and made a kettle of it. This was the fashion of their dishes.

Also Old Man said to the people: "Now, if you are overcome, you may go and sleep, and get power. Something will come to you in your dream that will help you. Whatever these animals tell you to do, you must obey them, as they appear to you in your sleep. Be guided by them. If anybody wants help, if you are alone and traveling, and cry aloud for help, your prayer will be answered. It may be by the eagles, perhaps by the buffalo, or by the bears. Whatever animal answers your prayer, you must listen to him."

That was how the first people got through the world, by the power of their dreams.

After this, Old Man kept on, traveling north. Many of the animals that he had made followed him as he went. The animals understood him when he spoke to them, and he used them as his servants. When he got to the north point of the Porcupine Mountains, there he made some more mud images of people, and blew breath upon them, and they became people. He made men and women. They asked him, "What are we to eat?" He made many images of clay in the form of buffalo. Then he blew breath on these, and they stood up; and when he made signs to them, they started to run. Then he said to the people, "Those are your food." They said to him, "Well, now, we have those animals; how are we to kill them?" "I will show you," he said. He took them to the cliff, and made them build rock piles . . .; and he taught them how to drive buffalo over a cliff.

After he had taught those people these things, he started off again, traveling north, until he came to where Bow and Elbow rivers meet. There he made some more people, and taught them the same things. From here he again went on northward. When he had come nearly to the Red Deer's River, he reached the hill where the Old Man sleeps. There he lay down and rested himself. The form of his body is to be seen there yet.

When he awoke from his sleep, he traveled farther northward and came to a fine high hill. He climbed to the top of it, and there sat down to rest. He looked over the country below him, and it pleased him. Before him the hill was steep, and he said to himself, "Well, this is a fine place for sliding; I will have some fun," and he began to slide down the hill. The marks where he slid down are to be seen yet, and the place is known to all people as the "Old Man's Sliding Ground."

This is as far as the Blackfeet followed Old Man. The Crees know what he did farther north.

In later times once, Na'pi said, "Here I will mark you off a piece of ground," and he did so. Then he said: "There is your land, and it is full of all kinds of animals, and many things grow in this land. Let no other people come into it. This is for you five tribes [Blackfeet, Bloods, Piegans, Gros Ventres, Sarcees]. When people come to cross the line, take your bows and arrows, your lances and your battle axes, and give them battle and keep them out. If they gain a footing, trouble will come to you."

Our forefathers gave battle to all people who came to cross these lines, and kept them out. Of late years we have let our friends, the white people, come in, and you know the result. We, his children, have failed to obey his laws.

RAVEN

A Legend of the Tlingit Indians

No ONE KNOWS just how the story of Raven really begins, so each starts from the point where he does know it. Here it was always begun in this way. . . . When Raven was born, his father tried to instruct him and train him in every way and, after he grew up, told him he would give him strength to make a world. After trying in all sorts of ways Raven finally succeeded. Then there was no light in this world, but it was told him that far up the Nass was a large house in which someone kept light just for himself.

Raven thought over all kinds of plans for getting this light into the world and finally he hit on a good one. The rich man living there had a daughter, and he thought, "I will make myself very small and drop into the water in the form of a small piece of dirt." The girl swallowed this dirt and became pregnant. When her time was completed, they made a hole for her, as was customary, in which she was to bring forth, and lined it with rich furs of all sorts. But the child did not wish to be born on those fine things. Then its grandfather felt sad and said, "What do you think it would be best to put into that hole? Shall we put in moss?" So they put moss inside and the baby was born on it. Its eyes were very bright and moved around rapidly.

Round bundles of varying shapes and sizes hung about on the walls of the house. When the child became a little larger it crawled around back of the people weeping continually, and as it cried it pointed to the bundles. This lasted many days. Then its grandfather said, "Give my grandchild what he is crying for. Give him that one hanging on the end. That is the bag of stars." So the child played with this, rolling it about on the floor back of the people, until suddenly he let it go up through the smoke hole. It went straight up into the sky and the stars scattered out of it, arranging themselves as you now see them. That was what he went there for.

Some time after this be began crying again, and he cried so much that it was thought he would die. Then his grandfather said, "Untie the next one and give it to him." He played and played with it around behind his mother. After a while he let that go up through the smoke hole also, and there was the big moon.

Now just one thing more remained, the box that held the daylight, and he cried for that. His eyes turned around and showed different colors, and the people began thinking that he must be something other than an ordinary baby. But it always happens that a grandfather loves his grandchild just as he does his own daughter, so the grandfather said, "Untie the last thing and give it to him." His grandfather felt very sad when he gave this to him. When the child had this in his hands, he uttered the raven cry, "Ga," and flew out with it through the smoke hole. Then the person from whom he had stolen it said, "That old manuring raven has gotten all of my things."

Journeying on, Raven was told of another place, where a man had an everlasting spring of water. This man was named Petrel [Ganù'k]. Raven wanted this water because there was none to drink in this world, but Petrel always slept by his spring, and he had a cover over it so as to keep it all to himself. Then Raven came in and said to him, "My brother-in-law, I have just come to see you. How are you?" He told Petrel of all kinds of things that were happening outside, trying to induce him to go out to look at them, but Petrel was too smart for him and refused.

When night came, Raven said, "I am going to sleep with you, brother-in-law." So they went to bed, and toward morning Raven heard Petrel sleeping very soundly. Then he went outside, took some dog manure and put it around Petrel's buttocks. When it was beginning to grow light, he said, "Wake up, wake up, wake up, brother-in-law, you have defecated all over your clothes." Petrel got up, looked at himself, and thought it was true, so he took his blankets and went outside. Then Raven went over to Petrel's spring, took off the cover and began drinking. After he had drunk up almost all of the water, Petrel came in and saw him. Then Raven flew straight, up, crying "Ga."

Before he got through the smoke hole, however, Petrel said, "My spirits up the smoke hole, catch him." So Raven stuck there, and Petrel put pitchwood on the fire under him so as to make a quantity of smoke. Raven was white before that time, but the smoke made him of the color you find him today. Still he did not drop the water. When the smoke-hole spirits let him go, he flew around the nearest point and rubbed himself all over so as to clear off as much of the soot as possible.

This happened somewhere about the Nass, and afterwards he started up this way. First he let some water fall from his mouth and made the Nass. By and by he spit more out and made the Stikine. Next he spit out Taku river, then Chilkat, then Alsek, and all the other large rivers. The small drops that came out of his mouth made the small salmon creeks.

After this Raven went on again and came to a large town where were people who had never seen daylight. They were out catching eulachon in the darkness when he came to the bank opposite, and he asked them to take him across but they would not. Then he said to them, "If you don't come over I will have daylight break on you." But they answered, "Where are you from? Do you come from far up the Nass where lives the man who has daylight?" At this Raven opened his box just a little and shed so great a light on them that they were nearly thrown down. He shut it quickly, but they quarreled with him so much across the creek that he became angry and opened the box completely, when the sun flew up into the sky. Then those people who had sea-otter or fur-seal skins, or the skins of any other sea animals, went into the ocean, while those who had land-otter, bear, or marten skins, or the skins of any other land animals, went into the woods becoming the animals whose skins they wore.

THE GARDEN

Andrew Marvell

How vainly men themselves amaze
To win the palm, the oak, or bays;
And their incessant labours see
Crowned from some single herb or tree,
Whose short and narrow-vergéd shade
Does prudently their toils upbraid;
While all flowers and all trees do close
To weave the garlands of repose.

　Fair Quiet, have I found thee here,
And Innocence, thy sister dear!
Mistaken long, I sought you then
In busy companies of men.
Your sacred plants, if here below,
Only among the plants will grow:
Society is all but rude
To this delicious solitude.

　No white nor red was ever seen
So amorous as this lovely green.
Fond lovers, cruel as their flame,
Cut in these trees their mistress' name:
Little, alas, they know or heed,
How far these beauties hers exceed!
Fair trees! wheres'e'er your barks I wound,
No name shall but your own be found.

　When we have run our passion's heat,
Love hither makes his best retreat.
The gods, that mortal beauty chase,
Still in a tree did end their race:
Apollo hunted Daphne so,
Only that she might laurel grow;
And Pan did after Syrinx speed,
Not as a nymph, but for a reed.

　What wondrous life in this I lead!
Ripe apples drop about my head;
The luscious clusters of the vine
Upon my mouth do crush their wine;
The nectarine, and curious peach,
Into my hands themselves do reach;

Stumbling on melons, as I pass,
Ensnared with flowers, I fall on grass.

   Meanwhile the mind, from pleasure less,
Withdraws into its happiness:
The mind, that ocean where each kind
Does straight its own resemblance find;
Yet it creates, transcending these,
Far other worlds, and other seas;
Annihilating all that's made
To a green thought in a green shade.

   Here at the fountain's sliding foot,
Or at some fruit-tree's mossy root,
Casting the body's vest aside,
My soul into the boughs does glide:
There like a bird it sits and sings,
Then whets, and combs its silver wings;
And, till prepared for longer flight,
Waves in its plumes the various light.

   Such was that happy garden-state,
While man there walked without a mate:
After a place so pure and sweet,
What other help could yet be meet?
But 'twas beyond a mortal's share
To wander solitary there:
Two Paradises 'twere in one,
To live in Paradise alone.

   How well the skilful gardener drew
Of flowers and herbs this dial new!
Where, from above, the milder sun
Does through a fragrant zodiac run;
And, as it works, the industrious bee
Computes its time as well as we.
How could such sweet and wholesome hours
Be reckoned but with herbs and flowers?

UPON NOTHING

The Earl Of Rochester

Nothing! Thou elder brother ev'n to shade,
Thou hadst a being ere the world was made,
And well-fixed art alone of ending not afraid.

Ere time and place were, time and place were not,
With primitive Nothing something straight begot,
Then all proceeded from the great united—what?

Something, the general attribute of all,
Severed from thee, its sole original,
Into thy boundless self must undistinguished fall.

Yet something did thy mighty power command,
And from thy fruitful emptiness's hand
Snatched men, beasts, birds, fire, air and land.

Matter, the wicked'st offspring of thy race,
By Form assisted flew from thy embrace,
And rebel Light obscured thy reverend dusky face.

With Form and Matter, Time and Place did join,
Body, thy foe, with thee did leagues combine,
To spoil thy peaceful realm, and ruin all thy line.

But turn-coat Time assists the foe in vain,
And bribed by thee assists thy short-lived reign,
And to thy hungry womb drives back thy slaves again.

Though mysteries are barred from laic eyes,
And the divine alone with warrant pries
Into thy bosom, where the truth in private lies;

Yet this of thee the wise may freely say,
Thou from the virtuous nothing tak'st away,
And to be part with thee the wicked wisely pray.

Great Negative, how vainly would the wise
Enquire, define, distinguish, teach, devise,
Didst thou not stand to point their dull philosophies!

Is or *is not,* the two great ends of Fate,
And, true or false, the subject of debate,
That perfect or destroy the vast designs of Fate.

When they have racked the politician's breast
Within thy bosom most securely rest,
And when reduced to thee are least unsafe and best.

But, Nothing, why does Something still permit
That sacred monarchs should at council sit,
With persons highly thought at best for nothing fit?

Whilst weighty something modestly abstains
From princes' coffers and from statesmen's brains,
And nothing there like stately Nothing reigns?

Nothing, who dwell'st with fools in grave disguise,
For whom they reverend shapes and forms devise,
Lawn sleeves and furs and gowns, when they like thee look wise.

French truth, Dutch prowess, British policy,
Hibernian learning, Scotch civility,
Spaniards' despatch, Danes' wit, are mainly seen in thee.

The great man's gratitude to his best friend,
Kings' promises, whores' vows towards thee they bend,
Flow swiftly into thee, and in thee ever end.

THE TYGER

William Blake

Tyger! Tyger! burning bright
In the forests of the night,
What immortal hand or eye
Could frame thy fearful symmetry?

In what distant deeps or skies
Burnt the fire of thine eyes?
On what wings dare he aspire?
What the hand dare seize the fire?

And what shoulder, and what art,
Could twist the sinews of thy heart?
And when thy heart began to beat,
What dread hand? and what dread feet?

What the hammer? what the chain?
In what furnace was thy brain?
What the anvil? what dread grasp
Dare its deadly terrors clasp?

When the stars threw down their spears
And watered heaven with their tears,
Did he smile his work to see?
Did he who made the Lamb make thee?

Tyger! Tyger! burning bright
In the forests of the night,
What immortal hand or eye
Dare frame thy fearful symmetry?

DREAMTIGERS

Jorge Luis Borges

IN MY CHILDHOOD I was a fervent worshiper of the tiger: not the jaguar, the spotted "tiger" of the Amazonian tangles and the isles of vegetation that float down the Paraná, but that striped, Asiatic, royal tiger, that can be faced only by a man of war, on a castle atop an elephant. I used to linger endlessly before one of the cages at the zoo; I judged vast encyclopedias and books of natural history by the splendor of their tigers. (I still remember those illustrations: I who cannot rightly recall the brow or the smile of a woman.) Childhood passed away, and the tigers and my passion for them grew old, but still they are in my dreams. At that submerged or chaotic level they keep prevailing. And so, as I sleep, some dream beguiles me, and suddenly I know I am dreaming. Then I think: This is a dream, a pure diversion of my will; and now that I have unlimited power, I am going to cause a tiger.

Oh, incompetence! Never can my dreams engender the wild beast I long for. The tiger indeed appears, but stuffed or flimsy, or with impure variations of shape, or of an implausible size, or all too fleeting, or with a touch of the dog or the bird.

THE OTHER TIGER

Jorge Luis Borges

And the craft that createth a semblance
MORRIS: SIGURD THE VOLSUNG (1876)

I think of a tiger. The gloom here makes
The vast and busy Library seem lofty
And pushes the shelves back;
Strong, innocent, covered with blood and new,
It will move through its forest and its morning
And will print its tracks on the muddy
Margins of a river whose name it does not know
(In its world there are no names nor past
Nor time to come, only the fixed moment)
And will overleap barbarous distances
And will scent out of the plaited maze
Of all the scents the scent of dawn
And the delighting scent of the deer.
Between the stripes of the bamboo I decipher
Its stripes and have the feel of the bony structure
That quivers under the glowing skin.
In vain do the curving seas intervene
And the deserts of the planet;
From this house in a far-off port
In South America, I pursue and dream you,
O tiger on the Ganges' banks.
In my soul the afternoon grows wider and I reflect
That the tiger invoked in my verse
Is a ghost of a tiger, a symbol,
A series of literary tropes
And memories from the encyclopaedia
And not the deadly tiger, the fateful jewel
That, under the sun or the varying moon,
In Sumatra or Bengal goes on fulfilling
Its round of love, of idleness and death.
To the symbolic tiger I have opposed
The real thing, with its warm blood,
That decimates the tribe of buffaloes
And today, the third of August, '59,
Stretches on the grass a deliberate
Shadow, but already the fact of naming it
And conjecturing its circumstance

Makes it a figment of art and no creature
Living among those that walk the earth.

We shall seek a third tiger. This
Will be like those others a shape
Of my dreaming, a system of words
A man makes and not the vertebrate tiger
That, beyond the mythologies,
Is treading the earth. I know well enough
That something lays on me this quest
Undefined, senseless and ancient, and I go on
Seeking through the afternoon time
The other tiger, that which is not in verse.

THE NIGHTINGALE

Hans Christian Andersen

IN CHINA, you must know, the Emperor is a Chinaman, and all whom he has about him are Chinamen too. It happened a good many years ago, but that's just why it's worth while to hear the story, before it is forgotten. The Emperor's palace was the most splendid in the world; it was made entirely of porcelain, very costly, but so delicate and brittle that one had to take care how one touched it. In the garden were to be seen the most wonderful flowers, and to the costliest of them silver bells were tied, which sounded, so that nobody should pass by without noticing the flowers. Yes, everything in the Emperor's garden was admirably arranged. And it extended so far, that the gardener himself did not know where the end was. If a man went on and on, he came into a glorious forest with high trees and deep lakes. The wood extended straight down to the sea, which was blue and deep; great ships could sail to and fro beneath the branches of the trees; and in the trees lived a nightingale, which sang so splendidly that even the poor Fisherman, who had many other things to do, stopped still and listened, when he had gone out at night to throw out his nets, and heard the Nightingale.

"How beautiful that is!" he said; but he was obliged to attend to his property, and thus forgot the bird. But when in the next night the bird sang again, and the Fisherman heard it, he exclaimed again, "How beautiful that is!"

From all the countries of the world travellers came to the city of the Emperor and admired it, and the palace, and the garden, but when they heard the Nightingale, they said, "That is the best of all!"

And the travellers told of it when they came home; and the learned men wrote many books about the town, the palace, and the garden. But they did not forget the Nightingale; that was placed highest of all; and those who were poets wrote most magnificent poems about the Nightingale in the wood by the deep lake.

The books went through all the world, and a few of them once came to the Emperor. He sat in his golden chair, and read, and read: every moment he nodded his head, for it pleased him to peruse the masterly descriptions of the city, the palace, and the garden. "But the Nightingale is the best of all!"—it stood written there.

"What's that?" exclaimed the Emperor. "I don't know the Nightingale at all! Is there such a bird in my empire, and even in my garden? I've never heard of that. To think that I should have to learn such a thing for the first time from books!"

And hereupon he called his Cavalier. This Cavalier was so grand that if any one lower in rank than himself dared to speak to him, or to ask him any question, he answered nothing but "P!"—and that meant nothing.

"There is said to be a wonderful bird here called a Nightingale!" said the Emperor. "They say it is the best thing in all my great empire. Why have I never heard anything about it?"

"I have never heard him named," replied the Cavalier. "He has never been introduced at court."

"I command that he shall appear this evening, and sing before me," said the Emperor. "All the world knows what I possess, and I do not know it myself!"

"I have never heard him mentioned," said the Cavalier, "I will seek for him. I will find him."

But where was he to be found? The Cavalier ran up and down all the staircases, through halls and passages, but no one among all those whom he met had heard talk of the Nightingale. And the Cavalier ran back to the Emperor, and said that it must be a fable invented by the writers of books.

"Your Imperial Majesty cannot believe how much is written that is fiction, besides something that they call the black art."

"But the book in which I read this," said the Emperor, "was sent to me by the high and mighty Emperor of Japan, and therefore it cannot be a falsehood. I will hear the Nightingale! It must be here this evening! It has my imperial favor; and if it does not come, all the court shall be trampled upon after the court has supped!"

"Tsing-pe!" said the Cavalier; and again he ran up and down all the staircases, and through all the halls and corridors; and half the court ran with him, for the courtiers did not like being trampled upon.

Then there was a great inquiry after the wonderful Nightingale, which all the world knew excepting the people at court.

At last they met with a poor little girl in the kitchen, who said,—

"The Nightingale? I know it well; yes, it can sing gloriously. Every evening I get leave to carry my poor sick mother the scraps from the table. She lives down by the strand, and when I get back and am tired, and rest in the wood, then I hear the Nightingale sing. And then the water comes into my eyes, and it is just as if my mother kissed me!"

"Little Kitchen Girl," said the Cavalier, "I will get you a place in the kitchen, with permission to see the Emperor dine, if you will lead us to the Nightingale, for it is announced for this evening."

So they all went out into the wood where the Nightingale was accustomed to sing; half the court went forth. When they were in the midst of their journey a cow began to low.

"O!" cried the court page, "now we have it! That shows a wonderful power in so small a creature! I have certainly heard it before."

"No, those are cows lowing!" said the little Kitchen Girl. "We are a long way from the place yet!"

Now the frogs began to croak in the marsh.

"Glorious!" said the Chinese Court Preacher. "Now I hear it—it sounds just like little church bells."

"No, those are frogs!" said the little Kitchen-maid. "But now I think we shall soon hear it."

And then the Nightingale began to sing.

"That is it!" exclaimed the little Girl. "Listen, listen! and yonder it sits."

And she pointed to a little gray bird up in the boughs.

"Is it possible?" cried the Cavalier. "I should never have thought it looked like that! How simple it looks! It must certainly have lost its color at seeing such grand people around."

"Little Nightingale!" called the Kitchen-maid, quite loudly, "our gracious Emperor wishes you to sing before him."

"With the greatest pleasure!" replied the Nightingale, and began to sing most delightfully.

"It sounds just like glass bells!" said the Cavalier. "And look at its little throat, how it's working! It's wonderful that we should never have heard it before. That bird will be a great success at court."

"Shall I sing once more before the Emperor?" asked the Nightingale, for it thought the Emperor was present.

"My excellent little Nightingale," said the Cavalier, "I have great pleasure in inviting you to a court festival this evening, when you shall charm his Imperial Majesty with your beautiful singing."

"My song sounds best in the greenwood!" replied the Nightingale; still it came willingly when it heard what the Emperor wished.

The palace was festively adorned. The walls and the flooring, which were of porcelain, gleamed in the rays of thousands of golden lamps. The most glorious flowers, which could ring clearly, had been placed in the passages. There was a running to and fro, and a thorough draught, and all the bells rang so loudly that one could not hear one's self speak.

In the midst of the great hall, where the Emperor sat, a golden perch had been placed, on which the Nightingale was to sit. The whole court was there, and the little Cook-maid had got leave to stand behind the door, as she had now received the title of a real court cook. All were in full dress, and all looked at the little gray bird, to which the Emperor nodded.

And the Nightingale sang so gloriously that the tears came into the Emperor's eyes, and the tears ran down over his cheeks; and then the Nightingale sang still more sweetly, that went straight to the heart. The Emperor was so much pleased that he said the Nightingale should have his golden slipper to wear round its neck. But the Nightingale declined this with thanks, saying it had already received a sufficient reward.

"I have seen tears in the Emperor's eyes—that is the real treasure to me. An emperor's tears have a peculiar power. I am rewarded enough!" And then it sang again with a sweet, glorious voice.

"That's the most amiable coquetry I ever saw!" said the ladies who stood round about, and then they took water in their mouths to gurgle when any one spoke to them. They thought they should be nightingales too. And the lackeys and chambermaids reported that they were satisfied too; and that was saying a good deal, for they are the most difficult to please. In short, the Nightingale achieved a real success.

It was now to remain at court, to have its own cage, with liberty to go out twice every day and once at night. Twelve servants were appointed when the Nightingale went out, each of whom had a silken string fastened to the bird's leg, which they held very tight. There was really no pleasure in an excursion of that kind.

The whole city spoke of the wonderful bird, and when two people met, one said nothing but "Nightin," and the other said "gale;" and then they sighed, and understood one another. Eleven peddlers' children were named after the bird, but not one of them could sing a note.

One day the Emperor received a large parcel, on which was written "The Nightingale."

"There we have a new book about this celebrated bird," said the Emperor.

But it was not a book, but a little work of art, contained in a box, an artificial nightingale, which was to sing like a natural one, and was brilliantly ornamented with diamonds, rubies, and sapphires. So soon as the artificial bird was wound up, he could sing one of the pieces that he really sang, and then his tail moved up and down, and shone with silver and gold. Round his neck hung a little ribbon, and on that was written, "The Emperor of China's Nightingale is poor compared to that of the Emperor of Japan."

"That is capital!" said they all, and he who had brought the artificial bird immediately received the title, Imperial Head-Nightingale-Bringer.

"Now they must sing together; what a duet that will be!"

And so they had to sing together; but it did not sound very well, for the real Nightingale sang in its own way, and the artificial bird sang waltzes.

"That's not his fault," said the Play-master; "he's quite perfect, and very much in my style."

Now the artificial bird was to sing alone. He had just as much success as the real one, and then it was much handsomer to look at—it shone like bracelets and breastpins.

Three-and-thirty times over did it sing the same piece, and yet was not tired. The people would gladly have heard it again, but the Emperor said that the living Nightingale ought to sing something now. But where was it? No one had noticed that it had flown away out of the open window, back to the greenwood.

"But what is become of that?" said the Emperor.

And all the courtiers abused the Nightingale, and declared that it was a very ungrateful creature.

"We have the best bird, after all," said they.

And so the artificial bird had to sing again, and that was the thirty-fourth time that they listened to the same piece. For all that they did not know it quite by heart, for it was so very difficult. And the Play-master praised the bird particularly; yes, he declared that it was better than a nightingale, not only with regard to its plumage and the many beautiful diamonds, but inside as well.

"For you see, ladies and gentlemen, and above all, your Imperial Majesty, with a real nightingale one can never calculate what is coming, but in this artificial bird everything is settled. One can explain it; one can open it, and make people understand where the waltzes come from, how they go, and how one follows up another."

"Those are quite our own ideas," they all said.

And the speaker received permission to show the bird to the people on the next Sunday. The people were to hear it sing too, the Emperor commanded; and they did hear it, and were as much pleased as if they had all got tipsy upon tea, for that's quite the Chinese fashion; and they all said, "O!" and held up their forefingers and nodded. But the poor Fisherman, who had heard the real Nightingale, said,—

"It sounds pretty enough, and the melodies resemble each other, but there's something wanting, though I know not what!"

The real Nightingale was banished from the country and empire. The artificial bird had its place on a silken cushion close to the Emperor's bed; all the presents it had received, gold and precious stones, were ranged about it; in title it had advanced to be the High Imperial After-Dinner-Singer, and in rank, to number one on the left hand; for the Emperor considered that side the most important in which the heart is placed, and even in an emperor the heart is on the left side; and the Play-master wrote a work of five-and-twenty volumes about the artificial bird; it was very learned and very long, full of the most difficult Chinese words; but yet all the people declared that they had read it, and understood it, for fear of being considered stupid, and having their bodies trampled on.

So a whole year went by. The Emperor, the court, and all the other Chinese knew every little twitter in the artificial bird's song by heart. But just for that reason it pleased them best—they could sing with it themselves, and they did so. The street boys sang, "Tsi-tsi-tsi-glug-glug!" and the Emperor himself sang it too. Yes, that was certainly famous.

But one evening, when the artificial bird was singing its best, and the Emperor lay in bed listening to it, something inside the bird said, "Whizz!" Something cracked. "Whir-r-r!" All the wheels ran round, and then the music stopped.

The Emperor immediately sprang out of bed, and caused his body physician to be called; but what could *he* do? Then they sent for a watchmaker, and after a good deal of talking and investigation, the bird was put into something like order; but the Watchmaker said that the bird must be carefully treated, for the barrels were worn, and it would be impossible to put new ones in in such a manner that the music would go. There was great lamentation; only once in a year was it permitted to let the bird sing, and that was almost too much. But then the Play-master made a little speech, full of heavy words, and said this was just as good as before—and so of course it was as good as before.

Now five years had gone by, and a real grief came upon the whole nation. The Chinese were really fond of their Emperor, and now he was ill, and could not, it was said, live much longer. Already a new Emperor had been chosen, and the people stood out in the street and asked the Cavalier how their old Emperor did.

"P!" said he, and shook his head.

Cold and pale lay the Emperor in his great gorgeous bed; the whole court thought him dead, and each one ran to pay homage to the new ruler. The chamberlains ran out to talk it over, and the ladies'-maids had a great coffee party. All about, in all the halls and passages, cloth had been laid down so that no footstep could be heard, and therefore it was quiet there, quite quiet. But the Emperor was not dead yet: stiff and pale he lay on the gorgeous bed with the long velvet curtains and the heavy gold tassels; high up, a window stood open, and the moon shone in upon the Emperor and the artificial bird.

The poor Emperor could scarcely breathe; it was just as if something lay upon his chest: he opened his eyes, and then he saw that it was Death who sat upon his chest, and had put on his golden crown, and held in one hand the Emperor's sword and in the other his beautiful banner. And all around, from among the folds of the splendid velvet curtains, strange heads peered forth; a few very ugly, the rest quite lovely and mild. These were all the Emperor's bad and good deeds, that stood before him now that Death sat upon his heart.

"Do you remember this?" whispered one to the other. "Do you remember that?" and then they told him so much that the perspiration ran from his forehead.

"I did not know that!" said the Emperor. "Music! music! the great

Chinese drum!" he cried, "so that I need not hear all they say!" And they continued speaking, and Death nodded like a Chinaman to all they said.

"Music! music!" cried the Emperor. "You little precious golden bird, sing, sing! I have given you gold and costly presents; I have even hung my golden slipper around your neck—sing now, sing!"

But the bird stood still; no one was there to wind him up, and he could not sing without that; but Death continued to stare at the Emperor with his great hollow eyes, and it was quiet, fearfully quiet.

Then there sounded from the window, suddenly, the most lovely song. It was the little live Nightingale, that sat outside on a spray. It had heard of the Emperor's sad plight, and had come to sing to him of comfort and hope. And as it sang the spectres grew paler and paler; the blood ran quicker and more quickly through the Emperor's weak limbs; and even Death listened, and said,—

"Go on, little Nightingale, go on!"

"But will you give me that splendid golden sword? Will you give me that rich banner? Will you give me the Emperor's crown?"

And Death gave up each of these treasures for a song. And the Nightingale sang on and on; and it sang of the quiet church-yard, where the white roses grow, where the elderblossom smells sweet, and where the fresh grass is moistened by the tears of survivors. Then Death felt a longing to see his garden, and floated out at the window in the form of a cold, white mist.

"Thanks! thanks!" said the Emperor. "You heavenly little bird! I know you well. I banished you from my country and empire, and yet you have charmed away the evil faces from my couch, and banished Death from my heart! How can I reward you?"

"You have rewarded me!" replied the Nightingale. "I have drawn tears from your eyes, when I sang the first time—I shall never forget that. Those are the jewels that rejoice a singer's heart. But now sleep and grow fresh and strong again. I will sing you something."

And it sang, and the Emperor fell into a sweet slumber. Ah! how mild and refreshing that sleep was! The sun shone upon him through the windows, when he awoke refreshed and restored; not one of his servants had yet returned, for they all thought he was dead; only the Nightingale still sat beside him and sang.

"You must always stay with me," said the Emperor. "You shall sing as you please; and I'll break the artificial bird into a thousand pieces."

"Not so," replied the Nightingale. "It did well as long as it could; keep it as you have done till now. I cannot build my nest in the palace to dwell in; but let me come when I feel the wish; then I will sit in the evening on the spray yonder by the window, and sing you something, so that you may be glad and thoughtful at once. I will sing of those who are happy and of those who suffer. I will sing of good and of evil that remain hidden round about you. The little singing bird flies far around, to the poor fisherman, to the peasant's roof, to every one who dwells far away from you and from your court. I love your heart more than your crown, and yet the crown has an air of sanctity about it. I will come and sing to you—but one thing you must promise me."

"Everything!" said the Emperor; and he stood there in his imperial robes, which he had put on himself, and pressed the sword which was heavy with gold to his heart.

"One thing I beg of you: tell no one that you have a little bird who tells you everything. Then it will go all the better."

And the Nightingale flew away.

The servants came in to look to their dead Emperor, and—yes, there he stood, and the Emperor said "Good morning!"

THE CREATION

James Weldon Johnson

And God stepped out on space,
And he looked around and said:
I'm lonely—
I'll make me a world.

And far as the eye of God could see
Darkness covered everything,
Blacker than a hundred midnights
Down in a cypress swamp.

Then God smiled,
And the light broke,
And the darkness rolled up on one side,
And the light stood shining on the other,
And God said: That's good!

Then God reached out and took the light in His hands,
And God rolled the light around in His hands
Until He made the sun;
And He set that sun a-blazing in the heavens.
And the light that was left from making the sun
God gathered up in a shining ball
And flung against the darkness,
Spangling the night with the moon and stars.
Then down between
The darkness and the light
He hurled the world;
And God said: That's good!

Then God himself stepped down—
And the sun was on His right hand,
And the moon was on His left;
The stars were clustered about His head,
And the earth was under His feet.
And God walked, and where He trod
His footsteps hollowed the valleys out
And bulged the mountains up.

Then He stopped and looked and saw
That the earth was hot and barren.
So God stepped over to the edge of the world
And He spat out the seven seas—

He batted His eyes, and the lightnings flashed—
He clapped His hands, and the thunders rolled—
And the waters above the earth came down,
The cooling waters came down.

Then the green grass sprouted,
And the little red flowers blossomed,
The pine tree pointed his finger to the sky,
And the oak spread out his arms,
The lakes cuddled down in the hollows of the ground,
And the rivers ran down to the sea;
And God smiled again,
And the rainbow appeared,
And curled itself around His shoulder.

Then God raised His arm and He waved His hand
Over the sea and over the land,
And He said: Bring forth! Bring forth!
And quicker than God could drop His hand,
Fishes and fowls
And beasts and birds
Swam the rivers and the seas,
Roamed the forests and the woods,
And split the air with their wings.
And God said: That's good!

Then God walked around,
And God looked around
On all that He had made.
He looked on His world
With all its living things,
And God said: I'm lonely still.

Then God sat down—
On the side of a hill where He could think;
By a deep, wide river He sat down;
With His head in His hands,
God thought and thought,
Till He thought: I'll make me a man!

Up from the bed of the river
God scooped the clay;
And by the bank of the river
He kneeled Him down;
And there the great God Almighty
Who lit the sun and fixed it in the sky,
Who flung the stars to the most far corner of the night,

Who rounded the earth in the middle of His hand;
This Great God,
Like a mammy bending over her baby,
Kneeled down in the dust
Toiling over a lump of clay
Till He shaped it in His own image;

Then into it He blew the breath of life,
And man became a living soul.
Amen. Amen.

LACANDON CREATION MYTH

Recorded by Howard Cline in Chiapas

In the beginning there were two brothers, Sukuyum and Nohotsakyum, and they are the main gods. Sukuyum is older and maybe more powerful. These two lived in the sky in a house, but Sukuyum wanted a house for himself. He ordered his younger brother to make him a house, but would not help him make it because he did not want to. Nohotsakyum made a round ball like masa for making tortillas. That is our world and the house of Sukuyum, who lives in the middle of it. Where he lives there is much fire, and he orders earthquakes and volcanos. Evil persons who kill other people and who lie and steal go down where he lives after they die. He burns them and punishes them by running hot irons up their penises. Nohotsakyum made the world and everything in it. First he made the land and then the water, and when he had finished he put in it all the things people would need. First he had to make the sun to have some light so he could work, and then came the moon and the stars. Of the things that grow he made them in this order: maize, bananas, garlic, beans, and cane. After that, there was no special order, because he made plants and vines and trees, but he made rice before he made fruit.

When the earth was all ready, he made men. He made them by peoples. First came the Kalsia, which is to say, people of the monkey; then came Koho-ka, people of the peccary; then Ka-puk, or people of the tiger; and then Chan-ka, or people of the pheasant. This is how he made people. He made them out of clay—men, women, and children—giving them eyes, a nose, all other parts, then he put the clay on the fire where he was cooking tortillas. The clay got hard from the fire, and the people lived. After they had life, he gave each people a place on earth to live. He had to make clay babies and children of all sizes so that there would be someone to be people on earth after the first adults died.

When he finished making men, he made animals in the same way. He made them in this order: tiger, snakes, monkey, howling ape, peccary, mountain deer, pheasant, wild turkey, and then the other birds and animals in no order.

Nohotsakyum and his wife Nainohotsakyum and all the good dead people and santos of various kinds live in the sky where there is land, with roads, and trees like here, but no animals and no chickens. When the world comes to an end by being eaten up by the big jaguar, everyone will go up there and live like Nohotsakyum, who works in his corn patch, smokes cigars, and eats tortillas and beans.

II

Transformation

Maid's failure to realize her dreams testifies to the difficulty of escaping from one's natural state. Yet the atmosphere of mystery and change in the world under the sea maintains the hope of miracles. The sea-scape is so beautiful and so mysterious that it is filled with the promise of magic transformations. In *The Tempest,* Shakespeare shows the same feeling for the world underwater as Andersen's in *The Little Sea Maid.* The island spirit Ariel informs a young prince that his father has drowned. He softens the news with a beautiful description of death, not as decay but as transformation.

> Full fathom five thy father lies,
>   Of his bones are coral made,
> Those are pearls that were his eyes.
>   Nothing of him that doth fade
> But doth suffer a sea change
> Into something rich and strange.

The sea change of death makes every part of the dead King's body into a precious and lasting jewel. The sea traditionally has this power to transform and ennoble what it touches.

That death is a transformation into "something rich and strange," something greater than the original human state, draws another parallel between Shakespeare's lines and Andersen's story. When the Sea Maid dies and finds that she has a soul at last, her discovery echoes the idea in many stories and poems, that death is the most mysterious transformation of all. This is one of the most important themes in "The Book of Thel."

Blake's heroine, Thel, is a glorious, innocent beauty. Like Daphne, she chooses to remain a virgin, to stay in her comfortable valley of Har. The necessity of death is so horrible to her that she flees in a deathlike retreat to her childhood. Yet the lily, cloud, worm, and clay try to assure her that death is part of her fate, a natural transformation to be accepted and glorified. Death is more real and more grim here than in *The Little Sea Maid,* but the speakers from the natural world try to make Thel understand that to reject death is to reject life. When she is finally confronted with this reality, she runs home in terror.

In "Blood, Sea" the narrator is transformed into one of the micro-scopic elements of the human blood. They invert all our frames of reference and suggest things about our physical beings we could never have imagined otherwise. The same is true to a lesser degree of the poems of Langston Huges and Welton Smith quoted here.

The idea of metamorphosis may lead one to a study of the *I Ching,* to understand the nature of change. It may lead to the mystic's accep-tance of change as illusion. It may lead to a laconic way of describing upheaval and turmoil in one's life; "I've been going through some changes." However it comes about, change shocks us. When the other-world seems to be involved, or the change is sudden and surprising, the joy or terror of change is doubled; then the globe does seem "to become winged in its orbit."

APOLLO AND DAPHNE

DAPHNE WAS APOLLO'S first love. It was not brought about by accident, but by the malice of Cupid. Apollo saw the boy playing with his bow and arrows; and being himself elated with his recent victory over Python, he said to him, "What have you to do with warlike weapons, saucy boy? Leave them for hands worthy of them. Behold the conquest I have won by means of them over the vast serpent who stretched his poisonous body over acres of the plain! Be content with your torch, child, and kindle up your flames, as you call them, where you will, but presume not to meddle with my weapons." Venus's boy heard these words, and rejoined, "Your arrows may strike all things else, Apollo, but mine shall strike you." So saying, he took his stand on a rock of Parnassus, and drew from his quiver two arrows of different workmanship, one to excite love, the other to repel it. The former was of gold and sharp pointed, the latter blunt and tipped with lead. With the leaden shaft he struck the nymph Daphne, the daughter of the river god Peneus, and with the golden one Apollo, through the heart. Forthwith the god was seized with love for the maiden, and she abhorred the thought of loving. Her delight was in woodland sports and in the spoils of the chase. Many lovers sought her, but she spurned them all, ranging the woods, and taking no thought of Cupid nor of Hymen. Her father often said to her, "Daughter, you owe me a son-in-law; you owe me grandchildren." She, hating the thought of marriage as a crime, with her beautiful face tinged all over with blushes, threw her arms around her father's neck, and said, "Dearest father, grant me this favor, that I may always remain unmarried, like Diana." He consented, but at the same time said, "Your own face will forbid it."

Apollo loved her, and longed to obtain her; and he who gives oracles to all the world was not wise enough to look into his own fortunes. He saw her hair flung loose over her shoulders, and said, "If so charming in disorder, what would it be if arranged?" He saw her eyes bright as stars; he saw her lips, and was not satisfied with only seeing them. He admired her hands and arms, naked to the shoulder, and whatever was hidden from view he imagined more beautiful still. He followed her; she fled, swifter than the wind, and delayed not a moment at his entreaties. "Stay," said he, "daughter of Peneus; I am not a foe. Do not fly me as a lamb flies the wolf, or a dove the hawk. It is for love I pursue you. You make me miserable, for fear you should fall and hurt yourself on these stones, and I should be the cause. Pray run slower, and I will follow slower. I am no clown, no rude peasant. Jupiter is my father, and I am lord of Delphos and Tenedos, and know all things, present and future. I am the god of song and the lyre. My arrows fly true to the mark; but, alas! an arrow more fatal than mine has pierced my heart! I am the god of medicine, and know the virtues of all healing plants. Alas! I suffer a malady that no balm can cure!

The nymph continued her flight, and left his plea half uttered. And even as she fled she charmed him. The wind blew her garments, and her unbound hair streamed loose behind her. The god grew impatient to find his wooings thrown away, and, sped by Cupid, gained upon her in the race. It was like a hound pursuing a hare, with open jaws ready to seize, while the feebler animal darts forward, slipping from the very grasp. So flew the god and the virgin—he on the wings of love, and she on those of fear. The pursuer is the more rapid, however, and gains upon her, and his panting breath blows upon her hair. Her strength begins to fail, and, ready to sink she calls upon her father, the river god: "Help me, Peneus! open the earth to enclose me, or change my form, which has brought me into this danger!" Scarcely had she spoken, when a stiffness seized all her limbs; her bosom began to be enclosed in a tender bark; her hair became leaves; her arms became branches; her foot stuck fast in the ground, as a root; her face became a tree-top, retaining nothing of its former self but its beauty. Apollo stood amazed. He touched the stem, and felt the flesh tremble under the new bark. He embraced the branches, and lavished kisses on the wood. The branches shrank from his lips. "Since you cannot be my wife," said he, "you shall assuredly be my tree. I will wear you for my crown; I will decorate with you my harp and my quiver; and when the great Roman conquerors lead up the triumphal pomp to the Capitol, you shall be woven into wreaths for their brows. And, as eternal youth is mine, you also shall be always green, and your leaf know no decay." The nymph, now changed into a Laurel tree, bowed its head in grateful acknowledgment.

CINDERELLA OR, THE LITTLE GLASS SLIPPER

Charles Perrault

Once there was a gentleman who married, for his second wife, the proudest and most haughty woman that was ever seen. She had, by a former husband, two daughters of her own humour, who were, indeed, exactly like her in all things. He had likewise, by another wife, a young daughter, but of unparalleled goodness and sweetness of temper, which she took from her mother, who was the best creature in the world.

No sooner were the ceremonies of the wedding over but the mother-in-law began to show herself in her true colours. She could not bear the good qualities of this pretty girl, and the less because they made her own daughters appear the more odious. She employed her in the meanest work of the house: she scoured the dishes, tables, etc., and rubbed madam's chamber, and those of misses, her daughters; she lay up in a sorry garret, upon a wretched straw bed, while her sisters lay in fine rooms, with floors all inlaid, upon beds of the very newest fashion, and where they had looking-glasses so large that they might see themselves at their full length from head to foot.

The poor girl bore all patiently, and dared not tell her father, who would have rattled her off; for his wife governed him entirely. When she had done her work, she used to go into the chimney-corner, and sit down among cinders and ashes, which made her commonly be called *Cinderwench;* but the youngest, who was not so rude and uncivil as the eldest, called her Cinderella. However, Cinderella, notwithstanding her mean apparel, was a hundred times handsomer than her sisters, though they were always dressed very richly.

It happened that the King's son gave a ball, and invited all persons of fashion to it. Our young misses were also invited, for they cut a very grand figure among the quality. They were mightily delighted at this invitation, and wonderfully busy in choosing out such gowns, petticoats, and head-clothes as might become them. This was a new trouble to Cinderella; for it was she who ironed her sister's linen, and plaited their ruffles; they talked all day long of nothing but how they should be dressed.

'For my part,' said the eldest, 'I will wear my red velvet suit with French trimming.'

'And I,' said the youngest, 'shall have my usual petticoat; but then, to make amends for that, I will put on my gold-flowered manteau, and my diamond stomacher, which is far from being the most ordinary one in the world.'

They sent for the best tire-woman they could get to make up their head-dresses and adjust their double pinners, and they had their red brushes and patches from Mademoiselle de la Poche.

Cinderella was likewise called up to them to be consulted in all these matters, for she had excellent notions, and advised them always for the best, nay, and offered her services to dress their heads, which they were very willing she should do. As she was doing this, they said to her:

'Cinderella, would you not be glad to go to the ball?'

'Alas!' said she, 'you only jeer me; it is not for such as I am to go thither.'

'Thou art in the right of it,' replied they; 'it would make the people laugh to see a Cinderwench at a ball.'

Anyone but Cinderella would have dressed their heads awry, but she was very good, and dressed them perfectly well. They were almost two days without eating, so much they were transported with joy. They broke above a dozen of laces in trying to be laced up close, that they might have a fine slender shape, and they were continually at their looking-glass. At last the happy day came; they went to Court, and Cinderella followed them with her eyes as long as she could, and when she had lost sight of them, she fell a-crying.

Her godmother, who saw her all in tears, asked her what was the matter.

'I wish I could—I wish I could—;' she was not able to speak the rest, being interrupted by her tears and sobbing.

This godmother of hers, who was a fairy, said to her, 'Thou wishest thou couldst go to the ball; is it not so?'

'Y—es,' cried Cinderella, with a great sigh.

'Well,' said her godmother, 'be but a good girl, and I will contrive that thou shalt go.' Then she took her into her chamber, and said to her, 'Run into the garden, and bring me a pumpkin.'

Cinderella went immediately to gather the finest she could get, and brought it to her godmother, not being able to imagine how this pumpkin could make her go to the ball. Her godmother scooped out all the inside of it, having left nothing but the rind; which done, she struck it with her wand, and the pumpkin was instantly turned into a fine coach, gilded all over with gold.

She then went to look into her mouse-trap, where she found six mice, all alive, and ordered Cinderella to lift up a little the trapdoor, when, giving each mouse, as it went out, a little tap with her wand, the mouse was that moment turned into a fine horse, which altogether made a very fine set of six horses of a beautiful mouse-coloured dapple-grey. Being at a loss for a coachman,

'I will go and see,' says Cinderella, 'if there is never a rat in the rat-trap—we may make a coachman of him.'

'Thou art in the right,' replied her godmother; 'go and look.'

Cinderella brought the trap to her, and in it there were three huge rats. The fairy made choice of one of the three which had the largest beard, and, having touched him with her wand, he was turned into a fat, jolly coachman, who had the smartest whiskers eyes ever beheld. After that, she said to her:

'Go again into the garden, and you will find six lizards behind the watering-pot, bring them to me.'

She had no sooner done so but her godmother turned them into six footmen, who skipped up immediately behind the coach, with their liveries all bedaubed with gold and silver, and clung as close behind each other as if they had done nothing else their whole lives. The Fairy then said to Cinderella:

'Well, you see here an equipage fit to go to the ball with; are you not pleased with it?'

'Oh! yes,' cried she; 'but must I go thither as I am, in these nasty rags?'

Her godmother only just touched her with her wand, and, at the same instant, her clothes were turned into cloth of gold and silver, all beset with jewels. This done, she gave her a pair of glass slippers, the prettiest in the whole world. Being thus decked out, she got up into her coach; but her godmother, above all things, commanded her not to stay till after midnight, telling her, at the same time, that if she stayed one moment longer, the coach would be a pumpkin again, her horses mice, her coachman a rat, her footmen lizards, and her clothes become just as they were before.

She promised her godmother she would not fail of leaving the ball before midnight; and then away she drives, scarce able to contain herself for joy. The King's son, who was told that a great princess, whom nobody knew, was come, ran out to receive her; he gave her his hand as she alighted out of the coach, and led her into the hall, among all the company. There was immediately a profound silence, they left off dancing, and the violins ceased to play, so attentive was everyone to contemplate the singular beauties of the unknown new-comer. Nothing was then heard but a confused noise of:

'Ha! how handsome she is! Ha! how handsome she is!'

The King himself, old as he was, could not help watching her, and telling the Queen softly that it was a long time since he had seen so beautiful and lovely a creature.

All the ladies were busied in considering her clothes and headdress, that they might have some made next day after the same pattern, provided they could meet with such fine materials and as able hands to make them.

The King's son conducted her to the most honourable seat, and afterwards took her out to dance with him; she danced so very gracefully that they all more and more admired her. A fine collation was served up, whereof the young prince ate not a morsel, so intently was he busied in gazing on her.

She went and sat down by her sisters, showing them a thousand civilities, giving them part of the oranges and citrons which the Prince had presented her with, which very much surprised them, for they did not know her. While Cinderella was thus amusing her sisters, she heard the clock strike eleven and three-quarters, whereupon she immediately made a courtesy to the company and hasted away as fast as she could.

Being got home, she ran to seek out her godmother, and, after having thanked her, she said she could not but heartily wish she might go next day to the ball, because the King's son had desired her.

As she was eagerly telling her godmother whatever had passed at the ball, her two sisters knocked at the door, which Cinderella ran and opened.

'How long you have stayed!' cried she, gaping, rubbing her eyes and stretching herself as if she had been just waked out of her sleep; she had not, however, any manner of inclination to sleep since they went from home.

'If thou hadst been at the ball,' says one of her sisters, 'thou wouldst not have been tired with it. There came thither the finest princess, the most beautiful ever was seen with mortal eyes; she showed us a thousand civilities, and gave us oranges and citrons.'

Cinderella seemed very indifferent in the matter; indeed, she asked them the name of that princess; but they told her they did not know it, and that the King's son was very uneasy on her account and would give all the world to know who she was. At this Cinderella, smiling, replied:

'She must, then, be very beautiful indeed; how happy you have been! Could not I see her? Ah! dear Miss Charlotte, do lend me your yellow suit of clothes which you wear every day.'

'Ay, to be sure!' cried Miss Charlotte; 'lend my clothes to such a dirty Cinderwench as thou art! I should be a fool.'

Cinderella, indeed, expected well such answer, and was very glad of the refusal; for she would have been sadly put to it if her sister had lent her what she asked for jestingly.

The next day the two sisters were at the ball, and so was Cinderella, but dressed more magnificently than before. The King's son was always by her, and never ceased his compliments and kind speeches to her; to whom all this was so far from being tiresome that she quite forgot what her godmother had recommended to her; so that she, at last, counted the clock striking twelve when she took it to be no more than eleven; she then rose up and fled, as nimble as a deer. The Prince followed, but could not overtake her. She left behind one of her glass slippers, which the Prince took up most carefully. She got home, but quite out of breath, and in her nasty old clothes, having nothing left her of all her finery but one of the little slippers, fellow to that she dropped. The guards at the palace gate were asked:

If they had not seen a princess go out.

Who said: They had seen nobody go out but a young girl, very meanly dressed, and who had more the air of a poor country wench than a gentlewoman.

When the two sisters returned from the ball Cinderella asked them: If they had been well diverted, and if the fine lady had been there.

They told her: Yes, but that she hurried away immediately when it struck twelve, and with so much haste that she dropped one of her little glass slippers, the prettiest in the world, which the King's son had taken up; that he had done nothing but look at her all the time at the ball, and that most certainly he was very much in love with the beautiful person who owned the glass slipper.

What they said was very true; for a few days after the King's son caused it to be proclaimed, by sound of trumpet, that he would marry her whose foot this slipper would just fit. They whom he employed began to try it upon the princesses, then the duchesses and all the Court, but in vain; it was brought to the two sisters, who did all they possibly could to thrust their foot into the slipper, but they could not effect it. Cinderella, who saw all this, and knew her slipper, said to them, laughing:

'Let me see if it will not fit me.'

Her sisters burst out a-laughing, and began to banter her. The gentleman who was sent to try the slipper looked earnestly at Cinderella, and, finding her very handsome, said:

It was but just that she should try, and that he had orders to let everyone make trial.

He obliged Cinderella to sit down, and, putting the slipper to her foot, he found it went on very easily, and fitted her as if it had been made of wax. The astonishment her two sisters were in was excessively great, but still abundantly greater when Cinderella pulled out of her pocket the other slipper, and put it on her foot. Thereupon, in came her godmother, who, having touched with her wand Cinderella's clothes, made them richer and more magnificent than any of those she had before.

And now her two sisters found her to be that fine, beautiful lady whom they had seen at the ball. They threw themselves at her feet to beg pardon for all the ill-treatment they had made her undergo. Cinderella took them up, and, as she embraced them, cried:

That she forgave them with all her heart, and desired them always to love her.

She was conducted to the young Prince, dressed as she was; he thought her more charming than ever, and, a few days after, married her. Cinderella, who was no less good than beautiful, gave her two sisters lodgings in the palace, and that very same day matched them with two great lords of the Court.

THE LITTLE SEA-MAID

Hans Christian Andersen

FAR OUT in the sea the water is as blue as the petals of the most beautiful corn-flower, and as clear as the purest glass. But it is very deep, deeper than any cable will sound; many steeples must be placed one above the other to reach from the ground to the surface of the water. And down there live the sea-people.

Now, you must not believe there is nothing down there but the naked sand; no,—the strangest trees and plants grow there, so pliable in their stalks and leaves that at the least motion of the water they move just as if they had life. All fishes, great and small, glide among the twigs, just as here the birds do in the trees. In the deepest spot of all lies the Sea-king's castle: the walls are of coral, and the tall, Gothic windows of the clearest amber; shells form the roof, and they open and shut according as the water flows. It looks lovely, for in each shell lie gleaming pearls, a single one of which would have great value in a queen's diadem.

The Sea-king below there had been a widower for many years, while his old mother kept house for him. She was a clever woman, but proud of her rank, so she wore twelve oysters on her tail, while the other great people were only allowed to wear six. Beyond this she was deserving of great praise, especially because she was very fond of her grand-daughters, the little Sea-princesses. These were six pretty children; but the youngest was the most beautiful of all. Her skin was as clear and as fine as a rose leaf; her eyes were as blue as the deepest sea; but, like all the rest, she had no feet, for her body ended in a fish-tail.

All day long they could play in the castle, down in the halls, where living flowers grew out of the walls. The great amber windows were opened, and then the fishes swam in to them, just as the swallows fly in to us when we open our windows; but the fishes swam straight up to the Princesses, ate out of their hands, and let themselves be stroked.

Outside the castle was a great garden with bright red and dark blue flowers; the fruit glowed like gold, and the flowers like flames of fire; and they continually kept moving their stalks and leaves. The earth itself was the finest sand, but blue as the flame of brimstone. A peculiar blue radiance lay upon everything down there: one would have thought oneself high in the air, with the canopy of heaven above and around, rather than at the bottom of the deep sea. During a calm the sun could be seen; it appeared like a purple flower, from which all light streamed out.

Each of the little Princesses had her own little place in the garden, where she might dig and plant at her good pleasure. One gave her flower-bed the form of a whale; another thought it better to make hers like a little sea-woman: but the youngest made hers quite round, like the sun and had flowers which gleamed red as the sun itself. She was a strange child, quiet and thoughtful, and when the other sisters made a display of the beautiful things they had received out of wrecked ships, she would have nothing beyond the red flowers which resembled the sun, except a pretty marble statue. This was a figure of a charming boy, hewn out of white clear stone, which had sunk down to the bottom of the sea from a wreck. She planted a pink weeping willow beside this statue; the tree grew famously, and hung its fresh branches over the statue towards the blue sandy ground, where the shadow showed violet, and moved like the branches themselves; it seemed as if the ends of the branches and the roots were playing together and wished to kiss each other.

There was no greater pleasure for her than to hear of the world of men above them. The old grandmother had to tell all she knew of ships and towns, of men and animals. It seemed particularly beautiful to her that up on the earth the flowers shed fragrance, for they had none down at the bottom of the sea, and that the trees were green, and that the fishes which one saw there among the trees could sing so loud and clear that it was a pleasure to hear them. What the grandmother called fishes were the little birds; the Princess could not understand them in any other way, for she had never seen a bird.

"When you have reached your fifteenth year," said the grandmother, "you shall have leave to rise up out of the sea, to sit on the rocks in the moonlight, and to see the great ships as they sail by. Then you will see forests and towns!"

In the next year one of the sisters was fifteen years of age, but each of the others was one year younger than the next; so that the youngest had full five years to wait before she could come up from the bottom of the sea, and find how our world looked. But one promised to tell the others what she had seen and what she had thought the most beautiful on the first day of her visit; for their grandmother could not tell them enough—there was so much about which they wanted information.

No one was more anxious about these things than the youngest—just that one who had the longest time to wait, and who was always quiet and thoughtful. Many a night she stood by the open window, and looked up through the dark blue water at the fishes splashing with their fins and tails. Moon and stars she could see; they certainly shone quite faintly, but through the water they looked much larger than they appear in our eyes. When something like a black cloud passed among them, she knew that it was either a whale swimming over her head, or a ship with many people: they certainly did not think that a pretty little sea-maid was standing down below stretching up her white hands towards the keel of their ship.

Now the eldest Princess was fifteen years old, and might mount up to the surface of the sea.

When she came back, she had a hundred things to tell,—but the finest thing, she said, was to lie in the moonshine on a sand-bank in the quiet sea, and to look at the neighboring coast, with the large town, where the lights twinkled like a hundred stars, and to hear the music and the noise and clamor of carriages and men, to see the many church steeples, and to hear the sound of the bells. Just because she could not get up to these, she longed for them more than for anything.

O how the youngest sister listened! and afterwards when she stood at the open window and looked up through the dark-blue water, she thought of the great city with all its bustle and noise; and then she thought she could hear the church bells ringing, even down to the depth where she was.

In the following year, the second sister received p ● mission to mount upward through the water and to swim whither she pleased. She rose up just as the sun was setting, and this spectacle, she said, was the most beautiful. The whole sky looked like gold, and as to the clouds, she could not properly describe their beauty. They sailed away over her head, purple and violet-colored, but far quicker than the clouds there flew a flight of wild swans, like a long white veil, over the water towards where the sun stood. She swam towards them; but the sun sank, and the roseate hue faded on the sea and in the clouds.

In the following year the next sister went up. She was the boldest of them all, and therefore she swam up a broad stream that poured its waters into the sea. She saw glorious green hills clothed with vines; palaces and castles shone forth from amid splendid woods; she heard how all the birds sang; and the sun shone so warm that she was often obliged to dive under the water to cool her glowing face. In a little bay she found a whole swarm of little mortals. They were quite naked, and splashed about in the water; she wanted to play with them, but they fled in affright and a little black animal came,—it was a dog, but she had never seen a dog,—and it barked at her so terribly that she became frightened, and tried to gain the open sea. But she could never forget the glorious woods, the green hills, and the pretty children, who could swim in the water, though they had not fish-tails.

The fourth sister was not so bold: she remained out in the midst of the wild sea, and declared that just there it was most beautiful. One could see for many miles around, and the sky above looked like a bell of glass. She had seen ships, but only in the far distance—they looked like seagulls; and the funny dolphins had thrown somersaults, and the great whales spouted out water from their nostrils, so that it looked like hundreds of fountains all around.

Now came the turn of the fifth sister. Her birthday came in the winter, and so she saw what the others had not seen the first time. The sea looked quite green, and great icebergs were floating about; each one separated like a pearl, she said, and yet was much taller than the church steeples built by men. They showed themselves in the strangest forms, and shone like diamonds. She had seated herself upon one of the greatest of all, and let the wind play with her long hair; and all the sailing ships tacked about in a very rapid way beyond where she sat: but toward evening the sky became covered with clouds, it thundered and lightened, and the black waves lifted the great ice-blocks high up, and let them glow in the red glare. On all the ships the sails were reefed, and there was fear and anguish. But she sat quietly upon her floating iceberg, and saw the forked blue flashes dart into the sea.

Each of the sisters, as she came up for the first time to the surface of the water, was delighted with the new and beautiful sights she saw; but as they now had permission, as grown-up girls, to go whenever they liked, it became indifferent to them. They wished themselves back again, and after a month had elapsed they said it was best of all down below, for there one felt so comfortably at home.

Many an evening hour the five sisters took one another by the arm and rose up in a row over the water. They had splendid voices, more charming than any mortal could have; and when a storm was approaching, so that they could apprehend that ships would go down, they swam on before the ships and sang lovely songs, which told how beautiful it was at the bottom of the sea, and exhorted the sailors not to be afraid to come down. But these could not understand the words, and thought it was the storm sighing; and they did not see the splendors below, for if the ships sank they were drowned, and came as corpses to the Sea-king's palace.

When the sisters thus rose up, arm in arm, in the evening time, through the water, the little sister stood all alone looking after them;

and she felt as if she must weep; but the sea-maid has no tears and for this reason she suffers far more acutely.

"O if I were only fifteen years old!" said she. "I know I shall love the world up there very much, and the people who live and dwell there."

At last she was really fifteen years old.

"Now, you see, you are grown up," said the grandmother, the old dowager. "Come, let me adorn you like your sisters."

And she put a wreath of white lilies in the little maid's hair, but each flower was half a pearl; and the old lady let eight great oysters attach themselves to the Princess's tail, in token of her high rank.

"But that hurts so!" said the little Sea-maid.

"Yes, pride must suffer pain," replied the old lady.

O how glad she would have been to shake off all the tokens of rank and lay aside the heavy wreath! Her red flowers in the garden suited her better; but she could not help it. "Farewell!" she said, and then she rose, light and clear as a water-bubble, up through the sea.

The sun had just set when she lifted her head above the sea, but all the clouds still shone like roses and gold, and in the pale red sky the evening-stars gleamed bright and beautiful. The air was mild and fresh, and the sea quite calm. There lay a great ship with three masts; one single sail only was set, for not a breeze stirred, and around in the shrouds and on the yards sat the sailors. There was music and singing, and as the evening closed in, hundreds of colored lanterns were lighted up, and looked as if the flags of every nation were waving in the air. The little Sea-maid swam straight to the cabin window, and each time the sea lifted her up, she could look through the panes, which were clear as crystal, and see many people standing within dressed in their best. But the handsomest of all was the young Prince with the great black eyes: he was certainly not much more than sixteen years old; it was his birthday, and that was the cause of all this feasting. The sailors were dancing upon deck; and when the young Prince came out, more than a hundred rockets rose into the air; they shone like day, so that the little Sea-maid was quite startled, and dived under the water; but soon she put out her head again, and then it seemed just as if all the stars of heaven were falling down upon her. She had never seen such fire-works. Great suns spurted fire all around, glorious fiery fishes flew up into the blue air, and everything was mirrored in the clear blue sea. The ship itself was so brightly lit up that every separate rope could be seen, and the people therefore appeared the more plainly. O how handsome the young Prince was! And he pressed the people's hands and smiled, while the music rang out in the glorious night.

It became late; but the little Sea-maid could not turn her eyes from the ship and from the beautiful Prince. The colored lanterns were extinguished, rockets ceased to fly into the air, and no more cannons were fired; but there was a murmuring and a buzzing deep down in the sea; and she sat on the water, swaying up and down, so that she could look into the cabin. But as the ship got more way, one sail after another was spread. And now the waves rose higher, great clouds came up, and in the distance there was lightning. O! it was going to be fearful weather, therefore the sailors furled the sails. The great ship flew in swift career over the wild sea: the waters rose up like great black mountains, which wanted to roll over the masts; but like a swan the ship dived into the valleys between these high waves, and then let itself be lifted on high again. To the little Sea-maid this seemed merry sport, but to the sailors it appeared very differently. The ship groaned and creaked; the thick planks were bent by the heavy blows; the sea broke into the ship; the mainmast snapped in two like a thin reed, and the ship lay over on her side, while the water rushed into the hold. Now the little Sea-maid saw that the people were in peril; she herself was obliged to take care to avoid the beams and fragments of the ship which were floating about on the waters. One moment it was so pitch dark that not a single object could be descried, but when it lightened it became so bright that she could distinguish every one on board. She looked particularly for the young prince, and when the ship parted she saw him sink into the sea. Then she was very glad, for now he would come down to her. But then she remembered that people could not live in the water, and that when he got down to her father's palace he would certainly be dead. No, he must not die: so she swam about among the beams and planks that strewed the surface, quite forgetting that one of them might have crushed her. Diving down deep under the water, she again rose high up among the waves, and in this way she at last came to the Prince, who could scarcely swim longer in that stormy sea. His arms and legs began to fail him, his beautiful eyes closed, and he would have died had the little Sea-maid not come. She held his head up over the water, and then allowed the waves to carry her and him whither they listed.

When the morning came the storm had passed by. Of the ship not a fragment was to be seen. The sun came up red and shining out of the water; it was as if its beams brought back the hue of life to the cheeks of the Prince, but his eyes remained closed. The Sea-maid kissed his high, fair forehead and put back his wet hair, and he seemed to her to be like the marble statue in her little garden: she kissed him again and hoped that he might live.

Now she saw in front of her the dry land—high blue mountains, on whose summits the white snow gleamed as if swans were lying there. Down on the coast were glorious green forests, and a building—she could not tell whether it was a church or a convent—stood there. In its garden grew orange and citron-trees, and high palms waved in front of the gate. The sea formed a little bay there; it was quite calm, but very deep. Straight toward the rock where the fine white sand had been cast up, she swam with the handsome Prince, and laid him upon the sand, taking especial care that his head was raised in the warm sunshine.

Now all the bells rang in the great white building, and many young girls came walking through the garden. Then the little Sea-maid swam farther out between some high stones that stood up out of the water, laid some sea-foam upon her hair and neck, so that no one could see her little countenance, and then she watched to see who would come to the poor Prince.

In a short time a young girl went that way. She seemed to be much startled, but only for a moment; then she brought more people, and the Sea-maid perceived that the Prince came back to life, and that he smiled at all around him. But he did not cast a smile at her: he did not know that she had saved him. And she felt very sorrowful; and when he was led away into the great building, she dived mournfully under the water and returned to her father's palace.

She had always been gentle and melancholy, but now she became much more so. Her sisters asked her what she had seen the first time she rose up to the surface, but she would tell them nothing.

Many an evening and many a morning she went up to the place where she had left the Prince. She saw how the fruits of the garden grew ripe and were gathered; she saw how the snow melted on the high mountain; but she did not see the Prince, and so she always returned home more sorrowful still. Then her only comfort was to sit in her little garden, and to wind her arm round the beautiful marble statue that resembled the Prince; but she did not tend her flowers; they grew as if in a wilderness over the paths and trailed their long leaves and stalks up into the branches of trees, so that it became quite dark there.

At last she could endure it no longer, and told all to one of her sisters, and then the others heard of it too; but nobody knew of it beyond these and a few other sea-maids, who told the secret to their intimate friends. One of these knew who the Prince was; she too had seen the festival on board the ship; and she announced whence he came and where his kingdom lay.

"Come, little sister," said the other Princesses; and linking their arms together, they rose up in a long row out of the sea, at the place where they knew the Prince's palace lay.

This palace was built of a kind of bright yellow stone, with great marble staircases, one of which led directly down into the sea. Over the roof rose splendid gilt cupolas, and between the pillars which surrounded the whole dwelling, stood marble statues which looked as if they were alive. Through the clear glass in the high windows one looked into the glorious halls, where costly silk hangings and tapestries were hung up, and all the walls were decked with splendid pictures, so that it was a perfect delight to see them. In the midst of the greatest of these halls a great fountain plashed; its jets shot high up toward the glass dome in the ceiling, through which the sun shone down upon the water and upon the lovely plants growing in the great basin.

Now she knew where he lived, and many an evening and many a night she spent there on the water. She swam far closer to the land than any of the others would have dared to venture; indeed, she went quite up the narrow channel under the splendid marble balcony, which threw a broad shadow upon the water. Here she sat and watched the young Prince, who thought himself quite alone in the bright moonlight.

Many an evening she saw him sailing, amid the sounds of music, in his costly boat with the waving flags; she peeped up through the green reeds, and when the wind caught her silver-white veil and any one saw it he thought it was a white swan spreading out its wings.

Many a night when the fishermen were on the sea with their torches, she heard much good told of the young Prince; and she rejoiced that she had saved his life when he was driven about, half dead, on the wild billows: she thought how quietly his head had reclined on her bosom, and how heartily she had kissed him; but he knew nothing of it, and could not even dream of her.

More and more she began to love mankind, and more and more she wished to be able to wander about among those whose world seemed far larger than her own. For they could fly over the sea in ships, and mount up the high hills far above the clouds, and the lands they possessed stretched out in woods and fields farther than her eyes could reach. There was much she wished to know, but her sisters could not answer all her questions; therefore she applied to the old grandmother; and the old lady knew the upper world, which she rightly called "the countries above the sea," very well.

"If people are not drowned," asked the little Sea-maid, "can they live forever? Do they not die as we die down here in the sea?"

"Yes," replied the old lady. "They too must die, and their life is even shorter than ours. We can live to be three hundred years old, but when we cease to exist here, we are turned into foam on the surface of the water, and have not even a grave down here among those we love. We have not an immortal soul; we never receive another life; we are like the green sea-weed, which, when once cut through, can never bloom again. Men, on the contrary, have a soul which lives forever, which lives on after the body has become dust; it mounts up through the clear air, up to all the shining stars! As we rise up out of the waters and behold all the lands of the earth, so they rise up to unknown glorious places which we can never see."

"Why did we not receive an immortal soul?" asked the little Sea-maid, sorrowfully. "I would gladly give all the hundreds of years I have to live to be a human being only for one day, and have a hope of partaking the heavenly kingdom."

"You must not think of that," replied the old lady. "We feel ourselves far more happy and far better than mankind yonder."

"Then I am to die and be cast as foam upon the sea, not hearing the music of the waves, nor seeing the pretty flowers and the red sun? Can I not do anything to win an immortal soul?"

"No!" answered the grandmother. "Only if a man were to love you so that you should be more to him than father or mother; if he should cling to you with his every thought and with all his love, and let the priest lay his right hand in yours with a promise of faithfulness here and in all eternity, then his soul would be imparted to your body, and you would receive a share of the happiness of mankind. He would give a soul to you and yet retain his own. But that can never come to pass. What is considered beautiful here in the sea—the fish-tail—they would consider ugly on the earth: they don't understand it; there one must have the clumsy supports which they call legs, to be called beautiful."

Then the little Sea-maid sighed and looked mournfully upon her fish-tail.

"Let us be glad!" said the old lady. "Let us dance and leap in the three hundred years we have to live. That is certainly long enough; after that we can rest ourselves all the better. This evening we shall have a court ball."

It was a splendid sight, such as is never seen on earth. The walls and the ceiling of the great dancing-saloon were of thick but transparent glass. Several hundreds of huge shells, pink and grass-green, stood on each side in rows, filled with a blue fire which lit up the whole hall and shone through the walls, so that the sea without was quite lit up; one could see all the innumerable fishes, great and small, swimming toward the glass walls; of some the scales gleamed with purple, while in others they shone like silver and gold. Through the midst of the hall flowed a broad stream, and on this the sea-men and sea-women danced to their own charming songs. Such beautiful voices the people of the earth have not. The little Sea-maid sang the most sweetly of all, and the whole court applauded with their hands and tails, and for a moment she felt gay in her heart, for she knew she had the loveliest voice of all in the sea or on the earth. But soon she thought again of the world above her; she could not forget the charming Prince, or her sorrow at not having an immortal soul like his. Therefore she crept out of her father's palace, and while everything within was joy and gladness, she sat melancholy in her little garden. Then she heard the bugle horn sounding through the waters, and thought, "Now he is certainly sailing above, he on whom my wishes hang, and in whose hand I should like to lay my life's happiness. I will dare everything to win him and an immortal soul. While my sisters dance yonder in my father's palace, I will go to the sea-witch of whom I have always been so much afraid: perhaps she can counsel and help me."

Now the little Sea-maid went out of her garden to the foaming whirlpools behind which the sorceress dwelt. She had never travelled that way before. No flowers grew there, no sea grass; only the naked gray sand stretched out toward the whirlpools, where the water rushed round like roaring mill-wheels and tore down everything it seized into the deep. Through the midst of these rushing whirlpools she was obliged to pass to get in to the domain of the witch; and for a long way there was no other road but one over warm gushing mud: this the witch called her turf-moor. Behind it lay her house in the midst of a singular forest, in which all the trees and bushes were polyps—half animals, half plants. They looked like hundred-headed snakes growing up out of the earth. All the branches were long, slimy arms, with fingers like supple worms, and they moved limb by limb from the root to the farthest point; all that they could seize on in the water they held fast and did not let it go. The little Sea-maid stopped in front of them quite frightened; her heart beat with fear, and she was near turning back; but then she thought of the Prince and the human soul, and her courage came back again. She bound her long flying hair closely around her head, so that the polyps might not seize it. She put her hands together on her breast and then shot forward, as a fish shoots through the water, among the ugly polyps, which stretched out their supple arms and fingers after her. She saw that each of them held something it had seized with hundreds of little arms, like strong iron bands. People who had perished at sea, and had sunk deep down, looked forth as white skeletons from among the polyps' arms; ships' oars and chests they also held fast, and skeletons of land animals, and a little sea-woman whom they had caught and strangled; and this seemed the most terrible of all to our little Princess.

Now she came to a great marshy place in the wood, where fat water-snakes rolled about, showing their ugly cream-colored bodies. In the midst of this marsh was a house built of white bones of shipwrecked men; there sat the Sea-witch, feeding a toad out of her mouth, just as a person might feed a little canary-bird with sugar. She called the ugly fat water-snakes her little chickens, and allowed them to crawl upward and all about her.

"I know what you want," said the Sea-witch. "It is stupid of you, but you shall have your way, for it will bring you to grief, my pretty Princess. You want to get rid of your fish-tail, and to have two supports instead of it, like those the people of the earth walk with, so that the young Prince may fall in love with you, and you may get an immortal soul." And with this the Witch laughed loudly and disagreeably, so that the toad and the water-snakes tumbled down to the ground, where they crawled about. "You come just in time," said the Witch: "after to-morrow at sunrise I could not help you until another year had gone by. I will prepare a draught for you, with which you must swim to land to-morrow before the sun rises, and seat yourself there and drink it; then your tail will shrivel up and become what the people of the earth call legs; but it will hurt you—it will seem as if you were cut with a sharp sword. All who see you will declare you to be the prettiest human being they every beheld. You will keep your graceful walk; no dancer will be able to move so lightly as you; but every step you take will be as if you trod upon sharp knives, and as if your blood must flow. If you will bear all this, I can help you."

"Yes!" said the little Sea-maid, with a trembling voice; and she thought of the Prince and the immortal soul.

"But remember," said the Witch, "when you have once received a human form, you can never be a sea-maid again; you can never return through the water to your sisters, or to your father's palace; and if you do not win the Prince's love, so that he forgets father and mother for your sake, is attached to you heart and soul, and tells the priest to join your hands, you will not receive an immortal soul. On the first morning after he has married another your heart will break, and you will become foam on the water."

"I will do it," said the little Sea-maid: but she became as pale as death.

"But you must pay me, too," said the Witch; "and it is not a trifle that I ask. You have the finest voice of all here at the bottom of the water; with that you think to enchant him; but this voice you must give to me. The best thing you possess I will have for my costly draught! I must give you my own blood in it, so that the draught may be as sharp as a two-edged sword."

"But if you take away my voice," said the little Sea-maid, "what will remain to me?"

"Your beautiful form," replied the Witch, "your graceful walk, and your speaking eyes: with those you can take captive a human heart. Well, have you lost your courage? Put out your little tongue, and then I will cut it off for my payment, and then you shall have the strong draught."

"It shall be so," said the little Sea-maid.

And the Witch put on her pot to brew the draught.

"Cleanliness is a good thing," said she; and she cleaned out the pot with the snakes, which she tied up in a big knot; then she scratched herself, and let her black blood drop into it. The stream rose up in the strangest forms, enough to frighten the beholder. Every moment the Witch threw something else into the pot; and when it boiled thoroughly, there was a sound like the weeping of a crocodile. At last the draught was ready. It looked like the purest water.

"There you have it," said the Witch.

And she cut off the little Sea-maid's tongue, so that now the Princess was dumb, and could neither sing nor speak.

She could see her father's palace. The torches were extinguished in the great hall, and they were certainly sleeping within, but she did not dare to go to them, now that she was dumb and was about to quit them forever. She felt as if her heart would burst with sorrow. She crept into the garden, took a flower from each bed of her sisters, blew a thousand kisses toward the palace, and rose up through the dark blue sea.

The sun had not yet risen when she beheld the Prince's castle, and mounted the splendid marble staircase. The moon shone beautifully clear. The little Sea-maid drank the burning sharp draught, and it seemed as if a two-edged sword went through her delicate body. She fell down in a swoon, and lay as if she were dead. When the sun shone out over the sea she awoke, and felt a sharp pain; but just before her stood the handsome young Prince. He fixed his coal-black eyes upon her, so that she cast down her own, and then she perceived that her fish-tail was gone, and that she had the prettiest pair of white feet a little girl could have. But she had no clothes, so she shrouded herself in her long hair. The Prince asked how she came there! and she looked at him mildly, but very mournfully, with her dark-blue eyes, for she could not speak. Then he took her by the hand, and led her into the castle. Each step she took was, as the Witch had told her, as if she had been treading on pointed needles and knives, but she bore it gladly. At the Prince's right hand she moved on, light as a soap-bubble, and he, like all the rest, was astonished at her graceful, swaying movements.

She now received splendid clothes of silk and muslin. In the castle she was the most beautiful creature to be seen; but she was dumb, and could neither sing nor speak. Lovely slaves, dressed in silk and gold, stepped forward, and sang before the Prince and his royal parents; one sang more charmingly than all the rest, and the Prince smiled at her and clapped his hands. Then the little Sea-maid became sad; she knew that she herself had sung far more sweetly, and thought,—

"O! that he only knew I had given away my voice forever to be with him!"

Now the slaves danced pretty waving dances to the loveliest music, then the little Sea-maid lifted her beautiful white arms, stood on the tips of her toes, and glided dancing over the floor as no one had yet danced. At each movement her beauty became more apparent, and her eyes spoke more directly to the heart than the song of the slaves.

All were delighted, and especially the Prince, who called her his little foundling; and she danced again and again, although every time she touched the earth it seemed as if she were treading upon sharp knives. The Prince said that she should always remain with him, and she received permission to sleep on a velvet cushion before his door.

He had a page's dress made for her, that she might accompany him on horseback. They rode through the blooming woods, where the green boughs swept their shoulders, and the little birds sang in the fresh leaves. She climbed with the Prince up the high mountains, and although her delicate feet bled so that even the others could see it, she laughed at it herself, and followed him until they saw the clouds sailing beneath them, like a flock of birds travelling to distant lands.

At home in the Prince's castle, when the others slept at night, she went out on to the broad marble steps. It cooled her burning feet to stand in the cold sea-water, and then she thought of the dear ones in the deep.

Once, in the night-time, her sisters came, arm in arm. Sadly they sang as they floated above the water; and she beckoned to them, and they recognized her, and told her how she had grieved them all. Then she visited them every night; and once she saw in the distance her old grandmother, who had not been above the surface for many years, and the Sea-king with his crown upon his head. They stretched out their hands toward her, but did not venture so near the land as her sisters.

Day by day the Prince grew more fond of her. He loved her as one loves a dear, good child, but it never came into his head to make her his wife; and yet she must become his wife, or she would not receive an immortal soul, and would have to become foam on the sea on his marriage morning.

"Do you not love me best of them all?" the eyes of the little Sea-maid seemed to say, when he took her in his arms and kissed her fair forehead.

"Yes, you are the dearest to me!" said the Prince, "for you have the best heart of them all. You are the most devoted to me, and are like a young girl whom I once saw, but whom I certainly shall not find again. I was on board a ship which was wrecked. The waves threw me ashore near a holy temple where several young girls performed the service. The youngest of them found me by the shore and saved my life. I only saw her twice: she was the only one in the world I could love, but you chase her picture out of my mind, you are so like her. She belongs to the holy temple, and therefore my good fortune has sent you to me. We will never part!"

"Ah! he does not know that I saved his life," thought the little Sea-maid. "I carried him over the sea to the wood where the temple stands. I sat there under the foam and looked to see if any one would come. I saw the beautiful girl whom he loves better than me." And the Sea-maid sighed deeply—she could not weep. "The maiden belongs to the holy temple," she said, "and will never come out into the world—they will meet no more. I am with him and see him every day; I will cherish him, love him, give up my life for him."

But now they said that the Prince was to marry, and that the beautiful daughter of a neighboring King was to be his wife, and that was why such a beautiful ship was being prepared. The story was, that the Prince travelled to visit the land of the neighboring King, but it was done that he might see the King's daughter. A great company was to go with him. The little Sea-maid shook her head and smiled; she knew the Prince's thoughts far better than any of the others.

"I must travel," he had said to her; "I must see the beautiful Princess: my parents desire it, but they do not wish to compel me to bring her home as my bride. I cannot love her. She is not like the beautiful maiden in the temple whom you resemble. If I were to choose a bride, I would rather choose you, my dear dumb foundling with the speaking eyes."

And he kissed her red lips and played with her long hair, so that she dreamed of happiness and of an immortal soul.

"You are not afraid of the sea, my dumb child?" said he, when they stood on the superb ship which was to carry him to the country of the neighboring King; and he told her of storm and calm, of strange fishes in the deep, and of what the divers had seen there. And she smiled at his tales for she knew better than any one what happened at the bottom of the sea.

In the moonlight night, when all were asleep, except the steersman who stood by the helm, she sat on the side of the ship gazing down through the clear water. She fancied she saw her father's palace. High on the battlements stood her old grandmother with the silver crown on her head, and looking through the rushing tide up to the vessel's keel. Then her sisters came forth over the water, and looked mournfully at her and wrung their white hands. She beckoned to them and smiled, and wished to tell them that she was well and happy; but the cabin-boy approached her and her sisters dived down, so that he thought the white objects he had seen were foam on the surface of the water.

The next morning the ship sailed into the harbor of the neighboring King's splendid city. All the church bells sounded, and from the high towers the trumpets were blown, while the soldiers stood there with flying colors and flashing bayonets. Each day brought some festivity with it; balls and entertainments followed one another; but the Princess was not yet there. People said she was being educated in a holy temple far away, where she was learning every royal virtue. At last she arrived.

The little Sea-maid was anxious to see the beauty of the Princess, and was obliged to acknowledge it. A more lovely apparition she had never beheld. The Princess's skin was pure and clear, and behind the long dark eyelashes there smiled a pair of faithful, dark-blue eyes.

"You are the lady who saved me when I lay like a corpse upon the shore!" said the Prince; and he folded his blushing bride to his heart. "O, I am too, too happy!" he cried to the little Sea-maid. "The best hope I could have is fulfilled. You will rejoice at my happiness, for you are the most devoted to me of them all!"

And the little Sea-maid kissed his hand; and it seemed already to her as if her heart was broken, for his wedding morning was to bring death to her, and change her into foam on the sea.

All the church bells were ringing, and heralds rode about the streets announcing the betrothal. On every altar fragrant oil was burning in gorgeous lamps of silver. The priests swung their censers, and bride and bridegroom laid hand in hand, and received the bishop's blessing. The little Sea-maid was dressed in cloth of gold, and held up the bride's train; but her ears heard nothing of the festive music, her eye marked not the holy ceremony; she thought of the night of her death, and of all that she had lost in this world.

On the same evening the bride and bridegroom went on board the ship. The cannon roared, all the flags waved; in the midst of the ship a costly tent of gold and purple, with the most beautiful cushions, had been set up, and there the married pair were to sleep in the cool, still night.

The sails swelled in the wind, and the ship glided smoothly and lightly over the clear sea. When it grew dark, colored lamps were lighted and the sailors danced merry dances on deck. The little Sea-maid thought of the first time when she had risen up out of the sea, and beheld a similar scene of splendor and joy; and she joined in the whirling dance, and flitted on as the swallow flits away when he is pursued; and all shouted and admired her, for she had danced so prettily. Her delicate feet were cut as if with knives, but she did not feel it, for her heart was wounded far more painfully. She knew this was the last evening on which she should see him for whom she had left her friends and her home, and had given up her beautiful voice, and had suffered unheard-of pains every day, while he was utterly unconscious of all. It was the last evening she should breathe the same air with him, and behold the starry sky and the deep sea; and everlasting night without thought or dream awaited her, for she had no soul, and could win none. And everything was merriment and gladness on the ship till past midnight, and she laughed and danced with thoughts of death in her heart. The Prince kissed his beautiful bride, and she played with his raven hair, and hand in hand they went to rest in the splendid tent. It became quiet on the ship; only the helmsman stood by the helm, and the little Sea-maid leaned her white arms upon the bulwark and gazed out toward the east for the morning dawn—the first ray, she knew, would kill her. Then she saw her sisters rising out of the flood; they were pale, like herself; their long, beautiful hair no longer waved in the wind; it had been cut off.

"We have given it to the witch, that we might bring you help, so that you may not die to-night. She has given us a knife; here it is—look! how sharp! Before the sun rises you must thrust it into the heart of the Prince, and when the warm blood falls upon your feet they will grow together again into a fish-tail, and you will become a sea-maid again, and come back to us, and live your three hundred years before you become dead salt sea-foam. Make haste! He or you must die before the sun rises! Our old grandmother mourns so that her white hair has fallen off, as ours did under the witch's scissors. Kill the Prince and come back! Make haste! Do you see that red streak in the sky? In a few minutes the sun will rise, and you must die!"

And they gave a very mournful sigh, and vanished beneath the waves. The little Sea-maid drew back the curtain from the tent, and saw the beautiful bride lying with her head on the Prince's breast; and she bent down and kissed his brow, and gazed up at the sky where the morning red was gleaming brighter and brighter; then she looked at the sharp knife, and again fixed her eyes upon the Prince, who in his sleep murmured his bride's name. She only was in his thoughts, and the knife trembled in the Sea-maid's hand. But then she flung it far away into the waves—they gleamed red where it fell, and it seemed as if drops of blood spurted up out of the water. Once more she looked with half-extinguished eyes upon the Prince; then she threw herself from the ship into the sea, and felt her frame dissolving into foam.

Now the sun rose up out of the sea. The rays fell mild and warm upon the cold sea-foam, and the little Sea-maid felt nothing of death. She saw the bright sun, and over her head sailed hundreds of glorious ethereal beings—she could see them through the white sails of the ship and the red clouds of the sky; their speech was melody, but of such a spiritual kind that no human ear could hear it, just as no human eye could see them; without wings they floated through the air. The little Sea-maid found that she had a frame like these, and was rising more and more out of the foam.

"Whither am I going?" she asked; and her voice sounded like that of other beings, so spiritual, that no earthly music could be compared to it.

"To the daughters of the air!" replied the others. "A sea-maid has no immortal soul, and can never gain one, except she win the love of a mortal. Her eternal existence depends upon the power of another. The daughters of the air have likewise no immortal soul, but they can make themselves one through good deeds. We fly to the hot countries, where the close, pestilent air kills men, and there we bring coolness. We disperse the fragrance of the flowers through the air, and spread refreshment and health. After we have striven for three hundred years to accomplish all the good we can bring about, we receive an immortal soul, and take part in the eternal happiness of men. You, poor little Sea-maid, have striven with your whole heart after the goal we pursue; you have suffered and endured; you have by good works raised yourself to the world of spirits, and can gain an immortal soul after three hundred years."

And the little Sea-maid lifted her glorified eyes toward God's sun, and for the first time she felt them fill with tears. On the ship there was again life and noise. She saw the Prince and his bride searching for her; then they looked mournfully at the pearly foam, as if they knew that she had thrown herself into the waves. Invisible, she kissed the forehead of the bride, fanned the Prince, and mounted with the other children of the air on the rosy cloud which floated through the ether. After three hundred years we shall thus float into Paradise!

"And we may even get there sooner," whispered a daughter of the air. "Invisibly we float into the houses of men where children are, and for every day on which we find a good child that brings joy to its parents and deserves their love, our time of probation is shortened. The child does not know when we fly through the room; and when we smile with joy at the child's conduct, a year is counted off from the three hundred; but when we see a naughty or a wicked child, we shed tears of grief, and for every tear a day is added to our time of trial."

THE BOOK OF THEL

William Blake

THEL'S MOTTO

Does the Eagle know what is in the pit?
Or wilt thou go ask the Mole?
Can Wisdom be put in a silver rod?
Or Love in a golden bowl?

I

The daughters of the Seraphim led round their sunny flocks,
All but the youngest: she in paleness sought the secret air,
To fade away like morning beauty from her mortal day:
Down by the river of Adona her soft voice is heard,
And thus her gentle lamentation falls like morning dew:

"O life of this our spring! why fades the lotus of the water,
Why fade these children of the spring, born but to smile & fall?
Ah! Thel is like a wat'ry bow, and like a parting cloud;
Like a reflection in a glass; like shadows in the water;
Like dreams of infants, like a smile upon an infant's face;
Like the dove's voice; like transient day; like music in the air.
Ah! gentle may I lay me down, and gentle rest my head.
And gentle sleep the sleep of death, and gentle hear the voice
Of him that walketh in the garden in the evening time."

The Lilly of the valley, breathing in the humble grass,
Answer'd the lovely maid and said: "I am a wat'ry weed,
And I am very small and love to dwell in lowly vales;
So weak, the gilded butterfly scarce perches on my head.
Yet I am visited from heaven, and he that smiles on all
Walks in the valley and each morn over me spreads his hand,
Saying, 'Rejoice, thou humble grass, thou new-born lilly flower,
Thou gentle maid of silent valleys and of modest brooks;
For thou shalt be clothed in light, and fed with morning manna,
Till summer's heat melts thee beside the fountains and the springs
To flourish in eternal vales.' Then why should Thel complain?
Why should the mistress of the vales of Har utter a sigh?"

She ceas'd & smil'd in tears, then sat down in her silver shrine.

Thel answer'd: "O thou little virgin of the peaceful valley,
Giving to those that cannot crave, the voiceless, the o'ertired;
Thy breath doth nourish the innocent lamb, he smells thy milky
    garments,
He crops thy flowers while thou sittest smiling in his face,
Wiping his mild and meekin mouth from all contagious taints.
Thy wine doth purify the golden honey; thy perfume,
Which thou dost scatter on every little blade of grass that springs,
Revives the milked cow, & tames the fire-breathing steed.
But Thel is like a faint cloud kindled at the rising sun:
I vanish from my pearly throne, and who shall find my place?"

"Queen of the vales," the Lilly answer'd,"ask the tender cloud,
And it shall tell thee why it glitters in the morning sky,
And why it scatters its bright beauty thro' the humid air.
Descend, O little Cloud, & hover before the eyes of Thel."

The Cloud descended, and the Lilly bow'd her modest head
And went to mind her numerous charge among the verdant grass.

II

"O little Cloud," the virgin said, "I charge thee tell to me
Why thou complainest not when in one hour thou fade away:
Then we shall seek thee, but not find. Ah! Thel is like to thee:
I pass away: yet I complain, and no one hears my voice."

The Cloud then shew'd his golden head & his bright form emerg'd,
Hovering and glittering on the air before the face of Thel.

"O virgin, know'st thou not our steeds drink of the golden springs
Where Luvah doth renew his horses? Look'st thou on my youth,
And fearest thou, because I vanish and am seen no more,
Nothing remains? O maid, I tell thee, when I pass away
It is to tenfold life, to love, to peace and raptures holy:
Unseen descending, weigh my light wings upon balmy flowers,
And court the fair-eyed dew to take me to her shining tent:
The weeping virgin, trembling kneels before the risen sun,
Till we arise link'd in a golden band and never part,
But walk united, bearing food to all our tender flowers."

"Dost thou, O little Cloud? I fear that I am not like thee,
For I walk thro' the vales of Har, and smell the sweetest flowers,
But I feed not the little flowers; I hear the warbling birds,
But I feed not the warbling birds; they fly and seek their food:
But Thel delights in these no more, because I fade away;

And all shall say, 'Without a use this shining woman liv'd,
Or did she only live to be at death the food of worms?' "

The Cloud reclin'd upon his airy throne and answer'd thus:

"Then if thou art the food of worms, O virgin of the skies,
How great thy use, how great they blessing! Every thing that lives
Lives not alone nor for itself. Fear not, and I will call
The weak worm from its lowly bed, and thou shalt hear its voice.
Come forth, worm of the silent valley, to thy pensive queen."

The helpless worm arose, and sat upon the Lilly's leaf,
And the bright Cloud sail'd on, to find his partner in the vale.

III

Then Thel astonish'd view'd the Worm upon its dewy bed.

"Art thou a Worm? Image of weakness, art thou but a Worm?
I see these like an infant wrapped in the Lilly's leaf.
Ah! weep not, little voice, thou canst not speak, but thou canst
    weep.
Is this a Worm? I see thee lay helpless & naked, weeping,
And none to answer, none to cherish thee with mother's smiles."

The Clod of Clay heard the Worm's voice & rais'd her pitying head:
She bow'd over the weeping infant, and her life exhal'd
In milky fondness: then on Thel she fix'd her humble eyes.

"O beauty of the vales of Har! we live not for ourselves.
Thou seest me the meanest thing, and so I am indeed.
My bosom of itself is cold, and of itself is dark;
But he, that loves the lowly, pours his oil upon my head,
And kisses me, and binds his nuptial bands around my breast,
And says: 'Thou mother of my children, I have loved thee
And I have given thee a crown that none can take away.'
But how this is, sweet maid, I know not, and I cannot know;
I ponder, and I cannot ponder; yet I live and love."

The daughter of beauty wip'd her pitying tears with her white veil,
And said: "Alas! I knew not this, and therefore did I weep.
That God would love a Worm I knew, and punish the evil foot
That wilful bruis'd its helpless form; but that he cherish'd it
With milk and oil I never knew, and therefore did I weep;
And I complain'd in the mild air, because I fade away,
And lay me down in thy cold bed, and leave my shining lot."

"Queen of the vales," the matron Clay answer'd, "I heard thy sighs,
And all thy moans flew o'er my roof, but I have call'd them down.
Wilt thou, O Queen, enter my house? 'Tis given thee to enter
And to return: fear nothing, enter with thy virgin feet."

IV

The eternal gates' terrific porter lifted the northern bar:
Thel enter'd in & saw the secrets of the land unknown.
She saw the couches of the dead, & where the fibrous roots
Of every heart on earth infixes deep its restless twists:
A land of sorrows & of tears where never smile was seen.

She wander'd in the land of clouds thro' valleys dark, list'ning
Dolours & lamentations; waiting oft beside a dewy grave
She stood in silence, list'ning to the voices of the ground,
Till to her own grave plot she came, & there she sat down,
And heard this voice of sorrow breathed from the hollow pit.

"Why cannot the Ear be closed to its own destruction?
Or the glist'ning Eye to the poison of a smile?
Why are Eyelids stor'd with arrows ready drawn,
Where a thousand fighting men in ambush lie?
Or an Eye of gifts & graces show'ring fruits & coined gold?
Why a Tongue impress'd with honey from every wind?
Why an Ear, a whirlpool fierce to draw creations in?
Why a Nostril wide inhaling terror, trembling, & affright?
Why a tender curb upon the youthful burning boy?
Why a little curtain of flesh on the bed of our desire?"

The Virgin started from her seat, & with a shriek
Fled back unhinder'd till she came into the vales of Har.

THE END

BLOOD, SEA

Italo Calvo

> *The conditions that obtained when life had not yet emerged
> from the oceans have not subsequently changed a great deal
> for the cells of the human body, bathed by the primordial
> wave which continues to flow in the arteries. Our blood in
> fact has a chemical composition analogous to that of the sea
> of our origins, from which the first living cells and the first
> multicellular beings derived the oxygen and the other ele-
> ments necessary to life. With the evolution of more complex
> organisms, the problem of maintaining a maximum number
> of cells in contact with the liquid environment could not be
> solved simply by the expansion of the exterior surface: those
> organisms endowed with hollow structures, into which the
> sea water could flow, found themselves at an advantage. But
> it was only with the ramification of these cavities into a
> system of blood circulation that distribution of oxygen was
> guaranteed to the complex of cells, thus making terrestrial
> life possible. The sea where living creatures were at one time
> immersed is now enclosed within their bodies.*

BASICALLY NOT MUCH has changed: I swim, I continue swimming in
the same warm area,—*Qfwfq said,*—or rather, the inside isn't changed,
what was formerly the outside, where I used to swim under the sun, and
where I now swim in darkness, is inside; what's changed is the outside,
the present outside, which was the inside before, that's changed all
right; however, it doesn't matter very much. I say it doesn't matter very
much and you promptly reply: What do you mean, the outside doesn't
matter much? What I mean is that if you look at it more closely, from
the point of view of the old outside, that is from the present inside, what
is the present outside? It's simply where it's dry, where there is no flux
or reflux, and as far as mattering goes, of course, that matters too,
inasmuch as it's the outside, since its been on the outside, since that
outside has been outside, and people believe it's more deserving of
consideration than the inside. When all is said and done, however, even
when it was inside it mattered, though in a more restricted range or
so it seemed then. This is what I mean: less deserving of consideration.
Well, let's start talking right now about the others, those who are not
I, our neighbor: we know our neighbor exists because he's outside,

agreed? Outside like the present outside. But before, when the outside was what we swam in, the very dense and very warm ocean, even then there were the others, slippery things, in that old outside, which is like the present inside, and so it is now when I've changed places and given the wheel to Signor Cècere, at the Codogno service station, and in front, next to him, Jenny Fumagalli has taken the passenger's seat, and I've moved in back with Zylphia: the outside, what is the outside? A dry environment, lacking in meaning, a bit crammed (there are four of us in a Volkswagen), where all is indifferent and interchangeable, Jenny Fumagalli, Codogno, Signor Cècere, the service station, and as far as Zylphia is concerned, at the moment when I placed my hand on her knee, at perhaps 15 kilometers from Casalpusterlengo, or else she was the one who started touching me, I don't remember, since outside events tend to be confused, what I felt, I mean the sensation that came from outside, was really a weak business compared to what went through my blood and to what I have felt ever since then, since the time when we were swimming together in the same torrid, blazing ocean, Zylphia and I.

The underwater depths were red like the color we see now only inside our eyelids, and the sun's rays penetrated to brighten them in flashes or else in sprays. We undulated with no sense of direction, drawn by an obscure current so light that it seemed downright impalpable and yet strong enough to drag us up in very high waves and down in their troughs. Zylphia would plunge headlong beneath me in a violet, almost black whirlpool, then soar over me rising toward the more scarlet stripes that ran beneath the luminous vault. We felt all this through the layers of our former surface dilated to maintain the most extended possible contact with that nourishing sea, because at every up and down of the waves there was stuff that passed from outside of us to our inside, all sustenance of every sort, even iron, healthful stuff, in short, and in fact I've never been so well as I was then. Or, to be more precise: I was well since in dilating my surface I increased the possibilities of contact between me and this outside of me that was so precious, but as the zones of my body soaked in marine solution were extended, my volume also increased at the same time, and a more and more volumi-nous zone within me became unreachable by the element outside, it became arid, dull, and the weight of this dry and torpid thickness I carried within me was the only shadow on my happiness, our happi-ness, Zylphia's and mine, because the more she splendidly took up space in the sea, the more the inert and opaque thickness grew in her too, unlaved and unlavable, lost to the vital flux, not reached by the messages I transmitted to her through the vibration of the waves. So perhaps I could say I'm better off now than I was then, now that the layers of our former surface, then stretched on the outside, have been turned inside out like a glove, now that all the outside has been turned inward and has entered and pervaded us through filiform ramifications, yes, I could really say this, were it not for the fact that the dull arid zone has been projected outward, has expanded to the extent of the distance between my tweed suit and the fleeting landscape of the Lodi plain, and it surrounds me, swollen with undesired presences such as Signor Cècere's, with all the thickness that Signor Cècere, formerly, would have enclosed within himself—in his foolish manner of dilating uniformly like a ball—now unfolded before me in a surface unsuitably irregular and detailed, especially in his pudgy neck dotted with pimples, taut in his half-starched collar at this moment when he is saying: "Oh, you two on the back seat!" and he has slightly shifted the rearview mirror and has certainly glimpsed what our hands are doing, mine and Zylphia's, our diminutive outside hands, our diminutively sensitive hands that pursue the memory of ourselves swimming, or rather our swimming memory, or rather the presence of what in me and Zylphia continues swimming or being swum, together, as then.

This is a distinction I might bring up to give a clearer idea of before and now: before, we swam, and now we are swum. But on sober reflection I prefer not to go into this, because in reality even when the sea was outside I swam in it the same way I do now, without any intervention of my will, that is to say I was swum even then, no more nor less than now, there was a current that enfolded me and carried me this way and that, a gentle and soft fluid, in which Zylphia and I wallowed, turning on ourselves, hovering over abysses of ruby-colored transparence, hiding among turquoise-colored filaments that wriggled up from the depths; but these sensations of movement—wait and I'll explain it to you—were due only to what? They were due to a kind of general pulsation, no, I don't want to confuse things with the way they are now, because since we've been keeping the sea closed inside us it's natural that in moving it should make this piston effect, but in those days you certainly couldn't have talked about pistons, because you would have had to imagine a piston without walls, a combustion chamber of infinite volume as the sea appeared infinite to us, or rather the ocean, in which we were immersed, whereas now everything is pulsation and beating and rumble and crackling, inside the arteries and outside, the sea within the arteries that accelerates its course as soon as I feel Zylphia's hand seeking mine, or rather, as soon as I feel the acceleration in the course of Zylphia's arteries as she feels my hand seeking hers (the two flows which are still the same flow of a same sea and which are joined beyond the contact of the thirsty fingertips); and also outside, the opaque thirsty outside that seeks dully to imitate the beat and rumble and crackling of inside, and vibrates in the accelerator under Signor Cècere's foot, and all the line of cars stopped at the exit from the superhighway tries to repeat the pulsating of the ocean now buried inside us, of the red ocean that was once without shores, under the sun.

It is a false sense of movement that this now-motionless line of cars transmits, crackling; then it moves and it's as if it were still, the movement is false, it merely repeats signs and white stripes and roadbeds; and the whole journey has been nothing but false movement in the immobility and indifference of everything that is outside. Only the sea moved and moves, outside or inside, only in that movement did Zylphia and I become aware of each other's presence, even if then we didn't so much as graze each other, even if I was undulating in this direction and she in that, but the sea had only to quicken its rhythm and I became aware of Zylphia's presence, her presence which was different, for example, from Signor Cècere, who was however also around even then and I could sense him as I felt an acceleration of the same sort as that other one but with a negative charge, that is the acceleration of the sea (and now of the blood) with regard to Zylphia was (is) like swimming toward each other, or else like swimming and chasing each other in play, while the acceleration (of the sea and now of the blood) with regard to Signor Cècere was (is) like a swimming away to avoid him, or else like swimming toward him to make him go away, all of this involving no change in the relationship of our respective distances.

Now it is Signor Cècere who accelerates (the words used are the same but the meanings change) and passes an Alfa Romeo in a curve, and it is with regard to Zylphia that he accelerates, to distract her with a risky maneuver, a false risky maneuver, from the swimming that unites her and me: false, I say, as a maneuver, not as a risk because the risk may well be real, that is to our inside which in a crash could spurt outside; whereas the maneuver in itself changes nothing at all, the distances between Alfa, curve, Volkswagen can assume different values and relationships but nothing essential happens, as nothing essential happens in Zylphia, who doesn't care a bit about Signor Cècere's driving, at most it is Jenny Fumagalli who exults: "My, isn't this car fast?" and her exultation, in the presumption that Signor Cècere's bold driving is for her benefit, is doubly unjustified, first because her inside transmits nothing to her that justifies exultation, and secondly because she is mistaken about Signor Cècere's intentions as he in turn is mistaken, believing he is achieving God knows what with his showing off, just as she, Jenny Fumagalli, was mistaken before about my intentions, when I was at the wheel and she at my side, and there in back next to Zylphia Signor Cècere, too, was mistaken, both concentrating—he and Jenny—on the reverse arrangement of dry layers of surface, unaware—dilated into balls as they were—that the only real things that happen are those that happen in the swimming of our immersed parts; and so this silly business of passing Alfas meaning nothing, like a passing of fixed, immobile, nailed-down objects which continues to be superimposed on the story of our free and real swimming, continues to seek meaning by interfering with it, in the only silly way it knows, risk of blood, a false return to a sea of blood which would no longer be blood or sea.

Here I must hasten to make clear—before by another idiotic passing of a trailer truck Signor Cècere makes all clarification pointless—the way that the common blood-sea of the past was common and at the same time individual to each of us and how we can continue swimming in it as such and how we can't: I don't know if I can make this sort of explanation in a hurry because, as always, when this general substance is discussed, the talk can't be in general terms but has to vary according to the relationship between one individual and the others, so it amounts practically to beginning all over again at the beginning. Now then: this business of having the vital element in common was a beautiful thing inasmuch as the separation between me and Zylphia was so to speak overcome and we could feel ourselves at the same time two distinct individuals and a single whole, which always has its advantages, but when you realize that this single whole also included absolutely insipid presences such as Jenny Fumagalli, or worse, unbearable ones such as Signor Cècere, then thanks all the same, the thing loses much of its interest. This is the point where the reproductive instinct comes into play: we had a great desire, Zylphia and I, or at least I had a great desire, and I think she must have had it too, since she was willing, to multiply our presence in the sea-blood so that there would be more and more of us to profit from it and less and less of Signor Cècere, and as we had our reproductive cells all ready for that very purpose, we fell to fertilizing with a will, that is to say I fertilized everything of hers that was fertilizable, so that our presence would increase in both absolute number and in percentage, and Signor Cècere —though he too made feverish clumsy efforts at reproducing himself —would remain in a minority—this was the dream, the virtual obsession that gripped me—a minority that would become smaller and smaller, insignificant, zero point zero zero etc. per cent, until he vanished into the dense cloud of our progeny as in a school of rapid and ravenous anchovies who would devour him bit by bit, burying him inside our dry inner layers, bit by bit, where the sea's flow would never reach him again, and then the sea-blood would have become one with us, that is, all blood would finally be our blood.

This is in fact the secret desire I feel, looking at the stiff collar of Signor Cècere up front: make him disappear, eat him up, I mean: not eat him up myself, because he turns my stomach slightly (in view of the pimples), but emit, project, outside myself (outside the Zylphia-me unit), a school of ravenous anchovies (of me-sardines, of Zylphia-sardines) to devour Signor Cècere, deprive him of the use of a circulatory system (as well as of a combustion engine, as well as the illusory use of an engine foolishly combustive), and while we're at it, devour also that pain in the neck Fumagalli, who because of the simple fact that I sat next to her before has got it into her head that I flirted with her somehow, when I wasn't paying the slightest attention to her, and now she says in that whiny little voice of hers: "Watch out, Zylphia" (just to cause trouble), "I know that gentleman back there . . ." just to suggest I behaved with her before as I'm behaving now with Zylphia, but what can la Fumagalli know about what is really happening between me and Zylphia, about how Zylphia and I are continuing our ancient swim through the scarlet depths?

I'll go back to what I was saying earlier, because I have the impression things have become a bit confused: to devour Signor Cècere, to ingurgitate him was the best way to separate him from the blood-sea when the blood was in fact the sea, when our present inside was outside and our outside, inside; but now, in reality, my secret desire is to make Signor Cècere become pure outside, deprive him of the inside he illicitly enjoys, make him expel the lost sea within his pleonastic person; in short, my dream is to eject against him not so much a swarm of me-anchovies as a hail of me-projectiles, rat-tat-tat to riddle him from head to foot, making him spurt his black blood to the last drop, and this idea is linked also to the idea of reproducing myself with Zylphia, of multiplying with her our blood circulation in a platoon or battalion of vindictive descendants armed with automatic rifles to riddle Signor Cècere, this in fact now prompts my sanguinary instinct (in all secrecy, given my constant mien as a civil, polite person just like the rest of you), the sanguinary instinct connected to the meaning of blood as "our blood" which I bear in me just as you do, civilly and politely.

Thus far everything may seem clear: however, you must bear in mind that to make it clear I have so simplified things that I'm not sure whether the step forward I've made is really a step forward. Because from the moment when blood becomes "our blood," the relationship between us and blood changes, that is, what counts is the blood insofar as it is "ours," and all the rest, us included, counts less. So there was in my impulse toward Zylphia, not only the drive to have all the ocean for us, but also the drive to lose it, the ocean, to annihilate ourselves in the ocean, to destroy ourselves, to torment ourselves, or rather—as a beginning—to torment her, Zylphia my beloved, to tear her to pieces, to eat her up. And with her it's the same: what she wanted was to torment me, devour me, swallow me, nothing but that. The orange stain of the sun seen from the water's depths swayed like a medusa, and Zylphia darted among the luminous filaments devoured by the desire to devour me, and I writhed in the tangles of darkness that rose from the depths like long strands of seaweed beringed with indigo glints, raving and longing to bite her. And finally there on the back seat of the Volkswagen in an abrupt swerve I fell on her and I sank my teeth into her skin just where the "American cut" of her sleeves left her shoulder bare, and she dug her sharp nails between the buttons of my shirt, and this is the same impulse as before, the impulse that tended to remove her (or remove me) from marine citizenship and now instead tends to remove the sea from her, from me, in any case to achieve the passage from the blazing element of life to the pale and opaque element which is our absence from the ocean and the absence of the ocean from us.

The same impulse acts then with amorous obstinacy between her and me and with hostile obstinacy against Signor Cècere: for each of us there is no other way of entering into a relationship with the others; I mean, it's always this impulse that nourishes our own relationship with the others in the most different and unrecognizable forms, as when Signor Cècere passes cars of greater horse-power than his, even a Porsche, through intentions of mastery toward these superior cars and through ill-advised amorous intentions toward Zylphia and also vindictive ones toward me and also self-destructive ones toward himself. So, through risk, the insignificance of the outside manages to interfere with the essential element, the sea where Zylphia and I continue our nuptial flights of fertilization and destruction: since the risk aims directly at the blood, at our blood, for if it were a matter only of the blood of Signor Cècere (a driver, after all, heedless of the traffic laws) we should hope that at the very least he would run off the road, but in effect it's a question of all of us, of the risk of a possible return of our blood from darkness to the sun, from the separate to the mixed, a false return, as all of us in our ambiguous game pretend to forget, because our present inside once it is poured out becomes our present outside and it can no longer return to being the outside of the old days.

So Zylphia and I in falling upon each other in the curves play at provoking vibrations in the blood, that is, at permitting the false thrills of the insipid outside to be added to those that vibrated from the depths of the millennia and of the marine abysses, and then Signor Cècere said: "Let's have a nice plate of spaghetti at the truck drivers' cafe," masking as generous love of life his constant torpid violence, and Jenny Fumagalli, acting clever, spoke up: "But you have to get to the spaghetti first, before the truck drivers, otherwise they won't leave you any," clever and always working in the service of the blackest destruction, and the black truck with the license Udine 38 96 21 was there ahead, roaring at its forty m.p.h. along the road that was nothing but curves, and Signor Cècere thought (and perhaps said): "I'll make it," and he swung out to the left, and we all thought (and didn't say): "You can't make it," and in fact, from the curve the Jaguar was already arriving full tilt, and to avoid it the Volkswagen scraped the wall and bounced back to scrape its side against the curved chrome bumper and, bouncing, it struck the plane tree, then went spinning down into the precipice, and the sea of common blood which floods over the crumpled metal isn't the blood-sea of our origin but only an infinitesimal detail of the outside, of the insignificant and arid outside, a number in the statistics of accidents over the weekend.

DREAM VARIATION

Langston Hughes

To fling my arms wide
In some place of the sun,
To whirl and to dance
Till the white day is done.

Then rest at cool evening
Beneath a tall tree
While night comes on gently,
    Dark like me——
That is my dream!

To fling my arms wide
In the face of the sun,
Dance! whirl! whirl!
Till the quick day is done.
Rest at pale evening. . . .
A tall, slim tree. . . .
Night coming tenderly
    Black like me.

A FOLDING AND UNFOLDING

Welton Smith

I am peopled by women
despondent men in hiding
continuous dark and wind
stealing sounds
from the lips of women
wind passing the heart
of a continent and stealing
sounds from the continent's heart

I am peopled by great shouts
dark people with lined faces
and ashy legs—tambourines
and low trumpet sounds
massive architectures
of sweetwater and swamp—
churches of rubble and sharp cries

I am peopled by men
sprawled in doorways
their hearts
blown away by the wind

I am peopled by huge people
who build barricades against the wind
and come together in alcoves
mute and blind
unable to hear—
and wipe the tears

in these alcoves
things occur
as if a soul were there;
we smile a toothless smile
and touch our damp
cheeks with our
crumbling black fingers

III

Bewitchment
and Enchantment

BEWITCHMENT
AND ENCHANTMENT

GUARDIAN ANGELS, fairy godmothers, geniis and spirit messengers of all kinds give supernatural assistance to the heroes and heroines of folk tales. The idea that these good spirits may exist rests on a belief in a world completely alive, in which every tree, river, house, rock, and person has its own protective spirit. But if these helpful spirits appeal to the imagination, it is almost impossible to keep from imagining their opposites, the witches, wizards, enchanters, werewolves, and space monsters of nightmares and horror stories. Devils, poltergeists, and other alien creatures may possess the souls of helpless mortals, and force their victims to perform uncharacteristically cruel or monstrous deeds. If the fairy godmother can rescue Cinderella from the ashes and send her off to meet Prince Charming, so can the wicked fairy put a lovely princess to sleep for a hundred years, as in "Sleeping Beauty."

The idea of bewitchment or enchantment resists all efforts to rationalize it away. Modern thought has banished fairies and werewolves. Scholars and scientists agree that magic was used by unscientific, primitive people to explain events—rain, thunderstorms, plagues, rainbows—which they did not understand in rational terms. As science provided reasonable explanations for more and more of the amazing events of the natural world, the need for supernatural explanations declined. Religion, magic, and miracles seem to disappear in a technological and systematic civilization. If the world really operates according to laws of cause and effect, there is no need for whimsical spirits of good and evil. If God is dead, so are legions of lesser gods, sorcerers, witches, and enchanters.

But enchantment dies hard. The psychiatric theories of Freud and Jung assert that a person may be possessed, seemingly ruled against his will, by the repressed or rejected qualities of his own mind. Freud views these visits from the subconscious mostly as illness, but Jung feels that each dream, vision, or fantasy may contain important messages from the subconscious mind of the dreamer. According to his theory, every person has a shadow, made up of the feelings, ambitions, and fantasies which have been rejected by the rational, conscious self. Jung insists that dreams must be considered as serious messages from the shadow, or *anima*. In choosing the word *anima,* derived from the

Latin word for soul, Jung shows his confidence that some sort of spirit or soul exists and must be considered in any complete theory of psychiatry. This view has earned him a low place in the history of psychology, but it is well supported by the stories and essays in this section. All of these works show the fascination men have felt at the idea that powers outside our knowledge or control may interfere or assist in our lives. The efforts of the rational intelligence to purge the world of its monsters and imaginary terrors also requires that the good fairies and friendly spirits be banished. But people continue to dream, to have visions, to imagine spirits and demons.

Shakespeare's *A Midsummer Night's Dream* has fantasy and magic as one of its central themes. A rare purple flower called love-in-idleness is used as a charm to make people fall in love. After an extremely complicated round of romantic and fantastic confusion, the Duke Theseus sums up the condition of fantasy. He is a nobleman, a ruler, and a man of reason. His point of view is sympathetic, but he speaks as a man rarely troubled by phantoms. Thus he describes three categories of people who are "of imagination all compact," or totally made up of fantasy.

> The lunatic, the lover, and the poet
> Are of imagination all compact.
> One sees more devils than vast Hell can hold,
> That is the madman.

The lover is full of fantasy because he always believes his lady to be a beautiful goddess, no matter how ugly she really is. The poet makes creatures out of "airy nothing," out of imagination. And like the lunatic, he is crazy; his rolling eye shows it. But it is the eye, the vision of the poet, which produces dreams and fantasies in every mind.

> The poet's eye, in a fine frenzy rolling,
> Doth glance from heaven to earth, from earth to heaven,
> And, as imagination bodies forth
> The forms of things unknown, the poet's pen
> Turns them into shapes, and gives to airy nothing
> A local habitation and a name.
> Such tricks hath strong imagination.

The poet gives a name and a "local habitation," or real setting, to the creatures of his imagination. Traditional stories like "Rip Van Winkle" or "The Headless Horseman" gain credibility by their settings in real places with real names. But the imaginary beings of the stories are not simply local; they are universal, part of the shared mind of all men, which we usually call imagination or fantasy. Jung calls it the "collective unconscious," and symbolizes it as a huge sea of myths and symbols, in which all our fantasies and dreams have their source. Dreams and myths float up to the surface of our minds like bubbles, and though they are our own, they are also links to the minds of the other dreamers of the world.

William Blake belongs to all three of Duke Theseus' categories. He is poet, lunatic, and lover, raging at the reasonable world which tries to destroy his dreams. At one level, "The Sick Rose" describes the worm of reason which gnaws and blights the rose of passion. The poem also suggests the mixture of good and evil, beauty and destruction, life and death, in nature. The devouring worm is time, or simply the process of blooming and dying. The rose, beautiful, fragile, and short-lived, often symbolizes this process for poets.

"Rapunzel" is a classic story of bewitchment. The evil old woman who locks the heroine away in a tower is like all the witches of fairy tales; old, ugly, cruel and spiteful. In every way she is the opposite of the beautiful, innocent Rapunzel. But she may represent the part of Rapunzel's soul which seeks solitude and rejects human company. The tower is often used to represent virginity; like Snow White's long sleep, it stands for the desire to resist marriage and adult life, to remain a child and therefore safe and perfect. Jung points out that the wicked old witch in many fairy tales turns out to be the *anima,* a good spirit in disguise. She stands for the hidden strength, wisdom, and guile which the innocent heroine will need in her adult life. Like the worm in the rose, the witch who possesses Rapunzel shows that evil accompanies good, and ugliness can imprison beauty.

In "Snow White" the evil stepmother is beautiful and proud; she shows that beauty may be a cloak for wickedness, and thus she is the opposite of more traditional witches whose moral ugliness is betrayed by warts, long noses, and hooked chins. The theme of the wicked stepmother runs through many fairy tales, and seems to relate to the unconscious rivalry between mothers and daughters. The desire of the Queen to be without competition as "fairest in the land" carries out the same theme. The seven dwarfs are classic examples of the helpful spirits of the woods. Sympathetic, earthy and simple, they offer shelter and love in contrast to the wicked stepmother's cruelty. Snow White herself is a perfect, unearthly beauty, white as snow, red as blood and black as ebony. Everything about her symbolizes the combined lure and danger of great beauty. Her frequent death and revival link this story to other tales of death and resurrection.

Fitzhugh Ludlow reports his discovery of second sight in "The Hasheesh Eater." It is particularly interesting that at the height of his vision, he felt himself to be two people; one completely carried away, bewitched, enchanted, possessed by the drug as by an alien spirit; and one calmly observing, guiding, and controlling his behavior. This parallels and reinforces the division between conscious and subconscious thought, and suggests that the state of vision or trance is often simply a rearrangement of the balance between conscious and subconscious thought, or reason and fantasy. Mr. Ludlow is a delightful narrator, communicating the excitement of his experiment, so intense that he rushes to his doctor for reassurance that he will not die of apoplexy, or brain hemorrhage. The terrifying old man he encounters seems to be an embodiment of evil and death like the witch in "Rapunzel," strange and yet horribly familiar. This *anima*-figure, the magnificent temple, the endless sea, and the ship of the soul which Ludlow experiences are universal symbols, the materials of all our dreams. They are, as he recognizes them to be, his meeting with eternity. But the wonderful old witches who *knit* other witches, though they are clearly related to universal *anima* figures, have details which are Ludlow's own fantasy. As in the other selections, it is very interesting to study the balance between familiar, universal symbolism in the major parts of a story and the specific, local, personal details added by individual dreamers or story-tellers.

"The Mark of the Beast" expands the idea of enchantment, showing that a man may be possessed by a spirit he does not believe in or understand. The story rests on the conflicts between alien cultures when one invades the other. Kipling conveys with a few details the ignorance and brutality of the drunken Englishmen and the mysterious, magical power of the natives. The Silver Man is a perfect symbol of evil; he is a leper, faceless and dangerous. He has power and knowledge which the intruders lack. Worst of all, he represents the terrors of the unknown. For men who customarily triumph by force, it is doubly frightening to be defeated by the very symbol of weakness and disease, without any outward show of force. There is a double irony in that Fleete, the "civilized" Englishman who is rendered a beast by the curse, has been shown already to be a savage. Thus the curse of the Silver Man seems only to have drawn out the inherent brutality of Fleete, and the Silver Man is seen to have acted honorably in defense of his gods.

"La Belle Dame Sans Merci" is an enchantress like Snow White's stepmother, beautiful and cruel. She shows the combined lure and danger of the Otherworld. An unearthly lover is infinitely more desirable than an ordinary person, but the loves of the fairies soon end, and to be chosen by one of them is to be spoiled ever after for human love. It is a great honor, a stroke of good luck, to be chosen by a fairy lover —but it is also one's doom. Once dropped off on the "cold hill's side" the knight-at-arms cannot rejoin human society. Like Coleridge's Ancient Mariner, or the man who dreamed of Xanadu, he is cursed even as he is blessed by his contact with the spirit world.

Nearer to us in time and place are the story of the Voodoo practices in "Anatol Pierre" and the sinister possessiveness of a natural force in "Monterrey Sun." Both demonstrate the persistence of the conviction that forces outside ourselves can help or harm us through our own creative imagination.

THE SICK ROSE

William Blake

O Rose, thou art sick!
The invisible worm,
That flies in the night,
In the howling storm,

Has found out thy bed
Of crimson joy;
And his dark secret love
Does thy life destroy.

RAPUNZEL

The Brothers Grimm

ONCE UPON A TIME there lived a man and his wife who were very
unhappy because they had no children. These good people had a little
window at the back of their house, which looked into the most lovely
garden, full of all manner of beautiful flowers and vegetables; but the
garden was surrounded by a high wall, and no one dared to enter it,
for it belonged to a witch of great power, who was feared by the whole
world. One day the woman stood at the window overlooking the garden,
and saw there a bed full of the finest rampion: the leaves looked so fresh
and green that she longed to eat them. The desire grew day by day, and
just because she knew she couldn't possibly get any, she pined away
and became quite pale and wretched. Then her husband grew alarmed
and said:

'What ails you, dear wife?'

'Oh,' she answered, 'if I don't get some rampion to eat out of the
garden behind the house, I know I shall die.'

The man, who loved her dearly, thought to himself, 'Come! rather
than let your wife die you shall fetch her some rampion, no matter the
cost.' So at dusk he climbed over the wall into the witch's garden, and,
hastily gathering a handful of rampion leaves, he returned with them
to his wife. She made them into a salad, which tasted so good that her
longing for the forbidden food was greater than ever. If she were to
know any peace of mind, there was nothing for it but that her husband
should climb over the garden wall again, and fetch her some more. So
at dusk over he got, but when he reached the other side he drew back
in terror, for there, standing before him, was the old witch.

'How dare you,' she said, with a wrathful glance, 'climb into my
garden and steal my rampion like a common thief? You shall suffer for
your foolhardiness.'

'Oh!' he implored, 'pardon my presumption; necessity alone drove me
to the deed. My wife saw your rampion from her window, and conceived
such a desire for it that she would certainly have died if her wish had
not been gratified.' Then the Witch's anger was a little appeased, and
she said:

'If it's as you say, you may take as much rampion away with you as
you like, but on one condition only—that you give me the child your
wife will shortly bring into the world. All shall go well with it, and I
will look after it like a mother.'

The man in his terror agreed to everything she asked, and as soon as the child was born the Witch appeared, and having given it the name of Rapunzel, which is the same as rampion, she carried it off with her.

Rapunzel was the most beautiful child under the sun. When she was twelve years old the Witch shut her up in a tower, in the middle of a great wood, and the tower had neither stairs nor doors, only high up at the very top a small window. When the old Witch wanted to get in she stood underneath and called out:

> 'Rapunzel, Rapunzel,
> Let down your golden hair,'

for Rapunzel had wonderful long hair, and it was as fine as spun gold. Whenever she heard the Witch's voice she unloosed her plaits, and let her hair fall down out of the window about twenty yards below, and the old Witch climbed up by it.

After they had lived like this for a few years, it happened one day that a Prince was riding through the wood and passed by the tower. As he drew near it he heard someone singing so sweetly that he stood still spell-bound, and listened. It was Rapunzel in her loneliness trying to while away the time by letting her sweet voice ring out into the wood. The Prince longed to see the owner of the voice, but he sought in vain for a door in the tower. He rode home, but he was so haunted by the song he had heard that he returned every day to the wood and listened. One day, when he was standing thus behind a tree, he saw the old Witch approach and heard her call out:

> 'Rapunzel, Rapunzel,
> Let down your golden hair.'

Then Rapunzel let down her plaits, and the Witch climbed up by them.

'So that's the staircase, is it?' said the Prince. 'Then I too will climb it and try my luck.'

So on the following day, at dusk, he went to the foot of the tower and cried:

> 'Rapunzel, Rapunzel,
> Let down your golden hair,'

and as soon as she had let it down the Prince climbed up.

At first Rapunzel was terribly frightened when a man came in, for she had never seen one before; but the Prince spoke to her so kindly, and told her at once that his heart had been so touched by her singing, that he felt he should know no peace of mind till he had seen her. Very soon Rapunzel forgot her fear, and when he asked her to marry him she consented at once. 'For,' she thought, 'he is young and handsome, and I'll certainly be happier with him than with the old Witch.' So she put her hand in his and said:

'Yes, I will gladly go with you, only how am I to get down out of the tower? Every time you come to see me you must bring a skein of silk with you, and I will make a ladder of them, and when it is finished I will climb down by it, and you will take me away on your horse.'

They arranged that, till the ladder was ready, he was to come to her every evening, because the old woman was with her during the day. The old Witch, of course, knew nothing of what was going on, till one day Rapunzel, not thinking of what she was about, turned to the Witch and said:

'How is it, good mother, that you are so much harder to pull up than the young Prince? He is always with me in a moment.'

'Oh! you wicked child,' cried the Witch. 'What is this I hear? I thought I had hidden you safely from the whole world, and in spite of it you have managed to deceive me.'

In her wrath she seized Rapunzel's beautiful hair, wound it round and round her left hand, and then grasping a pair of scissors in her right, snip snap, off it came, and the beautiful plaits lay on the ground. And, worse than this, she was so hard-hearted that she took Rapunzel to a lonely desert place, and there left her to live in loneliness and misery.

But on the evening of the day in which she had driven poor Rapunzel away, the Witch fastened the plaits on to a hook in the window, and when the Prince came and called out:

'Rapunzel, Rapunzel,
Let down your golden hair,'

she let them down, and the Prince climbed up as usual, but instead of his beloved Rapunzel he found the old Witch, who fixed her evil, glittering eyes on him, and cried mockingly:

'Ah, ah! you thought to find your lady love, but the pretty bird has flown and its song is dumb; the cat caught it, and will scratch out your eyes too. Rapunzel is lost to you for ever—you will never see her more.'

The Prince was beside himself with grief, and in his despair he jumped right down from the tower, and, though he escaped with his life, the thorns among which he fell pierced his eyes out. Then he wandered, blind and miserable, through the wood, eating nothing but roots and berries, and weeping and lamenting the loss of his lovely bride. So he wandered about for some years, as wretched and unhappy as he could well be, and at last he came to the desert place where Rapunzel was living. Of a sudden he heard a voice which seemed strangely familiar to him. He walked eagerly in the direction of the sound, and when he was quite close, Rapunzel recognised him and fell on his neck and wept. But two of her tears touched his eyes, and in a moment they became quite clear again, and he saw as well as he had ever done. Then he led her to his kingdom, where they were received and welcomed with great joy, and they lived happily ever after.

LITTLE SNOW-WHITE

The Brothers Grimm

Once upon a time in the middle of winter, when the flakes of snow were falling like feathers from the sky, a queen sat at a window sewing, and the frame of the window was made of black ebony. And whilst she was sewing and looking out of the window at the snow, she pricked her finger with the needle, and three drops of blood fell upon the snow. And the red looked pretty upon the white snow, and she thought to herself, "Would that I had a child as white as snow, as red as blood, and as black as the wood of the window frame."

Soon after that she had a little daughter, who was as white as snow, and as red as blood, and her hair was as black as ebony; and she was therefore called Little Snow-white. And when the child was born, the Queen died.

After a year had passed the King took to himself another wife. She was a beautiful woman, but proud and haughty, and she could not bear that any one else should surpass her in beauty. She had a wonderful looking-glass, and when she stood in front of it and looked at herself in it, and said—

> "Looking-glass, Looking-glass, on the wall,
> Who in this land is the fairest of all?"

the looking-glass answered—

> "Thou, O Queen, art the fairest of all!"

Then she was satisfied, for she knew that the looking-glass spoke the truth.

But Snow-white was growing up, and grew more and more beautiful; and when she was seven years old she was as beautiful as the day, and more beautiful than the Queen herself. And once when the Queen asked her looking-glass—

> "Looking-glass, Looking-glass, on the wall,
> Who in this land is the fairest of all?"

it answered—

> "Thou art fairer than all who are here, Lady Queen,
> But more beautiful still is Snow-white, as I ween."

Then the Queen was shocked, and turned yellow and green with envy.

From that hour, whenever she looked at Snow-white, her heart heaved in her breast, she hated the girl so much.

And envy and pride grew higher and higher in her heart like a weed, so that she had no peace day or night. She called a huntsman, and said, "Take the child away into the forest; I will no longer have her in my sight. Kill her, and bring me back her heart as a token." The huntsman obeyed, and took her away; but when he had drawn his knife, and was about to pierce Snow-white's innocent heart, she began to weep, and said, "Ah, dear huntsman, leave me my life! I will run away into the wild forest and never come home again."

And as she was so beautiful the huntsman had pity on her and said, "Run away, then, you poor child." "The wild beasts will soon have devoured you," thought he, and yet it seemed as if a stone had been rolled from his heart since it was no longer needful for him to kill her. And as a young boar just then came running by he stabbed it and cut out its heart and took it to the Queen as a proof that the child was dead. The cook had to salt this, and the wicked Queen ate it, and thought she had eaten the heart of Snow-white.

But now the poor child was all alone in the great forest, and so terrified that she looked at every leaf of every tree, and did not know what to do. Then she began to run, and ran over sharp stones and through thorns, and the wild beasts ran past her, but did her no harm.

She ran as long as her feet would go until it was almost evening; then she saw a little cottage and went into it to rest herself. Everything in the cottage was small, but neater and cleaner than can be told. There was a table on which was a white cover, and seven little plates, and on each plate a little spoon; moreover, there were seven little knives and forks, and seven little mugs. Against the wall stood seven little beds side by side, and covered with snow-white counterpanes.

Little Snow-white was so hungry and thirsty that she ate some vegetables and bread from each plate and drank a drop of wine out of each mug, for she did not wish to take all from one only. Then, as she was so tired, she laid herself down on one of the little beds, but none of them suited her; one was too long, another too short, but at last she found that the seventh one was right, and so she remained in it, said a prayer and went to sleep.

When it was quite dark the owners of the cottage came back; they were seven dwarfs who dug and delved in the mountains for ore. They lit their seven candles, and as it was now light within the cottage they saw that some one had been there, for everything was not in the same order in which they had left it.

The first said, "Who has been sitting on my chair?"

The second, "Who has been eating off my plate?"

The third, "Who has been taking some of my bread?"

The fourth, "Who has been eating my vegetables?"

The fifth, "Who has been using my fork?"

The sixth, "Who has been cutting with my knife?"

The seventh, "Who has been drinking out of my mug?"

Then the first looked round and saw that there was a little hole on his bed, and he said, "Who has been getting into my bed?" The others came up and each called out, "Somebody has been lying in my bed too." But the seventh when he looked at his bed saw little Snow-white, who was lying asleep therein. And he called the others, who came running up, and they cried out with astonishment, and brought their seven little candles and let the light fall on little Snow-white. "Oh, heavens! oh, heavens!" cried they, "what a lovely child!" and they were so glad that they did not wake her up, but let her sleep on in the bed. And the seventh dwarf slept with his companions, one hour with each, and so got through the night.

When it was morning little Snow-white awoke, and was frightened when she saw the seven dwarfs. But they were friendly and asked her what her name was. "My name is Snow-white," she answered. "How have you come to our house?" said the dwarfs. Then she told them that her step-mother had wished to have her killed, but that the huntsman had spared her life, and that she had run for the whole day, until at last she had found their dwelling. The dwarfs said, "If you will take care of our house, cook, make the beds, wash, sew, and knit, and if you will keep everything neat and clean, you can stay with us and you shall want for nothing." "Yes," said Snow-white, "with all my heart," and she stayed with them. She kept the house in order for them; in the mornings they went to the mountains and looked for copper and gold, in the evenings they came back, and then their supper had to be ready. The girl was alone the whole day, so the good dwarfs warned her and said, "Beware of your step-mother, she will soon know that you are here; be sure to let no one come in."

But the Queen, believing that she had eaten Snow-white's heart, could not but think that she was again the first and most beautiful of all; and she went to her looking-glass and said—

> "Looking-glass, Looking-glass, on the wall,
> Who in this land is the fairest of all?"

and the glass answered—

> "Oh, Queen, thou art fairest of all I see,
> But over the hills, where the seven dwarfs dwell,
> Snow-white is still alive and well,
> And none is so fair as she."

Then she was astounded, for she knew that the looking-glass never spoke falsely, and she knew that the huntsman had betrayed her, and that little Snow-white was still alive.

And so she thought and thought again how she might kill her, for so long as she was not the fairest in the whole land, envy let her have no rest. And when she had at last thought of something to do, she painted her face, and dressed herself like an old pedler-woman, and no one could have known her. In this disguise she went over the seven mountains to the seven dwarfs, and knocked at the door and cried, "Pretty things to sell, very cheap, very cheap." Little Snow-white looked out of the window and called out, "Good-day, my good woman, what have you to sell?" "Good things, pretty things," she answered; "stay-laces of all colours," and she pulled out one which was woven of bright-coloured silk. "I may let the worthy old woman in," thought Snow-white, and she unbolted the door and bought the pretty laces. "Child," said the old woman, "what a fright you look; come, I will lace you properly for once." Snow-white had no suspicion, but stood before her, and let herself be laced with the new laces. But the old woman laced so quickly and laced so tightly that Snow-white lost her breath and fell down as if dead. "Now I am the most beautiful," said the Queen to herself, and ran away.

Not long afterwards, in the evening, the seven dwarfs came home, but how shocked they were when they saw their dear little Snow-white lying on the ground, and that she neither stirred nor moved, and seemed to be dead. They lifted her up, and, as they saw that she was laced too tightly, they cut the laces; then she began to breathe a little, and after a while came to life again. When the dwarfs heard what had happened they said, "The old pedler-woman was no one else than the wicked Queen; take care and let no one come in when we are not with you."

But the wicked woman when she had reached home went in front of the glass and asked—

> "Looking-glass, Looking-glass, on the wall,
> Who in this land is the fairest of all?"

and it answered as before—

> "Oh, Queen, thou art fairest of all I see,
> But over the hills, where the seven dwarfs dwell,
> Snow-white is still alive and well,
> And none is so fair as she."

When she heard that, all her blood rushed to her heart with fear, for she saw plainly that little Snow-white was again alive. "But now," she said, "I will think of something that shall put an end to you," and by the help of witchcraft, which she understood, she made a poisonous comb. Then she disguised herself and took the shape of another old woman. So she went over the seven mountains to the seven dwarfs, knocked at the door, and cried, "Good things to sell cheap, cheap!"

Little Snow-white looked out and said, "Go away; I cannot let any one come in." "I suppose you can look," said the old woman, and pulled the poisonous comb out and held it up. It pleased the girl so well that she let herself be beguiled, and opened the door. When they had made a bargain the old woman said, "Now I will comb you properly for once." Poor little Snow-white had no suspicion, and let the old woman do as she pleased, but hardly had she put the comb in her hair than the poison in it took effect, and the girl fell down senseless. "You paragon of beauty," said the wicked woman, "you are done for now," and she went away.

But fortunately it was almost evening, when the seven dwarfs came home. When they saw Snow-white lying as if dead upon the ground they at once suspected the step-mother, and they looked and found the poisoned comb. Scarcely had they taken it out when Snow-white came to herself, and told them what had happened. Then they warned her once more to be upon her guard and to open the door to no one.

The Queen, at home, went in front of the glass and said—

"Looking-glass, Looking-glass, on the wall,
Who in this land is the fairest of all?"

then it answered as before—

"Oh, Queen, thou art fairest of all I see,
But over the hills, where the seven dwarfs dwell,
Snow-white is still alive and well,
And none is so fair as she."

When she heard the glass speak thus she trembled and shook with rage. "Snow-white shall die," she cried, "even if it costs me my life!"

Thereupon she went into a quite secret, lonely room, where no one ever came, and there she made a very poisonous apple. Outside it looked pretty, white with a red cheek, so that every one who saw it longed for it; but whoever ate a piece of it must surely die.

When the apple was ready she painted her face, and dressed herself up as a country-woman, and so she went over the seven mountains to the seven dwarfs. She knocked at the door. Snow-white put her head out of the window and said, "I cannot let any one in; the seven dwarfs have forbidden me." "It is all the same to me," answered the woman, "I shall soon get rid of my apples. There, I will give you one."

"No," said Snow-white, "I dare not take anything." "Are you afraid of poison?" said the old woman; "look, I will cut the apple in two pieces; you eat the red cheek, and I will eat the white." The apple was so cunningly made that only the red cheek was poisoned. Snow-white longed for the fine apple, and when she saw that the woman ate part of it she could resist no longer, and stretched out her hand and took the poisonous half. But hardly had she a bit of it in her mouth than she fell down dead. Then the Queen looked at her with a dreadful look, and laughed aloud and said, "White as snow, red as blood, black as ebony-wood! this time the dwarfs cannot wake you up again."

And when she asked of the Looking-glass at home—

"Looking-glass, Looking-glass, on the wall,
Who in this land is the fairest of all?"

it answered at last—

"Oh, Queen, in this land thou art fairest of all."

Then her envious heart had rest, so far as an envious heart can have rest.

The dwarfs, when they came home in the evening, found Snow-white lying upon the ground; she breathed no longer and was dead. They lifted her up, looked to see whether they could find anything poisonous, unlaced her, combed her hair, washed her with water and wine, but it was all of no use; the poor child was dead, and remained dead. They laid her upon a bier, and all seven of them sat round it and wept for her, and wept three days long.

Then they were going to bury her, but she still looked as if she were living, and still had her pretty red cheeks. They said, "We could not bury her in the dark ground," and they had a transparent coffin of glass made, so that she could be seen from all sides, and they laid her in it, and wrote her name upon it in golden letters, and that she was a king's daughter. Then they put the coffin out upon the mountain, and one of them always stayed by it and watched it. And birds came too, and wept for Snow-white; first an owl, then a raven, and last a dove.

And now Snow-white lay a long, long time in the coffin, and she did not change, but looked as if she were asleep; for she was as white as snow, as red as blood, and her hair was as black as ebony.

It happened, however, that a king's son came into the forest, and went to the dwarfs' house to spend the night. He saw the coffin on the mountain, and the beautiful Snow-white within it, and read what was written upon it in golden letters. Then he said to the dwarfs, "Let me have the coffin, I will give you whatever you want for it." But the dwarfs answered, "We will not part with it for all the gold in the world." Then he said, "Let me have it as a gift, for I cannot live without seeing Snow-white. I will honour and prize her as my dearest possession." As he spoke in this way the good dwarfs took pity upon him, and gave him the coffin.

And now the King's son had it carried away by his servants on their shoulders. And it happened that they stumbled over a tree-stump, and with the shock the poisonous piece of apple which Snow-white had bitten off came out of her throat. And before long she opened her eyes, lifted up the lid of the coffin, sat up, and was once more alive. "Oh, heavens, where am I?" she cried. The King's son, full of joy, said, "You are with me," and told her what had happened, and said, "I love you more than everything in the world; come with me to my father's palace, you shall be my wife."

And Snow-white was willing, and went with him, and their wedding was held with great show and splendour. But Snow-white's wicked step-mother was also bidden to the feast. When she had arrayed herself in beautiful clothes she went before the Looking-glass, and said—

> "Looking-glass, Looking-glass, on the wall,
> Who in this land is the fairest of all?"

the glass answered—

> "Oh, Queen, of all here the fairest art thou,
> But the young Queen is fairer by far as I trow."

Then the wicked woman uttered a curse, and was so wretched, so utterly wretched, that she knew not what to do. At first she would not go to the wedding at all, but she had no peace, and must go to see the young Queen. And when she went in she knew Snow-white; and she stood still with rage and fear, and could not stir. But iron slippers had already been put upon the fire, and they were brought in with tongs, and set before her. Then she was forced to put on the red-hot shoes, and dance until she dropped down dead.

THE HASHEESH EATER

Fitzhugh Ludlow

> *Apparently to satisfy the nineteenth–century American taste for stories and events of a supernatural cast, Fitzhugh Ludlow, an American journalist, produced* The Hasheesh Eater.
>
> *Apologists for the kind of imaginative writing of which this is an example suggest that the authors are actually exploring the ranges of human consciousness. Ludlow would certainly seem to substantiate this contention. Certainly in contemporary society there has been much said and written about experimenting with various hallucinogens to increase artistic creativity—but few writers have achieved the balance displayed by Ludlow in this selection. At all times he seems able to render a dispassionate account of his own state. This in turn enhances his vivid recollections of hallucinations.*
>
> *Ludlow also made much of the fact that the hasheesh–eater could extend his boundaries, so to speak. The conclusion to his book, in fact, states his belief that there is no limit to the capacity of the mind of man.*

ONE MORNING, in the spring of 185—, I dropped in upon the doctor for my accustomed lounge.

"Have you seen," said he, "my new acquisitions?"

I looked toward the shelves in the direction of which he pointed, and saw, added since my last visit, a row of comely pasteboard cylinders inclosing vials of the various extracts prepared by Tilden & Co. Arranged in order according to their size, they confronted me, as pretty a little rank of medicinal sharpshooters as could gratify the eye of an amateur. I approached the shelves, that I might take them in review.

A rapid glance showed most of them to be old acquaintances. "Conium, taraxacum, rhubarb—ha! what is this? Cannabis Indica?" "That," answered the doctor, looking with a parental fondness upon his new treasure, "is a preparation of the East Indian hemp, a powerful agent in cases of lock-jaw." On the strength of this introduction, I took down the little archer, and, removing his outer verdant coat, began the further prosecution of his acquaintance. To pull out a broad and shallow cork was the work of an instant, and it revealed to me an olive-brown extract, of the consistency of pitch, and a decided aromatic odor. Drawing out a small portion upon the point of my penknife, I was just going to put it to my tongue, when "Hold on!" cried the doctor; "do you want to kill yourself? That stuff is deadly poison." "Indeed!" I replied; "no, I can not say that I have any settled determination of that kind;" and with that I replaced the cork, and restored the extract, with all its appurtenances, to the shelf.

The remainder of my morning's visit in the sanctum was spent in consulting the Dispensatory under the title "Cannabis Indica." The sum of my discoveries there may be found, with much additional information, in that invaluable popular work, Johnston's Chemistry of Common Life. This being universally accessible, I will allude no further to the result of that morning's researches than to mention the three following conclusions to which I came.

First, the doctor was both right and wrong; right, inasmuch as a sufficiently large dose of the drug, if it could be retained in the stomach, would produce death, like any other narcotic, and the ultimate effect of its habitual use had always proved highly injurious to mind and body; wrong, since moderate doses of it were never immediately deadly, and many millions of people daily employed it as an indulgence similarly to opium. Second, it was the hasheesh referred to by Eastern travelers, and the subject of a most graphic chapter from the pen of Bayard Taylor, which months before had moved me powerfully to curiosity and admiration. Third, I would add it to the list of my former experiments.

In pursuance of this last determination, I waited till my friend was out of sight, that I might not terrify him by that which he considered a suicidal venture, and then quietly uncapping my little archer a second time, removed from his store of offensive armor a pill sufficient to balance the ten grain weight of the sanctorial scales. This, upon the authority of Pereira and the Dispensatory, I swallowed without a tremor as to the danger of the result.

Making all due allowance for the fact that I had not taken my hasheesh bolus fasting, I ought to experience its effects within the next four hours. That time elapsed without bringing the shadow of a phenomenon. It was plain that my dose had been insufficient.

For the sake of observing the most conservative prudence, I suffered several days to go by without a repetition of the experiment, and then, keeping the matter equally secret, I administered to myself a pill of fifteen grains. This second was equally ineffectual with the first.

Gradually, by five grains at a time, I increased the dose to thirty grains, which I took one evening half an hour after tea. I had now almost come to the conclusion that I was absolutely unsusceptible of the hasheesh influence. Without any expectation that this last experiment would be more successful than the former ones, and indeed with no realization of the manner in which the drug affected those who did make the experiment successfully, I went to pass the evening at the house of an intimate friend. In music and conversation the time passed pleasantly. The clock struck ten, reminding me that three hours had elapsed since the dose was taken, and as yet not an unusual symptom had appeared. I was provoked to think that this trial was as fruitless as its predecessors.

Ha! what means this sudden thrill? A shock, as of some unimagined vital force, shoots without warning through my entire frame, leaping to my fingers' ends, piercing my brain, startling me till I almost sprang from my chair.

I could not doubt it. I was in the power of the hasheesh influence. My first emotion was one of uncontrollable terror—a sense of getting something which I had not bargained for. That moment I would have given all I had or hoped to have to be as I was three hours before.

No pain anywhere—not a twinge in any fibre—yet a cloud of unutterable strangeness was settling upon me, and wrapping me impenetrably in from all that was natural or familiar. Endeared faces, well known to me of old, surrounded me, yet they were not with me in my loneliness. I had entered upon a tremendous life which they could not share. If the disembodied ever return to hover over the hearth-stone which once had a seat for them, they look upon their friends as I then looked upon mine. A nearness of place, with an infinite distance of state, a connection which had no possible sympathies for the wants of that hour of revelation, an isolation none the less perfect for seeming companionship.

Still I spoke; a question was put to me, and I answered it; I even laughed at a bon mot. Yet it was not my voice which spoke; perhaps one which I once had far away in another time and another place. For a while I knew nothing that was going on externally, and then the remembrance of the last remark which had been made returned slowly and indistinctly, as some trait of a dream will return after many days, puzzling us to say where we have been conscious of it before.

A fitful wind all the evening had been sighing down the chimney; it now grew into the steady hum of a vast wheel in accelerating motion. For a while this hum seemed to resound through all space. I was stunned by it—I was absorbed in it. Slowly the revolution of the wheel came to a stop, and its monotonous din was changed for the reverberating peal of a grand cathedral organ. The ebb and flow of its inconceivably solemn tone filled me with a grief that was more than human. I sympathized with the dirge-like cadence as spirit sympathizes with spirit. And then, in the full conviction that all I heard and felt was real, I looked out of my isolation to see the effect of the music on my friends. Ah! we were in separate worlds indeed. Not a trace of appreciation on any face.

Perhaps I was acting strangely. Suddenly a pair of busy hands, which had been running neck and neck all the evening with a nimble little crochet-needle over a race-ground of pink and blue silk, stopped at their goal, and their owner looked at me steadfastly. Ah! I was found out—I had betrayed myself. In terror I waited, expecting every instant to hear the word "hasheesh." No, the lady only asked me some question connected with the previous conversation. As mechanically as an automaton I began to reply. As I heard once more the alien and unreal tones of my own voice, I became convinced that it was some one else who spoke, and in another world. I sat and listened; still the voice kept speaking. Now for the first time I experienced that vast change which hasheesh makes in all measurements of time. The first word of the reply occupied a period sufficient for the action of a drama; the last left me in complete ignorance of any point far enough back in the past to date the commencement of the sentence. Its enunciation might have occupied years. I was not in the same life which had held me when I heard it begun.

And now, with time, space expanded also. At my friend's house one particular arm-chair was always reserved for me. I was sitting in it at a distance of hardly three feet from the centre-table around which the members of the family were grouped. Rapidly that distance widened. The whole atmosphere seemed ductile, and spun endlessly out into great spaces surrounding me on every side. We were in a vast hall, of which my friends and I occupied opposite extremities. The ceiling and the walls ran upward with a gliding motion, as if vivified by a sudden force of resistless growth.

Oh! I could not bear it. I should soon be left alone in the midst of an infinity of space. And now more and more every moment increased the conviction that I was watched. I did not know then, as I learned afterward, that suspicion of all earthly things and persons was the characteristic of the hasheesh delirium.

In the midst of my complicated hallucination, I could perceive that I had a dual existence. One portion of me was whirled unresistingly along the track of this tremendous experience, the other sat looking down from a height upon its double, observing, reasoning, and serenely weighing all the phenomena. This calmer being suffered with the other by sympathy, but did not lose its self-possession. Presently it warned me that I must go home, lest the growing effect of the hasheesh should incite me to some act which might frighten my friends. I acknowledged the force of this remark very much as if it had been made by another person, and rose to take my leave. I advanced toward the centre-table. With every step its distance increased. I nerved myself as for a long pedestrian journey. Still the lights, the faces, the furniture receded. At last, almost unconsciously, I reached them. It would be tedious to attempt to convey the idea of the time which my leave-taking consumed, and the attempt, at least with all minds that have not passed through the same experience, would be as impossible as tedious. At last I was in the street.

Beyond me the view stretched endlessly away. It was an unconverging vista, whose nearest lamps seemed separated from me by leagues. I was doomed to pass through a merciless stretch of space. A soul just disenthralled, setting out for his flight beyond the farthest visible star, could not be more overwhelmed with his newly-acquired conception of the sublimity of distance than I was at the moment. Solemnly I began my infinite journey.

Before long I walked in entire unconsciousness of all around me. I dwelt in a marvelous inner world. I existed by turns in different places and various states of being. Now I swept my gondola through the moon-lit lagoons of Venice. Now Alp on Alp towered above my view, and the glory of the coming sun flashed purple light upon the topmost icy pinnacle. Now in the primeval silence of some unexplored tropical forest I spread my feathery leaves, a giant fern, and swayed and nodded in the spice-gales over a river whose waves at once sent up clouds of music and perfume. My soul changed to a vegetable essence, thrilled with a strange and unimagined ectasy. The palace of Al Haroun could not have brought me back to humanity.

I will not detail all the transmutations of that walk. Ever and anon I returned from my dreams into consciousness, as some well-known house seemed to leap out into my path, awaking me with a shock. The whole way homeward was a series of such awakings and relapses into abstraction and delirium until I reached the corner of the street in which I lived.

Here a new phenomenon manifested itself. I had just awaked for perhaps the twentieth time, and my eyes were wide open. I recognized all surrounding objects, and began calculating the distance home. Suddenly, out of a blank wall at my side a muffled figure stepped into the path before me. His hair, white as snow, hung in tangled elf-locks on his shoulders, where he carried also a heavy burden, like unto the well-filled sack of sins which Bunyan places on the back of his pilgrim. Not liking his manner, I stepped aside, intending to pass around him and go on my way. This change of our relative position allowed the blaze of a neighboring streetlamp to fall full on his face, which had hitherto been totally obscured. Horror unspeakable! I shall never, till the day I die, forget that face. Every lineament was stamped with the records of a life black with damning crime; it glared upon me with a ferocious wickedness and a stony despair which only he may feel who is entering on the retribution of the unpardonable sin. He might have sat to a demon painter as the ideal of Shelley's Cenci. I seemed to grow blasphemous in looking at him, and, in an agony of fear, began to run away. He detained me with a bony hand, which pierced my wrist like talons, and, slowly taking down the burden from his own shoulders, laid it upon mine. I threw it off and pushed him away. Silently he returned and restored the weight. Again I repulsed him, this time crying out, "Man, what do you mean?" In a voice which impressed me with the sense of wickedness as his face had done, he replied, "You *shall* bear my burden with me," and a third time laid it on my shoulders. For the last time I hurled it aside, and, with all my force, dashed him from me. He reeled backward and fell, and before he could recover his disadvantage I had put a long distance between us.

Through the excitement of my struggle with this phantasm the effects of the hasheesh had increased mightily. I was bursting with an uncontrollable life; I strode with the thews of a giant. Hotter and faster came my breath; I seemed to pant like some tremendous engine. An electric energy whirled me resistlessly onward; I feared for myself lest it should burst its fleshly walls, and glance on, leaving a wrecked frame-work behind it.

At last I entered my own house. During my absence a family connection had arrived from abroad, and stood ready to receive my greeting. Partly restored to consciousness by the naturalness of home-faces and the powerful light of a chandelier which shed its blaze through the room, I saw the necessity of vigilance against betraying my condition, and with an intense effort suppressing all I felt, I approached my friend, and said all that is usual on such occasions. Yet recent as I was from my conflict with the supernatural, I cast a stealthy look about me, that I might learn from the faces of the others if, after all, I was shaking hands with a phantom, and making inquiries about the health of a family of hallucinations. Growing assured as I perceived no symptoms of astonishment, I finished the salutation and sat down.

It soon required all my resolution to keep the secret which I had determined to hold inviolable. My sensations began to be terrific—not from any pain that I felt, but from the tremendous mystery of all around me and within me. By an appalling introversion, all the operations of vitality which, in our ordinary state, go on unconsciously, came vividly into my experience. Through every thinnest corporeal tissue and minutest vein I could trace the circulation of the blood along each inch of its progress. I knew when every valve opened and when it shut; every sense was preternaturally awakened; the room was full of a great glory. The beating of my heart was so clearly audible that I wondered to find it unnoticed by those who were sitting by my side. Lo, now, that heart became a great fountain, whose jet played upward with loud vibrations, and, striking upon the roof of my skull as on a gigantic dome, fell back with a splash and echo into its reservoir. Faster and faster came the pulsations, until at last I heard them no more, and the stream became one continuously pouring flood, whose roar resounded through all my frame. I gave myself up for lost, since judgment, which still sat unimpaired above my perverted senses, argued that congestion must take place in a few moments, and close the drama with my death. But my clutch would not yet relax from hope. The thought struck me, Might not this rapidity of circulation be, after all, imaginary? I determined to find out.

Going to my own room, I took out my watch, and placed my hand upon my heart. The very effort which I made to ascertain the reality gradually brought perception back to its natural state. In the intensity of my observations, I began to perceive that the circulation was not as rapid as I had thought. From a pulseless flow it gradually came to be apprehended as a hurrying succession of intense throbs, then less swift and less intense, till finally, on comparing it with the second-hand, I found that about 90 a minute was its average rapidity. Greatly comforted, I desisted from the experiment. Almost instantly the hallucination returned. Again I dreaded apoplexy, congestion, hemorrhage, a multiplicity of nameless deaths, and drew my picture as I might be found on the morrow, stark and cold, by those whose agony would be redoubled by the mystery of my end. I reasoned with myself; I bathed my forehead—it did no good. There was one resource left: I would go to a physician.

With this resolve, I left my room and went to the head of the staircase. The family had all retired for the night, and the gas was turned off from the burner in hall below. I looked down the stairs: the depth was fathomless; it was a journey of years to reach the bottom! The dim light of the sky shone through the narrow panes at the sides of the front door, and seemed a demon-lamp in the middle darkness of the abyss. I never could get down! I sat me down despairingly upon the topmost step.

Suddenly a sublime thought possessed me. If the distance be infinite, I am immortal. It shall be tried. I commenced the descent, wearily, wearily down through my league-long, year-long journey. To record my impressions in that journey would be to repeat what I have said of the time of hasheesh. Now stopping to rest as a traveler would turn aside at a wayside inn, now toiling down through the lonely darkness, I came by-and-by to the end, and passed out into the street.

II. UNDER THE SHADOW OF ESCULAPIUS

On reaching the porch of the physician's house, I rang the bell, but immediately forgot whom to ask for. No wonder; I was on the steps of a palace in Milan—no (and I laughed at myself for the blunder), I was on the staircase of the Tower of London. So I should not be puzzled through my ignorance of Italian. But whom to ask for? This question recalled me to the real bearings of the place, but did not suggest its requisite answer. Whom shall I ask for? I began setting the most cunning traps of hypothesis to catch the solution of the difficulty. I looked at the surrounding houses; of whom had I been accustomed to think as living next door to them? This did not bring it. Whose daughter had I seen going to school from this house but the very day before? Her name was Julia—Julia—and I thought of every combination which had been made with this name from Julia Domna down to Giulia Grisi. Ah! now I had it—Julia H.; and her father naturally bore the same name. During this intellectual rummage I had rung the bell half a dozen times, under the impression that I was kept waiting a small eternity. When the servant opened the door she panted as if she had run for her life. I was shown up stairs to Dr. H.'s room, where he had thrown himself down to rest after a tedious operation. Locking the door after me with an air of determined secrecy, which must have conveyed to him pleasant little suggestions of a design upon his life, I approached his bedside.

"I am about to reveal to you," I commenced, "something which I would not for my life allow to come to other ears. Do you pledge me your eternal silence?"

"I do; what is the matter?"

"I have been taking hasheesh—Cannabis Indica, and I fear that I am going to die."

"How much did you take?"

"Thirty grains."

"Let me feel your pulse." He placed his finger on my wrist and counted slowly, while I stood waiting to hear my death-warrant. "Very regular," shortly spoke the doctor; "triflingly accelerated. Do you feel any pain?" "None at all." "Nothing the matter with you; go home and go to bed." "But—is there—is there—no—danger of—apoplexy?" "Bah!" said the doctor; and, having delivered himself of this very Abernethy-like opinion of my case, he lay down again. My hand was on the knob, when he stopped me with, "Wait a minute; I'll give you a powder to carry with you, and if you get frightened again after you leave me, you can take it as a sedative. Step out on the landing, if you please, and call my servant."

I did so, and my voice seemed to reverberate like thunder from every recess in the whole building. I was terrified at the noise I had made. I learned in after days that this impression is only one of the many due to the intense susceptibility of the sensorium as produced by hasheesh. At one time, having asked a friend to check me if I talked loudly or immoderately while in a state of fantasia among persons from whom I wished to conceal my state, I caught myself shouting and singing from very ecstasy, and reproached him with a neglect of his friendly office. I could not believe him when he assured me that I had not uttered an audible word. The intensity of the inward emotion had affected the external through the internal ear.

I returned and stood at the foot of the doctor's bed. All was perfect silence in the room, and had been perfect darkness also but for the small lamp which I held in my hand to light the preparation of the powder when it should come. And now a still sublimer mystery began to enwrap me. I stood in a remote chamber at the top of a colossal building, and the whole fabric beneath me was steadily growing into the air. Higher than the topmost pinnacle of Bel's Babylonish temple

—higher than Ararat—on, on forever into the lonely dome of God's infinite universe we towered ceaselessly. The years flew on; I heard the musical rush of their wings in the abyss outside of me, and from cycle to cycle, from life to life I careered, a mote in eternity and space. Suddenly emerging from the orbit of my transmigrations, I was again at the foot of the doctor's bed, and thrilled with wonder to find that we were both unchanged by the measureless lapse of time. The servant had not come.

"Shall I call her again?" "Why, you have this moment called her." "Doctor," I replied solemnly, and in language that would have seemed bombastic enough to any one who did not realize what I felt. "I will not believe you are deceiving me, but to me it appears as if sufficient time has elapsed since then for all the Pyramids to have crumbled back to dust." "Ha! ha! you are very funny to-night," said the doctor; "but here she comes, and I will send her for something which will comfort you on that score, and re-establish the Pyramids in your confidence." He gave the girl his orders, and she went out again.

The thought struck me that I would compare *my time* with other people's. I looked at my watch, found that its minute-hand stood at the quarter mark past eleven, and, returning it to my pocket, abandoned myself to my reflections.

Presently I saw myself a gnome imprisoned by a most weird enchanter, whose part I assigned to the doctor before me, in the Domdaniel caverns, "under the roots of the ocean." Here, until the dissolution of all things, was I doomed to hold the lamp that lit that abysmal darkness, while my heart, like a giant clock, ticked solemnly the remaining years of time. Now, this hallucination departing, I heard in the solitude of the night outside the sound of a wondrous heaving sea. Its waves, in sublime cadence, rolled forward till they met the foundations of the building; they smote them with a might which made the very topstone quiver, and then fall back, with hiss and hollow murmur, into the broad bosom whence they had arisen. Now through the street, with measured tread, an armed host passed by. The heavy beat of their footfall and the griding of their brazen corslet-rings alone broke the silence, for among them all there was no more speech nor music than in a battalion of the dead. It was the army of the ages going by into eternity. A godlike sublimity swallowed up my soul. I was overwhelmed in a fathomless barathrum of time, but I leaned on God, and was immortal through all changes.

And now, in another life, I remembered that far back in the cycles I had looked at my watch to measure the time through which I passed. The impulse seized me to look again. The minutehand stood half way between fifteen and sixteen minutes past eleven. The watch must have stopped; I held it to my ear; no, it was still going. I had traveled through all that immeasurable chain of dreams in thirty seconds. "My God!" I cried, "I am in eternity." In the presence of that first sublime revelation of the soul's own time, and her capacity for an infinite life, I stood trembling with breathless awe. Till I die, that moment of unveiling will stand in clear relief from all the rest of my existence. I hold it still in unimpaired remembrance as one of the unutterable sanctities of my being. The years of all my earthly life to come can never be as long as those thirty seconds.

Finally the servant reappeared. I received my powder and went home. There was a light in one of the upper windows, and I hailed it with unspeakable joy, for it relieved me from a fear which I could not conquer, that while I had been gone all familiar things had passed away from earth. I was hardly safe in my room before I doubted having ever been out of it. "I have experienced some wonderful dream," said I, "as I lay here after coming from the parlor." If I had not been out, I reasoned that I would have no powder in my pocket. The powder was there, and it steadied me a little to find that I was not utterly hallucinated on every point. Leaving the light burning, I set out to travel to my bed, which gently invited me in the distance. Reaching it after a sufficient walk, I threw myself down.

III. THE KINGDOM OF THE DREAM

The moment that I closed my eyes a vision of celestial glory burst upon me. I stood on the silver strand of a translucent, boundless lake, across whose bosom I seemed to have been just transported. A short way up the beach, a temple, modeled like the Parthenon, lifted its spotless and gleaming columns of alabaster sublimely into a rosy air —like the Parthenon, yet as much excelling it is the godlike ideal of architecture must transcend that ideal realized by man. Unblemished in its purity of whiteness, faultless in the unbroken symmetry of every line and angle, its pediment was draped in odorous clouds, whose tints outshone the rainbow. It was the work of an unearthly builder, and my soul stood before it in a trance of ecstasy. Its folded doors were resplendent with the glory of a multitude of eyes of glass, which were inlaid throughout the marble surfaces at the corners of diamond figures from the floor of the porch to the topmost moulding. One of these eyes was golden, like the midday sun, another emerald, another sapphire, and thus onward through the whole gamut of hues, all of them set in such collocations as to form most exquisite harmonies, and whirling upon their axes with the rapidity of thought. At the mere vestibule of the temple I could have sat and drunk in ecstasy forever; but lo! I am yet more blessed. On silent hinges the doors swing open, and I pass in.

I did not seem to be in the interior of a temple. I beheld myself as truly in the open air as if I had never passed the portals, for whichever way I looked there were no walls, no roof, no pavement. An atmosphere of fathomless and soul-satisfying serenity surrounded and transfused me. I stood upon the bank of a crystal stream, whose waters, as they slid on, discoursed notes of music which tinkled on the ear like the tones of some exquisite bell-glass. The same impression which such tones produce, of music refined to its ultimate ethereal spirit and borne from a far distance, characterized every ripple of those translucent waves. The gently sloping banks of the stream were luxuriant with a velvety cushioning of grass and moss, so living green that the eye and the soul reposed on them at the same time and drank in peace. Through this amaranthine herbage strayed the gnarled, fantastic roots of giant cedars of Lebanon, from whose primeval trunks great branches spread above me, and interlocking, wove a roof of impenetrable shadow; and wandering down the still avenues below those grand arboreal arches went glorious bards, whose snowy beards fell on their breasts beneath countenances of ineffable benignity and nobleness.

They were all clad in flowing robes, like God's high-priests, and each one held in his hand a lyre of unearthly workmanship. Presently one stops midway down a shady walk, and, baring his right arm, begins a prelude. While his celestial chords were trembling up into their sublime fullness, another strikes his strings, and now they blend upon my ravished ear in such a symphony as was never heard elsewhere, and I shall never hear again out of the Great Presence. A moment more, and three are playing in harmony; now the fourth joins the glorious rapture of his music to their own, and in the completeness of the chord my soul is swallowed up. I can bear no more. But yes, I am sustained, for suddenly the whole throng break forth in a chorus, upon whose wings I am lifted out of the riven walls of sense, and music and spirit thrill in immediate communion. Forever rid of the intervention of pulsing air and vibrating nerve, my soul dilates with the swell of that transcendent harmony, and interprets from it arcana of a meaning which words can never tell. I am borne aloft upon the glory of sound. I float in a trance among the burning choir of the seraphim. But, as I am melting through the purification of that sublime ecstasy into oneness with the Deity himself, one by one those pealing lyres faint away, and as the last throb dies down along the measureless ether, visionless arms swiftly as lightning carry me far into the profound, and set me down before another portal. Its leaves, like the first, are of spotless marble, but ungemmed with wheeling eyes of burning color.

Before entering on the record of this new vision I will make a digression for the purpose of introducing two laws of the hasheesh operation, which, as explicatory, deserve a place here. First, after the completion of any one fantasia has arrived, there almost invariably succeeds a shifting of the action to some other stage entirely different in its surroundings. In this transition the general character of the emotion may remain unchanged. I may be happy in Paradise and happy at the sources of the Nile, but seldom, either in Paradise or on the Nile, twice in succession. I may writhe in Etna and burn unquenchably in Gehenna, but almost never, in the course of the same delirium, shall Etna or Gehenna witness my torture a second time.

Second, after the full storm of a vision of intense sublimity has blown past the hasheesh-eater, his next vision is generally of a quiet, relaxing, and recreating nature. He comes down from his clouds or up from his abyss into a middle ground of gentle shadows, where he may rest his eyes from the splendor of the seraphim or the flames of fiends. There is a wise philosophy in this arrangement, for otherwise the soul would soon burn out in the excess of its own oxygen. Many a time, it seems to me, has my own thus been saved from extinction.

This next vision illustrated both, but especially the latter of these laws. The temple-doors opened noiselessly before me, but it was no scene of sublimity which thus broke in upon my eyes. I stood in a large apartment, which resembled the Senate-chamber at Washington more than any thing else to which I can compare it. Its roof was vaulted, and at the side opposite the entrance the floor rose into a dais surmounted by a large arm-chair. The body of the house was occupied by similar chairs disposed in arcs; the heavy paneling of the walls was adorned with grotesque frescoes of every imaginable bird, beast, and monster, which, by some hidden law of life and motion, were forever changing, like the figures of the kaleidoscope. Now the walls bristled with hippo-griffs; now, from wainscot to ceiling, toucans and maccataws swung and nodded from their perches amid emerald palms; now Centaurs and Lapithæ clashed in ferocious turmoil, while crater and cyathus were crushed beneath ringing hoof and heel. But my attention was quickly distracted from the frescoes by the sight of a most witchly congress, which filled all the chairs of that broad chamber. On the dais sat an old crone, whose commanding position first engaged my attention to her personal appearance, and, upon rather impolite scrutiny, I beheld that she was the product of an art held in pre-eminent favor among persons of her age and sex. She was *knit* of purple yarn! In faultless order the stitches ran along her face; in every pucker of her re-entrant mouth, in every wrinkle of her brow, she was a yarny counterfeit of the gran-dam of actual life, and by some skillful process of stuffing her nose had received its due peak and her chin its projection. The occupants of the seats below were all but reproductions of their president, and both she and they were constantly swaying from side to side, forward and back, to the music of some invisible instruments, whose tone and style were most intensely and ludicrously Ethiopian. Not a word was spoken by any of the woolly conclave, but with untiring industry they were all knitting, knitting, knitting ceaselessly, as if their lives depended on it. I looked to see the objects of their manufacture. They were knitting old women like themselves! One of the sisterhood had nearly brought her double to completion; earnestly another was engaged in rounding out an eyeball; another was fastening the gathers at the corner of a mouth; another was setting up stitches for an old woman in petto.

With marvelous rapidity this work went on; ever and anon some completed crone sprang from the needles which had just achieved her, and, instantly vivified, took up the instruments of reproduction, and fell to work as assiduously as if she had been a member of the congress since the world began. "Here," I cried, "here, at last do I realize the meaning of endless progression!" and, though the dome echoed with my peals of laughter, I saw no motion of astonishment in the stitches of a single face, but, as for dear life, the manufacture of old women went on unobstructed by the involuntary rudeness of the stranger.

An irresistible desire to aid in the work possessed me: I was half determined to snatch up a quartette of needles and join the sisterhood. My nose began to be ruffled with stitches, and the next moment I had been a partner in their yarny destinies but for a hand which pulled me backward through the door, and shut the congress forever from my view.

For a season I abode in an utter void of sight and sound, but I waited patiently in the assurance that some new changes of magnificence were preparing for me. I was not disappointed. Suddenly, at a far distance, three intense luminous points stood on the triple wall of darkness, and through each of them shot twin attenuated rays of magic light and music. Without being able to perceive any thing of my immediate surroundings, I still felt that I was noiselessly drifting toward those radiant and vocal points. With every moment they grew larger, the light and the harmony came clearer, and before long I could distinguish plainly three colossal arches rising from the bosom of a waveless water. The mid arch towered highest; the two on either side were equal to each other. Presently I beheld that they formed the portals of an enormous cavern, whose dome rose above me into such sublimity that its cope was hidden from my eyes in wreaths of cloud. On each side of me ran a wall of gnarled and rugged rock, from whose jutting points, as high as the eye could reach, depended stalactites of every imagined form and tinge of beauty, while below me, in the semblance of an ebon pavement, from the reflection of its overshadowing crags, lay a level lake, whose exquisite transparency wanted but the smile of the sun to make it glow like a floor of adamant. On this lake I lay in a little boat divinely carved from pearl after the similitude of Triton's shelly shallop; its rudder and its oarage were my own unconscious will, and, without the labors of especial volition, I floated as I list with a furrowless keel swiftly toward the central giant arch. With every moment that brought me nearer to my exit, the harmony that poured through it developed into a grander volume and an intenser beauty.

And now I passed out.

Claude Lorraine, freed from the limitations of sense, and gifted with an infinite canvas, may, for aught I know, be upon some halcyon island of the universe painting such a view as now sailed into my vision. Fitting employment would it be for his immortality were his pencil dipped into the very fountains of the light. Many a time in the course of my life have I yearned for the possession of some grand old master's soul and culture in the presence of revelations of Nature's loveliness which I dared not trust to memory; before this vision, as now in the remembrance of it, that longing became a heartfelt pain. Yet, after all, it was well; the mortal limner would have fainted in his task. Alas! how does the material in which we must embody the spiritual cramp and resist its execution! Standing before windows where the invisible spirit of the frost had traced his exquisite algae, his palms and his ferns, have I said to myself, with a sigh, Ah! Nature alone, of all artists, is gifted to work out her ideals!

Shall I be so presumptuous as to attempt in words that which would beggar the palette and the pencil of old-time disciples of the beautiful? I will, if it be only to satisfy a deep longing.

From the arches of my cavern I had emerged upon a horizonless sea. Through all the infinitudes around me I looked out, and met no boundaries of space. Often in after times have I beheld the heavens and the earth stretching out in parallel lines forever, but this was the first time I had ever stood un-"ringed by the azure world," and I exulted in all the sublimity of the new conception. The whole atmosphere was one measureless suffusion of golden motes, which throbbed continually in cadence, and showered radiance and harmony at the same time. With ecstasy vision spread her wings for a flight against which material laws locked no barrier, and every moment grew more and more entranced at further and fuller glimpses of a beauty which floated like incense from the pavement of that eternal sea. With ecstasy the spiritual ear gathered in continually some more distant and unimaginable tone, and grouped the growing harmonies into one sublime chant of benediction. With ecstasy the whole soul drank in revelations from every province, and cried out, "Oh, awful loveliness!" And now out of my shallop I was borne away into the full light of the mid firmament; now seated on some toppling peak of a cloud-mountain, whose yawning rifts disclosed far down the mines of reserved lightning; now bathed in my ethereal travel by the rivers of the rainbow, which, side by side, coursed through the valleys of heaven; now dwelling for a season in the environment of unbroken sunlight, yet bearing it like the eagle with undazzled eye; now crowned with a coronal of prismatic beads of dew. Through whatever region of circumstances I passed, one characteristic of the vision remained unchanged: peace—everywhere godlike peace, the sum of all conceivable desires satisfied.

Slowly I floated down to earth again. There Oriental gardens waited to receive me. From fountain to fountain I danced in graceful mazes with inimitable houris, whose foreheads were bound with fillets of jasmine. I pelted with figs the rare exotic birds, whose gold and crimson wings went flashing from branch to branch, or wheedled them to me with Arabic phrases of endearment. Through avenues of palm I walked arm-in-arm with Hafiz, and heard the hours flow singing through the channels of his matchless poetry. In gay kiosques I quiffed my sherbet, and in the luxury of lawlessness kissed away by drops that other juice which is contraband unto the faithful. And now beneath citron shadows I laid me down to sleep. When I awoke it was morning—actually morning, and not a hasheesh hallucination. The first emotion that I felt upon opening my eyes was happiness to find things again wearing a natural air. Yes; although the last experience of which I had been conscious had seemed to satisfy every human want, physical or spiritual, I smiled on the four plain white walls of my bedchamber, and hailed their familiar unostentatiousness with a pleasure which had no wish to transfer itself to arabesque or rainbows. It was like returning home from an eternity spent in loneliness among the palaces of strangers. Well may I say an eternity, for during the whole day I could not rid myself of the feeling that I was separated from the preceding one by an immeasurable lapse of time. In fact, I never got wholly rid of it.

I rose that I might test my reinstated powers, and see if the restoration was complete. Yes, I felt not one trace of bodily weariness nor mental depression. Every function had returned to its normal state, with the one exception mentioned; memory could not efface the traces of my having passed through a great mystery. I recalled the events of the past night, and was pleased to think that I had betrayed myself to no one but Dr. H. I was satisfied with my experiment.

Ah! would that I had been satisfied! Yet history must go on.

THE MARK
OF THE BEAST

Rudyard Kipling

Your Gods and my Gods—do you or I know which are the stronger?
—NATIVE PROVERB.

EAST OF SUEZ, some hold, the direct control of Providence ceases; Man being there handed over to the power of the gods and devils of Asia, and the Church of England Providence only exercising an occasional and modified supervision in the case of Englishmen.

This theory accounts for some of the more unnecessary horrors of life in India: it may be stretched to explain my story.

My friend Strickland of the Police, who knows as much of natives of India as is good for any man, can bear witness to the facts of the case. Dumoise, our doctor, also saw what Strickland and I saw. The inference which he drew from the evidence was entirely incorrect. He is dead now; he died in a rather curious manner, which has been elsewhere described.

When Fleete came to India he owned a little money and some land in the Himalayas, near a place called Dharmsala. Both properties had been left him by an uncle, and he came out to finance them. He was a big, heavy, genial, and inoffensive man. His knowledge of natives was, of course, limited, and he complained of the difficulties of the language.

He rode in from his place in the hills to spend New Year in the station, and he stayed with Strickland. On New Year's Eve there was a big dinner at the club, and the night was excusably wet. When men foregather from the uttermost ends of the Empire, they have a right to be riotous. The Frontier had sent down a contingent o' Catch-'em-Alive-O's who had not seen twenty white faces for a year, and were used to ride fifteen miles to dinner at the next Fort at the risk of a Khyberee bullet where their drinks should lie. They profited by their new security, for they tried to play pool with a curled-up hedgehog found in the garden, and one of them carried the marker round the room in his teeth. Half a dozen planters had come in from the south and were talking "horse" to the Biggest Liar in Asia, who was trying to cap all their stories at once. Everybody was there, and there was a general closing up of ranks and taking stock of our losses in dead or disabled that had fallen during the past year. It was a very wet night, and I remember that we sang "Auld Lang Syne" with our feet in the Polo Championship Cup, and our heads among the stars, and swore that we were all dear friends. Then some of us went away and annexed Burma, and some tried to open up the Soudan and were opened up by Fuzzies in that cruel scrub outside Suakim, and some found stars and medals, and some were married, which was bad, and some did other things which were worse, and the others of us stayed in our chains and strove to make money on insufficient experiences.

Fleete began the night with sherry and bitters, drank champagne steadily up to dessert, then raw, rasping Capri with all the strength of whisky, took Benedictine with his coffee, four or five whiskies and sodas to improve his pool strokes, beer and bones at half-past two, winding up with old brandy. Consequently, when he came out, at half-past three in the morning into fourteen degrees of frost, he was very angry with his horse for coughing, and tried to leap-frog into the saddle. The horse broke away and went to his stables; so Strickland and I formed a Guard of Dishonor to take Fleete home.

Our road lay through the bazaar, close to a little temple of Hanuman, the Monkey-god, who is a leading divinity worthy of respect. All gods have good points, just as have all priests. Personally, I attach much importance to Hanuman, and am kind to his people—the great gray apes of the hills. One never knows when one may want a friend.

There was a light in the temple, and as we passed, we could hear the voices of men chanting hymns. In a native temple, the priests rise at all hours of the night to do honor to their god. Before we could stop him, Fleete dashed up the steps, patted two priests on the back, and was gravely grinding the ashes of his cigar-butt into the forehead of the red, stone image of Hanuman. Strickland tried to drag him out, but he sat down and said solemnly:

"Shee that? 'Mark of the B—beasht! I made it. Ishn't it fine?"

In half a minute the temple was alive and noisy, and Strickland, who knew what came of polluting gods, said that things might occur. He, by virtue of his official position, long residence in the country, and weakness for going among the natives, was known to the priests and he felt unhappy. Fleete sat on the ground and refused to move. He said that "good old Hanuman" made a very soft pillow.

Then, without any warning, a Silver Man came out of a recess behind the image of the god. He was perfectly naked in that bitter, bitter cold, and his body shone like frosted silver, for he was what the Bible calls "a leper as white as snow." Also he had no face, because he was a leper of some years' standing, and his disease was heavy upon him. We stooped to haul Fleete up, and the temple was filling and filling with folk who seemed to spring from the earth, when the Silver Man ran in under our arms, making a noise exactly like the mewing of an otter, caught Fleete round the body and dropped his head on Fleete's breast before we could wrench him away. Then he retired to a corner and sat mewing while the crowd blocked all the doors.

The priests were very angry until the Silver Man touched Fleete. That nuzzling seemed to sober them.

At the end of a few minutes' silence one of the priests came to Strickland and said, in perfect English, "Take your friend away. He has done with Hanuman, but Hanuman has not done with him." The crowd gave room and we carried Fleete into the road.

Strickland was very angry. He said that we might all three have been knifed, and that Fleete should thank his stars that he had escaped without injury.

Fleete thanked no one. He said that he wanted to go to bed. He was gorgeously drunk.

We moved on, Strickland silent and wrathful, until Fleete was taken with violent shivering fits and sweating. He said that the smells of the bazaar were overpowering, and he wondered why slaughter-houses were permitted so near English residences. "Can't you smell the blood?" said Fleete.

We put him to bed at last, just as dawn was breaking, and Strickland invited me to have another whisky and soda. While we were drinking he talked of the trouble in the temple, and admitted that it baffled him completely. Strickland hates being mystified by natives, because his business in life is to overmatch them with their own weapons. He has not yet succeeded in doing this, but in fifteen or twenty years he will have made some small progress.

"They should have mauled us," he said, "instead of mewing at us. I wonder what they meant. I don't like it one little bit."

I said that the Managing Committee of the temple would in all probability bring a criminal action against us for insulting their religion. There was a section of the Indian Penal Code which exactly met Fleete's offense. Strickland said he only hoped and prayed that they would do this. Before I left I looked into Fleet's room, and saw him lying on his right side and scratching his left breast. Then I went to bed cold, depressed, and unhappy, at seven o'clock in the morning.

At one o'clock I rode over to Strickland's house to inquire after Fleete's head. I imagined that it would be a sore one. Fleete was breakfasting and seemed unwell. His temper was gone, for he was abusing the cook for not supplying him with an underdone chop. A man who can eat raw meat after a wet night is a curiosity. I told Fleete this and he laughed.

"You breed queer mosquitoes in these parts," he said. "I've been bitten to pieces, but only in one place."

"Let's have a look at the bite," said Strickland. "It may have gone down since this morning."

While the chops were being cooked, Fleete opened his shirt and showed us, just over his left breast, a mark, the perfect double of the black rosettes—the five or six irregular blotches arranged in a circle —on a leopard's hide. Strickland looked and said, "It was only pink this morning. It's grown black now."

Fleete ran to a glass.

"By Jove!" he said, "this is nasty. What is it?"

We could not answer. Here the chops came in, all red and juicy, and Fleete bolted three in a most offensive manner. He ate on his right grinders only, and threw his head over his right shoulder as he snapped the meat. When he had finished, it struck him that he had been behaving strangely, for he said, apologetically, "I don't think I ever felt so hungry in my life. I've bolted like an ostrich."

After breakfast Strickland said to me, "Don't go. Stay here, and stay for the night."

Seeing that my house was not three miles from Strickland's this request was absurd. But Strickland insisted, and was going to say something when Fleete interrupted by declaring in a shame-faced way that he felt hungry again. Strickland sent a man to my house to fetch over my bedding and a horse, and we three went down to Strickland's stables to pass the hours until it was time to go out for a ride. The man who has a weakness for horses never wearies of inspecting them; and when two men are killing time in this way they gather knowledge and lies the one from the other.

There were five horses in the stables, and I shall never forget the scene as we tried to look them over. They seemed to have gone mad. They reared and screamed and nearly tore up their pickets; they sweated and shivered and lathered and were distraught with fear. Strickland's horses used to know him as well as his dogs; which made the matter more curious. We left the stable for fear of the brutes throwing themselves in their panic. Then Strickland turned back and called me. The horses were still frightened, but they let us "gentle" and make much of them, and put their heads in our bosoms.

"They aren't afraid of *us*," said Strickland. "D'you know, I'd give three months' pay if *Outrage* here could talk."

But *Outrage* was dumb, and could only cuddle up to his master and blow out his nostrils, as is the custom of horses when they wish to explain things but can't. Fleete came up when we were in the stalls, and as soon as the horses saw him, their fright broke out afresh. It was all that we could do to escape from the place unkicked. Strickland said, "They don't seem to love you, Fleete."

"Nonsense," said Fleete; "my mare will follow me like a dog." He went to her; she was in a loose-box; but as he slipped the bars she plunged, knocked him down, and broke away into the garden. I laughed, but Strickland was not amused. He took his mustache in both fists and pulled at it till it nearly came out. Fleete, instead of going off to chase his property, yawned, saying that he felt sleepy. He went to the house to lie down, which was a foolish way of spending New Year's Day.

Strickland sat with me in the stables and asked if I had noticed anything peculiar in Fleete's manner. I said that he ate his food like a beast: but that this might have been the result of living alone in the hills out of the reach of society as refined and elevating as ours, for instance. Strickland was not amused. I do not think that he listened to me, for his next sentence referred to the mark on Fleete's breast and I said that it might have been caused by blister-flies, or that it was possibly a birthmark newly born and now visible for the first time. We both agreed that it was unpleasant to look at, and Strickland found occasion to say that I was a fool.

"I can't tell you what I think now," said he, "because you would call me a madman; but you must stay with me for the next few days, if you can. I want you to watch Fleete, but don't tell me what you think till I have made up my mind."

"But I am dining out tonight," I said.

"So am I," said Strickland, "and so is Fleete. At least if he doesn't change his mind."

We walked about the garden smoking, but saying nothing—because we were friends, and talking spoils good tobacco—till our pipes were out. Then we went to wake up Fleete. He was wide awake and fidgeting about his room.

"I say, I want some more chops," he said. "Can I get them?"

We laughed and said, "Go and change. The ponies will be round in a minute."

"All right," said Fleete. "I'll go when I get the chops—underdone ones, mind."

He seemed to be quite in earnest. It was four o'clock and we had had breakfast at one; still, for a long time, he demanded those underdone chops. Then he changed into riding clothes and went out into the veranda. His pony—the mare had not been caught—would not let him come near. All three horses were unmanageable—mad with fear—and finally Fleete said that he would stay at home and get something to eat. Strickland and I rode out wondering. As we passed the temple of Hanuman, the Silver Man came out and mewed at us.

"He is not one of the regular priests of the temple," said Strickland. "I think I should peculiarly like to lay my hands on him."

There was no spring in our gallop on the race-course that evening. The horses were stale, and moved as though they had been ridden out.

"The fright after breakfast has been too much for them," said Strickland.

That was the only remark he made through the remainder of the ride. Once or twice I think he swore to himself; but that did not count.

We came back in the dark at seven o'clock, and saw that there were no lights in the bungalow. "Careless ruffians my servants are!" said Strickland.

My horse reared at something on the carriage drive, and Fleete stood up under its nose.

"What are you doing, groveling about the garden?" said Strickland.

But both horses bolted and nearly threw us. We dismounted by the stables and returned to Fleete, who was on his hands and knees under the orange-bushes.

"What the devil's wrong with you?" said Strickland.

"Nothing, nothing in the world," said Fleete, speaking very quickly and thickly. "I've been gardening—botanizing, you know. The smell of the earth is delightful. I think I'm going for a walk—a long walk—all night."

Then I saw that there was something excessively out of order somewhere, and I said to Strickland, "I am not dining out."

"Bless you!" said Strickland. "Here, Fleete, get up. You'll catch fever there. Come in to dinner and let's have the lamps lit. We'll all dine at home."

Fleete stood up unwillingly, and said, "No lamps—no lamps. It's much nicer here. Let's dine outside and have some more chops—lots of 'em and underdone—bloody ones with gristle."

Now a December evening in Northern India is bitterly cold, and Fleete's suggestion was that of a maniac.

"Come in," said Strickland, sternly. "Come in at once."

Fleete came, and when the lamps were brought, we saw that he was literally plastered with dirt from head to foot. He must have been rolling in the garden. He shrank from the light and went to his room. His eyes were horrible to look at. There was a green light behind them, not in them, if you understand, and the man's lower lip hung down.

Strickland said, "There is going to be trouble—big trouble—tonight. Don't you change your riding-things."

We waited and waited for Fleete's reappearance, and ordered dinner in the meantime. We could hear him moving about his own room, but there was no light there. Presently from the room came the long-drawn howl of a wolf.

People write and talk lightly of blood running cold and hair standing up and things of that kind. Both sensations are too horrible to be trifled with. My heart stopped as though a knife had been driven through it, and Strickland turned as white as the table-cloth.

The howl was repeated, and was answered by another howl far across the fields.

That set the gilded roof on the horror. Strickland dashed into Fleete's room. I followed, and we saw Fleete getting out of the window. He made beast-noises in the back of his throat. He could not answer us when we shouted at him. He spat.

I don't quite remember what followed, but I think that Strickland must have stunned him with the long bootjack or else I should never have been able to sit on his chest. Fleete could not speak, he could only snarl, and his snarls were those of a wolf, not of a man. The human spirit must have been giving away all day and have died out with the twilight. We were dealing with a beast that had once been Fleete.

The affair was beyond any human and rational experience. I tried to say "Hydrophobia," but the word wouldn't come, because I knew that I was lying.

We bound this beast with leather thongs of the punkahrope, and tied its thumbs and big toes together, and gagged it with a shoe-horn, which makes a very efficient gag if you know how to arrange it. Then we carried it into the dining-room and set a man to Dumoise, the doctor, telling him to come over at once. After we had despatched the messenger and were drawing breath, Strickland said, "It's no good. This isn't any doctor's work." I, also, knew that he spoke the truth.

The beast's head was free, and it threw it about from side to side. Anyone entering the room would have believed that we were curing a wolf's pelt. That was the most loathsome accessory of all.

Strickland sat with his chin in the heel of his fist, watching the beast as it wriggled on the ground, but saying nothing. The shirt had been torn open in the scuffle and showed the black rosette mark on the left breast. It stood out like a blister.

In the silence of the watching we heard something without mewing like a she-otter. We both rose to our feet, and, I answer for myself, not Strickland, felt sick—actually and physically sick. We told each other, as did the men in *Pinafore,* that it was the cat.

Dumoise arrived, and I never saw a little man so unprofessionally shocked. He said that it was a heart-rending case of hydrophobia, and that nothing could be done. At least any palliative measures would only prolong the agony. The beast was foaming at the mouth. Fleete, as we told Dumoise, had been bitten by dogs once or twice. Any man who keeps half a dozen terriers must expect a nip now and again. Dumoise could offer no help. He could only certify that Fleete was dying of hydrophobia. The beast was then howling, for it had managed to spit out the shoe-horn. Dumoise said that he would be ready to certify to the cause of death, and that the end was certain. He was a good little man, and he offered to remain with us; but Strickland refused the kindness. He did not wish to poison Dumoise's New Year. He would only ask him not to give the real cause of Fleete's death to the public.

So Dumoise left, deeply agitated; and as soon as the noise of the cart wheels had died away, Strickland told me, in a whisper, his suspicions.

They were so wildly improbable that he dared not say them out aloud; and I, who entertained all Strickland's beliefs, was so ashamed of owning to them that I pretended to disbelieve.

"Even if the Silver Man had bewitched Fleete for polluting the image of Hanuman, the punishment could not have fallen so quickly."

As I was whispering this the cry outside the house rose again, and the beast fell into a fresh paroxysm of struggling till we were afraid that the thongs that held it would give away.

"Watch!" said Strickland. "If this happens six times I shall take the law into my own hands. I order you to help me."

He went into his room and came out in a few minutes with the barrels of an old shot-gun, a piece of fishing line, some thick cord, and his heavy wooden bedstead. I reported that the convulsions had followed the cry by two seconds in each case, and the beast seemed perceptibly weaker.

Strickland muttered. "But he can't take away the life! He can't take away the life!"

I said, though I knew that I was arguing against myself, "It may be a cat. It must be a cat. If the Silver Man is responsible, why does he dare to come here?"

Strickland arranged the wood on the hearth, put the gun-barrels into the glow of the fire, spread the twine on the table and broke a walking stick in two. There was one yard of fishing line, gut, lapped with wire, such as is used for *mahseer*-fishing, and he tied the two ends together in a loop.

Then he said, "How can we catch him? He must be taken alive and unhurt."

I said that we must trust in Providence, and go out softly with polo-sticks into the shrubbery at the front of the house. The man or animal that made the cry was evidently moving round the house as regularly as a night-watchman. We could wait in the bushes till he came by and knock him over.

Strickland accepted this suggestion, and we slipped out from a bathroom window into the front veranda and then across the carriage drive into the bushes.

In the moonlight we could see the leper coming round the corner of the house. He was perfectly naked, and from time to time he mewed and stopped to dance with his shadow. It was an unattractive sight, and thinking of poor Fleete, brought to such degradation by so foul a creature, I put away all my doubts and resolved to help Strickland from the heated gun-barrels to the loop of twine—from the loins to the head and back again—with all the tortures that might be needful.

The leper halted in the front porch for a moment and we jumped out on him with the sticks. He was wonderfully strong, and we were afraid that he might escape or be fatally injured before we caught him. We had an idea that lepers were frail creatures, but this proved to be incorrect. Strickland knocked his legs from under him and I put my foot on his neck. He mewed hideously, and even through my riding-boots I could feel that his flesh was not the flesh of a clean man.

He struck at us with his hand and feet-stumps. We looped the lash of a dog-whip round him, under the armpits, and dragged him backward into the hall and so into the dining-room where the beast lay. There we tied him with trunk-straps. He made no attempt to escape, but mewed.

When we confronted him with the beast the scene was beyond description. The beast doubled backward into a bow as though he had been poisoned with strychnine, and moaned in the most pitiable fashion. Several other things happened also, but they cannot be put down here.

"I think I was right," said Strickland. "Now we will ask him to cure this case."

But the leper only mewed. Strickland wrapped a towel round his hand and took the gun-barrels out of fire. I put the half of the broken walking stick through the loop of the fishing-line and buckled the leper comfortably to Strickland's bedstead. I understood then how men and women and little children can endure to see a witch burned alive; for the beast was moaning on the floor, and though the Silver Man had no face, you could see horrible feelings passing through the slab that took its place, exactly as waves of heat play across red-hot iron-gun-barrels for instance.

Strickland shaded his eyes with his hands for a moment and we got to work. This part is not to be printed.

* * *

The dawn was beginning to break when the leper spoke. His mewings had not been satisfactory up to that point. The beast had fainted from exhaustion and the house was very still. We unstrapped the leper and told him to take away the evil spirit. He crawled to the beast and laid his hand upon the left breast. That was all. Then he fell face down and whined, drawing in his breath as he did so.

We watched the face of the beast, and saw the soul of Fleete coming back into the eyes. Then a sweat broke out on the forehead and the eyes —they were human eyes—closed. We waited for an hour but Fleete still slept. We carried him to his room and bade the leper go, giving him the bedstead and the sheet on the bedstead to cover his nakedness, the gloves and the towels with which we had touched him, and the whip that had been hooked round his body. He put the sheet about him and went out into the early morning without speaking or mewing.

Strickland wiped his face and sat down. A night-gong, far away in the city, made seven o'clock.

"Exactly four-and-twenty hours!" said Strickland. "And I've done enough to ensure my dismissal from the service, besides permanent quarters in a lunatic asylum. Do you believe that we are awake?"

The red-hot gun-barrel had fallen on the floor and was singeing the carpet. The smell was entirely real.

That morning at eleven we two together went to wake up Fleete. We looked and saw that the black leopard-rosette on his chest had disappeared. He was very drowsy and tired, but as soon as he saw us, he said, "Oh! Confound you fellows. Happy New Year to you. Never mix your liquors, I'm nearly dead."

"Thanks for your kindness, but you're overtime," said Strickland. "Today is the morning of the second. You've slept the clock round with a vengeance."

The door opened, and little Dumoise put his head in. He had come on foot, and fancied that we were laying out Fleete.

"I've brought a nurse," said Dumoise. "I suppose that she can come in for . . . what is necessary."

"By all means," said Fleete, cheerily, sitting up in bed. "Bring on your nurses."

Dumoise was dumb. Strickland led him out and explained that there must have been a mistake in the diagnosis. Dumoise remained dumb and left the house hastily. He considered that his professional reputation had been injured, and was inclined to make a personal matter of the recovery. Strickland went out too. When he came back, he said that he had been to call on the Temple of Hanuman to offer redress for the pollution of the god, and had been solemnly assured that no white man had ever touched the idol and that he was an incarnation of all the virtues laboring under a delusion. "What do you think?" said Strickland.

I said, " 'There are more things . . . ' "

But Strickland hates that quotation. He says that I have worn it threadbare.

One other curious thing happened which frightened me as much as anything in all the night's work. When Fleete was dressed he came into the dining-room and sniffed. He had a quaint trick of moving his nose when he sniffed. "Horrid doggy smell here," said he. "You should really keep those terriers of yours in better order. Try sulphur, Strick."

But Strickland did not answer. He caught hold of the back of a chair, and, without warning, went into an amazing fit of hysterics. It is terrible to see a strong man overtaken with hysteria. Then it struck me that we had fought for Fleete's soul with the Silver Man in that room, and had disgraced ourselves as Englishmen forever, and I laughed and gasped and gurgled just as shamefully as Strickland, while Fleete thought that we had both gone mad. We never told him what we had done.

Some years later, when Strickland had married and was a church-going member of society for his wife's sake, we reviewed the incident dispassionately, and Strickland suggested that I should put it before the public.

I can not myself see that this step is likely to clear up the mystery; because, in the first place, no one will believe a rather unpleasant story, and, in the second, it is well known to every right-minded man that the gods of the heathen are stone and brass, and any attempt to deal with them otherwise is justly condemned.

LA BELLE DAME SANS MERCI

John Keats

O what can ail thee, knight-at-arms,
    Alone and palely loitering?
The sedge has wither'd from the lake,
    And no birds sing.

O what can ail thee, knight-at-arms!
    So haggard and so woe-begone?
The squirrel's granary is full,
    And the harvest's done.

I see a lily on thy brow
    With anguish moist and fever dew,
And on thy cheeks a fading rose
    Fast withereth too.

I met a lady in the meads,
    Full beautiful—a faery's child,
Her hair was long, her foot was light,
    And her eyes were wild.

I made a garland for her head,
    And bracelets too, and fragrant zone;
She look'd at me as she did love,
    And made sweet moan.

I set her on my pacing steed,
    And nothing else saw all day long,
For sidelong would she bend, and sing
    A faery's song.
She found me roots of relish sweet,
    And honey wild, and manna dew,
And sure in language strange she said—
    "I love thee true."

She took me to her elfin grot,
    And there she wept, and sigh'd full sore,
And there I shut her wild eyes
    With kisses four.

And there she lulled me asleep,
    And there I dream'd—Ah! woe betide!
The latest dream I ever dream'd
    On the cold hill's side.

I saw pale kings and princes too,
   Pale warriors, death-pale were they all;
They cried—"La Belle Dame sans Merci
   Hath thee in thrall!"

I saw their starved lips in the gloam,
   With horrid warning gaped wide,
And I awoke and found me here,
   On the cold hill's side.

And this is why I sojourn here,
   Alone and palely loitering,
Though the sedge is wither'd from the lake,
   And no birds sing.

MONTERREY SUN

Alfonso Reyes

No doubt: the sun
dogged me when a child.

It followed at my heels
like a Pekinese;
    dishevely and soft,
    luminous and gold:
    the sun that sleepy dogs
    the footsteps of the child.

It frisked from court to court,
in my bedroom weltered.
I even think they sometimes
shooed it with a broom.
And next morning there
it was with me again,
    dishevely and soft,
    luminous and gold,
    the sun that sleepy dogs
    the footsteps of the child.

    (I was dubbed a knight
    by the fire of May:
    I was the Child-Errant
    and the sun my squire.)

Indigo all the sky,
all the house of gold.
How it poured into me,
the sun, through my eyes!
A sea inside my skull,
go where I may,
and though the clouds be drawn,
oh what weight of sun
upon me, oh what hurt
within me of that cistern
of sun that journeys with me!

No shadow in my childhood
but was red with sun.
Every window was sun,
windows every room.

The corridors bent bows
of sun through the house.
On the trees the coals
of the oranges burned redhot,
and in the burning light
the orchard turned to gold.
The royal peacocks were
kinsmen of the sun.
The heron at every step
it took went aflame.

And me the sun stripped bare
the fiercer to cleave to me,
    dishevely and soft,
    luminous and gold,
    the sun that sleepy dogs
    the footsteps of the child.

When I with my stick
and bundle went from home,
to my heart I said:
Now bear the sun awhile!
It is a hoard—unending,
unending—that I squander.
I bear within me so
much sun that so much sun
already wearies me.

No shadow in my childhood
but was red with sun.

ANATOL PIERRE

Zora Neale Hurston

ANATOL PIERRE, of New Orleans, was a middle-aged octoroon. He is a Catholic and lays some feeble claim to kinship with Marie Leveau. He had the most elaborate temple of any of the practitioners. His altar room was off by itself and absolutely sacrosanct. He made little difficulty about taking me after I showed him that I had worked with others. Pierre was very emotional and sometimes he would be sharp with his clients, indifferent as to whether they hired him or not. But he quickly adjusted himself to my being around him and at the end of the first week began to prepare me for the crown.

The ceremony was as follows:

On Saturday I was told to have the materials for my initiation bath ready for the following Tuesday at eleven o'clock. I must have a bottle of lavender toilet water, Japanese honeysuckle perfume, and orange blossom water. I must get a full bunch of parsley and brew a pint of strong parsley water. I must have at hand sugar, salt and Vacher Balm. Two long pink candles must be provided, one to be burned at the initiation, one to be lit on the altar for me in Pierre's secret room.

He came to my house in Belville Court at a quarter to eleven to see if all was right. The tub was half-filled with warm water and Pierre put in all of the ingredients, along with a handful of salt and three tablespoons of sugar.

The candles had been dressed on Saturday and one was already burning on the secret altar for me. The other long pink candle was rolled around the tub three times, "In nomina patria, et filia, et spiritu sanctus, Amen." Then it was marked for a four day burning and lit. The spirit was called three times. "Kind spirit, whose name is Moccasin, answer me." This I was told to repeat three times, snapping my fingers.

Then I, already prepared, stepped into the tub and was bathed by the teacher. Particular attention was paid to my head and back and chest since there the "controls" lie. While in the tub, my left little finger was cut a little and his finger was cut and the blood bond made. "Now you are of my flesh and of the spirit, and neither one of us will ever deny you."

He dried me and I put on new underwear bought for the occasion and dressed with oil of geranium, and was told to stretch upon the couch and read the third chapter of Job night and morning for nine days. I was given a little Bible that had been "visited" by the spirit and told the names of the spirits to call for any kind of work I might want to perform. I am to call on Great Moccasin for all kinds of power and also to have him stir up the particular spirit I may need for a specific task. I must call on Kangaroo to stop worrying; call on Jenipee spirit for marriages; call on Death spirit for killing, and the seventeen "quarters" of spirit to aid me if one spirit seems insufficient.

I was told to burn the marked candle every day for two hours—from eleven till one, in the northeast corner of the room. While it is burning I must go into the silence and talk to the spirit through the candle.

On the fifth day Pierre called again and I resumed my studies, but now as an advanced pupil. In the four months that followed these are some of the things I learned from him:

A man called Muttsy Ivins came running to Pierre soon after my initiation was over. Pierre looked him over with some instinctive antipathy. So he wouldn't help him out by asking questions. He just let Mr. Muttsy tell him the best way he could. So he began by saying, "A lot of hurting things have been done to me, Pierre, and now it done got to de place Ah'm skeered for mah life."

"That's a lie, yes," Pierre snapped.

"Naw it 'tain't!" Muttsy insisted. "Ah done found things 'round mah door step and in mah yard and Ah knows who's doin' it too."

"Yes, you find things in your yard because you continue to sleep with the wife of another man and you are afraid because he has said that he will kill you if you don't leave her alone. You are crazy to think that you lie to me. Tell me the truth and then tell me what you want me to do."

"Ah want him out de way—kilt, cause he swear he's gointer kill me. And since one of us got to die, Ah'd ruther it to be him than me."

"I knew you wanted a death the minute you got in here. I don't like to work for death."

"Please, Pierre, Ah'm skeered to walk de streets after dark, and me and de woman done gone too far to turn back. And he got de consumption nohow. But Ah don't wanter die before he do. Ah'm a well man."

"That's enough about that. How much money have you got?"

"Two hundred dollars."

"Two fifty is my terms, and I ain't a bit anxious for the job at that."

Pierre turned to me and began to give me a list of things to get for my own use and seemed to forget the man behind him.

"Maybe Ah kin get dat other fifty dollars and maybe not. These ain't no easy times. Money is tight."

"Well, goodbye, we're busy folks here. You don't have to do this thing, anyway. You can leave town."

"And leave mah good trucking business? Dat'll never happen. Ah kin git yo' money. When yo' goin' ter do de work?"

"You pay the money and go home. It is not for you to know how and when the work is done. Go home with faith."

The next morning soon, Pierre sent me out to get a beef brain, a beef tongue, a beef heart and a live black chicken. When I returned he had prepared a jar of bad vinegar. He wrote Muttsy's enemy's name nine times on a slip of paper. He split open the heart, placed the paper in it, pinned up the opening with eighteen steel needles, and dropped it into the jar of vinegar, point downward.

The main altar was draped in black and the crudely carved figure of Death was placed upon it to shield us from the power of death.

Black candles were lit on the altar. A black crown was made and placed on the head of Death. The name of the man to die was written on paper nine times and placed on the altar one degree below Death, and the jar containing the heart was set on this paper. The candles burned for twelve hours.

Then Pierre made a coffin six inches long. I was sent out to buy a small doll. It was dressed in black to represent the man and placed in the coffin with his name under the doll. The coffin was left open upon the altar. Then we went far out to a lonely spot and dug a grave which was much longer and wider than the coffin. A black cat was placed in the grave and the whole covered with a cloth that we fastened down so that the cat could not get out. The black chicken was then taken from its confinement and fed a half glass of whiskey in which a paper had been soaked that bore the name of the man who was to die. The chicken was put in with the cat, and left there for a full month.

The night after the entombment of the cat and the chicken, we began to burn the black candles. Nine candles were set to burn in a barrel and every night at twelve o'clock we would go to the barrel and call upon the spirit of Death to follow the man. The candles were dressed by biting off the bottoms, as Pierre called for vengeance. Then the bottom was lighted instead of the top.

At the end of the month, the coffin containing the doll was carried out to the grave of the cat and chicken and buried upon their remains. A white bouquet was placed at the head and foot of the grave.

The beef brain was placed on a plate with nine hot peppers around it to cause insanity and brain hemorrhages, and placed on the altar. The tongue was slit, the name of the victim inserted, the slit was closed with a pack of pins and buried in the tomb.

"The black candles must burn for ninety days," Pierre told me. "He cannot live. No one can stand that."

Every night for ninety days Pierre slept in his holy place in a black draped coffin. And the man died.

IV

The Other

THE OTHER

We like to believe that we know ourselves, that we are a unity which integrates statistical data such as age, occupation, and hair color, social circumstances, memories, opinions, imaginings and emotions; a totality comfortably comprehensible to our own awareness.

Because we want to be so lucid to ourselves, the possibility of unknowns within us can be threatening, even frightening. This unknown exists beyond our rational control, often only a disturbing sensation that reveals itself in nightmares and moments of weakness. This other may feel things and do things which shock our conscious selves; it may even be the enemy of our consciousness, undermining all that we think we are.

Most of us at some point in our lives have occasion to see X-ray pictures of the bones and organs within our flesh. But the other can never be photographed. It lurks hidden behind the shadows of an X-ray. We can imagine it squatting inside the cage of our skeleton, peering out from between the ribs, smirking at the person we think we are because it knows much more than our rationality. This other annoys our nervous system and sends mysterious messages to us; occasionally it projects itself outside our bodies and moves about the surrounding environment, luring us or even worse pursuing us.

A thin line divides the category of "The Other" from that which precedes it in this collection, "Bewitchment and Enchantment." Perhaps the other is the source of the bewilderment. The answer is one of origins. If the invisible worm, which, through "dark, secret love" destroys the life of Blake's sick rose, has entered the rose from without it is an enemy apart. But if that worm has always dwelt inside the rose, coexistent, grimly waiting for its chance to destroy, then it is the other.

These two categories have by far the greatest tendency to terrify us because they are so personal and strike us where we are most vulnerable. Sigmund Freud analyzes the reasons for this condition in a significant essay called "The Uncanny." Defining the "uncanny" as the province of all that is terrible, of all that arouses dread and creeping horror, both in life and in art, he concludes that the source of the uncanny is much more than the unknown. On the contrary, the uncanny is not just new or strange, "but something familiar and old-established in the mind that has been estranged only by a process of repression"; it is the working of forces which the individual is "dimly aware of in a remote corner of his own being."

   Usually when it is dealt with in literature, the other is embodied outside the individual in an object or character which appears physically separate. Yet that individual is really engaging some hidden aspect of himself in a manner more appropriate for dramatic presentation. The poems, tales, and stories in this section all externalize the other, but each in a different way, a significant shading of method which alters meaning, so that in these selections we encounter varieties of the other.

   The fairytale "The Goose Girl" by the Grimm brothers presents a complexity of others. Here the good princess is actually displaced by a wicked pretender who steals her identity, but only after the princess has made herself vulnerable by losing the handkerchief her mother had given her, and with it the power to survive the long journey unharmed. Unprotected by the security of her mother, the princess is cast out from her safe life into the role of a goose girl, and an evil creature now assumes her role as princess. The decapitated horse that emphasizes shame—what her mother would say if she knew—can be considered a manifestation of her conscience, a more familiar other.

   If the basic fear of "The Goose Girl" is loss of the mother's love, that of Coleridge's "Christabel" is loss of the father's. The poem, unlike the fairytale, does not have a happy ending which restores the good self. Instead, before her eyes Christabel watches her father reject her pleas and walk off arm in arm with the treacherous Geraldine, the daughter of his mortal enemy. The relationship is even more complex. Not only has Geraldine displaced Christabel from her father's affection, she has overcome the guardian spirit of Christabel's dead mother to embrace the girl to her own malevolent bosom. Christabel is literally in the hands of the other. Here the invisible worm takes manifest form in Geraldine's sinister dream as a snake coiled around the neck of a gentle dove.

   In one sense the force which pursues the speaker in Francis Thompson's "The Hound of Heaven" is external, God himself. The fugitive flees because he fears that if he were captured, he would lose possession of himself: "Yet was I sore adread/Lest, having Him, I must have naught beside." Thinking to protect himself, he chooses the miserable condition of an outcast. However, the irony of the poem is that the speaker in denying God is actually denying himself. This is an irony fundamental to Christianity: he who would find himself must lose himself; that is, he must embrace God to realize the spiritual fulfillment of his being. In this case, the other from whom the speaker has been in constant flight is actually the goal he should have sought.

   A contemporary Mexican author expresses his own experience with the other in terms of a love-hate relationship in "The Vampire." Since the other may consume us as a vampire does, it is not surprising to find Anthony Boucher, a contemporary writer, combining the archetypal idea of the (external) ogre with the internal retribution for sins. In "They Bite" the other does just that and the evil protagonist is overwhelmed by a fate as horrible as that he has dealt to his victim. In a similar category is the Black folk tale "Tailypo," in which retribution comes to the inhumane man. This American Negro story is more simple and less sinister, however, than its fellows in this section.

These selections begin with one victory and one defeat. The common lesson of all is that, in one form or another, the other cannot be cast off. It is part of us, and we cannot truly be ourselves without recognition of the other.

THE GOOSE-GIRL

The Brothers Grimm

ONCE UPON A TIME an old queen, whose husband had been dead for many years, had a beautiful daughter. When she grew up she was betrothed to a prince who lived a great way off. Now, when the time drew near for her to be married and to depart into a foreign kingdom, her old mother gave her much costly baggage, and many ornaments, gold and silver, trinkets and knicknacks, and, in fact, everything that belonged to a royal trousseau, for she loved her daughter very dearly. She gave her a waiting-maid also, who was to ride with her and hand her over to the bridegroom, and she provided each of them with a horse for the journey. Now the Princess's horse was called Falada, and could speak.

When the hour for departure drew near the old mother went to her bedroom, and taking a small knife she cut her fingers till they bled; then she held a white rag under them, and letting three drops of blood fall into it, she gave it to her daughter, and said: 'Dear child, take great care of this rag: it may be of use to you on the journey.'

So they took a sad farewell of each other, and the Princess stuck the rag in front of her dress, mounted her horse, and set forth on the journey to her bridegroom's kingdom. After they had ridden for about an hour the Princess began to feel very thirsty, and said to her waiting-maid: 'Pray get down and fetch me some water in my golden cup out of yonder stream: I would like a drink.' 'If you're thirsty,' said the maid, 'dismount yourself, and lie down by the water and drink; I don't mean to be your servant any longer.' The Princess was so thirsty that she got down, bent over the stream, and drank, for she wasn't allowed to drink out of the golden goblet. As she drank she murmured: 'Oh! heaven, what am I to do?' and the three drops of blood replied:

> 'If your mother only knew,
> Her heart would surely break in two.'

But the Princess was meek, and said nothing about her maid's rude behaviour, and quietly mounted her horse again. They rode on their way for several miles, but the day was hot, and the sun's rays smote fiercely on them, so that the Princess was soon overcome by thirst again. And as they passed a brook she called once more to her waiting-maid: 'Pray get down and give me a drink from my golden cup,' for she had long ago forgotten her maid's rude words. But the waiting-maid replied, more haughtily even than before: 'If you want a drink, you can

> Till my locks of ruddy gold,
> Now astray and hanging down,
> Be combed and plaited in a crown.'

Then a puff of wind came and blew Curdken's hat far away, so that he had to run after it; and when he returned she had long finished putting up her golden locks, and he couldn't get any hair; so they watched the geese till it was dark.

But that evening when they got home Curdken went to the old King, and said: 'I refuse to herd geese any longer with that girl.' 'For what reason?' asked the old King. 'Because she does nothing but annoy me all day long,' replied Curdken; and he proceeded to relate all her iniquities, and said: 'Every morning as we drive the flock through the dark gate she says to a horse's head that hangs on the wall:

'Oh! Falada, 'tis you hang there;" and the head replies:

> ''Tis you; pass under, Princess fair:
> If your mother only knew,
> Her heart would surely break in two.'

And Curdken went on to tell what passed on the common where the geese fed, and how he had always to chase his hat.

The old King bade him go and drive forth his flock as usual next day; and when morning came he himself took up his position behind the dark gate, and heard how the goose-girl greeted Falada. Then he followed her through the field, and hid himself behind a bush on the common. He soon saw with his own eyes how the goose-boy and the goose-girl looked after the geese, and how after a time the maiden sat down and loosed her hair, that glittered like gold, and repeated:

> 'Wind, wind, gently sway,
> Blow Curdken's hat away;
> Let him chase o'er field and wold
> Till my locks of ruddy gold,
> Now astray and hanging down,
> Be combed and plaited in a crown.'

Then a gust of wind came and blew Curdken's hat away, so that he had to fly over hill and dale after it, and the girl in the meantime quietly combed and plaited her hair: all this the old King observed, and returned to the palace without any one having noticed him. In the evening when the goose-girl came home he called her aside, and asked her why she behaved as she did. 'I mayn't tell you why; how dare I confide my woes to anyone? for I swore not to by heaven, otherwise I should have lost my life.' The old King begged her to tell him all, and left her no peace, but he could get nothing out of her. At last he said: 'Well, if you won't tell me, confide your trouble to the iron stove there;' and he went away. Then she crept to the stove, and began to sob and cry and to pour out her poor little heart, and said: 'Here I sit, deserted by all the world, I who am a king's daughter, and a false waiting-maid has forced me to take off my own clothes, and has taken my place with my bridegroom, while I have to fulfil the lowly office of goose-girl.

'If my mother only knew,
Her heart would surely break in two.'

But the old King stood outside at the stove chimney, and listened to her words. Then he entered the room again, and bidding her leave the stove, he ordered royal apparel to be put on her, in which she looked amazingly lovely. Then he summoned his son, and revealed to him that he had got the false bride, who was nothing but a waiting-maid, while the real one, in the guise of the ex-goose-girl, was standing at his side. The young King rejoiced from his heart when he saw her beauty and learnt how good she was, and a great banquet was prepared, to which everyone was bidden. The bridegroom sat at the head of the table, the Princess on one side of him and the waiting-maid on the other; but she was so dazzled that she did not recognise the Princess in her glittering garments. Now when they had eaten and drunk, and were merry, the old King asked the waiting-maid to solve a knotty point for him. 'What,' said he, 'should be done to a certain person who had deceived everyone?' and he proceeded to relate the whole story, ending up with, 'Now what sentence should be passed?' Then the false bride answered: 'She deserves to be put stark naked into a barrel lined with sharp nails, which should be dragged by two white horses up and down the street till she is dead.'

'You are the person,' said the King, 'and you have passed sentence on yourself; and even so it shall be done to you.' And when the sentence had been carried out the young King was married to his real bride, and both reigned over the kingdom in peace and happiness.

CHRISTABEL

Samuel Taylor Coleridge

PREFACE

The first part of the following poem was written in the year 1797, at Stowey, in the county of Somerset. The second part, after my return from Germany, in the year 1800, at Keswick, Cumberland. It is probable that if the poem had been finished at either of the former periods, or if even the first and second part had been published in the year 1800, the impression of its originality would have been much greater than I dare at present expect. But for this I have only my own indolence to blame. The dates are mentioned for the exclusive purpose of precluding charges of plagiarism or servile imitation from myself. For there is amongst us a set of critics, who seem to hold, that every possible thought and image is traditional; who have no notion that there are such things as fountains in the world, small as well as great; and who would therefore charitably derive every rill they behold flowing, from a perforation made in some other man's tank. I am confident, however, that as far as the present poem is concerned, the celebrated poets whose writings I might be suspected of having imitated, either in particular passages, or in the tone and the spirit of the whole, would be among the first to vindicate me from the charge, and who, on any striking coincidence, would permit me to address them in this doggerel version of two monkish Latin hexameters.

> *'Tis mine and it is likewise yours;*
> *But an' if this will not do,*
> *Let it be mine, good friend! for I*
> *Am the poorer of the two.*

I have only to add that the metre of Christabel is not, properly speaking, irregular, though it may seem so from its being founded on a new principle: namely, that of counting in each line the accents, not the syllables. Though the latter may vary from seven to twelve, yet in each line the accents will be found to be only four. Nevertheless, this occasional

variation in number of syllables is not introduced wantonly,
or for the mere ends of convenience, but in correspondence
with some transition in the nature of the imagery of passion.

PART I

'Tis the middle of night by the castle clock,
And the owls have awakened the crowing cock;
Tu—whit!——Tu—Whoo!
And hark, again! the crowing cock,
How drowsily it crew.

Sir Leoline, the Baron rich
Hath a toothless mastiff bitch;
From her kennel beneath the rock
She maketh answer to the clock,
Four for the quarters, and twelve for the hour;
Ever and aye, by shine and shower,
Sixteen short howls, not over loud;
Some say, she sees my lady's shroud.

Is the night chilly and dark?
The night is chilly, but not dark.
The thin gray cloud is spread on high,
It covers but not hides the sky.
The moon is behind, and at the full;
And yet she looks both small and dull.
The night is chill, the cloud is gray:
'Tis a month before the month of May,
And the Spring comes slowly up this way.

The lovely lady, Christabel,
Whom her father loves so well,
What makes her in the wood so late,
A furlong from the castle gate?
She had dreams all yesternight
Of her own bethrothéd knight;
And she in the midnight wood will pray
For the weal of her lover that's far away.

She stole along, she nothing spoke,
The sighs she heaved were soft and low,
And naught was green upon the oak
But moss and rarest mistletoe:
She kneels beneath the huge oak tree,
And in silence prayeth she.

The lady sprang up suddenly,
The lovely lady, Christabel!
It moaned as near, as near can be,
But what it is she cannot tell.—
On the other side it seems to be,
Of the huge, broad-breasted, old oak tree.

The night is chill; the forest bare;
Is it the wind that moaneth bleak?
There is not wind enough in the air
To move away the ringlet curl
From the lovely lady's cheek—
There is not wind enough to twirl
The one red leaf, the last of its clan,
That dances as often as dance it can,
Hanging so light, and hanging so high,
On the topmost twig that looks up at the sky.

Hush, beating heart of Christabel!
Jesu, Maria, shield her well!
She folded her arms beneath her cloak,
And stole to the other side of the oak.
    What sees she there?

There she sees a damsel bright,
Drest in a silken robe of white,
That shadowy in the moonlight shone:
The neck that made that white robe wan,
Her stately neck, and arms were bare;
Her blue-veined feet unsandal'd were,
And wildly glittered here and there
The gems entangled in her hair.
I guess, 'twas frightful there to see
A lady so richly clad as she—
Beautiful exceedingly!

Mary mother, save me now!
(Said Christabel,) And who art thou?

The lady strange made answer meet,
And her voice was faint and sweet:—
Have pity on my sore distress,
I scarce can speak for weariness:
Stretch forth thy hand, and have no fear!
Said Christabel, How camest thou here?
And the lady, whose voice was faint and sweet,
Did thus pursue her answer meet:—

My sire is of a noble line,
And my name is Geraldine:
Five warriors seized me yestermorn,
Me, even me, a maid forlorn:
They choked my cries with force and fright,
And tied me on a palfrey white.
The palfrey was as fleet as wind,
And they rode furiously behind.
They spurred amain, their steeds were white:
And once we crossed the shade of night.
As sure as Heaven shall rescue me,
I have no thought what men they be;
Nor do I know how long it is
(For I have lain entranced I wis)
Since one, the tallest of the five,
Took me from the palfrey's back,
A weary woman, scarce alive.
Some muttered words his comrades spoke:
He placed me underneath this oak;
He swore they would return with haste;
Whither they went I cannot tell—
I thought I heard, some minutes past,
Sounds as of a castle bell.
Stretch forth thy hand (thus ended she),
And help a wretched maid to flee.

Then Christabel stretched forth her hand,
And comforted fair Geraldine:
O well, bright dame! may you command
The service of Sir Leoline;
And gladly our stout chivalry
Will he send forth and friends withal
To guide and guard you safe and free
Home to your noble father's hall.

She rose: and forth with steps they passed
That strove to be, and were not, fast.
Her gracious stars the lady blest,
And thus spake on sweet Christabel:
All our household are at rest,
The hall as silent as the cell;
Sir Leoline is weak in health,
And may not well awakened be,
But we will move as if in stealth,
And I beseech your courtesy,
This night, to share your couch with me.

They crossed the moat, and Christabel
Took the key that fitted well;
A little door she opened straight,
All in the middle of the gate;
The gate that was ironed within and without,
Where an army in battle array had marched out.
The lady sank, belike through pain,
And Christabel with might and main
Lifted her up, a weary weight,
Over the threshold of the gate:
Then the lady rose again,
And moved, as she were not in pain.

So free from danger, free from fear,
They crossed the court: right glad they were.
And Christabel devoutly cried
To the lady by her side,
Praise we the Virgin all divine
Who hath rescued thee from thy distress!
Alas, alas! said Geraldine,
I cannot speak for weariness.
So free from danger, free from fear,
They crossed the court: right glad they were.

Outside her kennel, the mastiff old
Lay fast asleep, in moonshine cold.
The mastiff old did not awake,
Yet she an angry moan did make!
And what can ail the mastiff bitch?
Never till now she uttered yell
Beneath the eye of Christabel.
Perhaps it is the owlet's scritch:
For what can ail the mastiff bitch?

They passed the hall, that echoes still,
Pass as lightly as you will!
The brands were flat, the brands were dying,
Amid their own white ashes lying;
But when the lady passed, there came
A tongue of light, a fit of flame;
And Christabel saw the lady's eye,
And nothing else saw she thereby,
Save the boss of the shield of Sir Leoline tall,
Which hung in a murky old niche in the wall.
O softly tread, said Christabel,
My father seldom sleepeth well.

Sweet Christabel her feet doth bare,
And jealous of the listening air
They steal their way from stair to stair,
Now in glimmer, and now in gloom,
And now they pass the Baron's room,
As still as death, with stifled breath!
And now have reached her chamber door;
And now doth Geraldine press down
The rushes of the chamber floor.

The moon shines dim in the open air,
And not a moonbeam enters here.
But they without its light can see
The chamber carved so curiously,
Carved with figures strange and sweet,
All made out of the carver's brain,
For a lady's chamber meet:
The lamp with twofold silver chain
Is fastened to an angel's feet.

The silver lamp burns dead and dim;
But Christabel the lamp will trim.
She trimmed the lamp, and made it bright,
And left it swinging to and fro,
While Geraldine, in wretched plight,
Sank down upon the floor below.

O weary lady, Geraldine,
I pray you, drink this cordial wine!
It is a wine of virtuous powers;
My mother made it of wild flowers.

And will your mother pity me,
Who am a maiden most forlorn?
Christabel answered—Woe is me!
She died the hour that I was born.
I have heard the grey-haired friar tell
How on her death-bed she did say,
That she should hear the castle-bell
Strike twelve upon my wedding-day.
O mother dear! that thou wert here!
I would, said Geraldine, she were!

But soon with altered voice, said she—
"Off, wandering mother! Peak and pine!
I have power to bid thee flee."
Alas! what ails poor Geraldine?

Why stares she with unsettled eye?
Can she the bodiless dead espy?
And why with hollow voice cries she,
"Off, woman, off! this hour is mine—
Though thou her guardian spirit be,
Off, woman, off! 'tis given to me."

Then Christabel knelt by the lady's side,
And raised to heaven her eyes so blue—
Alas! said she, this ghastly ride—
Dear lady! it hath wildered you!
The lady wiped her moist cold brow,
And faintly said, " 'tis over now!"

Again the wild-flower wine she drank:
Her fair large eyes 'gan glitter bright,
And from the floor whereon she sank,
The lofty lady stood upright:
She was most beautiful to see,
Like a lady of a far countrée.

And thus the lofty lady spake—
"All they who live in the upper sky,
Do love you, holy Christabel!
And you love them, and for their sake
And for the good which me befel,
Even I in my degree will try,
Fair maiden, to requite you well.
But now unrobe yourself; for I
Must pray, ere yet in bed I lie."

Quoth Christabel, So let it be!
And as the lady bade, did she.
Her gentle limbs did she undress,
And lay down in her loveliness.

But through her brain of weal and woe
So many thoughts moved to and fro,
That vain it were her lids to close;
So half-way from the bed she rose,
And on her elbow did recline
To look at the lady Geraldine.

Beneath the lamp the lady bowed,
And slowly rolled her eyes around;
Then drawing in her breath aloud,
Like one that shuddered, she unbound
The cincture from beneath her breast:

Her silken robe, and inner vest,
Dropt to her feet, and full in view,
Behold! her bosom and half her side——
A sight to dream of, not to tell!
O shield her! shield sweet Christabel!

Yet Geraldine nor speaks nor stirs;
Ah! what a stricken look was hers!
Deep from within she seems half-way
To lift some weight with sick assay,
And eyes the maid and seeks delay;
Then suddenly, as one defied,
Collects herself in scorn and pride,
And lay down by the Maiden's side!—
And in her arms the maid she took,
  Ah wel-a-day!
And with low voice and doleful look
These words did say:
"In the touch of this bosom there worketh a spell,
Which is lord of thy utterance, Christabel!
Thou knowest to-night, and wilt know to-morrow,
This mark of my shame, this seal of my sorrow;
  But vainly thou warrest,
   For this is alone in
  Thy power to declare,
   That in the dim forest
  Thou heard'st a low moaning,
And found'st a bright lady, surpassingly fair;
And didst bring her home with thee in love and in charity,
To shield her and shelter her from the damp air."

THE CONCLUSION TO PART I

  It was a lovely sight to see
  The lady Christabel, when she
  Was praying at the old oak tree.
   Amid the jaggéd shadows
   Of mossy leafless boughs,
   Kneeling in the moonlight,
   To make her gentle vows;
  Her slender palms together prest,
  Heaving sometimes on her breast;
  Her face resigned to bliss or bale—

Her face, oh call it fair not pale,
And both blue eyes more bright than clear,
Each about to have a tear.

With open eyes (ah woe is me!)
Asleep, and dreaming fearfully,
Fearfully dreaming, yet, I wis,
Dreaming that alone, which is—
O sorrow and shame! Can this be she,
The lady, who knelt at the old oak tree?
And lo! the worker of these harms,
That holds the maiden in her arms,
Seems to slumber still and mild,
As a mother with her child.

A star hath set, a star hath risen,
O Geraldine! since arms of thine
Have been the lovely lady's prison.
O Geraldine! one hour was thine—
Thou'st had thy will! By tairn and rill,
The night-birds all that hour were still.
But now they are jubilant anew,
From cliff and tower, tu—whoo! tu—whoo!
Tu—whoo! tu—whoo! from wood and fell!

And see! the lady Christabel
Gathers herself from out her trance;
Her limbs relax, her countenance
Grows sad and soft; the smooth thin lids
Close o'er her eyes; and tears she sheds—
Large tears that leave the lashes bright!
And oft the while she seems to smile
As infants at a sudden light!

Yea, she doth smile, and she doth weep,
Like a youthful hermitess,
Beauteous in a wilderness,
Who, praying always, prays in sleep.
And, if she move unquietly,
Perchance, 'tis but the blood so free
Comes back and tingles in her feet.
No doubt, she hath a vision sweet.
What if her guardian spirit 'twere,
What if she knew her mother near?
But this she knows, in joys and woes,
That saints will aid if men will call:
For the blue sky bends over all!

PART II

Each matin bell, the Baron saith,
Knells us back to a world of death.
These words Sir Leoline first said,
When he rose and found his lady dead:
These words Sir Leoline will say
Many a morn to his dying day!

And hence the custom and law began
That still at dawn the sacristan,
Who duly pulls the heavy bell,
Five and forty beads must tell
Between each stroke—a warning knell,
Which not a soul can choose but hear
From Bratha Head to Wyndermere.

Saith Bracy the bard, So let it knell!
And let the drowsy sacristan
Still count as slowly as he can!
There is no lack of such, I ween,
As well fill up the space between.
In Langdale Pike and Witch's Lair,
And Dungeon-ghyll so foully rent,
With ropes of rock and bells of air
Three sinful sextons' ghosts are pent,
Who all give back, one after t'other,
The death-note to their living brother;
And oft too, by the knell offended,
Just as their one! two! three! is ended,
The devil mocks the doleful tale
With a merry peal from Borodale.

The air is still! through mist and cloud
That merry peal comes ringing loud;
And Geraldine shakes off her dread,
And rises lightly from the bed;
Puts on her silken vestments white,
And tricks her hair in lovely plight,
And nothing doubting of her spell
Awakens the lady Christabel.
"Sleep you, sweet lady Christabel?
I trust that you have rested well."

And Christabel awoke and spied
The same who lay down by her side—

O rather say, the same whom she
Raised up beneath the old oak tree!
Nay, fairer yet! and yet more fair!
For she belike hath drunken deep
Of all the blessedness of sleep!
And while she spake, her looks, her air
Such gentle thankfulness declare,
That (so it seemed) her girded vests
Grew tight beneath her heaving breasts.
"Sure I have sinn'd!" said Christabel,
"Now heaven be praised if all be well!"
And in low faltering tones, yet sweet,
Did she the lofty lady greet
With such perplexity of mind
As dreams too lively leave behind.

So quickly she rose, and quickly arrayed
Her maiden limbs, and having prayed
That He, who on the cross did groan,
Might wash away her sins unknown,
She forthwith led fair Geraldine
To meet her sire, Sir Leoline.

The lovely maid and the lady tall
Are pacing both into the hall,
And pacing on through page and groom,
Enter the Baron's presence-room.

The Baron rose, and while he prest
His gentle daughter to his breast,
With cheerful wonder in his eyes
The lady Geraldine espies,
And gave such welcome to the same,
As might beseem so bright a dame!

But when he heard the lady's tale,
And when she told her father's name,
Why waxed Sir Leoline so pale,
Murmuring o'er the name again,
Lord Roland de Vaux of Tryermaine?

Alas! they had been friends in youth;
But whispering tongues can poison truth;
And constancy lives in realms above;
And life is thorny; and youth is vain;
And to be wroth with one we love
Doth work like madness in the brain.

And thus it chanced, as I divine,
With Roland and Sir Leoline.
Each spake words of high disdain
And insult to his heart's best brother:
They parted—ne'er to meet again!
But never either found another
To free the hollow heart from paining—
They stood aloof, the scars remaining,
Like cliffs which had been rent asunder;
A dreary sea now flows between;—
But neither heat, nor frost, nor thunder,
Shall wholly do away, I ween,
The marks of that which once hath been.

Sir Leoline, a moment's space,
Stood gazing on the damsel's face:
And the youthful Lord of Tryermaine
Came back upon his heart again.

O then the Baron forgot his age,
His noble heart swelled high with rage;
He swore by the wounds in Jesu's side
He would proclaim it far and wide,
With trump and solemn heraldry,
That they, who thus had wronged the dame,
Were base as spotted infamy!
"And if they dare deny the same,
My herald shall appoint a week,
And let the recreant traitors seek
My tourney court—that there and then
I may dislodge their reptile souls
From the bodies and forms of men!"
He spake: his eye in lightning rolls!
For the lady was ruthlessly seized; and he kenned
In the beautiful lady the child of his friend!

And now the tears were on his face,
And fondly in his arms he took
Fair Geraldine, who met the embrace,
Prolonging it with joyous look.
Which when she viewed, a vision fell
Upon the soul of Christabel,
The vision of fear, the touch and pain!
She shrunk and shuddered, and saw again—
(Ah, woe is me! Was it for thee,
Thou gentle maid! such sights to see?)

Again she saw that bosom old,
Again she felt that bosom cold,
And drew in her breath with a hissing sound:
Whereat the Knight turned wildly round,
And nothing saw, but his own sweet maid
With eyes upraised, as one that prayed.

The touch, the sight, had passed away,
And in its stead that vision blest,
Which comforted her after-rest
While in the lady's arms she lay,
Had put a rapture in her breast,
And on her lips and o'er her eyes
Spread smiles like light!
                    With new surprise,
"What ails then my belovéd child?"
The Baron said—His daughter mild
Made answer, "All will yet be well!"
I ween, she had no power to tell
Aught else: so mighty was the spell.

Yet he, who saw this Geraldine,
Had deemed her sure a thing divine:
Such sorrow with such grace she blended,
As if she feared she had offended
Sweet Christabel, that gentle maid!
And with such lowly tones she prayed
She might be sent without delay
Home to her father's mansion.
                    "Nay!
Nay, by my soul!" said Leoline.
"Ho! Bracy the bard, the charge be thine!
Go thou, with music sweet and loud,
And take two steeds with trappings proud,
And take the youth whom thou lov'st best
To bear thy harp, and learn thy song,
And clothe you both in solemn vest,
And over the mountains haste along,
Lest wandering folk, that are abroad,
Detain you on the valley road.

"And when he has crossed the Irthing flood,
My merry bard! he hastes, he hastes
Up Knorren Moor, through Halegarth Wood,
And reaches soon that castle good
Which stands and threatens Scotland's wastes.

"Bard Bracy! bard Bracy! your horses are fleet,
Ye must ride up the hall, your music so sweet,
More loud than your horses' echoing feet!
And loud and loud to Lord Roland call,
Thy daughter is safe in Langdale hall!
Thy beautiful daughter is safe and free—
Sir Leoline greets thee thus through me!
He bids thee come without delay
With all thy numerous array
And take thy lovely daughter home:
And he will meet thee on the way
With all his numerous array
White with their panting palfreys' foam:
And, by mine honour! I will say,
That I repent me of the day
When I spake words of fierce disdain
To Roland de Vaux of Tryermaine!—
—For since that evil hour hath flown,
Many a summer's sun hath shone;
Yet ne'er found I a friend again
Like Roland de Vaux of Tryermaine."

The lady fell, and clasped his knees,
Her face upraised, her eyes o'erflowing;
And Bracy replied, with faltering voice,
His gracious Hail on all bestowing!—
"Thy words, thou sire of Christabel,
Are sweeter than my harp can tell;
Yet might I gain a boon of thee,
This day my journey should not be,
So strange a dream hath come to me,
That I had vowed with music loud
To clear yon wood from thing unblest,
Warned by a vision in my rest!
For in my sleep I saw that dove,
That gentle bird, whom thou dost love,
And call'st by thy own daughter's name—
Sir Leoline! I saw the same
Fluttering, and uttering fearful moan,
Among the green herbs in the forest alone.
Which when I saw and when I heard,
I wonder'd what might ail the bird;
For nothing near it could I see,
Save the grass and green herbs underneath the old tree.

"And in my dream methought I went

To search out what might there be found;
And what the sweet bird's trouble meant,
That thus lay fluttering on the ground.
I went and peered, and could descry
No cause for her distressful cry;
But yet for her dear lady's sake
I stooped, methought, the dove to take,
When lo! I saw a bright green snake
Coiled around its wings and neck.
Green as the herbs on which it couched,
Close by the dove's its head it crouched;
And with the dove it heaves and stirs,
Swelling its neck as she swelled hers!
I woke; it was the midnight hour,
The clock was echoing in the tower;
But though my slumber was gone by,
This dream it would not pass away—
It seems to live upon my eye!
And thence I vowed this self-same day
With music strong and saintly song
To wander through the forest bare,
Lest aught unholy loiter there."

Thus Bracy said: the Baron, the while,
Half-listening heard him with a smile;
Then turned to Lady Geraldine,
His eyes made up of wonder and love;
And said in courtly accents fine,
"Sweet maid, Lord Roland's beauteous dove,
With arms more strong than harp or song,
Thy sire and I will crush the snake!"
He kissed her forehead as he spake,
And Geraldine in maiden wise
Casting down her large bright eyes,
With blushing cheek and courtesy fine
She turned her from Sir Leoline;
Softly gathering up her train,
That o'er her right arm fell again;
And folded her arms across her chest,
And couched her head upon her breast,
And looked askance at Christabel——
Jesu, Maria, shield her well!

A snake's small eye blinks dull and shy;
And the lady's eyes they shrunk in her head,
Each shrunk up to a serpent's eye,

And with somewhat of malice, and more of dread,
At Christabel she looked askance!—
One moment—and the sight was fled!
But Christabel in dizzy trance
Stumbling on the unsteady ground
Shuddered aloud, with a hissing sound;
And Geraldine again turned round,
And like a thing, that sought relief,
Full of wonder and full of grief,
She rolled her large bright eyes divine
Wildly on Sir Leoline.

The maid, alas! her thoughts are gone,
She nothing sees—no sight but one!
The maid, devoid of guile and sin,
I know not how, in fearful wise,
So deeply had she drunken in
That look, those shrunken serpent eyes,
That all her features were resigned
To this sole image in her mind:
And passively did imitate
That look of dull and treacherous hate!
And thus she stood, in dizzy trance,
Still picturing that look askance
With forced unconscious sympathy
Full before her father's view——
As far as such a look could be
In eyes so innocent and blue!

And when the trance was o'er, the maid
Paused awhile, and inly prayed:
Then falling at the Baron's feet,
"By my mother's soul do I entreat
That thou this woman send away!"
She said: and more she could not say:
For what she knew she could not tell,
O'er-mastered by the mighty spell.

Why is thy cheek so wan and wild,
Sir Leoline? Thy only child
Lies at thy feet, thy joy, thy pride,
So fair, so innocent, so mild;
The same, for whom thy lady died!
O by the pangs of her dear mother
Think thou no evil of thy child!
For her, and thee, and for no other,

She prayed the moment ere she died:
Prayed that the babe for whom she died,
Might prove her dear lord's joy and pride!
   That prayer her deadly pangs beguiled,
      Sir Leoline!
   And wouldst thou wrong thy only child,
      Her child and thine?

Within the Baron's heart and brain
If thoughts, like these, had any share,
They only swelled his rage and pain,
And did but work confusion there.
His heart was cleft with pain and rage,
His cheeks they quivered, his eyes were wild,
Dishonoured thus in his old age;
Dishonoured by his only child,
And all his hospitality
To the wronged daughter of his friend
By more than woman's jealousy
Brought thus to a disgraceful end—
He rolled his eye with stern regard
Upon the gentle minstrel bard,
And said in tones abrupt, austere—
"Why, Bracy! dost thou loiter here?
I bade thee hence!" The bard obeyed;
And turning from his own sweet maid,
The agéd knight, Sir Leoline,
Led forth the lady Geraldine!

THE CONCLUSION TO PART II

A little child, a limber elf,
Singing, dancing to itself,
A fairy thing with red round cheeks,
That always finds, and never seeks,
Makes such a vision to the sight
As fills a father's eyes with light;
And pleasures flow in so thick and fast
Upon his heart, that he at last
Must needs express his love's excess
With words of unmeant bitterness.
Perhaps 'tis pretty to force together
Thoughts so all unlike each other;

To mutter and mock a broken charm,
To dally with wrong that does no harm.
Perhaps 'tis tender too and pretty
At each wild word to feel within
A sweet recoil of love and pity.
And what, if in a world of sin
(O sorrow and shame should this be true!)
Such giddiness of heart and brain
Comes seldom save from rage and pain,
So talks as it's most used to do.

THE HOUND OF HEAVEN

Francis Thompson

I fled Him, down the nights and down the days;
  I fled Him, down the arches of the years;
I fled Him, down the labyrinthine ways
    Of my own mind; and in the mist of tears
I hid from Him, and under running laughter.
        Up vistaed hopes I sped;
        And shot, precipitated,
Adown Titanic glooms of chasmed fears,
  From those strong Feet that followed, followed after.
        But with unhurrying chase,
        And unperturbéd pace,
Deliberate speed, majestic instancy,
        They beat—and a Voice beat
        More instant than the Feet—
  "All things betray thee, who betrayest Me."
        I pleaded, outlaw-wise,
By many a hearted casement, curtained red,
  Trellised with intertwining charities
(For, though I knew His love Who followéd,
        Yet was I sore adread
Lest, having Him, I must have naught beside);
But, if one little casement parted wide,
  The gust of His approach would clash it to:
  Fear wist not to evade, as Love wist to pursue.
Across the margent of the world I fled,
  And troubled the gold gateways of the stars,
  Smiting for shelter on their clanged bars;
        Fretted to dulcet jars
And silvern chatter the pale ports o' the moon.
I said to Dawn: Be sudden—to Eve: Be soon;
  With thy young skiey blossoms heap me over
        From this tremendous Lover—
Float thy vague veil about me, lest He see!
  I tempted all His servitors, but to find
My own betrayal in their constancy,
In faith to Him their fickleness to me,
  Their traitorous trueness, and their loyal deceit.
To all swift things for swiftness did I sue;
  Clung to the whistling mane of every wind.
        But whether they swept, smoothly fleet,

The long savannahs of the blue;
    Or whether, Thunder-driven,
    They clanged his chariot 'thwart a heaven,
Plashy, with flying lightnings round the spurn o' their feet:—
  Fear wist not to evade as Love wist to pursue.
      Still with unhurrying chase,
      And unperturbéd pace,
    Deliberate speed, majestic instancy,
      Came on the following Feet,
      And a Voice above their beat—
"Naught shelters thee, who wilt not shelter Me."

I sought no more that after which I strayed
      In face of man or maid;
But still within the little children's eyes
      Seems something, something that replies,
They at least are for me, surely for me!
I turned me to them very wistfully;
But just as their young eyes grew sudden fair
      With dawning answers there,
Their angel plucked them from me by the hair.
"Come then, ye other children, Nature's—share
With me" (said I) "your delicate fellowship;
      Let me greet you lip to lip,
      Let me twine with you caresses,
        Wantoning
      With our Lady-Mother's vagrant tresses,
        Banqueting
      With her in her wind-walled palace,
      Underneath her azured daïs,
      Quaffing, as your taintless way is,
        From a chalice
Lucent-weeping out of the dayspring."
      So it was done:
I in their delicate fellowship was one—
Drew the bolt of Nature's secrecies.
      I knew all the swift importings
      On the willful face of skies;
      I knew how the clouds arise
      Spumed of the wild sea-snortings;
      All that's born or dies
      Rose and drooped with; made them shapers
Of mine own moods, or wailful or divine;
      With them joyed and was bereaven.
      I was heavy with the even,

When she lit her glimmering tapers
    Round the day's dead sanctities.
    I laughed in the morning's eyes.
I triumphed and I saddened with all weather,
    Heaven and I wept together,
And its sweet tears were salt with mortal mine;

Against the red throb of its sunset-heart
    I laid my own to beat,
    And share commingling heat;
But not by that, by that, was eased my human smart.
In vain my tears were wet on Heaven's gray cheek.
For ah! we know not what each other says,
    These things and I; in sound I speak—
Their sound is but their stir, they speak by silences.
Nature, poor stepdame, cannot slake my drouth;
    Let her, if she would owe me,
Drop yon blue bosom-veil of sky, and show me
    The breasts o' her tenderness:
Never did any milk of hers once bless
      My thirsting mouth.
      Nigh and nigh draws the chase,
      With unperturbéd pace,
    Deliberate speed, majestic instancy;
      And past those noiséd Feet
      A Voice comes yet more fleet—
"Lo! naught contents thee, who content'st not Me."

Naked I wait Thy love's uplifted stroke!
My harness piece by piece Thou hast hewn from me,
    And smitten me to my knee;
    I am defenseless utterly.
    I slept, methinks, and woke,
And, slowly gazing, find me stripped in sleep.
In the rash lustihead of my young powers,
    I shook the pillaring hours
And pulled my life upon me; grimed with smears,
I stand amid the dust o' the mounded years—
My mangled youth lies dead beneath the heap.
My days have crackled and gone up in smoke,
Have puffed and burst as sun-starts on a stream.
    Yea, faileth now even dream
The dreamer, and the lute the lutanist;
Even the linked fantasies, in whose blossomy twist
I swung the earth a trinket at my wrist,
Are yielding; cords of all too weak account

For earth with heavy griefs so overpulsed.
  Ah! is Thy love indeed
A weed, albeit an amaranthine weed,
Suffering no flowers except its own to mount?
  Ah! must—
  Designer infinite!—
Ah! must Thou char the wood ere Thou canst limn with it?
My freshness spent its wavering shower i' the dust;
And now my heart is as a broken fount,
Wherein tear-drippings stagnate, split down ever
  From the dank thoughts that shiver
Upon the sighful branches of my mind.
  Such is; what is to be?
The pulp so bitter, how shall taste the rind?
I dimly guess what Time in mists confounds;
Yet ever and anon a trumpet sounds
From the hid battlements of Eternity;
Those shaken mists a space unsettle, then
Round the half-glimpsed turrets slowly wash again.
  But not ere him who summoneth
  I first have seen, enwound
With glooming robes purpureal, cypress-crowned;
His name I know, and what his trumpet saith.
Whether man's heart or life it be which yields
  Thee harvest, must Thy harvest-fields
  Be dunged with rotten death?

   Now of that long pursuit
   Comes on at hand the bruit;
  That Voice is round me like a bursting sea:
   "And is thy earth so marred,
   Shattered in shard on shard?
  Lo, all things fly thee, for thou fliest me!
  Strange, piteous, futile thing!
Wherefore should any set thee love apart?
Seeing none but I makes much of naught" (He said),
"And human love needs human meriting:
  How hast thou merited—
Of all man's clotted clay the dingiest clot?
  Alack, thou knowest not
How little worthy of any love thou art!
Whom wilt thou find to love ignoble thee
  Save Me, save only Me?
All which I took from thee I did but take,
  Not for thy harms,

But just that thou might'st seek it in My arms.
    All which thy child's mistake
Fancies as lost, I have stored for thee at home:
    Rise, clasp My hand, and come!"

        Halts by me that footfall:
        Is my gloom, after all,
    Shade of His hand, outstretched caressingly?
        "Ah, fondest, blindest, weakest,
        I am He Whom thou seekest!
    Thou dravest love from thee, who dravest Me."

THE VAMPIRE

Efrén Rebolledo

Whirling your deep and gloomy tresses pour
Over your candid body like a torrent,
and on the shadowy and curling flood
I strew the fiery roses of my kisses.

As I disenmesh the tangled locks
I feel the light chill chafing of your hand,
and a great shudder courses over me
and penetrates me to the very bone.

Your chaotic and disdainful eyes
glitter like stars when they hear the sigh
that from my vitals issue rendingly,

and you, thirsting, as I agonize,
assume the form of an implacable
black vampire battening on my burning blood.

THEY BITE

Anthony Boucher

THERE WAS NO PATH, only the almost vertical ascent. Crumbled rock for a few yards, with the roots of sage finding their scanty life in the dry soil. Then jagged outcroppings of crude crags, sometimes with accidental footholds, sometimes with overhanging and untrustworthy branches of greasewood, sometimes with no aid to climbing but the leverage of your muscles and the ingenuity of your balance.

The sage was as drably green as the rock was drably brown. The only color was the occasional rosy spikes of a barrel cactus.

Hugh Tallant swung himself up onto the last pinnacle. It had a deliberate, shaped look about it—a petrified fortress of Lilliputians, a Gibraltar of pygmies. Tallant perched on its battlements and unslung his field glasses.

The desert valley spread below him. The tiny cluster of buildings that was Oasis, the exiguous cluster of palms that gave name to the town and shelter to his own tent and to the shack he was building, the dead-ended highway leading straightforwardly to nothing, the oiled roads diagraming the vacant blocks of an optimistic subdivision.

Tallant saw none of these. His glasses were fixed beyond the oasis and the town of Oasis on the dry lake. The gliders were clear and vivid to him, and the uniformed men busy with them were as sharply and minutely visible as a nest of ants under glass. The training school was more than usually active. One glider in particular, strange to Tallant, seemed the focus of attention. Men would come and examine it and glance back at the older models in comparison.

Only the corner of Tallant's left eye was not preoccupied with the new glider. In that corner something moved, something little and thin and brown as the earth. Too large for a rabbit, much too small for a man. It darted across that corner of vision, and Tallant found gliders oddly hard to concentrate on.

He set down the bifocals and deliberately looked about him. His pinnacle surveyed the narrow, flat area of the crest. Nothing stirred. Nothing stood out against the sage and rock but one barrel of rosy spikes. He took up the glasses again and resumed his observations. When he was done, he methodically entered the results in the little black notebook.

His hand was still white. The desert is cold and often sunless in winter. But it was a firm hand, and as well trained as his eyes, fully capable of recording faithfully the designs and dimensions which they had registered so accurately.

Once his hand slipped, and he had to erase and redraw, leaving a smudge that displeased him. The lean, brown thing had slipped across the edge of his vision again. Going toward the east edge, he would swear, where that set of rocks jutted like the spines on the back of a stegosaur.

Only when his notes were completed did he yield to curiosity, and even then with cynical self-reproach. He was physically tired, for him an unusual state, from this daily climbing and from clearing the ground for his shack-to-be. The eye muscles play odd nervous tricks. There could be nothing behind the stegosaur's armor.

There was nothing. Nothing alive and moving. Only the torn and half-plucked carcass of a bird, which looked as though it had been gnawed by some small animal.

It was halfway down the hill—hill in Western terminology, though anywhere east of the Rockies it would have been considered a sizable mountain—that Tallant again had a glimpse of a moving figure.

But this was no trick of a nervous eye. It was not little nor thin nor brown. It was tall broad and wore a loud red-and-black lumberjacket. It bellowed, "Tallant!" in a cheerful and lusty voice.

Tallant drew near the man and said, "Hello." He paused and added, "Your advantage, I think."

The man grinned broadly. "Don't know me? Well, I daresay ten years is a long time, and the California desert ain't exactly the Chinese rice fields. How's stuff? Still loaded down with Secrets for Sale?"

Tallant tried desperately not to react to that shot, but he stiffened a little. "Sorry. The prospector getup had me fooled. Good to see you again, Morgan."

The man's eyes had narrowed. "Just having my little joke," he smiled. "Of course you wouldn't have no serious reason for mountain climbing around a glider school, now, would you? And you'd kind of need field glasses to keep an eye on the pretty birdies."

"I'm out here for my health." Tallant's voice sounded unnatural even to himself.

"Sure, sure. You were always in it for your health. And come to think of it, my own health ain't been none too good lately. I've got me a little cabin way to hell-and-gone around here, and I do me a little prospecting now and then. And somehow it just strikes me, Tallant, like maybe I hit a pretty good lode today."

"Nonsense, old man. You can see—"

"I'd sure hate to tell any of them Army men out at the field some of the stories I know about China and the kind of men I used to know out there. Wouldn't cotton to them stories a bit, the Army wouldn't. But if I was to have a drink too many and get talkative-like—"

"Tell you what," Tallant suggested brusquely. "It's getting near sunset now, and my tent's chilly for evening visits. But drop around in the morning and we'll talk over old times. Is rum still your tipple?"

"Sure is. Kind of expensive now, you understand—"

"I'll lay some in. You can fine the place easily—over by the oasis. And we . . . we might be able to talk about your prospecting, too."

Tallant's thin lips were set firm as he walked away.

The bartender opened a bottle of beer and plunked it on the damp-circled counter. "That'll be twenty cents," he said, then added as an afterthought, "Want a glass? Sometimes tourists do."

Tallant looked at the others sitting at the counter—the red-eyed and unshaven old man, the flight sergeant unhappily drinking a Coke—it was after Army hours for beer—the young man with the long, dirty trench coat and the pipe and the new-looking brown beard—and saw no glasses. "I guess I won't be a tourist," he decided.

This was the first time Tallant had had a chance to visit the Desert Sport Spot. It was as well to be seen around in the community. Otherwise people begin to wonder and say, "Who is that man out by the oasis? Why don't you ever see him anyplace?"

The Sport Spot was quiet that night. The four of them at the counter, two Army boys shooting pool, and a half-dozen of the local men gathered about a round poker table, soberly and wordlessly cleaning a construction worker whose mind seemed more on his beer than on his cards.

"You just passing through?" the bartender asked sociably.

Tallant shook his head. "I'm moving in. When the Army turned me down for my lungs, I decided I better do something about it. Heard so much about your climate here I thought I might as well try it."

"Sure thing," the bartender nodded. "You take up until they started this glider school, just about every other guy you meet in the desert is here for his health. Me, I had sinus, and look at me now. It's the air."

Tallant breathed the atmosphere of smoke and beer suds, but did not smile, "I'm looking forward to miracles."

"You'll get 'em. Whereabouts you staying?"

"Over that way a bit. The agent called it 'the old Carker place.'"

Tallant felt the curious listening silence and frowned. The bartender had started to speak and then thought better of it. The young man with the beard looked at him oddly. The old man fixed him with red and watery eyes that had a faded glint of pity in them. For a moment, Tallant felt a chill that had nothing to do with the night air of the desert.

The old man drank his beer in quick gulps and frowned as though trying to formulate a sentence. At last he wiped beer from his bristly lips and said, "You wasn't aiming to stay in the adobe, was you?"

"No. It's pretty much gone to pieces. Easier to rig me up a little shack than try to make the adobe livable. Meanwhile, I've got a tent."

"That's all right, then, m'bbe. But mind you don't go poking around that there adobe."

"I don't think I'm apt to. But why not? Want another beer?"

The old man shook his head reluctantly and slid from his stool to the ground. "No thanks, I don't rightly know as I—"

"Yes?"

"Nothing. Thanks all the same." He turned and shuffled to the door.

Tallant smiled. "But why should I stay clear of the adobe?" he called after him.

The old man mumbled.

"What?"

"They bite," said the old man, and went out shivering into the night.

The bartender was back at his post. "I'm glad he didn't take that beer you offered him," he said. "Along about this time in the evening I have to stop serving him. For once he had the sense to quit."

Tallant pushed his own empty bottle forward. "I hope I didn't frighten him away."

"Frighten? Well, mister, I think maybe that's just what you did do. He didn't want beer that sort of came, like you might say, from the old Carker place. Some of the old-timers here, they're funny that way."

Tallant grinned. "Is it haunted?"

"Not what you'd call haunted, no. No ghosts there that I ever heard of." He wiped the counter with a cloth and seemed to wipe the subject away with it.

The flight sergeant pushed his Coke bottle away, hunted in his pocket for nickels, and went over to the pinball machine. The young man with the beard slid onto his vacant stool. "Hope old Jake didn't worry you," he said.

Tallant laughed. "I suppose every town has its deserted homestead with a grisly tradition. But this sounds a little different. No ghosts, and they bite. Do you know anything about it?"

"A little," the young man said seriously. "A little. Just enough to—"

Tallant was curious. "Have one on me and tell me about it."

The flight sergeant swore bitterly at the machine.

Beer gurgled through the beard, "You see," the young man began, "the desert's so big you can't be alone in it. Ever notice that? It's all empty and there's nothing in sight, but there's always something moving over there where you can't quite see it. It's something very dry and thin and brown, only when you look around it isn't there. Ever see it?"

"Optical fatigue—" Tallant began

"Sure, I know. Every man to his own legend. There isn't a tribe of Indians hasn't got some way of accounting for it. You've heard of the Watchers? And the twentieth-century white man comes along, and it's optical fatigue. Only in the nineteenth century things weren't quite the same, and there were the Carkers."

"You've got a special localized legend?"

"Call it that. You glimpse things out of the corner of your mind, same like you glimpse lean, dry things out of the corner of your eye. You encase 'em in solid circumstance and they're not so bad. That is known as the Growth of Legend. The Folk Mind in Action. You take the Carkers and the things you don't quite see and you put 'em together. And they bite."

Tallant wondered how long that beard had been absorbing beer. "And what were the Carkers?" he prompted politely.

"Ever hear of Sawney Bean? Scotland—reign of James First, or maybe the Sixth, though I think Roughead's wrong on that for once. Or let's be more modern—ever hear of the Benders? Kansas in the 1870s? No? Ever hear of Procrustes? Or Polyphemus? Or Fee-fi-fo-fum?

"There are ogres, you know. They're no legend. They're fact, they are. The inn where nine guests left for every ten that arrived, the mountain cabin that sheltered travelers from the snow, sheltered them all winter till the melting spring uncovered their bones, the lonely stretches of road that so many passengers traveled halfway—you'll find 'em everywhere. All over Europe and pretty much in this country too before communications became what they are. Profitable business. And it wasn't just the profit. The Benders made money, sure; but that wasn't why they killed all their victims as carefully as a kosher butcher. Sawney Bean got so he didn't give a damn about the profit; he just needed to lay in more meat for the winter.

"And think of the chances you'd have at an oasis."

"So these Carkers of yours were, as you call them, ogres?"

"Carkers, ogres—maybe they were Benders. The Benders were never seen alive, you know, after the townspeople found those curiously butchered bodies. There's a rumor they got this far west. And the time checks pretty well. There wasn't any town here in the eighties. Just a couple of Indian families, last of a dying tribe living on at the oasis. They vanished after the Carkers moved in. That's not so surprising. The white race is a sort of super-ogre, anyway. Nobody worried about them. But they used to worry about why so many travelers never got across this stretch of desert. The travelers used to stop over at the Carkers', you see, and somehow they often never got any farther. Their wagons'd be found maybe fifteen miles beyond in the desert. Sometimes they found the bones, too, parched and white. Gnawed-looking, they said sometimes."

"And nobody ever did anything about these Carkers?"

"Oh, sure. We didn't have King James Sixth—only I still think it was First—to ride up on a great white horse for a gesture, but twice Army detachments came here and wiped them all out."

"Twice? One wiping-out would do for most families." Tallant smiled.

"Uh-uh. That was no slip. They wiped out the Carkers twice because, you see, once didn't do any good. They wiped 'em out and still travelers vanished and still there were gnawed bones. So they wiped 'em out again. After that they gave up, and people detoured the oasis. It made a longer, harder trip, but after all—"

Tallant laughed. "You mean to say these Carkers were immortal?"

"I don't know about immortal. They somehow just didn't die very easy. Maybe, if they were the Benders—and I sort of like to think they were—they learned a little more about what they were doing out here on the desert. Maybe they put together what the Indians knew and what they knew, and it worked. Maybe Whatever they made their sacrifices to understood them better out here than in Kansas."

"And what's become of them—aside from seeing them out of the corner of the eye?"

"There's forty years between the last of the Carker history and this new settlement at the oasis. And people won't talk much about what they learned here in the first year or so. Only that they stay away from that old Carker adobe. They tell some stories— The priest says he was sitting in the confessional one hot Saturday afternoon and thought he heard a penitent come in. He waited a long time and finally lifted the gauze to see was anybody there. Something was there, and it bit. He's got three fingers on his right hand now, which looks funny as hell when he gives a benediction."

Tallant pushed their two bottles toward the bartender. "That yarn, my young friend, has earned another beer. How about it, bartender? Is he always cheerful like this, or is this just something he's improvised for my benefit?"

The bartender set out the fresh bottles with great solemnity. "Me, I wouldn't've told you all that myself, but then, he's a stranger too and maybe don't feel the same way we do here. For him it's just a story."

"It's more comfortable that way," said the young man with the beard, and he took a firm hold on his beer bottle.

"But as long as you've heard that much," said the bartender, "you might as well— It was last winter, when we had that cold spell. You heard funny stories that winter. Wolves coming into prospectors' cabins just to warm up. Well, business wasn't so good. We don't have a license for hard liquor, and the boys don't drink much beer when it's that cold. But they used to come in anyway because we've got that big oil burner.

"So one night there's a bunch of 'em in here—old Jake was here, that you was talking to, and his dog Jigger—and I think I hear somebody else come in. The door creaks a little. But I don't see nobody, and the poker game's going, and we're talking just like we're talking now, and all of a sudden I hear a kind of a noise like *crack!* over there in that corner behind the juke box near the burner.

"I go over to see what goes and it gets away before I can see it very good. But it was little and thin and it didn't have no clothes on. It must've been damned cold that winter."

"And what was the cracking noise?" Tallant asked dutifully.

"That? That was a bone. It must've strangled Jigger without any noise. He was a little dog. It ate most of the flesh, and if it hadn't cracked the bone for the marrow it could've finished. You can still see the spots over there. The blood never did come out."

There had been silence all through the story. Now suddenly all hell broke loose. The flight sergeant let out a splendid yell and began pointing excitedly at the pinball machine and yelling for his payoff. The construction worker dramatically deserted the poker game, knocking his chair over in the process, and announced lugubriously that these guys here had their own rules, see?

Any atmosphere of Carker-inspired horror was dissipated. Tallant whistled as he walked over to put a nickel in the jukebox. He glanced casually at the floor. Yes, there was a stain, for what that was worth.

He smiled cheerfully and felt rather grateful to the Carkers. They were going to solve his blackmail problem very neatly.

Tallant dreamed of power that night. It was a common dream with him. He was a ruler of the new American Corporate State that would follow the war; and he said to this man, "Come!" and he came, and to that man, "Go!" and he went, and to his servants, "Do this!" and they did it.

Then the young man with the beard was standing before him, and the dirty trench coat was like the robes of an ancient prophet. And the young man said, "You see yourself riding high, don't you? Riding the crest of the wave—the Wave of the Future, you call it. But there's a deep, dark undertow that you don't see, and that's a part of the Past. And the Present and even your Future. There is evil in mankind that is blacker even than your evil, and infinitely more ancient."

And there was something in the shadows behind the young man, something little and lean and brown.

Tallant's dream did not disturb him the following morning. Nor did the thought of the approaching interview with Morgan. He fried his bacon and eggs and devoured them cheerfully. The wind had died down for a change, and the sun was warm enough so that he could strip to the waist while he cleared land for his shack. His machete glinted brilliantly as it swung through the air and struck at the roots of the brush.

When Morgan arrived his full face was red and sweating.

"It's cool over there in the shade of the adobe," Tallant suggested. "We'll be more comfortable." And in the comfortable shade of the adobe he swung the machete once and clove Morgan's full, red, sweating face in two.

It was so simple. It took less effort than uprooting a clump of sage. And it was so safe. Morgan lived in a cabin way to hell-and-gone and was often away on prospecting trips. No one would notice his absence for months, if then. No one had any reason to connect him with Tallant. And no one in Oasis would hunt for him in the Carker-haunted adobe.

The body was heavy, and the blood dripped warm on Tallant's bare skin. With relief he dumped what had been Morgan on the floor of the adobe. There were no boards, no flooring. Just the earth. Hard, but not too hard to dig a grave in. And no one was likely to come poking around in this taboo territory to notice the grave. Let a year or so go by, and the grave and the bones it contained would be attributed to the Carkers.

The corner of Tallant's eye bothered him again. Deliberately he looked about the interior of the adobe.

The little furniture was crude and heavy, with no attempt to smooth down the strokes of the ax. It was held together with wooden pegs or half-rotted thongs. There were age-old cinders in the fireplace, and the dusty shards of a cooking jar among them.

And there was a deeply hollowed stone, covered with stains that might have been rust, if stone rusted. Behind it was a tiny figure, clumsily fashioned of clay and sticks. It was something like a man and something like a lizard, and something like the things that flit across the corner of the eye.

Curious now, Tallant peered about further. He penetrated to the corner that the one unglassed window lighted but dimly. And there he let out a little choking gasp. For a moment he was rigid with horror. Then he smiled and all but laughed aloud.

This explained everything. Some curious individual had seen this, and from his accounts had burgeoned the whole legend. The Carkers had indeed learned something from the Indians, but that secret was the art of embalming.

It was a perfect mummy. Either the Indian art had shrunk bodies, or this was that of a ten-year-old boy. There was no flesh. Only skin and bone and taut, dry stretches of tendon between. The eyelids were closed; the sockets looked hollow under them. The nose was sunken and almost lost. The scant lips were tightly curled back from the long and very white teeth, which stood forth all the more brilliantly against the deep-brown skin.

It was a curious little trove, this mummy. Tallant was already calculating the chances for raising a decent sum of money from an interested anthropologist—murder can produce such delightfully profitable chance by-products—when he noticed the infinitesimal rise and fall of the chest.

The Carker was not dead. It was sleeping.

Tallant did not dare stop to think beyond the instant. This was no time to pause to consider if such things were possible in a well-ordered world. It was no time to reflect on the disposal of the body of Morgan. It was a time to snatch up your machete and get out of there.

But in the doorway he halted. There, coming across the desert, heading for the adobe, clearly seen this time, was another—a female.

He made an involuntary gesture of indecision. The blade of the machete clanged ringingly against the adobe wall. He heard the dry shuffling of a roused sleeper behind him.

He turned fully now, the machete raised. Dispose of this nearer one first, then face the female. There was no room even for terror in his thoughts, only for action.

The lean brown shape darted at him avidly. He moved lightly away and stood poised for its second charge. It shot forward again. He took one step back, machete arm raised, and fell headlong over the corpse of Morgan. Before he could rise, the thin thing was upon him. Its sharp teeth had met through the palm of his left hand.

The machete moved swiftly. The thin dry body fell headless to the floor. There was no blood.

The grip of the teeth did not relax. Pain coursed up Tallant's left arm —a sharper, more bitter pain than you would expect from the bite. Almost as though venom—

He dropped the machete, and his strong white hand plucked and twisted at the dry brown lips. The teeth stayed clenched, unrelaxing. He sat bracing his back against the wall and gripped the head between his knees. He pulled. His flesh ripped, and blood formed dusty clots on the dirt floor. But the bite was firm.

His world had become reduced now to that hand and that head. Nothing outside mattered. He must free himself. He raised his aching arm to his face, and with his own teeth he tore at that unrelenting grip. The dry flesh crumbled away in desert dust, but the teeth were locked fast. He tore his lip against their white keenness, and tasted in his mouth the sweetness of blood and something else.

He staggered to his feet again. He knew what he must do. Later he could use cautery, a tourniquet, see a doctor with a story about a Gila monster—their heads grip too, don't they?—but he knew what he must do now.

He raised the machete and struck again.

His white hand lay on the brown floor, gripped by the white teeth in the brown face. He propped himself against the adobe wall, momentarily unable to move. His open wrist hung over the deeply hollowed stone. His blood and his strength and his life poured out before the little figure of sticks and clay.

The female stood in the doorway now, the sun bright on her thin brownness. She did not move. He knew that she was waiting for the hollow stone to fill.

TAILYPO

A Black Folk Tale

Once upon a time, way down in de big woods ob Tennessee, dey lived a man all by hisself. His house didn't hab but one room in it, an' dat room was his pahlor, his settin' room, his bedroom, his dinin' room, an' his kitchen, too. In one end ob de room was a great, big, open fiahplace, an' dat's wha' de man cooked an' et his suppah. An' one night atter he had cooked an' et his suppah, dey crep' in troo de cracks ob de logs de curiestes creetur dat you ebber did see, an' it had a *great, big, long tail.*

Jis' as soon as dat man see dat varmint, he reached fur his hatchet, an' wid one lick, he cut dat thing's tail off. De creeter crep' out troo de cracks ob de logs an' run away, an' de man, fool like, he took an' cooked dat tail, he did, an' et it. Den he went ter bed, an' atter a while, he went ter sleep.

He hadn't been 'sleep berry long, till he waked up, an' heerd sumpin' climbin' up de side ob his cabin. It sounded jis' like a cat, an' he could hear it *scratch, scratch, scratch,* an' by-an'-by, he heerd it say, *"Tailypo, tailypo; all I want's my tailypo."*

Now dis yeer man had t'ree dogs: one wuz called Uno, an' one wuz called Ino, an' de udder one wuz called Cumptico-Calico. An' when he heerd dat thing he called his dawgs, huh! huh! huh! an' dem dawgs cum bilin' out from under de floo', an' dey chased dat thing way down in de big woods. An' de man went back ter bed an' went ter sleep.

Well, way long in de middle ob de night, he waked up an' he heerd sumpin' right above his cabin doo', tryin' ter git in. He listened, an' he could heer it *scratch, scratch, scratch,* an' den he heerd it say, *"Tailypo, tailypo; all I want's my tailypo."* An' he sot up in bed and called his dawgs, huh! huh! huh! an' dem dawgs cum bustin' round de corner ob de house an' dey cotched up wid dat thing at de gate an' dey jis' tore de whole fence down, tryin' ter git at it. An' dat time, dey chased it way down in de big swamp. An' de man went back ter bed agin an' went ter sleep.

Way long toward mornin' he waked up, an he heerd sumpin' down in de big swamp. He listened, an' he heerd it say, *"You know, I know; all I want's my tailypo."* An' dat man sot up in bed an' called his dawgs, huh! huh! huh! an' you know dat time dem dawgs didn' cum. Dat thing had carried 'em way off down in de big swamp an' killed 'em, or los' 'em. An' de man went back ter bed an' went ter sleep agin.

Well, jis' befo' daylight, he waked up an' he heerd sumpin' in his room, an' it sounded like a cat, climbin' up de civers at de foot ob his bed. He listened an' he could hear it scratch, scratch, scratch, an' he looked ober de foot ob his bed an' he saw two little pinted ears, an' in a minute, he saw two big roun', fiery eyes lookin' at him. He wanted to call his dawgs, but he too skeered ter holler. Dat thing kep' creepin' up until by-an-by it wuz right on top ob dat man, an' den it said in a low voice, "Tailypo, tailypo; all I want's my tailypo." An' all at once dat man got his voice an' he said, "I hain't got yo' tailypo." An dat thing said, "Yes you has," an' it jumped on dat man an' scratched him all to pieces. An' sum folks say he got his tailypo.

Now dey ain't nothin' lef' ob dat man's cabin way down in de big woods ob Tennessee, 'ceptin' the chimbley, an' folks w'at lib in de big valley say dat when de moon shines bright an' de win' blows down de valley you can heer sumpin' say, "Tailypo. . . . . ," An' den, die away in de distance.

V

Strange Journeys

STRANGE JOURNEYS

FICTIONAL JOURNEYS have always fascinated man because there are so many places we have not been and so many places we fear to go. The journey removes us to a reality different from the one we usually dwell in, physically and mentally. Through fictional journeys we travel in time and space, but mainly in mind. If during the journey we encounter things foreign and unknown, the journey is a strange one.

Many of the greatest works of world literature are variations of the strange journey: Homer's *Odyssey,* Dante's *Divine Comedy,* Swift's *Gulliver's Travels,* Conrad's *Heart of Darkness,* Melville's *Moby Dick,* Shakespeare's *The Tempest,* the Indian epic *The Ramayana,* the Babylonian *Gilgamesh,* and many others.

When most of the planet was unknown to civilized man, strange journeys could be conceived of literally on earth. Primitive men feared horrible monsters lurking over the horizon. A brilliant man of the 14th century such as Dante believed the mountain of Purgatory, populated with souls of the dead, arose from a vast ocean on the other side of the earth. During the age of exploration which began with the Renaissance, travel books, records of actual journeys, achieved great popularity. Even what really existed—great cities in China, golden empires in Peru, redskinned natives in America—struck European man as bizarre phenomena. Yet writers were stimulated to construct fictions of even stranger places, some of them ideal civilizations, as in More's *Utopia* and Bacon's *New Atlantis.*

Beyond earth, man has always found magic in the moon and planets and longed to visit them. Despite occasional imaginary voyages created over the ages, it was not until the technological developments of the late 19th and 20th centuries that space travel became such a widespread fictional subject. Little green men, bugeyed monsters, and six-headed giants populated the planets in this makebelieve, though in some cases Utopian human societies were now found on Saturn or Mercury or in galaxies thousands of light years away. Space gave a new location to our dreams.

However, we have reduced our geographical unknowns greatly over the past few centuries, most strikingly in our own. Very little of the earth remains uncharted and unexplored; astronauts have travelled to the moon. Unmanned space probes to Mars and Venus confirm that these planets are barren of intelligent life. Scientific evidence concludes that man is alone in his solar system. Rockets to Jupiter or Pluto would find not the alien civilizations which enlivened so much science fiction only a decade ago; rather nothing but gases and mists and minerals.

Yet fictional journeys still fascinate us. The strange journeys of contemporary writing occur within fantastic worlds, such as that of J. R. R. Tolkein's hobbits, or in the still mysterious inner world of the mind. Strange journeys, wherever their physical setting, have really been trips of the imagination all along. The imagination is personal and private, infinite in its resources, beyond technology. As long as the imagination exists, strange journeys will exist.

The literary critic Northrop Frye has written of such fictions:

> Of all fictions, the marvelous journey is the one formula that is never exhausted. ... Its episodic theme is perhaps best described as the theme of the boundary of consciousness, the sense of the poetic mind as passing from one world to another, or as simultaneously aware of both.

It is obvious why strange journeys fascinate man so much when we consider the circumstances of our existence. We come into the world through one strange journey—birth—and leave it through another—death. While we are here, unknowns overwhelm us. Personally and collectively we seek reasons, purposes, and goals; we long for understanding. The fictions of journeys are attempts to answer our ignorance. They transcend the seeming limitations of our realities and give shape to our dreams and wishes and to our fears. Fictional journeys take us where life does not allow us to go.

Andrew Marvell's poem "Bermudas," written in the seventeenth century when America was a new hope to European man, envisions these small isles as a refuge from the stormy seas of this world, a religious sanctuary. The journey across the ocean would find the Garden of Eden restored. Writing in the early twentieth century, William Butler Yeats also evoked a past paradise in "Sailing to Byzantium." For Yeats the Byzantine civilization of the fifth century was the ideal age. The paradise of the poem is an artistic one, a shelter from aging flesh in a world of artificial beauty.

Walt Whitman's "Passage to India" is an even more triumphant journey because in his poem the issue is not one of escaping a painful place to one of happiness, but rather a condition of transcendence which unites all existence—past and present, matter and spirit, East and West, religion and technology—in the fulfillment of mankind's eternal dream of perfect harmony.

Unfortunately, not all journeys reach their goals. The next selection takes us to the bottom of the sea. It is a journey unfulfilled. Matthew Arnold's "The Forsaken Merman" and his children are abandoned by their human wife and mother, who has rejected the enchanted realm and chosen to remain earthbound. Paradoxically, it is the creatures from the strange place who travel to this world and fail.

"Childe Roland to the Dark Tower Came," by Robert Browning, is a journey to an ultimate test. But the poem ends on the verge of that test; its focus is upon the journey which Roland must make through the terrifying wasteland to reach that dark tower with its unknown horrors. This threatening landscape is as much a state of mind as it is a physical setting, and more fearful precisely because of that. In legend Childe Roland was a son of King Arthur, who rescued his sister from the castle of the king of Elfland after she had been abducted by fairies. The words of the title are taken from Edgar's song of feigned madness in Shakespeare's *King Lear.*

Probably the two most unusual selections are "Kōgi the Priest" and "Paraguay." Lafcadio Hearn's retelling of a Japanese tale typifies many of the differences between Eastern and Western art with its delicate, almost whimsical, use of the supernatural. Here the journey is twofold: a journey of transformation of man into fish and a journey into the realm after death. And this is also a story of rebirth.

We are not sure exactly where Donald Barthelme's Paraguay exists, although we are told definitely that it is not the Paraguay we know from our maps. Much of this other Paraguay is similar to the world we know, populated with recognizable humanity, activities, and objects. Perhaps it is because so much of this Paraguay is known to us that its differences are so jarring. Here creatures much like us shed their skins in green official receptacles, silence is sold powdered in sacks, and snow is red. We know we are on a journey, but feel disturbed because we do not know where Barthelme has taken us. His story reaffirms the limitlessness of the regions of strange journeys, and Margaret Walker reminds us that even ordinary travel awakens in us the knowledge that we travel beyond time and space, into the dark secret places in mind and heart.

BERMUDAS

Andrew Marvell

Where the remote Bermudas ride
In th' ocean's bosom unespied,
From a small boat that rowed along
The listening winds received this song:
   What should we do but sing His praise
Who led us through the watery maze,
Unto an isle so long unknown,
And yet far kinder than our own?
Where He the huge sea-monsters wracks
That lift the deep upon their backs.
He lands us on a grassy stage,
Safe from the storms and prelate's rage.
He gave us this eternal spring
Which here enamels every thing;
And sends the fowls to us in care
On daily visits through the air.
He hangs in shades the orange bright,
Like golden lamps in a green night;
And does in the pomegranates close
Jewels more rich than Ormus shows.
He makes the figs our mouths to meet,
And throws the melons at our feet;
But apples plants of such a price
No tree could ever bear them twice.
With cedars chosen by His hand
From Lebanon He stores the land;
And makes the hollow seas that roar
Proclaim the ambergris on shore.
He cast (of which we rather boast)
The gospel's pearl upon our coast,
And in these rocks for us did frame
A temple, where to sound His name.
Oh, let our voice His praise exalt
Till it arrive at Heaven's vault,
Which then perhaps rebounding may
Echo beyond the Mexique bay.
   Thus sung they in the English boat
A holy and a cheerful note,
And all the way to guide their chime
With falling oars they kept the time.

SAILING TO BYZANTIUM

William Butler Yeats

1

That is no country for old men. The young
In one another's arms, birds in the trees
—Those dying generations—at their song,
The salmon-falls, the mackerel-crowded seas,
Fish, flesh, or fowl, commend all summer long
Whatever is begotten, born, and dies.
Caught in that sensual music all neglect
Monuments of unageing intellect.

2

An aged man is but a paltry thing,
A tattered coat upon a stick, unless
Soul clap its hands and sing, and louder sing
For every tatter in its mortal dress,
Nor is there singing school but studying
Monuments of its own magnificence;
And therefore I have sailed the seas and come
To the holy city of Byzantium.

3

O sages standing in God's holy fire
As in the gold mosaic of a wall,
Come from the holy fire, perne[1] in a gyre,
And be the singing-masters of my soul.
Consume my heart away; sick with desire
And fastened to a dying animal
It knows not what it is; and gather me
Into the artifice of eternity.

4

Once out of nature I shall never take
My bodily form from any natural thing,

---

[1]spin

But such a form as Grecian goldsmiths make
Of hammered gold and gold enamelling
To keep a drowsy Emperor awake;
Or set upon a golden bough to sing
To lords and ladies of Byzantium
Of what is past, or passing, or to come.

PASSAGE TO INDIA

Walt Whitman

1

Singing my days,
Singing the great achievements of the present,
Singing the strong light works of engineers,
Our modern wonders, (the antique ponderous Seven outvied,)
In the Old World the east the Suez canal,
The New by its mighty railroad spann'd,
The seas inlaid with eloquent gentle wires;
Yet first to sound, and ever sound, the cry with thee O soul,
The Past! the Past! the Past!

The Past—the dark unfathom'd retrospect!
The teeming gulf—the sleepers and the shadows!
The past—the infinite greatness of the past!
For what is the present after all but a growth out of the past?
(As a projectile form'd, impell'd, passing a certain line, still keeps
        on,
So the present, utterly form'd, impell'd by the past.)

2

Passage O soul to India!
Eclaircise the myths Asiatic, the primitive fables.
Not you alone proud truths of the world,
Nor you alone ye facts of modern science,
But myths and fables of eld, Asia's, Africa's fables,
The far-darting beams of the spirit, the unloos'd dreams,
The deep diving bibles and legends,
The daring plots of the poets, the elder religions;
O you temples fairer than lilies pour'd over by the rising sun!
O you fables spurning the known, eluding the hold of the known,
        mounting to heaven!
You lofty and dazzling towers, pinnacled, red as roses, burnish'd
        with gold!
Towers of fables immortal fashion'd from mortal dreams!
You too I welcome and fully the same as the rest!
You too with joy I sing.

Passage to India!
Lo, soul, seest thou not God's purpose from the first?

The earth to be spann'd, connected by network,
The races, neighbors, to marry and be given in marriage,
The oceans to be cross'd, the distant brought near,
The lands to be welded together.

A worship new I sing,
You captains, voyagers, explorers, yours,
You engineers, you architects, machinists, yours,
You, not for trade or transportation only,
But in God's name, and for thy sake O soul.

3

Passage to India!
Lo soul for thee of tableaus twain,
I see in one the Suez canal initiated, open'd,
I see the procession of steamships, the Empress Eugenie's leading
    the van,
I mark from on deck the strange landscape, the pure sky, the level
    sand in the distance,
I pass swiftly the picturesque groups, the workmen gather'd,
The gigantic dredging machines.
In one again, different, (yet thine, all thine, O soul, the same,)
I see over my own continent the Pacific railroad surmounting every
    barrier,
I see continual trains of cars winding along the Platte carrying
    freight and passengers,
I hear the locomotives rushing and roaring, and the shrill
    steam-whistle,
I hear the echoes reverberate through the grandest scenery in the
    world,
I cross the Laramie plains, I note the rocks in grotesque shapes, the
    buttes,
I see the plentiful larkspur and wild onions, the barren, colorless,
    sage-deserts,
I see in glimpses afar or towering immediately above me the great
    mountains, I see the Wind river and the Wahsatch mountains,
I see the Monument mountain and the Eagle's Nest, I pass the
    Promontory, I ascend the Nevadas,
I scan the nobel Elk mountain and wind around its base,
I see the Humboldt range, I thread the valley and cross the river,
I see the clear waters of lake Tahoe, I see forests of majestic pines,
Or crossing the great desert, the alkaline plains, I behold
    enchanting mirages of waters and meadows,
Marking through these and after all, in duplicate slender lines,

Bridging the three or four thousand miles of land travel,
Tying the Eastern to the Western sea,
The road between Europe and Asia.

(Ah Genoese thy dream! thy dream!
Centuries after thou art laid in thy grave,
The shore thou foundest verifies thy dream.)

4

Passage to India!
Struggles of many a captain, tales of many a sailor dead,
Over my mood stealing and spreading they come,
Like clouds and cloudlets in the unreach'd sky.
Along all history, down the slopes,
As a rivulet running, sinking now, and now again to the surface
    rising,
A ceaseless thought, a varied train—lo, soul, to thee, thy sight, they
    rise,
The plans, the voyages again, the expeditions;
Again Vasco de Gama sails forth,
Again the knowledge gain'd, the mariner's compass,
Lands found and nations born, thou born America,
For purpose vast, man's long probation fill'd,
Thou rondure of the world at last accomplish'd.

5

O vast Rondure, swimming in space,
Cover'd all over with visible power and beauty,
Alternate light and day and the teeming spiritual darkness,
Unspeakable high processions of sun and moon and countless stars
    above,
Below, the manifold grass and waters, animals, mountains, trees,
With inscrutable purpose, some hidden prophetic intention,
Now first it seems my thought begins to span thee.

Down from the gardens of Asia descending radiating,
Adam and Eve appear, then their myriad progeny after them,
Wandering, yearning, curious, with restless explorations,
With questionings, baffled, formless, feverish, with never-happy
    hearts,
With that sad incessant refrain, *Wherefore unsatisfied soul?* and
    Whither O mocking life?

Ah who shall soothe these feverish children?

Who justify these restless explorations?
Who speak the secret of impassive earth?
Who bind it to us? what is this separate Nature so unnatural?
What is this earth to our affections? (unloving earth, without a
    throb to answer ours,
Cold earth, the place of graves.)

Behold him sail from Palos leading his little fleet,
His voyage behold, his return, his great fame,
His misfortunes, calumniators, behold him a prisoner, chain'd,
Behold his dejection, poverty, death.

(Curious in time I stand, noting the efforts of heroes,
Is the deferment long? bitter the slander, poverty, death?
Lies the seed unreck'd for centuries in the ground? lo, to God's due
    occasion,
Uprising in the night, it sprouts, blooms,
And fills the earth with use and beauty.)

7

Passage indeed O soul to primal thought,
Not lands and seas alone, thy own clear freshness,
The young maturity of brood and bloom,
To realms of budding bibles.

O soul, repressless, I with thee and thou with me,
Thy circumnavigation of the world begin,
Of man, the voyage of his mind's return,
To reason's early paradise,
Back, back to wisdom's birth, to innocent intuitions,
Again with fair creation.

8

O we can wait no longer,
We too take ship O soul,
Joyous we too launch out on trackless seas,
Fearless for unknown shores on waves of ecstasy to sail,
Amid the wafting winds, (thou pressing me to thee, I thee to me, O
    soul,)
Caroling free, singing our song of God,
Chanting our chant of pleasant exploration.

With laugh and many a kiss,
(Let others deprecate, let others weep for sin, remorse, humiliation,)
O soul thou pleasest me, I thee.

Ah more than any priest O soul we too believe in God,
But with the mystery of God we dare not dally.

O soul thou pleasest me, I thee,
Sailing these seas or on the hills, or waking in the night,
Thoughts, silent thoughts, of Time and Space and Death, like
    waters flowing,
Bear me indeed as through the regions infinite,
Whose air I breathe, whose ripples hear, lave me all over,
Bathe me O God in thee, mounting to thee,
I and my soul to range in range of thee.

O Thou transcendent,
Nameless, the fibre and the breath,
Light of the light, shedding forth universes, thou centre of them,
Thou mightier centre of the true, the good, the loving,
Thou moral, spiritual fountain—affection's source—thou reservoir,
(O pensive soul of me—O thirst unsatisfied—waitest not there?
Waitest not haply for us somewhere there the Comrade perfect?)
Thou pulse—thou motive of the stars, suns, systems,
That, circling, move in order, safe, harmonious,
Athwart the shapeless vastnesses of space,
How should I think, how breathe a single breath, how speak, if, out
    of myself,
I could not launch, to those, superior universes?

Swiftly I shrivel at the thought of God,
At Nature and its wonders, Time and Space and Death,
But that I, turning, call to thee O soul, thou actual Me,
And lo, thou gently masterest the orbs,
Thou matest Time, smilest content at Death,
And fillest, swellest full the vastnesses of Space.

Greater than stars or suns,
Bounding O soul thou journeyest forth;
What love than thine and ours could wider amplify?
What aspirations, wishes, outvie thine and ours O soul?
What dreams of the ideal? what plans of purity, perfection,
    strength,
What cheerful willingness for others' sake to give up all?
For others' sake to suffer all?

Reckoning ahead O soul, when thou, the time achiev'd,
The seas all cross'd, weather'd the capes, the voyage done,
Surrounded, copest, frontest God, yieldest, the aim attain'd,
As fill'd with friendship, love complete, the Elder Brother found,
The Younger melts in fondness in his arms.

9

Passage to more than India!
Are thy wings plumed indeed for such far flights?
O soul, voyagest thou indeed on voyages like those?
Disportest thou on waters such as those?
Soundest below the Sanscrit and the Vedas?
Then have thy bent unleash'd.

Passage to you, your shores, ye aged fierce enigmas!
Passage to you, to mastership of you, ye strangling problems!
You, strew'd with the wrecks of skeletons, that, living, never
       reach'd you.

Passage to more than India!
O secret of the earth and sky!
Of you O waters of the sea! O winding creeks and rivers!
Of you O woods and fields! of you strong mountains of my land!
Of you O prairies! of you gray rocks!
O morning red! O clouds! O rain and snows!
O day and night, passage to you!
O sun and moon and all you stars! Sirius and Jupiter!
Passage to you!

Passage, immediate passage! the blood burns in my veins!
Away O soul! hoist instantly the anchor!
Cut the hawsers—haul out—shake out every sail!
Have we not stood here like trees in the ground long enough?
Have we not grovel'd here long enough, eating and drinking like
       mere brutes?
Have we not darken'd and dazed ourselves with books long enough?

Sail forth—steer for the deep waters only,
Reckless O soul, exploring, I with thee, and thou with me.
For we are bound where mariner has not yet dared to go,
And we will risk the ship, ourselves and all.

O my brave soul!
O farther farther sail!
O daring joy, but safe! are they not all the seas of God?
O farther, farther, farther sail!

THE FORSAKEN MERMAN

Matthew Arnold

Come, dear children, let us away;
Down and away below.
Now my brothers call from the bay;
Now the great winds shoreward blow;
Now the salt tides seaward flow;
Now the wild white horses play,
Champ and chafe and toss in the spray.
Children dear, let us away.
This way, this way.

Call her once before you go.
Call once yet.
In a voice that she will know:
"Margaret! Margaret!"
Children's voices should be dear
(Call once more) to a mother's ear:
Children's voices, wild with pain.
Surely she will come again.
Call her once and come away.
This way, this way.
"Mother dear, we cannot stay."
The wild white horses foam and fret.
Margaret! Margaret!

Come, dear children, come away down.
Call no more.
One last look at the white-wall'd town,
And the little grey church on the windy shore.
Then come down.
She will not come though you call all day.
Come away, come away.

Children dear, was it yesterday
We heard the sweet bells over the bay?
In the caverns where we lay,
Through the surf and through the swell,
The far-off sound of a silver bell?
Sand-strewn caverns, cool and deep,
Where the winds are all asleep;
Where the spent lights quiver and gleam;
Where the salt weed sways in the stream;

Where the sea-beasts rang'd all round
Feed in the ooze of their pasture-ground;
Where the sea-snakes coil and twine,
Dry their mail and bask in the brine;
Where great whales come sailing by,
Sail and sail, with unshut eye,
Round the world for ever and aye?
When did music come this way?
Children dear, was it yesterday?

Children dear, was it yesterday
(Call yet once) that she went away?
Once she sate with you and me,
On a red gold throne in the heart of the sea,
And the youngest sate on her knee.
She comb'd its bright hair, and she tended it well,
When down swung the sound of the far-off bell.
She sigh'd, she look'd up through the clear green sea.
She said: "I must go, for my kinsfolk pray
In the little grey church on the shore to-day.
'Twill be Easter-time in the world—ah me!
And I lose my poor soul, Merman, here with thee."
I said: "Go up, dear heart, through the waves;
Say thy prayer, and come back to the kind sea-caves."
She smil'd, she went up through the surf in the bay.
Children dear, was it yesterday?

Children dear, were we long alone?
"The sea grows stormy, the little ones moan.
Long prayers," I said, "in the world they say.
Come," I said, and we rose through the surf in the bay.
We went up the beach, by the sandy down
Where the sea-stocks bloom, to the white-wall'd town.
Through the narrow pav'd streets, where all was still,
To the little grey church on the windy hill.
From the church came a murmur of folk at their prayers,
For we stood without in the cold blowing airs.
We climb'd on the graves, on the stones, worn with rains,
And we gaz'd up the aisle through the small leaded panes.
She sate by the pillar; we saw her clear:
"Margaret, hist! come quick, we are here.
Dear heart," I said, "we are long alone.
The sea grows stormy, the little ones moan,"
But, ah, she gave me never a look,
For her eyes were seal'd to the holy book.
Loud prays the priest; shut stands the door.

Come away, children, call no more.
Come away, come down, call no more.

Down, down, down.
Down to the depths of the sea.
She sits at her wheel in the humming town,
Singing most joyfully.
Hark, what she sings: "O joy, O joy,
For the humming street, and the child with its toy.
For the priest, and the bell, and the holy well.
For the wheel where I spun,
And the blessed light of the sun."
And so she sings her fill,
Singing most joyfully,
Till the shuttle falls from her hand,
And the whizzing wheel stands still.
She steals to the window, and looks at the sand;
And over the sand at the sea;
And her eyes are set in a stare;
And anon there breaks a sigh,
And anon there drops a tear,
From a sorrow-clouded eye,
And a heart sorrow-laden,
A long, long sigh,
For the cold strange eyes of a little Mermaiden,
And the gleam of her golden hair.

Come away, away children.
Come children, come down.
The hoarse wind blows colder;
Lights shine in the town.
She will start from her slumber
When gusts shake the door;
She will hear the winds howling,
Will hear the waves roar.
We shall see, while above us
The waves roar and whirl,
A ceiling of amber,
A pavement of pearl.
Singing, "Here came a mortal,
But faithless was she.
And alone dwell for ever
The kings of the sea."

But, children, at midnight,
When soft the winds blow;

When clear falls the moonlight;
When spring-tides are low:
When sweet airs come seaward
From heaths starr'd with broom;
And high rocks throw mildly
On the blanch'd sands a gloom:
Up the still, glistening beaches,
Up the creeks we will hie;
Over banks of bright seaweed
The ebb-tide leaves dry.
We will gaze, from the sand-hills,
At the white sleeping town;
At the church on the hill-side—
　And then come back down.
Singing, "There dwells a lov'd one,
But cruel is she.
She left lonely for ever
The kings of the sea."

"CHILDE ROLAND[1]
TO THE DARK TOWER CAME"

Robert Browning

I

My first thought was, he lied in every word,
    That hoary cripple, with malicious eye
    Askance to watch the working of his lie
On mine, and mouth scarce able to afford
Suppression of the glee, that pursed and scored
    Its edge, at one more victim gained thereby.

II

What else should he be set for, with his staff?
    What, save to waylay with his lies, ensnare
    All travellers who might find him posted there,
And ask the road? I guessed what skull-like laugh
Would break, what crutch 'gin write my epitaph
    For pastime in the dusty thoroughfare,

III

If at his counsel I should turn aside
    Into that ominous tract which, all agree,
    Hides the Dark Tower. Yet acquiescingly
I did turn as he pointed: neither pride
Nor hope rekindling at the end descried,
    So much as gladness that some end might be.

IV

For, what with my whole world-wide wandering,
    What with my search drawn out through years, my hope
    Dwindled into a ghost not fit to cope
With that obstreperous joy success would bring,
I hardly tried now to rebuke the spring
    My heart made, finding failure in its scope.

---

[1]Childe Roland, in legend, was a son of King Arthur whose sister was carried away by fairies to the castle of the king of Elfland. He rescues her. In Shakespeare's *King Lear,* Edgar, in feigned madness, sings "Child Rowland to the dark tower came."

V

As when a sick man very near to death
    Seems dead indeed, and feels begin and end
    The tears and takes the farewell of each friend,
And hears one bid the other go, draw breath
Freelier outside, ("since all is o'er," he saith,
    "And the blow fallen no grieving can amend;")

VI

While some discuss if near the other graves
    Be room enough for this, and when a day
    Suits best for carrying the corpse away,
With care about the banners, scarves and staves:
And still the man hears all, and only craves
    He may not shame such tender love and stay.

VII

Thus, I had so long suffered in this quest,
    Heard failure prophesied so oft, been writ
    So many times among "The Band"—to wit,
The knights who to the Dark Tower's search addressed
Their steps—that just to fail as they, seemed best,
    And all the doubt was now—should I be fit?

VIII

So, quiet as despair, I turned from him,
    That hateful cripple, out of his highway
    Into the path he pointed. All the day
Had been a dreary one at best, and dim[2]
Was settling to its close, yet shot one grim
    Red leer to see the plain catch its estray.[3]

IX

For mark! no sooner was I fairly found
    Pledged to the plain, after a pace or two,
    Than, pausing to throw backward a last view
O'er the safe road, 'twas gone; grey plain all round:
Nothing but plain to the horizon's bound.
    I might go on; nought else remained to do

---

[2]Twilight.
[3]Stray (red glow).

X

So, on I went, I think I never saw
    Such starved ignoble nature; nothing throve:
    For flowers—as well expect a cedar grove!
But cockle, spurge, according to their law
Might propagate their kind, with none to awe,
    You'd think; a burr had been[4] a treasure-trove.

XI

No! penury, inertness and grimace,
    In some strange sort, were the land's portion. "See
    Or shut your eyes," said Nature peevishly,
"It nothing skills:[5] I cannot help my case:
'Tis the Last Judgment's fire must cure this place,
    Calcine its clods and set my prisoners[6] free."

XII

If there pushed any ragged thistle-stalk
    Above its mates, the head was chopped; the bents[7]
    Were jealous else. What made those holes and rents
In the dock's harsh swarth leaves,[8] bruised as to balk
All hope of greenness? 'tis a brute must walk
    Pashing[9] their life out, with a brute's intents.

XIII

As for the grass, it grew as scant as hair
    In leprosy; thin dry blades pricked the mud
    Which underneath looked kneaded up with blood.
One stiff blind horse, his every bone a-stare,
Stood stupefied, however he came there:[10]
    Thrust out past service from the devil's stud![11]

[4]Would have been (had it been there).
[5]It doesn't matter, makes no difference.
[6]My possessions, that is, plants that grow in the "clods" (soil).
[7]Stalks of stiff coarse grass.
[8]The dock is a coarse weedy plant.
[9]Smashing.
[10]That is, he looked as if he wondered however he came there.
[11]Place for keeping a group of animals, especially horses.

XIV

Alive? he might be dead for aught I know,
    With that red gaunt and colloped[12] neck a-strain,
    And shut eyes underneath the rusty mane;
Seldom went such grotesqueness with such woe;
I never saw a brute I hated so;
    He must be wicked to deserve such pain.

XV

I shut my eyes and turned them on my heart.
    As a man calls for wine before he fights,
    I asked one draught of earlier, happier sights,
Ere fitly I could hope to play my part.
Think first, fight afterwards—the soldier's art:
    One taste of the old time sets all to rights.

XVI

Not it! I fancied Cuthbert's reddening face[13]
    Beneath its garniture of curly gold,
    Dear fellow, till I almost felt him fold
An arm in mine to fix me to the place,
That way he used. Alas, one night's disgrace!
    Out went my heart's new fire and left it cold.

XVII

Giles then, the soul of honour—there he stands
    Frank as ten years ago when knighted first.
    What honest man should dare (he said) he durst.
Good—but the scene shifts—faugh! what hangman hands
Pin to his breast a parchment? His own bands
    Read it. Poor traitor, spit upon and curst!

XVIII

Better this present than a past like that;
    Back therefore to my darkening path again!
    No sound, no sight as far as eye could strain.

---

[12]Having fatty folds; wrinkled.
[13]Cuthbert and Giles are former companions of Roland.

Will the night send a howlet[14] or a bat?
I asked: when something on the dismal flat[15]
    Came to arrest my thoughts and change their train.

XIX

A sudden little river crossed my path
    As unexpected as a serpent comes.
    No sluggish tide congenial to the glooms;
This, as it frothed by, might have been a bath
For the fiend's glowing hoof[16] —to see the wrath
    Of its black eddy bespate[17] with flakes and spumes.

XX

So petty yet so spiteful! All along,
    Low scrubby alders kneeled down over it;
    Drenched willows flung them headlong in a fit
Of mute despair, a suicidal throng:
The river which had done them all the wrong,
    Whate'er that was, rolled by, deterred no whit.

XXI

Which, while I forded,—good saints, how I feared
    To set my foot upon a dead man's cheek,
    Each step, or feel the spear I thrust to seek
For hollows, tangled in his hair or beard!
—It may have been a water-rat I speared,
    But, ugh! it sounded like a baby's shriek.

XXII

Glad was I when I reached the other bank.
    Now for a better country. Vain presage!
    Who were the strugglers, what war did they wage,
Whose savage trample thus could pad the dank
Soil to a plash?[18] Toads in a poisoned tank,
    Or wild cats in a red-hot iron cage—

[14]Owlet.
[15]Plain.
[16]The cloven hoof often attributed to Satan.
[17]Bespattered.
[18]Puddle.

XXIII

The fight must so have seemed in that fell cirque.[19]
 What penned them there, with all the plain to choose?
 No foot-print leading to that horrid mews,[20]
None out of it. Mad brewage set to work
Their brains, no doubt, like galley-slaves the Turk
 Pits for his pastime, Christians against Jews.

XXIV

And more than that—a furlong on—why, there!
 What bad use was that engine for, that wheel,
 Or brake, not wheel—that harrow fit to reel
Men's bodies out like silk? with all the air
Of Tophet's tool,[21] on earth left unaware,
 Or brought to sharpen its rusty teeth of steel.

XXV

Then came a bit of stubbed ground, once a wood,
 Next a marsh, it would seem, and now mere earth
 Desperate and done with; (so a fool finds mirth,
Makes a thing and then mars it, till his mood
Changes and off he goes!) within a rood—[22]
 Bog, clay and rubble, sand and stark black dearth.

XXVI

Now blotches rankling, coloured gay and grim,
 Now patches where some leanness of the soil's
 Broke into moss or substances like boils;
Then came some palsied oak, a cleft in him
Like a distorted mouth that splits its rim
 Gaping at death, and dies while it recoils.

XXVII

And just as far as ever from the end!
 Nought in the distance but the evening, nought

---

[19]A theatre or arena (a "circle").
[20]Stable or collection of cages.
[21]Tophet was a place near Jerusalem where Jews were supposed to have made human sacrifices (Jeremiah 19:4). Later the place was used to burn rubbish and, partly because bonfires burned continually, became symbolic of the torments of hell.
[22]About one-fourth of an acre.

To point my footstep further! At the thought,
A great black bird, Apollyon's bosom-friend,[23]
Sailed past, nor beat his wide wing dragon-penned[24]
    That brushed my cap—perchance the guide I sought.

XXVIII

For, looking up, aware I somehow grew,
    'Spite of the dusk, the plain had given place
    All round to mountains—with such name to grace
Mere ugly heights and heaps now stolen in view.
How thus they had surprised me,—solve it, you!
    How to get from them was no clearer case.

XXIX

Yet half I seemed to recognize some trick
    Of mischief happened to me, God knows when—
    In a bad dream perhaps. Here ended, then,
Progress this way. When, in the very nick
Of giving up, one time more, came a click
    As when a trap shuts—you're inside the den!

XXX

Burningly it came on me all at once,
    This was the place! those two hills on the right,
    Crouched like two bulls locked horn in horn in fight;
While to the left, a tall scalped mountain . . . Dunce,
Dotard, a-dozing at the very nonce,[25]
    After a life spent training for the sight!

XXXI

What in the midst lay but the Tower itself?
    The round squat turret, blind as the fool's heart,
    Built of brown stone, without a counterpart
In the whole world. The tempest's mocking elf
Points to the shipman thus the unseen shelf
    He strikes on, only when the timbers start.[26]

[23]Apollyon, or "The Destroyer," according to Revelation 9:11, is the "angel of the bottom-less pit."
[24]Having the feathers (pens) of a dragon.
[25]Occasion.
[26]Become loosened or forced out of place.

XXXII

Not see? because of night perhaps?—why, day
 Came back again for that! before it left,
 The dying sunset kindled through a cleft:
The hills, like giants at a hunting, lay,
Chin upon hand, to see the game at bay,—
 "Now stab and end the creature—to the heft!"

XXXIII

Not hear? when noise was everywhere! it tolled
 Increasing like a bell. Names in my ears
 Of all the lost adventurers my peers,—
How such a one was strong, and such was bold,
And such was fortunate, yet each of old
 Lost, lost! one moment knelled the woe of years.

XXXIV

There they stood, ranged along the hillsides, met
 To view the last of me, a living frame
 For one more picture! in a sheet of flame
I saw them and I knew them all. And yet
Dauntless the slug-horn[27] to my lips I set,
 And blew. *"Childe Roland to the Dark Tower came."*

[27]Trumpet.

THE STORY OF
KŌGI THE PRIEST

Lafcadio Hearn

NEARLY ONE THOUSAND years ago there lived in the famous temple called Miidera, at Ōtsu in the province of Ōmi, a learned priest named Kōgi. He was a great artist. He painted, with almost equal skill, pictures of the Buddhas, pictures of beautiful scenery, and pictures of animals or birds; but he liked best to paint fishes. Whenever the weather was fair, and religious duty permitted, he would go to Lake Biwa, and hire fishermen to catch fish for him, without injuring them in any way, so that he could paint them afterwards as they swam about in a large vessel of water. After having made pictures of them, and fed them like pets, he would set them free again,—taking them back to the lake himself. His pictures of fish at last became so famous that people travelled from great distances to see them. But the most wonderful of all his drawings of fish was not drawn from life, but was made from the memory of a dream. For one day, as he sat by the lake-side to watch the fishes swimming, Kōgi had fallen into a doze, and had dreamed that he was playing with the fishes under the water. After he awoke, the memory of the dream remained so clear that he was able to paint it; and this painting, which he hung up in the alcove of his own room in the temple, he called "Dream-Carp."

Kōgi could never be persuaded to sell any of his pictures of fish. He was willing to part with his drawings of landscapes, of birds, or of flowers; but he said that he would not sell a picture of living fish to any one who was cruel enough to kill or to eat fish. And as the persons who wanted to buy his paintings were all fish-eaters, their offers of money could not tempt him.

One summer Kōgi fell sick; and after a week's illness he lost all power of speech and movement, so that he seemed to be dead. But after his funeral service had been performed, his disciples discovered some warmth in the body, and decided to postpone the burial for awhile, and to keep watch by the seeming corpse. In the afternoon of the same day he suddenly revived, and questioned the watchers, asking:—

"How long have I remained without knowledge of the world?"

"More than three days," an acolyte made answer. "We thought that you were dead; and this morning your friends and parishioners assembled in the temple for your funeral service. We performed the service;

but afterwards, finding that your body was not altogether cold, we put off the burial; and now we are very glad that we did so."

Kōgi nodded approvingly: then he said:—

"I want some one of you to go immediately to the house of Taira no Suké, where the young men are having a feast at the present moment —(they are eating fish and drinking wine),—and say to them:—'Our master has revived; and he begs that you will be so good as to leave your feast, and to call upon him without delay, because he has a wonderful story to tell you.' ... At the same time"—continued Kōgi—"observe what Suké and his brothers are doing;—see whether they are not feasting as I say."

Then an acolyte went at once to the house of Taira no Suké, and was surprised to find that Suké and his brother Jūrō, with their attendant, Kamori, were having a feast, just as Kōgi had said. But, on receiving the message, all three immediately left their fish and wine, and hastened to the temple. Kōgi, lying upon the couch to which he had been removed, received them with a smile of welcome; and, after some pleasant words had been exchanged, he said to Suké:—

"Now, my friend, please reply to some questions that I am going to ask you. First of all, kindly tell me whether you did not buy a fish to-day from the fisherman Bunshi."

"Why, yes," replied Suké—"but how did you know?"

"Please wait a moment," said the priest. ... "That fisherman Bunshi to-day entered your gate, with a fish three feet long in his basket: it was early in the afternoon, just after you and Jūrō had begun a game of go;—and Kamori was watching the game, and eating a peach—was he not?"

"That is true," exclaimed Suké and Kamori together, with increasing surprise.

"And when Kamori saw that big fish," proceeded Kōgi, "he agreed to buy it at once; and, besides paying the price of the fish, he also gave Bunshi some peaches, in a dish, and three cups of wine. Then the cook was called; and he came and looked at the fish, and admired it; and then, by your order, he sliced it and prepared it for your feast. ... Did not all this happen just as I have said?"

"Yes," responded Suké; "but we are very much astonished that you should know what happened in our house to-day. Please tell us how you learned these matters."

"Well, now for my story," said the priest. "You are aware that almost everybody believed me to be dead;—you yourselves attended my funeral service. But I did not think three days ago, that I was at all dangerously ill: I remember only that I felt weak and very hot, and that I wanted to go out into the air to cool myself. And I thought that I got up from my bed, with a great effort, and went out,—supporting myself with a stick. ... Perhaps this may have been imagination; but you will

presently be able to judge the truth for yourselves: I am going to relate
everything exactly as it appeared to happen. . . . As soon as I got outside
of the house, into the bright air, I began to feel quite light,—light as
a bird flying away from the net or the basket in which it has been
confined. I wandered on and on till I reached the lake; and the water
looked so beautiful and blue that I felt a great desire to have a swim.
I took off my clothes, and jumped in, and began to swim about; and I
was astonished to find that I could swim very fast and very skilfully,
—although before my sickness I had always been a very poor swimmer.
. . . You think that I am only telling you a foolish dream—but listen!
. . . While I was wondering at this new skill of mine, I perceived many
beautiful fishes swimming below me and around me; and I felt suddenly envious of their happiness,—reflecting that, no matter how good
a swimmer a man may become, he never can enjoy himself under the
water as a fish can. Just then, a very big fish lifted its head above the
surface in front of me, and spoke to me with the voice of a man, saying:
—'That wish of yours can very easily be satisfied: please wait there a
moment!' The fish then went down, out of sight; and I waited. After a
few minutes there came up, from the bottom of the lake,—riding on the
back of the same big fish that had spoken to me,—a man wearing the
headdress and the ceremonial robes of a prince; and the man said to
me:—'I come to you with a message from the Dragon-King, who knows
of your desire to enjoy for a little time the condition of a fish. As you
have saved the lives of many fish, and have always shown compassion
to living creatures, the God now bestows upon you the attire of the
Golden Carp, so that you will be able to enjoy the pleasures of the
Water-World. But you must be very careful not to eat any fish, or any
food prepared from fish,—no matter how nice may be the smell of it;
—and you must also take great care not to get caught by the fishermen,
or to hurt your body in any way.' With these words, the messenger and
his fish went below and vanished in the deep water. I looked at myself,
and saw that my whole body had become covered with scales that shone
like gold;—I saw that I had fins;—I found that I had actually been
changed into a Golden Carp. Then I knew that I could swim wherever
I pleased.

"Thereafter it seemed to me that I swam away, and visited many
beautiful places. [*Here, in the original narrative, are introduced some
verses describing the Eight Famous Attractions of the Lake of Ōmi;—
"Ōmi-Hakkei."*] Sometimes I was satisfied only to look at the sunlight
dancing over the blue water, or to admire the beautiful reflection of
hills and trees upon still surfaces sheltered from the wind. . . . I remember especially the coast of an island—either Okitsushima or Chikubu-
shima—reflected in the water like a red wall. . . . Sometimes I would
approach the shore so closely that I could see the faces and hear the
voices of people passing by; sometimes I would sleep on the water until

startled by the sound of approaching oars. At night there were beautiful moonlight-views; but I was frightened more than once by the approaching torchfires of the fishing-boats of Katasé. When the weather was bad, I would go below,—far down,—even a thousand feet,—and play at the bottom of the lake. But after two or three days of this wandering pleasure, I began to feel very hungry; and I returned to this neighborhood in the hope of finding something to eat. Just at that time the fisherman Bunshi happened to be fishing; and I approached the hook which he had let down into the water. There was some fish-food upon it that was good to smell. I remembered in the same moment the warning of the Dragon-King, and swam away, saying to myself:—'In any event I must not eat food containing fish;—I am a disciple of the Buddha.' Yet after a little while my hunger became so intense that I could not resist the temptation; and I swam back again to the hook, thinking,—'Even if Bunshi should catch me, he would not hurt me;— he is my old friend.' I was not able to loosen the bait from the hook; and the pleasant smell of the food was too much for my patience; and I swallowed the whole thing at a gulp. Immediately after I did so, Bunshi pulled in his line, and caught me. I cried out to him, 'What are you doing?—you hurt me!'—but he did not seem to hear me, and he quickly put a string through my jaws. Then he threw me into his basket, and took me to your house. When the basket was opened there, I saw you and Jūrō playing *go* in the south room, and Kamori watching you— eating a peach the while. All of you presently came out upon the veranda to look at me; and you were delighted to see such a big fish. I called out to you as loud as I could:—'I am not a fish!—I am Kōgi— Kōgi the priest! please let me go back to my temple!' But you clapped your hands for gladness, and paid no attention to my words. Then your cook carried me into the kitchen, and threw me down violently upon a cutting-board, where a terribly sharp knife was lying. With his left hand he pressed me down, and with his right hand he took up that knife,—and I screamed to him:—'How can you kill me so cruelly! I am a disciple of the Buddha!—help! help!' But in the same instant I felt his knife dividing me—a frightful pain!—and then I suddenly awoke, and found myself here in the temple."

When the priest had thus finished his story, the brothers wondered at it; and Suké said to him:—"I now remember noticing that the jaws of the fish were moving all the time that we were looking at it; but we did not hear any voice. . . . Now I must send a servant to the house with orders to throw the remainder of that fish into the lake."

Kōgi soon recovered from his illness, and lived to paint many more pictures. It is related that, long after his death, some of his fish-pictures once happened to fall into the lake, and that the figures of the fish immediately detached themselves from the silk or the paper upon which they had been painted, and swam away!

NIGHT-SEA JOURNEY

John Barth

ONE WAY OR ANOTHER, no matter which theory of our journey is correct, it's myself I address; to whom I rehearse as to a stranger our history and condition, and will disclose my secret hope though I sink for it.

"Is the journey my invention? Do the night, the sea, exist at all, I ask myself, apart from my experience of them? Do I myself exist, or is this a dream? Sometimes I wonder. And if I am, who am I? The Heritage I supposedly transport? But how can I be both vessel and contents? Such are the questions that beset my intervals of rest.

"My trouble is, I lack conviction. Many accounts of our situation seem plausible to me—where and what we are, why we swim and whither. But implausible ones as well, perhaps especially those, I must admit as possibly correct. Even likely. If at times, in certain humors—striking in unison, say, with my neighbors and chanting with them 'Onward! Upward!'—I have supposed that we have after all a common Maker, Whose nature and motives we may not know, but Who engendered us in some mysterious wise and launched us forth toward some end known but to Him—if (for a moodslength only) I have been able to entertain such notions, very popular in certain quarters, it is because our night-sea journey partakes of their absurdity. One might even say: I can believe them *because* they are absurd.

"Has that been said before?

"Another paradox: it appears to be these recesses from swimming that sustain me in the swim. Two measures onward and upward, flailing with the rest, then I float exhausted and dispirited, brood upon the night, the sea, the journey, while the flood bears me a measure back and down: slow progress, but I live, I live, and make my way, aye, past many a drownèd comrade in the end, stronger, worthier than I, victims of their unremitting *joie de nager*. I have seen the best swimmers of my generation go under. Numberless the number of the dead! Thousands drown as I think this thought, millions as I rest before returning to the swim. And scores, hundreds of millions have expired since we surged forth, brave in our innocence, upon our dreadful way. 'Love! Love!' we sang then, a quarter-billion strong, and churned the warm sea white with joy of swimming! Now all are gone down—the buoyant, the sodden, leaders and followers, all gone under, while wretched I swim on. Yet these same reflective intervals that keep me afloat have led me into wonder, doubt, despair—strange emotions for a swimmer!

—have led me, even, to suspect . . . that our night-sea journey is without meaning.

"Indeed, if I have yet to join the hosts of the suicides, it is because (fatigue apart) I find it no meaningfuller to drown myself than to go on swimming.

"I know that there are those who seem actually to enjoy the night-sea; who claim to love swimming for its own sake, or sincerely believe that 'reaching the Shore,' 'transmitting the Heritage' (*Whose* Heritage, I'd like to know? And to whom?) is worth the staggering cost. I do not. Swimming itself I find at best not actively unpleasant, more often tiresome, not infrequently a torment. Arguments from function and design don't impress me: granted that we can and do swim, that in a manner of speaking our long tails and streamlined heads are 'meant for' swimming; it by no means follows—for me, at least—that we *should* swim, or otherwise endeavor to 'fulfill our destiny.' Which is to say, Someone Else's destiny, since ours, so far as I can see, is merely to perish, one way or another, soon or late. The heartless zeal of our (departed) leaders, like the blind ambition and good cheer of my own youth, appalls me now; for the death of my comrades I am inconsolable. If the night-sea journey has justification, it is not for us swimmers ever to discover it.

"Oh, to be sure, 'Love!' one heard on every side: 'Love it is that drives and sustains us!' I translate: we don't know *what* drives and sustains us, only that we are most miserably driven and, imperfectly, sustained. *Love* is how we call our ignorance of what whips us. 'To reach the Shore,' then: but what if the Shore exists in the fancies of us swimmers merely, who dream it to account for the dreadful fact that we swim, have always and only swum, and continue swimming without respite (myself excepted) until we die? Supposing even that there *were* a Shore —that, as a cynical companion of mine once imagined, we rise from the drowned to discover all those vulgar superstitions and exalted metaphors to be literal truth: the giant Maker of us all, the Shores of Light beyond our night-sea journey!—whatever would a swimmer do there? The fact is, when we imagine the Shore, what comes to mind is just the opposite of our condition: no more night, no more sea, no more journeying. In short, the blissful estate of the drowned.

" 'Ours not to stop and think; ours but to swim and sink. . . .' Because a moment's thought reveals the pointlessness of swimming. 'No matter,' I've heard some say, even as they gulped their last: 'The night-sea journey may be absurd, but here we swim, will-we nill-we, against the flood, onward and upward, toward a Shore that may not exist and couldn't be reached if it did.' The thoughtful swimmer's choices, then, they say, are two: give over thrashing and go under for good, or embrace the absurdity; affirm in and for itself the night-sea journey; swim on with neither motive nor destination, for the sake of swimming, and

compassionate moreover with your fellow swimmer, we being all at sea
and equally in the dark. I find neither course acceptable. If not even
the hypothetical Shore can justify a sea-full of drowned comrades, to
speak of the swim-in-itself as somehow doing so strikes me as obscene.
I continue to swim—but only because blind habit, blind instinct, blind
fear of drowning are still more strong than the horror of our journey.
And if on occasion I have assisted a fellow-thrasher, joined in the cheers
and songs, even passed along to others strokes of genius from the
drowned great, it's that I shrink by temperament from making myself
conspicuous. To paddle off in one's own direction, assert one's indepen-
dent right-of-way, overrun one's fellows without compunction, or dedi-
cate oneself entirely to pleasures and diversions without regard for
conscience—I can't finally condemn those who journey in this wise; in
half my moods I envy them and despise the weak vitality that keeps
me from following their example. But in reasonabler moments I re-
mind myself that it's their very freedom and self-responsibility I reject,
as more dramatically absurd, in our senseless circumstances, than
tailing along in conventional fashion. Suicides, rebels, affirmers of the
paradox—nay-sayers and yea-sayers alike to our fatal journey—I
finally shake my head at them. And splash sighing past their corpses,
one by one, as past a hundred sorts of others: friends, enemies, brothers;
fools, sages, brutes—and nobodies, million upon million. I envy them
all.

"A poor irony: that I, who find abhorrent and tautological the doctrine of survival of the fittest (*fitness* meaning, in my experience, nothing more than survival-ability, a talent whose only demonstration is
the fact of survival, but whose chief ingredients seem to be strength,
guile, callousness), may be the sole remaining swimmer! But the doctrine is false as well as repellent: Chance drowns the worthy with the
unworthy, bears up the unfit with the fit by whatever definition, and
makes the night-sea journey essentially *haphazard* as well as murder-
ous and unjustified.

" 'You only swim once.' Why bother, then?

" 'Except ye drown, ye shall not reach the Shore of Light.' Poppycock.

"One of my late companions—that same cynic with the curious
fancy, among the first to drown—entertained us with odd conjectures
while we waited to begin our journey. A favorite theory of his was that
the Father does exist, and did indeed make us and the sea we swim—
but not a-purpose or even consciously; He made us, as it were, despite
Himself, as we make waves with every tail-thrash, and may be unaware of our existence. Another was that He knows we're here but
doesn't care what happens to us, inasmuch as He creates (voluntarily
or not) other seas and swimmers at more or less regular intervals. In
bitterer moments, such as just before he drowned, my friend even
supposed that our Maker wished us unmade; there was indeed a Shore,

he'd argue, which could save at least some of us from drowning and toward which it was our function to struggle—but for reasons unknowable to us He wanted desperately to prevent our reaching that happy place and fulfilling our destiny. Our 'Father,' in short, was our adversary and would-be killer! No less outrageous, and offensive to traditional opinion, were the fellow's speculations on the nature of our Maker: that He might well be no swimmer Himself at all, but some sort of monstrosity, perhaps even tailless; that He might be stupid, malicious, insensible, perverse, or asleep and dreaming; that the end for which He created and launched us forth, and which we flagellate ourselves to fathom, was perhaps immoral, even obscene. Et cetera, et cetera: there was no end to the chap's conjectures, or the impoliteness of his fancy; I have reason to suspect that his early demise, whether planned by 'our Maker' or not, was expedited by certain fellow-swimmers indignant at his blasphemies.

"In other moods, however (he was as given to moods as I), his theorizing would become half-serious, so it seemed to me, especially upon the subjects of Fate and Immortality, to which our youthful conversations often turned. Then his harangues, if no less fantastical, grew solemn and obscure, and if he was still baiting us, his passion undid the joke. His objection to popular opinions of the hereafter, he would declare, was their claim to general validity. Why need believers hold that *all* the drowned rise to be judged at journey's end, and non-believers that drowning is final without exception? In *his* opinion (so he'd vow at least), nearly everyone's fate was permanent death; indeed he took a sour pleasure in supposing that every 'Maker' made thousands of separate seas in His creative lifetime, each populated like ours with millions of swimmers, and that in almost every instance both sea and swimmers were utterly annihilated, whether accidentally or by malevolent design. (Nothing if not pluralistic, he imagined there might be millions and billions of 'Fathers,' perhaps in some 'night-sea' of their own!) However—and here he turned infidels against him with the faithful—he professed to believe that in possibly a single night-sea per thousand, say, one of its quarter-billion swimmers (that is, one swimmer in two hundred fifty billions) achieved a qualified immortality. In some cases the rate might be slightly higher; in others it was vastly lower, for just as there are swimmers of every degree of proficiency, including some who drown before the journey starts, unable to swim at all, and others created drowned, as it were, so he imagined what can only be termed impotent Creators, Makers unable to Make, as well as uncommonly fertile ones and all grades between. And it pleased him to deny any necessary relation between a Maker's productivity and His other virtues—including, even, the quality of His creatures.

"I could go on (*he* surely did) with his elaboration of these mad notions—such as that swimmers in other night-seas needn't be of our kind; that Makers themselves might belong to different *species,* so to speak; that our particular Maker mightn't Himself be immortal, or that we might be not only His emissaries but His 'immortality,' continuing His life and our own, transmogrified, beyond our individual deaths. Even this modified immortality (meaningless to me) he conceived as relative and contingent, subject to accident or deliberate termination: his pet hypothesis was that Makers and swimmers *each generate the other*—against all odds, their number being so great— and that any given 'immortality-chain' could terminate after any number of cycles, so that what was 'immortal' (still speaking relatively) was only the cyclic process of incarnation, which itself might have a beginning and an end. Alternatively he liked to imagine cycles within cycles, either finite or infinite: for example, the 'night-sea,' as it were, in which Makers 'swam' and created night-seas and swimmers like ourselves, might be the creation of a larger Maker, Himself one of many, Who in turn et cetera. Time itself he regarded as relative to our experience, like magnitude: who knew but what, with each thrash of our tails, minuscule seas and swimmers, whole eternities, came to pass—as ours, perhaps, and our Maker's Maker's, was elapsing between the strokes of some supertail, in a slower order of time?

Naturally I hooted with the others at this nonsense. We were young then, and had only the dimmest notion of what lay ahead; in our ignorance we imagined night-sea journeying to be a positively heroic enterprise. Its meaning and value we never questioned; to be sure, some must go down by the way, a pity no doubt, but to win a race requires that others lose, and like all my fellows I took for granted that I would be the winner. We milled and swarmed, impatient to be off, never mind where or why, only to try our youth against the realities of night and sea; if we indulged the skeptic at all, it was as a droll, half-contemptible mascot. When he died in the initial slaughter, no one cared.

"And even now I don't subscribe to all his views—but I no longer scoff. The horror of our history has purged me of opinions, as of vanity, confidence, spirit, charity, hope, vitality, everything—except dull dread and a kind of melancholy, stunned persistence. What leads me to recall his fancies is my growing suspicion that I, of all swimmers, may be the sole survivor of this fell journey, tale-bearer of a generation. This suspicion, together with the recent sea-change, suggests to me now that nothing is impossible, not even my late companion's wildest visions, and brings me to a certain desperate resolve, the point of my chronicling.

"Very likely I have lost my senses. The carnage at our setting out; our decimation by whirlpool, poisoned cataract, sea-convulsion; the panic stampedes, mutinies, slaughters, mass suicides; the mounting evidence that none will survive the journey—add to these anguish and fatigue; it were a miracle if sanity stayed afloat. Thus I admit, with the other possibilities, that the present sweetening and calming of the sea, and what seems to be a kind of vasty presence, song, or summons from the near upstream, may be hallucinations of disordered sensibility. . . .

"Perhaps, even, I am drowned already. Surely I was never meant for the rough-and-tumble of the swim; not impossibly I perished at the outset and have only imaged the night-sea journey from some final deep. In any case, I'm no longer young, and it is we spent old swimmers, disabused of every illusion, who are most vulnerable to dreams.

"Sometimes I think I am my drowned friend.

"Out with it: I've begun to believe, not only that *She* exists, but that She lies not far ahead, and stills the sea, and draws me Herward! Aghast, I recollect his maddest notion: that our destination (which existed, mind, in but one night-sea out of hundreds and thousands) was no Shore, as commonly conceived, but a mysterious being, indescribable except by paradox and vaguest figure: wholly different from us swimmers, yet our complement; the death of us, yet our salvation and resurrection; simultaneously our journey's end, mid-point, and commencement; not membered and thrashing like us, but a motionless or hugely gliding sphere of unimaginable dimension; self-contained, yet dependent absolutely, in some wise, upon the chance (always monstrously improbable) that one of us will survive the night-sea journey and reach . . . Her! *Her,* he called it, or *She,* which is to say, Other-than-a-he. I shake my head; the thing is too preposterous; it is myself I talk to, to keep my reason in this awful darkness. There is no She! There is no You! I rave to myself; it's Death alone that hears and summons. To the drowned, all seas are calm. . . .

"Listen: my friend maintained that in every order of creation there are two sorts of creators, contrary yet complementary, one of which gives rise to seas and swimmers, the other to the Night-which-contains-the-sea and to What-waits-at-the-journey's-end: the former, in short, to destiny, the latter to destination (and both profligately, involuntarily, perhaps indifferently or unwittingly). The 'purpose' of the night-sea journey—but not necessarily of the journeyer or of either Maker!—my friend could describe only in abstractions: *consummation, transfiguration, union of contraries, transcension of categories.* When we laughed, he would shrug and admit that he understood the business no better than we, and thought it ridiculous, dreary, possibly obscene. 'But one of you,' he'd add with his wry smile, 'may be the Hero destined to complete the night-sea journey and be one with Her. Chances are, of course, you won't make it.' He himself, he declared, was not even going to try; the whole idea repelled him; if we chose to dismiss it as an ugly fiction, so much the better for us; thrash, splash, and be merry, we were soon enough drowned. But there it was, he could not say how he knew or why he bothered to tell us, any more that he could say what would happen after She and Hero, Shore and Swimmer, 'merged identities' to become something both and neither. He quite agreed with me that if the issue of that magical union had no memory of the night-sea journey, for example, it enjoyed a poor sort of immortality; even poorer if, as he rather imagined, a swimmer-hero plus a She equaled or became merely another Maker of future night-seas and the rest, at such incredible expense of life. This being the case—he was persuaded it was—the merciful thing to do was refuse to participate; the genuine heroes, in his opinion, were the suicides, and the hero of heroes would be the swimmer who, in the very presence of the Other, refused Her proffered 'immortality' and thus put an end to at least one cycle of catastrophes.

"How we mocked him! Our moment came, we hurtled forth, pretending to glory in the adventure, thrashing, singing, cursing, strangling, rationalizing, rescuing, killing, inventing rules and stories and relationships, giving up, struggling on, but dying all, and still in darkness, until only a battered remnant was left to croak 'Onward, upward,' like a bitter echo. Then they too fell silent—victims, I can only presume, of the last frightful wave—and the moment came when I also, utterly desolate and spent, thrashed my last and gave myself over to the current, to sink or float as might be, but swim no more. Whereupon, marvelous to tell, in an instant the sea grew still! Then warmly, gently, the great tide turned, began to bear me, as it does now, onward and upward will-I nill-I, like a flood of joy—and I recalled with dismay my dead friend's teaching.

"I am not deceived. This new emotion is Her doing; the desire that possesses me is Her bewitchment. Lucidity passes from me; in a moment I'll cry 'Love!' bury myself in Her side, and be 'transfigured.' Which is to say, I die already; this fellow transported by passion is not I; I *am he who abjures and rejects the night-sea journey!* I. . . .

"I am all love. 'Come!' She whispers, and I have no will.

"You who I may be about to become, whatever You are: with the last twitch of my real self I beg You to listen. It is *not* love that sustains me! No; though Her magic makes me burn to sing the contrary, and though I drown even now for the blasphemy, I will say truth. What has fetched me across this dreadful sea is a single hope, gift of my poor dead comrade: that You may be stronger-willed than I, and that by sheer force of concentration I may transmit to You, along with Your official Heritage, a private legacy of awful recollection and negative resolve. Mad as it may be, my dream is that some unimaginable embodiment of myself (or myself plus Her if that's how it must be) will come to find itself expressing, in however garbled or radical a translation, some reflection of these reflections. If against all odds this comes to pass, may You to whom, through whom I speak, do what I cannot: terminate this aimless, brutal business! Stop Your hearing against Her song! Hate love!

"Still alive, afloat, afire. Farewell then my penultimate hope: that one may be sunk for direst blasphemy on the very shore of the Shore. Can it be (my old friend would smile) that only utterest nay-sayers survive the night? But even that were Sense, and there is no sense, only senseless love, senseless death. Whoever echoes these reflections: be more courageous than their author! An end to night-sea journeys! Make no more! And forswear me when I shall forswear myself, deny myself, plunge into Her who summons, singing . . .
    " 'Love! Love! Love!' "

PARAGUAY

Donald Barthelme

THE UPPER PART of the plain that we had crossed the day before was now white with snow, and it was evident that there was a storm raging behind us and that we had only just crossed the Burji La in time to escape it. We camped in a slight hollow at Sekbachan, eighteen miles from Malik Mar, the night as still as the previous one and the temperature the same; it seemed as if the Deosai Plains were not going to be so formidable as they had been described; but the third day a storm of hail, sleet, and snow alternately came at noon when we began to ascend the Sari Sangar Pass, 14,200 feet, and continued with only a few minutes' intermission till four o' clock. The top of the pass is a fairly level valley containing two lakes, their shores formed of boulders that seemed impossible to ride over. The men slid and stumbled so much that I would not let anyone lead my pony for fear of pulling him over; he was old and slow but perfectly splendid here, picking his way among the rocks without a falter. At the summit there is a cairn on which each man threw a stone, and here it is customary to give payment to the coolies. I paid each man his agreed-upon wage, and alone, began the descent. Ahead was Paraguay.[1]

Where Paraguay Is
    Thus I found myself in a strange country. This Paraguay is not the Paraguay that exists on our maps. It is not to be found on the continent,

---

[1]Quoted from *A Summer Ride Through Western Tibet,* by Jane E. Duncan, Collins, London, 1906. Slightly altered.

South America; it is not a political subdivision of that continent, with a population of 2,161,000 and a capital city named Asunción. This Paraguay exists elsewhere. Now, moving toward the first of the "silver cities," I was tired but also elated and alert. Flights of white meat moved through the sky overhead in the direction of the dim piles of buildings.

Jean Mueller

Entering the city I was approached, that first day, by a dark girl wrapped in a red shawl. The edges of the shawl were fringed, and the tip of each strand of fringe was a bob of silver. The girl at once placed her hands on my hips, standing facing me; she smiled, and exerted a slight pull. I was claimed as her guest; her name was Jean Mueller. *"Teníamos grandes deseos de conocerlo,"* she said. I asked how she knew I had arrived and she said, "Everyone knows." We then proceeded to her house, a large, modern structure some distance from the center of the city; there I was shown into a room containing a bed, a desk, a chair, bookcases, a fireplace, a handsome piano in a cherrywood case. I was told that when I had rested I might join her downstairs and might then meet her husband; before leaving the room she sat down before the piano, and, almost mischievously, played a tiny sonata of Bibblemann's.

Temperature

Temperature controls activity to a remarkable degree. By and large, adults here raise their walking speed and show more spontaneous movement as the temperature rises. But the temperature-dependent pattern of activity is complex. For instance, the males move twice as fast at 60 degrees as they do at 35 degrees, but above 60 degrees speed decreases. The females show more complicated behavior; they increase spontaneous activity as the temperature rises from 40 to 48 degrees, become less active between 49 and 66 degrees, and above 66 degrees again go into a rising tempo of spontaneous movements up to the lethal temperature of 77 degrees. Temperature also (here as elsewhere) plays a critical role in the reproductive process. In the so-called "silver cities" there is a particular scale—66, 67, 68, 69 degrees—at which intercourse occurs (and only within that scale). In the "gold" areas, the scale does not, apparently, apply.

Herko Mueller

Herko Mueller walks through gold and silver leaves, awarded, in the summer months, to those who have produced the best pastiche of the emotions. He is smiling because he did not win one of these prizes, which the people of Paraguay seek to avoid. He is tall, brown, wears a funny short beard, and is fond of zippered suits in brilliant colors:

yellow, green, violet. He is, professionally, an arbiter of comedy. "A sort of drama critic?" "More what you would term an umpire. The members of the audience are given a set of rules and the rules constitute the comedy. Our comedies seek to reach the imagination. When you are looking at something, you cannot imagine it." In the evenings I have wet sand to walk upon—long stretches of beach with the sea tasting the edges. Getting back into my clothes after a swim, I discover a strange thing: a sand dollar under my shirt. It is strange because this sand is sifted twice daily to remove impurities and maintain whiteness. And the sea itself, the New Sea, is not programmed for echinoderms.

Error

A government error resulting in the death of a statistically insignificant portion of the population (less than one-fortieth of one per cent) has made people uneasy. A skelp of questions and answers is fused at high temperature (1400° C) and then passed through a series of protracted caresses. Amelioration of the condition results. Paraguay is not old. It is new, a new country. Rough sketches suggest its "look." Heavy yellow drops like pancake batter fall from its sky. I hold a bouquet of umbrellas in each hand. A phrase of Herko Mueller's: *"Y un 60% son mestizos: gloria, orgullo, presente y futuro del Paraguay"* (" ... the glory, pride, present and future of Paraguay"). The country's existence is "predictive," he says, and I myself have noticed a sort of frontier ambience. There are problems. The problem of shedding skin. Thin discarded shells like disposable plastic gloves are found in the street.

Rationalization

The problems of art. New artists have been obtained. These do not object to, and indeed argue enthusiastically for, the rationalization process. Production is up. Quality-control devices have been installed at those points where the interests of artists and audience intersect. Shipping and distribution have been improved out of all recognition. (It is in this area, they say in Paraguay, that traditional practices were most blameworthy.) The rationalized art is dispatched from central art dumps to regional art dumps, and from there into the lifestreams of cities. Each citizen is given as much art as his system can tolerate. Marketing considerations have not been allowed to dictate product mix; rather, each artist is encouraged to maintain, in his software, highly personal, even idiosyncratic, standards (the so-called "hand of the artist" concept). Rationalization produces simpler circuits and, therefore, a saving in hardware. Each artist's product is translated into a statement in symbolic logic. The statement is then "minimized" by various clever methods. The simpler statement is translated back into the design of a simpler circuit. Foamed by a number of techniques, the art is then run through heavy steel rollers. Flip-flop switches control its further development. Sheet art is generally dried in smoke and is dark brown in color. Bulk art is air-dried, and changes color in particular historical epochs.

Skin

Ignoring a letter from the translator Jean sat on a rubber pad doing exercises designed to loosen the skin. Scores of diamond-shaped lights abraded her arms and legs. The light placed a pattern of false information in those zones most susceptible to tearing. Whistling noises accompanied the lights. The process of removing the leg skin is private. Tenseness is eased by the application of a cream, heavy yellow drops like pancake batter. I held several umbrellas over her legs. A man across the street pretending not to watch us. Then the skin placed in the green official receptacles.

The Wall

Our design for the lift tower left us with a vast blind wall of *in situ* concrete. There was thus the danger of having a dreary expanse of blankness in that immensely important part of the building. A solution had to be found. The great wall space would provide an opportunity for a gesture of thanks to the people of Paraguay; a stone would be placed in front of it, and, instead of standing in the shadows, the Stele of the Measures would be brought there also. The wall would be divided, by means of softly worn paths, into doors. These, varying in size from the very large to the very small, would have different colors and thicknesses. Some would open, some would not, and this would change from week to week, or from hour to hour, or in accord with sounds made by people standing in front of them. Long lines or tracks would run from the doors into the roaring public spaces.[2]

Silence

In the larger stores silence (damping materials) is sold in paper sacks like cement. Similarly, the softening of language usually lamented as a falling off from former practice is in fact a clear response to the proliferation of surfaces and stimuli. Imprecise sentences lessen the strain of close tolerances. Silence is also available in the form of white noise. The extension of white noise to the home by means of leased wire from a central generating point has been useful, Herko says. The analogous establishment of "white space" in a system paralleling the existing park system has also been beneficial. Anechoic chambers placed randomly about the city (on the model of telephone booths) are said to have actually saved lives. Wood is becoming rare. They are now paying

---

[2]Quoted from *The Modular,* by Le Corbusier, M.I.T. Press, Cambridge, 1954. Slightly altered.

for yellow pine what was formerly paid for rosewood. Relational methods govern the layout of cities. Curiously, in some of the most successful projects the design has been swung upon small collections of rare animals spaced (on the lost-horse principle) on a lack of grid. Carefully calculated mixes: mambas, the black wrasse, the giselle. Electrolytic jelly exhibiting a capture ratio far in excess of standard is used to fix the animals in place.

Terror

We rushed down to the ends of the waves, apertures through which threatening lines might be seen. Arbiters registered serial numbers of the (complex of threats) with ticks on a great, brown board. Jean meanwhile, unaffected, was casting about on the beach for driftwood, brown washed pieces of wood laced with hundreds of tiny hairline cracks. Such is the smoothness of surfaces in Paraguay that anything not smooth is valuable. She explains to me that in demanding (and receiving) explanations you are once more brought to a stop. You have got, really, no farther than you were before. "Therefore we try to keep everything open, go forward avoiding the final explanation. If we inadvertently receive it, we are instructed to 1) pretend that it is just another error, or 2) misunderstand it. Creative misunderstanding is crucial." Creation of new categories of anxiety which must be bandaged or "patched." The expression "put a patch on it." There are "hot" and "cold" patches and specialists in the application of each. Rhathymia is the preferred mode of presentation of the self.

The Temple

Turning sharply to the left I came upon, in a grove of trees, a temple of some sort, abandoned, littered with empty boxes, the floor coated with a thin layer of lime. I prayed. Then drawing out my flask I refreshed myself with apple juice. Everyone in Paraguay has the same fingerprints. There are crimes but people chosen at random are punished for them. Everyone is liable for everything. An extension of the principle, there but for the grace of God go I. Sexual life is very free. There are rules but these are like the rules of chess, intended to complicate and enrich the game. I made love to Jean Mueller while her husband watched. There have been certain technical refinements. The procedures we use (called here "impalement") are used in Paraguay but also new techniques I had never before encountered, "dimidiation" and "quartering." These I found very refreshing.

Microminiaturization

Microminiaturization leaves enormous spaces to be filled. Disposability of the physical surround has psychological consequences. The example of the child's anxiety occasioned by the family's move to a new home may be cited. Everything physical in Paraguay is getting smaller and smaller. Walls thin as a thought, locomotive-substitutes no bigger than ball-point pens. Paraguay, then, has big empty spaces in which men wander, trying to touch something. Preoccupation with skin (on and off, wrinkling, the new skin, pink fresh, taut) possibly a response to this. Stories about skin, histories of particular skins. But no jokes! Some 700,000 photographs of nuclear events were lost when the great library of Paraguay burned. Particle identification was set back many years. Rather than recreate the former physics, a new physics based on the golden section (proliferation of golden sections) was constructed. As a system of explanation almost certain to be incorrect it enjoys enormous prestige here.

Behind the Wall

Behind the wall there is a field of red snow. I had expected that to enter it would be forbidden, but Jean said no, walk about in it, as much as you like. I had expected that walking in it one would leave no footprints, or that there would be some other anomaly of that kind, but there were no anomalies; I left footprints and felt the cold of red snow underfoot. I said to Jean Mueller, "What is the point of this red snow?" "The intention of the red snow, the reason it is isolated behind the wall, yet not forbidden, is its soft glow—as if it were lighted from beneath. You must have noticed it; you've been standing here for twenty minutes." "But what does it do?" "Like any other snow, it invites contemplation and walking about in." The snow rearranged itself into a smooth, red surface without footprints. It had a red glow, as if lighted from beneath. It seemed to proclaim itself a mystery, but one there was no point in solving—an ongoing low-grade mystery.

Departure

Then I was shown the plan, which is kept in a box. Herko Mueller opened the box with a key (everyone has a key). "Here is the plan," he said, "It governs more or less everything. It is a way of allowing a very wide range of tendencies to interact." The plan was a number of analyses of Brownian motion equipped, at each end, with alligator clips. Then the bell rang and the space became crowded, hundreds of men and women standing there waiting for the marshals to establish some sort of order. I had been chosen, Herko said, to head the column (on the principle of the least-likely-leader). We robed; I folded my arms around the mace. We began the descent (into? out of?) Paraguay.

OCTOBER JOURNEY

Margaret Walker

Traveller take heed for journeys undertaken in the dark of the
    year.
Go in the bright blaze of Autumn's equinox.
Carry protection against ravages of a sun-robber, a vandal, and a
    thief.
Cross no bright expanse of water in the full of the moon.
Choose no dangerous summer nights;
no heady tempting hours of spring;
October journeys are safest, brightest, and best.

I want to tell you what hills are like in October
when colors gush down mountainsides
and little streams are freighted with a caravan of leaves.

I want to tell you how they blush and turn in fiery shame and joy,
how their love burns with flames consuming and terrible
until we wake one morning and woods are like a smoldering plain—
    a glowing caldron full of jewelled fire:
the emerald earth a dragon's eye
the poplars drenched with yellow light
and dogwoods blazing bloody red.

Travelling southward earth changes from gray rock to green velvet.
Earth changes to red clay
with green grass growing brightly
with saffron skies of evening setting dully
with muddy rivers moving sluggishly.

In the early spring when the peach tree blooms
wearing a veil like a lavender haze
and the pear and plum in their bridal hair
gently snow their petals on earth's grassy bosom below
then the soughing breeze is soothing
and the world seems bathed in tenderness,
but in October
blossoms have long since fallen.
A few red apples hang on leafless boughs;
wind whips bushes briskly.
And where a blue stream sings cautiously
a barren land feeds hungrily.

An evil moon bleeds drops of death

The earth burns brown.
Grass shrivels and dries to a yellowish mass.
Earth wears a dun-colored dress
like an old woman wooing the sun to be her lover,
be her sweetheart and her husband bound in one.
Farmers heap hay in stacks and bind corn in shocks
against the biting breath of frost.

The train wheels hum, "I am going home, I am going home,
I am moving toward the South."

Soon cypress swamps and muskrat marshes
and black fields touched with cotton will appear.
I dream again of my childhood land
of a neighbor's yard with a redbud tree
the smell of pine for turpentine
an Easter dress, a Christmas eve
and winding roads from the top of a hill.
A music sings within my flesh
I feel the pulse within my throat
my heart fills up with hungry fear
while hills and flatlands stark and staring
before my dark eyes sad and haunting
appear and disappear.

Then when I touch this land again
the promise of a sun-lit hour dies.
The greenness of an apple seems
to dry and rot before my eyes.
The sullen winter rains
are tears of grief I cannot shed.
The windless days are static lives.
The clock runs down
timeless and still.
The days and nights turn hours to years
and water in a gutter marks the circle of another world
hating, resentful, and afraid
stagnant, and green, and full of slimy things.

VI

Death and Resurrection

DEATH AND RESURRECTION

O<small>F ALL THE STATES</small> a human being must confront, death is the most difficult for us to imagine. Even birth is more accessible. We know about, perhaps have seen pictures of, the development from egg to embryo to foetus. We can curl up in a warm bed, pass into an easeful sleep, and approximate our condition in the womb. Although the source of the spark of life is a mystery, we know where we came from and we know how we got here.

The process of birth is singular; but we can die in so many ways—from disease, from war, from accident, from famine, from fire, from cold. More significantly, what does it mean to be dead? What does it feel like? In death are we just a corpse of decaying flesh? Does some immaterial part of us live on? If so, where does it live?

In recent years medical science has conducted spectacular research into life. The genetic code has been broken, operations have been performed on foetuses, beginnings have been made toward producing life in a test tube. Though meters and gauges and probes and graphs can measure, record and analyze all the functions of living, all these instruments and machines cannot penetrate death; in death all the scales read zero. Even those who have been there technically for seconds or minutes have no tales to tell.

When we try to imagine our own death, it is usually no different from a good night's sleep, often a sentimental scene where we lie in an open coffin and those dear to us in life weep our praises. But all we have done is picture the death of our body; our mind lives on, sharing that room with the mourners as an unseen presence, perhaps even a bit smug at its secret of survival. It is much easier to comprehend the death of the body than the annihilation of consciousness.

Existentialist philosophers of this century tell us that this block is a misfortune. We regard death as something that happens to other people, while we ourselves possess a kind of immortality. But—paradoxically—this attitude hinders our living because it lures us into taking life for granted, as if it were a gift forever ours to be wasted at whim. These philosophers stress the contrary, that measured against the billions of years of existence our individual selves flicker for an instant and are quickly gone. An urgency should pervade our living; a truly experienced life requires an authentic recognition of one's impending death.

These philosophers set us a difficult standard. To ask the mind to conceive of a time when it will not exist may be beyond the power of mind. Obliteration exceeds our range; we cannot look into the void. Even myth and fantasy falter at such a leap of the imagination. They tend either to picture death as another form of life, perhaps even as a superior state, or to triumph over death through rebirth. Here the rationalistic norm is reversed; death becomes transitory and life permanent.

Resurrection is a prevalent theme in many religions and mythologies. In the myths the process is associated with the yearly cycle of nature, the seasons of seeding, growth, and withering. The Egyptian and Greek deities Osiris, Attis, and Adonis are examples of gods associated with fertility who undergo an annual pattern of death and renewal. Christianity, of course, gives central importance to rebirth. The three-day period from Good Friday to Easter Sunday is a movement from crucifixion to resurrection. But rather than an annual occurrence, the rebirth of Jesus was final and eternal, and it is the hope of all Christian believers to enjoy the salvation of eternal life. Yet, although his religion promises eternity, Western man has long held a confused attitude toward dying; he clings to this life as if he was not sure.

The first poems in this section make death seductive, a condition of release and fulfillment from the inadequacies of life. In "Ode to the West Wind" Percy Bysshe Shelley celebrates the wind of Autumn because it is a force of death. He longs to be one with the wind, to be carried with it and have his dead thoughts driven over the universe. But his ultimate hope is not death, but renewal. Autumn, in the natural cycle, bodes not oblivion, but the coming of a new Spring. Henry Vaughan, a Christian poet of the 17th century, sings a hymn of praise to death because in his orthodox outlook death is not a finality; it is a transcendence into the true eternal liberty.

The next two poems envision the realm in foreboding rather than desirable imagery. Edgar Allen Poe depicts the place of the dead as an ominous city in the sea where Death looks down from a proud tower at gaping graves. And an even more terrifying realm—that of Hell— is threatened. In "The Garden of Proserpine" A. C. Swinburne contrasts the sterile garden of the underworld's queen with the abundance of earthly harvest. Yet Swinburne attributes a luring quality to this underworld because it is an escape from love and dreams and joy, from too much living. Unlike the triumphant deaths described by Shelley and Vaughan, Swinburne's is a denial of desire, a submission to nothingness.

Mythology often presents literal visits to the land of the dead in which humans confront the powers of death in defense of the values of life. The two myths presented here are American Indian—Modoc and Wishram. They display different degrees of failure and success in the struggle against death. "How Death Came into the World" is strikingly similar to the Greek Orpheus–Eurydice legend. Kumokums' attempt to return his daughter from the Land of the Dead is an ultimate test of mankind in overcoming death. His failure makes the fact of death permanent. In "Coyote and Eagle Visit the Land of the Dead" a potential of cyclical rebirth of the dead exists, but the dead are not eager and the living find them a burden. A choice is made to return them to death, affirming that death will last forever.

John Donne's Holy Sonnet X, "Death Be Not Proud," unlike the preceding selections in this section, displays no awe or respect for death. Death is belittled because it is a trivial circumstance for the true Christian, who, looking forward to an eternity of salvation, is beyond the fear of dying.

Can death bring release from all worldly cares? Using a river as the figure for tranquility, the Mexican author Alfonso Reyes suggests the temptation to let go of life, to allow oneself to slip into a dream of perpetual calm, directly opposed by that hectic and desperate life portrayed by Ramirez, who dies without fear or hope.

Not all primitive men see life after death as entirely unworldly. While it shares with many other stories elements of the strange journey and transformation, the Tzeltal Indian tale of the afterlife carries on the human traits all too well-known to the Mexican Indian who related it.

All these writers and tales cope with dying; a few attempt to describe the conditions of death. Yet not one of them gives us death as a pure state. Myth and poetry must use language to tell of death, and language is an agency of life. Words take their lives from existence. Perhaps absolute death is meaningless to us, impossible to convey apart from what we know in life.

ODE TO THE WEST WIND

Percy Bysshe Shelley

I

O wild West Wind, thou breath of Autumn's being,
Thou, from whose unseen presence the leaves dead
Are driven, like ghosts from an enchanter fleeing,

Yellow, and black, and pale, and hectic red,
Pestilence-stricken multitudes: O thou,
Who chariotest to their dark wintry bed

The wingéd seeds, where they lie cold and low,
Each like a corpse within its grave, until
Thine azure sister of the Spring shall blow

Her clarion o'er the dreaming earth, and fill
(Driving sweet buds like flocks to feed in air)
With living hues and odours plain and hill:

Wild Spirit, which art moving everywhere;
Destroyer and preserver; hear, oh, hear!

II

Thou on whose stream, mid the steep sky's commotion,
Loose clouds like earth's decaying leaves are shed,
Shook from the tangled boughs of Heaven and Ocean,

Angels of rain and lightning: there are spread
On the blue surface of thine aëry surge,
Like the bright hair uplifted from the head

Of some fierce Maenad, even from the dim verge
Of the horizon to the zenith's height,
The locks of the approaching storm. Thou dirge

Of the dying year, to which this closing night
Will be the dome of a vast sepulchre,
Vaulted with all thy congregated might

Of vapours, from whose solid atmosphere
Black rain, and fire, and hail will burst: oh, hear!

III

Thou who didst waken from his summer dreams
The blue Mediterranean, where he lay,
Lulled by the coil of his crystálline streams,

Beside a pumice isle in Baiae's bay,
And saw in sleep old palaces and towers
Quivering within the wave's intenser day,

All overgrown with azure moss and flowers
So sweet, the sense faints picturing them! Thou
For whose path the Atlantic's level powers

Cleave themselves into chasms, while far below
The sea-blooms and the oozy woods which wear
The sapless foliage of the ocean, know

Thy voice, and suddenly grow gray with fear,
And tremble and despoil themselves: oh, hear!

IV

If I were a dead leaf thou mightest bear;
If I were a swift cloud to fly with thee;
A wave to pant beneath thy power, and share

The impulse of thy strength, only less free
Than thou, O uncontrollable! If even
I were as in my boyhood, and could be

The comrade of thy wanderings over Heaven,
As then, when to outstrip thy skiey speed
Scarce seemed a vision; I would ne'er have striven

As thus with thee in prayer in my sore need.
Oh, lift me as a wave, a leaf, a cloud!
I fall upon the thorns of life! I bleed!

A heavy weight of hours has chained and bowed
One too like thee: tameless, and swift, and proud.

V

Make me thy lyre, even as the forest is;
What if my leaves are falling like its own!
The tumult of thy mighty harmonies

Will take from both a deep, autumnal tone,
Sweet though in sadness. Be thou, Spirit fierce,
My spirit! Be thou me, impetuous one!

Drive my dead thoughts over the universe
Like withered leaves to quicken a new birth!
And, by the incantation of this verse,

Scatter, as from an unextinguished hearth
Ashes and sparks, my words among mankind!
Be through my lips to unawakened earth

The trumpet of a prophecy! O, Wind,
If Winter comes, can Spring be far behind?

"THEY ARE ALL GONE ..."

Henry Vaughan

They are all gone into the world of light!
  And I alone sit lingering here;
Their very memory is fair and bright,
    And my sad thoughts doth clear.

It glows and glitters in my cloudy breast,
  Like stars upon some gloomy grove,
Or those faint beams in which this hill is dressed,
    After the sun's remove.

I see them walking in an air of glory,
  Whose light doth trample on my days;
My days, which are at best but dull and hoary,
    Mere glimmering and decays.

O holy Hope! and high Humility!
  High as the heavens above!
These are your walks, and you have showed them me,
    To kindle my cold love.

Dear beauteous Death! the jewel of the just,
  Shining nowhere but in the dark;
What mysteries do lie beyond thy dust,
    Could man outlook that mark!

He that hath found some fledged bird's nest may know
  At first sight if the bird be flown;
But what fair well or grove he sings in now,
    That is to him unknown.

And yet, as angels in some brighter dreams
  Call to the soul when man doth sleep,
So some strange thoughts transcend our wonted themes,
    And into glory peep.

If a star were confined into a tomb,
  Her captive flames must needs burn there;
But when the hand that locked her up gives room,
    She'll shine through all the sphere.

O Father of eternal life, and all
  Created glories under Thee!
Resume Thy spirit from this world of thrall
    Into true liberty.

Either disperse these mists, which blot and fill
  My perspective still as they pass;
Or else remove me hence unto that hill
    Where I shall need no glass.

THE CITY IN THE SEA

Edgar Allen Poe

Lo! Death has reared himself a throne
In a strange city lying alone
Far down within the dim West,
Where the good and the bad and the worst and the best
Have gone to their eternal rest.
There shrines and palaces and towers
(Time-eaten towers that tremble not!)
Resemble nothing that is ours.
Around, by lifting winds forgot,
Resignedly beneath the sky
The melancholy waters lie.

No rays from the holy heaven come down
On the long night-time of that town:
But light from out the lurid sea
Streams up the turrets silently—
Gleams up the pinnacles far and free—
Up domes—up spires—up kingly halls—
Up fanes—up Babylon-like walls—
Up shadowy long-forgotten bowers
Of sculptured ivy and stone flowers—
Up many and many a marvellous shrine
Whose wreathéd friezes intertwine
The viol, the violet, and the vine.
Resignedly beneath the sky
The melancholy waters lie.
So blend the turrets and shadows there
That all seem pendulous in air,
While from a proud tower in the town
Death looks gigantically down.

There open fanes and gaping graves
Yawn level with the luminous waves;
But not the riches there that lie
In each idol's diamond eye—
Not the gaily-jewelled dead
Tempt the waters from their bed;
For no ripples curl, alas!
Along that wilderness of glass—
No swellings tell that winds may be
Upon some far-off happier sea—

No heavings hint that winds have been
On seas less hideously serene.

But lo, a stir is in the air!
The wave—there is a movement there!
As if the towers had thrust aside,
In slightly sinking, the dull tide—
As if their tops had feebly given
A void within the filmy Heaven.
The waves have now a redder glow—
The hours are breathing faint and low—
And when, amid no earthly moans,
Down, down that town shall settle hence,
Hell, rising from a thousand thrones,
Shall do it reverence.

THE GARDEN OF PROSERPINE

Algernon C. Swinburne

Here, where the world is quiet;
   Here, where all trouble seems
Dead winds' and spent waves' riot
   In doubtful dreams of dreams;
I watch the green field growing
For reaping folk and sowing,
For harvest-time and mowing,
   A sleepy world of streams.

I am tired of tears and laughter,
   And men that laugh and weep;
Of what may come hereafter
   For men that sow to reap:
I am weary of days and hours,
Blown buds of barren flowers,
Desires and dreams and powers
   And everything but sleep.

Here night has death for neighbour,
   And far from eye or ear
Wan waves and wet winds labour,
   Weak ships and spirits steer;
They drive adrift, and whither
They wot not who make thither;
But no such winds blow hither,
   And no such things grow here.

No growth of moor or coppice,
   No heather-flower or vine,
But bloomless buds of poppies,
   Green grapes of Proserpine,
Pale beds of blowing rushes
Where no leaf blooms or blushes
Save this whereout she crushes
   For dead men deadly wine.

Pale, without name or number,
   In fruitless fields of corn,
They bow themselves and slumber
   All night till light is born;
And like a soul belated,
In hell and heaven unmated,

By cloud and mist abated,
  Comes out of darkness morn.

Though one were strong as seven,
  He too with death shall dwell,
Nor wake with wings in heaven,
  Nor weep for pains in hell;
Though one were fair as roses,
His beauty clouds and closes;
And well though love reposes,
  In the end it is not well.

Pale, beyond porch and portal,
  Crowned with calm leaves, she stands,
Who gathers all things mortal
  With cold immortal hands;
Her languid lips are sweeter
Than love's who fears to greet her
To men that mix and meet her
  From many times and lands.

She waits for each and other,
  She waits for all men born;
Forgets the earth her mother,
  The life of fruits and corn;
And spring and seed and swallow
Take wing for her and follow
Where summer song rings hollow,
  And flowers are put to scorn.

There go the old loves that wither,
  The old loves with wearier wings;
And all dead years draw thither,
  And all disastrous things;
Dead dreams of days forsaken,
Blind buds that snows have shaken,
Wild leaves that winds have taken,
  Red strays of ruined springs.

We are not sure of sorrow,
  And joy was never sure;
To-day will die to-morrow;
  Time stoops to no man's lure;
And love, grown faint and fretful,
With lips but half regretful
Sighs, and with eyes forgetful
  Weeps that no loves endure.

good they are happy. Well, everybody in this village is well fed and contented, so they have been good. Why not let them go to the Land of the Dead, and they can be happy there?"

Kumokums sat and thought it over for a long time. Then he said, "I believe you are right. People should leave this earth forever when they die. The chief of the Land of the Dead is a good man, and they will be happy in his village."

"I'm glad you see it that way," said Porcupine, and waddled off.

Five days later, Kumokums came home from fishing up Sprague River, and he heard a sound of crying in his house. He threw down his catch, and rushed to the door in the roof of his house. He climbed down the pole ladder through the smoke hole. His daughter was lying on the ground and his wives were standing around, wringing their hands and crying.

"What has happened? What is the matter with her?" Kumokums cried. He loved his daughter very dearly.

"She has left us," his wives cried. "She has gone to the Land of the Dead."

"No! She can't do that!" Kumokums exclaimed, and he stroked his daughter's head, and called her name. "Come back to me," Kumokums begged. "Stay with us here in our villages."

Kumokums sent his wife through the village to bring in the most powerful medicine men. They sang and prayed over the girl's body, but no one could bring her back.

Finally, Porcupine came waddling backward down the pole ladder through the smoke hole.

"Kumokums," he said, "this is the way you said it should be. You were the one who set death in the world for everybody. Now you must suffer for it like everyone else."

"Is there no way to bring her back?" Kumokums pleaded.

"There is a way," said Porcupine, and Bear, who is as wise as Porcupine, nodded his head. "There is a way, but it is hard and it is dangerous. You yourself must go to the Land of the Dead, and ask its chief, who is your friend, to give you your daughter back."

"No matter how hard or how dangerous it is, I am willing to do it," Kumokums assured them. He lay down on the opposite side of the house, and sent his spirit out of his body, away and away to the Land of the Dead.

"What do you want and whom do you come for?" the chief asked. He was a skeleton, and all the people in his village were skeletons, too.

"I have come to take my daughter home," Kumokums answered. "I love her dearly, and I want her with me, but I do not see her here."

"She is here," replied the chief of the Land of the Dead. "I, too, love her. I have taken her into my own house to be my own daughter." He turned his head and called, "Come out, daughter," and a slim young girl's skeleton came out of the hole in the roof. "There she is," said the chief of the Land of the Dead. "Do you think you would know her now, or want her in your village the way she is?"

"However she is, she is my daughter and I want her," Kumokums said.

"You are a brave man," observed the chief of the Land of the Dead. "Nobody else who has ever come here has been able to say that. If I give her to you, and she returns to the Land of the Living, it will not be easy. You must do exactly what I tell you."

"I will do whatever you say," Kumokums vowed.

"Then listen to me carefully," said the chief of the Land of the Dead. "Take your daughter by the hand and lead her behind you. Walk as straight as you can to your own place. Four times you may press her hand, and it will be warmer and rounder. When you reach your own village, she will be herself again. But whatever you do, do—not—look —back. If you do, your daughter will return to me."

"I will do as you say," Kumokums promised.

Kumokums held out his hand behind his back, and felt his daughter's finger bones take hold of it. Together they set out for their own village. Kumokums led the way. Once he stopped and pressed his daughter's hand. There was some flesh on it, and Kumokums' heart began to feel lighter than it had since his daughter died.

Four times Kumokums stopped and pressed his daughter's hand, and each time it was warmer and firmer and more alive in his own. Their own village was ahead of them. They were coming out of the Land of the Dead and into the Land of the Living. They were so close Kumokums decided they were safe now. He looked back at his daughter. A pile of bones lay on the ground for a moment, and then was gone. Kumokums opened his eyes in his own house.

"I told you it was hard and dangerous," Porcupine reminded him. "Now there will always be death in the world."

COYOTE AND EAGLE VISIT THE LAND OF THE DEAD

A Wishram Indian Legend

In the days of the animal people, Coyote was sad because people died and went away to the land of the spirits. All around him was the sound of mourning. He wondered and wondered how he could bring the dead back to the land of the living.

Coyote's sister had died. Some of his friends had died. Eagle's wife had died and Eagle was mourning for her. To comfort him Coyote said, "The dead shall not remain forever in the land of the dead. They are like the leaves that fall, brown and dead, in the autumn. They shall come back again. When the grass grows and the birds sing, when the leaf buds open and the flowers bloom, the dead shall come back again."

But Eagle did not want to wait until spring. He thought that the dead should be brought back without any delay. So Coyote and Eagle started out together to the land of the dead, Eagle flying along over Coyote's head. After several days they came to a big body of water, on the other side of which were a great many houses.

"Bring a boat and take us across the water!" shouted Coyote.

But there was no answer—no sound and no movement.

"There is no one there," said Eagle. "We have come all the way for nothing."

"They are asleep," explained Coyote. "The dead sleep during the day and come out at night. We will wait here until dark."

After sunset, Coyote began to sing. In a short time, four spirit men came out of the houses, got into a boat, and started toward Coyote and Eagle. Coyote kept on singing, and soon the spirits joined him, keeping time with their paddles. But the boat moved without them. It skimmed over the water by itself.

When the spirits reached the shore, Eagle and Coyote stepped into the boat and started back with them. As they drew near the island of the dead, the sound of drums and of dancing met them across the water.

"Do not go into the house," warned the spirits as they were landing. "Do not look at the things around you. Keep your eyes closed, for this is a sacred place."

"But we are hungry and cold. Do let us go in," begged Eagle and Coyote.

So they were allowed to go into a large lodge made of tule mats, where the spirits were dancing and singing to the beating of the drums. An old woman brought to them some seal oil in a basket bottle. Dipping a feather into it, she fed them from the oil until their hunger was gone.

Then Eagle and Coyote looked around. Inside the lodge everything was beautiful, and there were many spirits. They were dressed in ceremonial robes, beautifully decorated with shells and with elks' teeth. Their faces were painted, and they wore feathers in their hair. The moon, hanging from above, filled the big lodge with light. Near the moon stood Frog, who has watched over it ever since he jumped into it long ago. He saw to it that the moon shone brightly on the crowd of dancers and singers.

Eagle and Coyote knew some of the spirits as their former friends, but no one paid any attention to the two strangers. No one saw the basket which Coyote had brought with him. In this basket he planned to carry the spirits back to the land of the living.

Early in the morning, the spirits left the lodge for their day of sleep. Then Coyote killed Frog, took his clothes, and put them on himself. At twilight the spirits returned and began again a night of singing and dancing. They did not know that Coyote, in Frog's clothing, stood beside the moon.

When the dancing and singing were at their gayest, Coyote swallowed the moon. In the darkness, Eagle caught the spirit people, put them into Coyote's basket, and closed the lid tight. Then the two started back to the land of the living, Coyote carrying the basket.

After traveling a great distance, they heard noises in the basket and stopped to listen.

"The people are coming to life," said Coyote.

After they had gone a little farther, they heard voices talking in the basket. The spirits were complaining.

"We are being bumped and banged around," groaned some.

"My leg is being hurt," groaned one spirit.

"My legs and arms are cramped," groaned another.

"Open the lid and let us out!" called several spirits together.

Coyote was tired, for the basket was getting heavier and heavier. The spirits were turning back into people.

"Let's let them out," said Coyote.

"No, no," answered Eagle quickly.

A little later, Coyote set the basket down. It was too heavy for him.

"Let's let them out," repeated Coyote. "We are so far from the spirit land now that they won't return."

So he opened the basket. The people took their spirit forms and, moving like the wind, went back to the island of the dead.

Eagle scolded at first, but soon he remembered Coyote's earlier thought. "It is now autumn. The leaves are falling, just as people die. Let us wait until spring. When the buds open and the flowers bloom, let us return to the land of the dead and try again."

"No," replied Coyote. "I am tired. Let the dead stay in the land of the dead forever and forever."

So Coyote made the law that, after people have died, they shall never come to life again. If he had not opened the basket and let the spirits out, the dead would have come to life every spring as the grass and flowers and trees do.

DEATH, BE NOT PROUD

John Donne

Death, be not proud though some have called thee
Mighty and dreadful, for thou art not so,
For those, whom thou think'st thou dost overthrow,
Die not, poor Death, nor yet canst thou kill me.
From rest and sleep, which but thy pictures be,
Much pleasure, then from thee much more must flow,
And soonest our best men with thee do go,
Rest of their bones and soul's delivery.
Thou art slave to Fate, Chance, kings and desperate men,
And dost with poison, war, and sickness dwell,
And poppy or charms can make us sleep as well,
And better than thy stroke; why swell'st thou then?
One short sleep past, we wake eternally,
And death shall be no more; Death, thou shalt die.

RIVER OF OBLIVION

Alfonso Reyes

Rio de Janeiro, Río de Enero,
you were a river and are a sea;
what comes to you impetuous
forth from you languid goes.

Day ripens on your breast
in calms of eternity;
every hour you cull
turns to an hour and more.

Sponges of clarity,
your mountains filter the clouds,
and even the down you sift
that drifts from the wings of storm.

What trouble can resist you
when for every smart of salt
sweetness is in the air
And pity in the light?

The earth plays in the water
and with the city the field
and night enters
evening open wide.

The nightingale's song mingles
with the house's stir
and fruit and woman give
their single effluence.

To know you is to have
solitude of you
and in you to rest
of the rest forgetfulness.

The soul's disorder seeks
your limpid crystal law,
sleep showers from the nodding
crest of your royal palm.

For I am as the wanderers,
my home is in my pack,
I captain of a bark
with never a mariner's chart.

Río de Enero,
and I ask no better hap
in my mishap than to roam
your shores in the hour of wrack.

—The hand sustained the brow,
seeking to give it calm.
No, not the hand, the wind,
no, not the wind, your peace.

A STORY OF
THE UNDERWORLD

A Tzeltal Indian Story Recorded by Anne Chapman in Chiapas

MEN AS WELL AS WOMEN go to the underworld when they die. Those who have not been very bad return to live again on earth after a short stay, while those who have been wicked remain below a long time, or until they have received their full punishment. But sooner or later everyone comes back to live on earth. One does not know how he will look the second time, nor where he will live, nor who will be his parents. The only thing that is known is that a man will be a man and a woman a woman; also that those who live to an old age the first time will do so again the second time—and the same is true of those who die young.

"But now I'm going to tell you something so that you may see how the underworld is," said Antonio Gómez Ichilick, a native of Oxchuc, Chiapas.

An Indian's wife died and he became very sad. He wept much, saying, "Where are you? You, my wife, who prepared my food, who took care of me, where are you?" He became sadder as the days passed, as he had to go from house to house among his neighbors to ask for a few tortillas and a little pozol (corn gruel).

One night he went to his wife's grave and throwing himself upon it, began to weep and talk to her, "Where are you? Why did you leave me so alone?" He was still weeping when suddenly there appeared before him a human figure—it may have been God—who knows? He was dressed like a Ladino (a citified man), in cloth trousers and a new shirt.

He asked the man, "Why are you weeping so much? What is the matter?" At first the man was too surprised to answer but finally he said, "My wife has died and I'm weeping because I am very lonely and want to see her." Upon hearing this the Ladino answered, "So you want to see your wife. Very well, I shall take you to her. Now close your eyes and don't open them until I tell you to." A moment later he said, "Open them."

The man opened his eyes and saw that he was below the earth, in the presence of the Lord of Death. The Ladino who had brought him had disappeared. The Lord said to him, "If you wish to see your wife, go on until you reach a river. There on its banks you will find a horse; bring it to me."

The man obeyed and went looking for the river, which he found without any difficulty, but he saw no horse, only women washing their hair and clothes. He looked and looked, but found no horse. Then he returned to the Lord of Death and told him that he had not seen any horse, just women.

Then the Lord of Death said to him, "Go to the river again and ask each one of the women if she is a horse. The woman who says she is a horse will be your wife; when you ask her the question, she will be transformed into one. Tie the horse well and bring him to me."

The man returned to the river, and just as the Lord of Death had said, he found the woman who admitted being a horse; who upon his asking the question, was immediately turned into one. He tied the ribbon his wife was wearing in her hair around the horse's neck. Upon feeling the ribbon around her neck, the horse said to him, "Don't tie me so tight; you are hurting my neck." So he took off the ribbon and tied her with the cotton girdle he was wearing. And thus he led her into the presence of the Lord of Death.

Upon passing a well within which a big fire was burning, near which there was a heap of bones, his wife, or rather the horse, explained to her husband that she had to go to the river daily to wash and to look for wood; she was converted into a woman to wash herself and into a horse to carry the wood. But upon reaching the well with her wood, she became nothing but bones.

"Every day the Lord of Death throws me into the fire to punish me," she went on. "He leaves me in the fire until I'm changed into ashes, and when I say that I have suffered sufficiently for one day, he takes my ashes and makes a woman of me again. This punishment is very severe and I have to suffer it all because you did not beat me when we lived there above on the earth."*

Then the wife led her husband to her hut, for all those below have huts like ours up here. She gave him some food, but only yellow corn and red beans. Down there they cannot eat white corn because it is the brains of man, nor black corn because it is our burned flesh, nor black beans because they are the pupils of our eyes.

Upon finishing their food, the wife said to him, "I'm going to sleep on the wooden bed, but you will have to sleep near the fire, for you already know that we cannot sleep together nor do as we did before when we lived on earth." The husband lay down near the fire, as his wife had said, but in a little while he had a desire to sleep with her as they used to. He moved closer to her but upon touching her he felt no

---

*When drunk, the men of that region, as elsewhere, beat their wives. When sober, they are ashamed of themselves and rationalize their actions by saying, "If I don't beat you here, the Lord of Death will punish you much harder." [Comment by Frances Toor, author of *A Treasury of Mexican Folkways* (Crown, 1947).]

flesh, only bones. The following day his wife scolded him, "Why did you touch me? You behaved very badly. Now I will be punished more, when I was already reducing the amount of punishment against me."

We do not know how many days the man stayed down there with his wife, because we cannot tell whether there are just days or just nights down there, for it is certain that it must be different.

One day or night, whichever it may have been, the woman said to her husband, "You will die in fifteen days after returning to the earth. If you had not come here, you would have lived a long life, for it is written that you should not die until you are old. But now that you have seen how it is down here, you will die within fifteen days." He answered, "That is all right; I don't care. I don't want to live up there any longer."

When the man was prepared to return to earth, the same Ladino who had brought him down, appeared and said to him, "Close your eyes as you did the other time and don't open them until I tell you to."

Upon opening his eyes, he found himself back on earth once more. At the end of fifteen days he died and went down below.

FOR THE DEAD GREGORIANS ...

Ignacio Ramírez

What! would you have the fatal sister lend
an ear to sorrow's pleas? Vain intercession!
Rabble of spectres, get you to your dens!

Separated brother was from brother!
To sit us down at table it is too late;
to get us gone with you it is too soon!

For you, unhappy ones, no longer burns
a single log upon the hearth; nor do
I see that any cup awaits your kisses.

A sigh goes after you, a sigh, no more!
Peace be with your going; and may fortune
not bar the way to your retreat to light.

I hate the sepulchre, changed to the cradle
of a vile insect or a venomous snake,
where the sun never rises, nor the moon.

May among your bones a rose take root,
reigned over by the painted butterfly,
and with its fragrance permeate the dew.

Hearken fearless to the impious thunder:
and smile in contemplation, near at hand,
of a stream swollen, overflowing with life.

To get us gone with you it is too soon!
Let her consent at least, the Furious One,
to wait until the cup slips from our hand.

Why, more swiftly still alas! than you,
why does she strip us of existence bare?
From one she steals his forehead's ornament,

another with her rude hand bends in twain:
some she envelops in a yellow veil:
and others in their entrails feel a claw

that rends, and in their veins an icy cold.
Alas! the spring will come again and find
sorrow in our gates, and lamentation.

And we shall watch the feasters from without.

Perhaps for one the hour has come to go!
The throng of spectres watches for his going.

The course that we are setting, do you know
for what port it is bound? The tomb. Our ship
already founders. Shivered, the mast falls.

Some lie drifting in the waters, dying.
Others commit them to the fragile raft;
and for him who climbed into the shrouds

hope's despairing light still gutters on,
while wind and wave concert their batteries
and the implacable sky lets loose its bolts.

The flames mount to the lowering of the pennons,
unknown to all save to the bird of rapine,
the sullen west and monsters of the deep.

What is our life but an ill-fashioned vase
whose worth is but the worth of the desire
shut up in it by nature and by chance?

When I see it spilt by age I know
that in the hand of the wise earth alone
it can receive new form and new employ.

Life is not life, but prison, in which want
and pain and lamentation pine in vain;
pleasure flown, who is afraid of death?

Mother nature, there are no more flowers
along the slow paths of my stumbling feet.
I was born without hope or fear;
fearless and hopeless I return to thee.

VII

Apocalypse

APOCALYPSE

APOCALYPSE, from the Greek *apokalupsis,* "to uncover," means simply a vision or a revelation. But apocalypse, as it is commonly used, refers to a special kind of vision—the vision of the end of the world.

Just as man has always been confronted with the fact of his own death and has attempted to envision what lies beyond his mortality, so has he also speculated about the course of the world and wondered if the world too will have an end. And just as there seems to be a universal impulse to conceptualize a beginning to the world, so is there perhaps a universal impulse to conceive of an end. It is no accident that the Bible begins with a clean-cut beginning ("In the beginning God created the heavens and the earth") and ends with a vision of the destruction of the earth ("Then I saw a new heaven and a new earth; for the first heaven and the first earth had passed away. . . ."). The myths of many societies posit some final end to the world. The Greek Stoics believed that time was a never ending cycle, but at certain points in the cycle (the Great Cosmic Year), the world would be destroyed in a great cosmic fire and then be created again. The Icelandic myths express a similar notion, showing the end of the world in a cataclysmic battle among the transcendent powers (accompanied by a universal conflagration and the loosing of the serpent which sleeps coiled around the trunk of the Cosmic Tree) but followed by a new creation. In Zoroastrian mythology, the world was conceived to have a limited duration (12,000 years) after which there would be a final battle between Ahura Mazda, the principle of light and good, and Angra Mainyu, the principle of darkness and evil, who controlled the world for much of its duration.

It will be noticed that all these conceptions suggest new beginnings as well as endings. They are expressions of an intense faith that there is a beneficent force operating in the cosmos, whether that force is a personal deity or an abstract cosmic principle. This intense faith in a beneficent purpose, behind even the cataclysmic end of the world, lies behind the conception of the end of the world in the Judeo-Christian tradition which had its first expression in the literature of apocalypse. Apocalypses were first written in the second century B.C. and continued to be produced into the early Christian centuries by both Jewish and Christian writers. No one knows how many apocalypses were written, but those that survived express a consistent attitude toward the course of history and time.

All the apocalypses assert that the present is a time of decisive importance in history. The powers of evil (symbolized as grotesque beasts) hold sway over the temporal world making the present the most evil of times. But coupled with this pessimism is a feeling that these evil times are merely the prelude to the fulfillment of the covenant which God had established with his people. The apocalypses predicted that an end to man's misery would soon come: God would intercede soon in the course of time, overthrow his enemies in a final battle, purge the world of evil and establish his kingdom on earth. It would be a kingdom of peace, tranquility, and fecundity, a kingdom which would be a return to the paradise men lost in Adam's fall. The advent of these "last times" could be perceived in the natural order, the apocalyptic writers argued, and in their prophecies, they outlined the signs which would precede the end—shakings of the natural order, portents in the heavens, cataclysmic events in the affairs of men. It is these signs which define the essential quality of the apocalyptic view of the world and lend to the term apocalypse a further connotation of cataclysm.

For the writers of Jewish apocalypses the cataclysmic last times were a prelude to the advent of the Messianic kingdom on earth; for the early Christians who inherited the tradition of apocalypse, the end was conceived as a moment in which all men will be called to a final judgment for their deeds in life. Beyond that last judgment, life on earth will not continue: the kingdom of God, announced by Jesus, is to be in heaven.

The idea of a last judgment was one of the most powerful images in the early Christian church, and throughout the early Christian centuries, homilies, poems, tracts, and commentaries reiterated its nearness: *when* it would come remained a mystery, but its imminence was never held in doubt. Early medieval man regarded each calamity—whether natural disasters or the invasion of barbarian tribes—as a fulfillment of Biblical prophecy of the nearness of Judgment Day.

With the secularization of Western Culture in the Renaissance, the image of the end of the world underwent a significant change. The notion of a final judgment still maintained its validity to devout Christians—and still does to this day among literal believers—but for mainstream Western society, since at least the eighteenth century, the idea of an open-ended world has replaced the closed apocalyptic sense of time.

Yet the myths of the modern world have assimilated essential features of the apocalyptic myth. The image of a world transformed into a place of peace, harmony, fecundity, justice, and brotherhood lies at the center of most revolutionary social movements from the American revolution and the nineteenth century vision of America as a "new world" and a "virgin land" to the Marxist vision of a worker's paradise. And in these revolutionary movements, there is a notion that the millenial kingdom on earth will follow a cataclysmic confrontation between the forces of revolutionary change and the entrenched powers of evil and reaction who seek to impede the transformation of society. Less dramatically, implicit in the myth of progress, which has dominated Western thinking for nearly 200 years, is the vision of a world transformed through the forces of science and technology, a millenial kingdom reached not through an apocalyptic battle but through the application of reason to the problems of humanity and nature.

Paradoxically, it is the same force of technology which promises a transformed world which has also brought about a reincarnation of the apocalyptic myth; for technology has also provided us with the means of our own extermination and has thus re-awakened the feeling that an end to the world is a real possibility. Wars of calamitous proportions, the possible unleashing of unimaginable destruction through nuclear weapons, and even the possibility of more subtle means of destruction through ecological imbalance have shaken our faith that the world can continue forever. Our sense of the future is ambiguous; we feel that technology controlled for human purposes can usher in the millenium. But we also are in despair of ever achieving that control and, like Yeats in "The Second Coming," we wonder "what rough beast, its hour come round at last, slouches toward Bethlehem to be born?"

The selections in this section illustrate various aspects of the apocalyptic myth. The first, the Revelation of St. John, is the definitive form of Judeo-Christian apocalypse. Although it has known antecedants which deal with the same subjects in the same or similar terms, it is still an act of inspired imagination. It is the most consistently focused and conceptualized of apocalypses: its predecessors are awkward compilations of numerous, often contradictory traditions. The steady unfolding of the vision through its various stages, the accumulation of details of cataclysm leading up to the final battle or Armageddon, and its ecstatic vision of the new Jerusalem descending, have been a source of literary imagery and inspiration from the Middle Ages to the present day. Even writers who, like D. H. Lawrence, reject its religious message, have felt the force of its symbolism. To paraphrase the critic Northrop Frye, The Revelation of John provides a "grammar" of all of Man's hopes and fears about the future.

The Icelandic vision of the end of the world is told several times in Icelandic literature. Its earliest version is in a series of prophetical poems known as the *Voluspa,* written down in the ninth century. The version presented here is translated from a thirteenth century retelling of these old myths known as the Younger *Edda* of Snorri Sturlusson. The piling up of cataclysmic horror and the understated style of the Icelandic vision are its outstanding features. The end conceived here is not just of the world but of the gods as well; in the final onslaught of the forces of the cosmos (embodied in Fenriswolf and the Midgarth serpent), the gods are the epitome of Germanic heroism as they die fighting against overwhelming odds. As opposed to the Christian apocalypse, the Icelandic vision does not predicate a purpose for the end. The end comes not as part of some divine plan for the world but as the inevitable conclusion of the cosmic flow. In this sense, the Icelandic vision is much more grim and foreboding than the inherently optimistic Judeo-Christian apocalypses. Yet the image of a world reborn and of men given sustenance by the morning dew and repopulating the earth mitigates the horror of the preceding catastrophe with a note of lyrical promise.

The remaining selections show the various ways apocalyptic imagery has had its impact on modern authors. Byron's "Darkness" is perhaps characteristic of one modern "sense of an ending." Its central point, like that of MacLeish's "The End of the World," emphasizes a conception of a universe without hope or purpose. Like the Revelation of John and the Icelandic Doom of the Gods, in "a dream which was not all a dream," Byron piles up images of cataclysm and horror often echoing very specifically the traditional signs of apocalypse. But what lies beyond the ending implied in the poem is not a world renewed but an eternal darkness. MacLeish's poem, although less intense than Byron's —it omits all of the "apocalyptic signs"—nevertheless is a striking statement of the "nothingness" which lies beyond the world's span. The ironic image of the end of the world erupting into the midst of the circus, narrated with Icelandic-like terseness, gives the poem its pointedness and allows the author to compress cosmic meaning into a short poem.

Tennyson's "Kraken" and Yeats' "The Second Coming" both draw from the imagery of apocalyptic beasts. Tennyson's poem, like MacLeish's, is an exercise in poetic compression, pointing to the imagery of apocalypse only indirectly. But Tennyson manages to strike a note which touches the deepest level of the collective consciousness in his description of the primordial sea monster. Like the Judeo-Christian apocalypses and the Icelandic Doom of the Gods, the end of the world is heralded by the unleashing of the most horrible forces man can imagine. Tennyson, poet-laureate in the reign of Queen Victoria, is usually associated with poems of determined optimism; the "Kraken" perhaps shows a darker side of Tennyson's vision.

Yeats' "The Second Coming" is a more personal statement of the dark vision of the world founded on a personal conception of the organization of history. Yeats thought that history was cyclical and the poem implies that one cycle of history—the Christian "2000 years of stony sleep"—is drawing to a close and another cycle is beginning. Thus the end of the world as such is not about to happen but what the nature of the new age will be is uncertain. What is certain is that the end of the present era is marked by radical upheavals in the natural and social orders. The image of the "rough beast" "out of the Spiritus

Mundi" draws on apocalyptic and other mythological beasts and symbolizes all of Yeats' uncertainty about the future. Written in the early 1920's, a period marked by conflict both in Yeats' native Ireland and throughout the rest of the world, the poem yet transcends its immediate temporal concerns and becomes a powerful statement of much of the feeling for the future in the twentieth century.

The next selections can be called "personal apocalypses"—moments of crisis in the individual soul which, seen in relation to the cosmic crisis of apocalypse, are given deeper significance and impact. Hopkins' "I Wake and Feel the Fell of Dark" is a statement of personal religious experience. An Anglican convert to Roman Catholicism and subsequently a Jesuit priest, Hopkins draws from the traditional religious imagery of Judgment Day to underscore the universality of his personal crisis. His troubled night of sleepless anguish becomes a symbol for man's life in a dark world cut off from God who "lives, alas! away." Hopkins sees his own sinful state, his human pride ("Selfyeast of spirit"), as the sin of the lost who at the last judgment will receive their punishment from God. Their suffering in the next life is like Hopkins' anguished night—only worse.

William Zander's "German" is a personal crisis of a different order from Hopkins'. One might say that this is a poem about an attempted creation which turns into an apocalypse. The failed attempt at bringing order out of chaos leads to more chaos as the speaker in frustration rages at and destroys his intractable surroundings. The imagery of apocalypse hinted at in the last lines is used somewhat ironically and light-heartedly but one nevertheless gets the feeling of intense personal despair on the part of the speaker, disordered in chaotic surroundings, who yet wishes for the order and authoritarianism embodied in his image of a German military officer.

The next piece is Flannery O'Connor's terrifying short story "Judgment Day." Like many other characters in Flannery O'Connor's fiction, Old Tanner is a man lost in his own vision of the world, confronting a world in which he is out of place. Raised in the rural south with all of its prejudices and preconceptions, he is unable to cope with the openness of life in the North where he is now living with his daughter. He accuses his daughter of disobedience and ingratitude and hurls at her the threat of judgment day, but with biting irony his confrontation with his black neighbors turns out to be judgment day for him, or more precisely, his own Armageddon.

In the final story Hawthorne tells of the intense personal Apocalypse that can befall one who searches in trust for an ideal in his own family or circle.

THE REVELATION OF ST. JOHN THE DIVINE

Chapter 1

THE REVELATION of Jesus Christ, which God gave unto him, to shew unto his servants things which must shortly come to pass; and he sent and signified it by his angel unto his servant John:

2 Who bare record of the word of God, and of the testimony of Jesus Christ, and of all things that he saw.

3 Blessed is he that readeth, and they that hear the words of this prophecy, and keep those things which are written therein: for the time is at hand.

4 John to the seven churches which are in Asia: Grace be unto you, and peace, from him which is, and which was, and which is to come; and from the seven Spirits which are before his throne;

5 And from Jesus Christ, who is the faithful witness, and the first begotten of the dead, and the prince of the kings of the earth. Unto him that loved us, and washed us from our sins in his own blood,

6 And hath made us kings and priests unto God and his Father; to him be glory and dominion for ever and ever. Amen.

7 Behold, he cometh with clouds; and every eye shall see him, and they also which pierced him: and all kindreds of the earth shall wail because of him. Even so, Amen.

8 ¶ I am Alpha and Omega, the beginning and the ending, saith the Lord, which is, and which was, and which is to come, the Almighty.

9 ¶ I John, who also am your brother, and companion in tribulation, and in the kingdom and patience of Jesus Christ, was in the isle that is called Patmos, for the word of God, and for the testimony of Jesus Christ.

10 I was in the Spirit on the Lord's day, and heard behind me a great voice, as of a trumpet,

11 Saying, I am Alpha and Omega, the first and the last: and, What thou seest, write in a book, and send it unto the seven churches which are in Asia; unto Ephesus, and unto Smyrna, and unto Pergamos, and unto Thyatira, and unto Sardis, and unto Philadelphia, and unto Laodicea.

12 And I turned to see the voice that spake with me. And being turned, I saw seven golden candlesticks;

13 And in the midst of the seven candlesticks one like unto the Son of man, clothed with a garment down to the foot, and girt about the paps with a golden girdle.

14 His head and his hairs were white like wool, as white as snow; and his eyes were as a flame of fire;

15 And his feet like unto fine brass, as if they burned in a furnace; and his voice as the sound of many waters.

16 And he had in his right hand seven stars: and out of his mouth went a sharp two-edged sword: and his countenance was as the sun shineth in his strength.

17 And when I saw him, I fell at his feet as dead. And he laid his right hand upon me, saying unto me, Fear not; I am the first and the last:

18 I am he that liveth, and was dead; and, behold, I am alive for evermore, Amen; and have the keys of hell and of death.

19 Write the things which thou hast seen, and the things which are, and the things which shall be hereafter;

20 The mystery of the seven stars which thou sawest in my right hand, and the seven golden candlesticks. The seven stars are the angels of the seven churches: and the seven candlesticks which thou sawest are the seven churches.

Chapter 2

Unto the angel of the church of Ephesus write; These things saith he that holdeth the seven stars in his right hand, who walketh in the midst of the seven golden candlesticks;

2 I know thy works, and thy labour, and thy patience, and how thou canst not bear them which are evil: and thou hast tried them which say they are apostles, and are not, and hast found them liars:

3 And hast borne, and hast patience, and for my name's sake hast laboured, and hast not fainted.

4 Nevertheless I have somewhat against thee, because thou hast left thy first love.

5 Remember therefore from whence thou art fallen, and repent, and do the first works; or else I will come unto thee quickly, and will remove thy candlestick out of his place, except thou repent.

6 But this thou hast, that thou hatest the deeds of the Nicolaitans, which I also hate.

7 He that hath an ear, let him hear what the Spirit saith unto the churches; To him that overcometh will I give to eat of the tree of life, which is in the midst of the paradise of God.

8 ¶ And unto the angel of the church in Smyrna write; These things saith the first and the last, which was dead, and is alive;

9 I know thy works, and tribulation, and poverty, (but thou art rich) and I know the blasphemy of them which say they are Jews, and are not, but are the synagogue of Satan.

10 Fear none of those things which thou shalt suffer: behold, the devil shall cast some of you into prison, that ye may be tried; and ye shall have tribulation ten days: be thou faithful unto death, and I will give thee a crown of life.

11 He that hath an ear, let him hear what the Spirit saith unto the churches; He that overcometh shall not be hurt of the second death.

12 ¶ And to the angel of the church in Pergamos write; These things saith he which hath the sharp sword with two edges;

13 I know thy works, and where thou dwellest, even where Satan's seat is: and thou holdest fast my name, and hast not denied my faith, even in those days wherein Antipas was my faithful martyr, who was slain among you, where Satan dwelleth.

14 But I have a few things against thee, because thou hast there them that hold the doctrine of Balaam, who taught Balac to cast a stumbling block before the children of Israel, to eat things sacrificed unto idols, and to commit fornication.

15 So hast thou also them that hold the doctrine of the Nicolaitans, which thing I hate.

16 Repent; or else I will come unto thee quickly, and will fight against them with the sword of my mouth.

17 He that hath an ear, let him hear what the Spirit saith unto the churches; To him that overcometh will I give to eat of the hidden manna, and will give him a white stone, and in the stone a new name written, which no man knoweth saving he that receiveth it.

18 ¶ And unto the angel of the church in Thyatira write; These things saith the Son of God, who hath his eyes like unto a flame of fire, and his feet are like fine brass;

19 I know thy works, and charity, and service, and faith, and thy patience, and thy works; and the last to be more than the first.

20 Notwithstanding I have a few things against thee, because thou sufferest that woman Jezebel, which calleth herself a prophetess, to teach and to seduce my servants to commit fornication, and to eat things sacrificed unto idols.

21 And I gave her space to repent of her fornication; and she repented not.

22 Behold, I will cast her into a bed, and them that commit adultery with her into great tribulation, except they repent of their deeds.

23 And I will kill her children with death; and all the churches shall know that I am he which searcheth the reins and hearts: and I will give unto every one of you according to your works.

24 But unto you I say, and unto the rest in Thyatira, as many as have not this doctrine, and which have not known the depths of Satan, as they speak; I will put upon you none other burden.
25 But that which ye have already hold fast till I come.
26 And he that overcometh, and keepeth my works unto the end, to him will I give power over the nations:
27 And he shall rule them with a rod of iron; as the vessels of a potter shall they be broken to shivers: even as I received of my Father.
28 And I will give him the morning star.
29 He that hath an ear, let him hear what the Spirit saith unto the churches.

Chapter 3

And unto the angel of the church in Sardis write; These things saith he that hath the seven Spirits of God, and the seven stars; I know thy works, that thou hast a name that thou livest, and art dead.
2 Be watchful, and strengthen the things which remain, that are ready to die: for I have not found thy works perfect before God.
3 Remember therefore how thou hast received and heard, and hold fast, and repent. If therefore thou shalt not watch, I will come on thee as a thief, and thou shalt not know what hour I will come upon thee.
4 Thou hast a few names even in Sardis which have not defiled their garments; and they shall walk with me in white: for they are worthy.
5 He that overcometh, the same shall be clothed in white raiment; and I will not blot out his name out of the book of life, but I will confess his name before my Father, and before his angels.
6 He that hath an ear, let him hear what the Spirit saith unto the churches.
7 ¶ And to the angel of the church in Philadelphia write; These things saith he that is holy, he that is true, he that hath the key of David, he that openeth, and no man shutteth; and shutteth, and no man openeth;
8 I know thy works: behold, I have set before thee an open door, and no man can shut it: for thou hast a little strength, and hast kept my word, and hast not denied my name.
9 Behold, I will make them of the synagogue of Satan, which say they are Jews, and are not, but do lie; behold, I will make them to come and worship before thy feet, and to know that I have loved thee.
10 Because thou hast kept the word of my patience, I also will keep thee from the hour of temptation, which shall come upon all the world, to try them that dwell upon the earth.
11 Behold, I come quickly: hold that fast which thou hast, that no man take thy crown.
12 Him that overcometh will I make a pillar in the temple of my God,

and he shall go no more out: and I will write upon him the name of my God, and the name of the city of my God, which is new Jerusalem, which cometh down out of heaven from my God: and I will write upon him my new name.

13 He that hath an ear, let him hear what the Spirit saith unto the churches.

14 ¶ And unto the angel of the church of the Laodiceans write; These things saith the Amen, the faithful and true witness, and beginning of the creation of God;

15 I know thy works, that thou are neither cold nor hot: I would thou wert cold or hot.

16 So then because thou art lukewarm, and neither cold nor hot, I will spue thee out of my mouth.

17 Because thou sayest, I am rich, and increased with goods, and have need of nothing; and knowest not that thou art wretched, and miserable, and poor, and blind, and naked:

18 I counsel thee to buy of me gold tried in the fire, that thou mayest be rich; and white raiment, that thou mayest be clothed, and that the shame of thy nakedness do not appear; and anoint thine eyes with eyesalve, that thou mayest see.

19 As many as I love, I rebuke and chasten: be zealous therefore, and repent.

20 Behold, I stand at the door, and knock: if any man hear my voice, and open the door, I will come in to him, and will sup with him, and he with me.

21 To him that overcometh will I grant to sit with me in my throne, even as I also overcame, and am set down with my Father in his throne.

22 He that hath an ear, let him hear what the Spirit saith unto the churches.

Chapter 4

After this I looked, and behold, a door was opened in heaven: and the first voice which I heard was as it were of a trumpet talking with me; which said, Come up hither, and I will shew thee things which must be hereafter.

2 And immediately I was in the spirit: and, behold, a throne was set in heaven, and one sat on the throne.

3 And he that sat was to look upon like a jasper and a sardine stone: and there was a rainbow round about the throne, in sight like unto an emerald.

4 And round about the throne were four and twenty seats: and upon the seats I saw four and twenty elders sitting, clothed in white raiment; and they had on their heads crowns of gold.

5 And out of the throne proceeded lightnings and thunderings and voices: and there were seven lamps of fire burning before the throne, which are the seven Spirits of God.

6 And before the throne there was a sea of glass like unto crystal: and in the midst of the throne, and round about the throne, were four beasts full of eyes before and behind.

7 And the first beast was like a lion, and the second beast like a calf, and the third beast had a face as a man, and the fourth beast was like a flying eagle.

8 And the four beasts had each of them six wings about him; and they were full of eyes within: and they rest not day and night, saying, Holy, holy, holy, Lord God Almighty, which was, and is, and is to come.

9 And when those beasts give glory and honour and thanks to him that sat on the throne, who liveth for ever and ever,

10 The four and twenty elders fall down before him that sat on the throne, and worship him that liveth for ever and ever, and cast their crowns before the throne, saying,

11 Thou art worthy, O Lord, to receive glory and honour and power: for thou hast created all things, and for thy pleasure they are and were created.

Chapter 5

And I saw in the right hand of him that sat on the throne a book written within and on the backside, sealed with seven seals.

2 And I saw a strong angel proclaiming with a loud voice, Who is worthy to open the book, and to loose the seals thereof?

3 And no man in heaven, nor in earth neither under the earth, was able to open the book, neither to look thereon.

4 And I wept much, because no man was found worthy to open and read the book, neither to look thereon.

5 And one of the elders saith unto me, Weep not: behold, the Lion of the tribe of Juda, the Root of David, hath prevailed to open the book, and to loose the seven seals thereof.

6 And I beheld, and, lo, in the midst of the throne and of the four beasts, and in the midst of the elders, stood a Lamb as it had been slain, having seven horns and seven eyes, which are the seven Spirits of God set forth into all the earth.

7 And he came and took the book out of the right hand of him that sat upon the throne.

8. And when he had taken the book, the four beasts and four and twenty elders fell down before the Lamb, having every one of them harps, and golden vials full of odours, which are the prayers of saints.

9 And they sung a new song, saying, Thou are worthy to take the book and to open the seals thereof: for thou wast slain, and hast redeemed

us to God by thy blood out of every kindred, and tongue, and people, and nation;

10 And hast made us unto our God kings and priests: and we shall reign on the earth.

11 And I beheld, and I heard the voice of many angels round about the throne and the beasts and the elders: and the number of them was ten thousand times ten thousand, and thousands of thousands;

12 Saying with a loud voice, Worthy is the Lamb that was slain to receive power, and riches, and wisdom, and strength, and honour, and glory, and blessing.

13 And every creature which is in heaven, and on the earth, and under the earth, and such as are in the sea, and all that are in them, heard I saying, Blessing, and honour, and glory, and power, be unto him that sitteth upon the throne, and unto the Lamb for ever and ever.

14 And the four beasts said, Amen. And the four and twenty elders fell down and worshipped him that liveth for ever and ever.

Chapter 6

And I saw when the Lamb opened one of the seals, and I heard, as it were the noise of thunder, one of the four beasts saying, Come and see.

2 And I saw, and behold a white horse: and he that sat on him had a bow; and a crown was given unto him: and he went forth conquering, and to conquer.

3 ¶ And when he had opened the second seal, I heard the second beast say, Come and see.

4 And there went out another horse that was red: and power was given to him that sat thereon to take peace from the earth, and that they should kill one another: and there was given unto him a great sword.

5 ¶ And when he had opened the third seal, I heard the third beast say, Come and see. And I beheld, and lo a black horse; and he that sat on him had a pair of balances in his hand.

6 And I heard a voice in the midst of the four beasts say, A measure of wheat for a penny, and three measures of barley for a penny; and see thou hurt not the oil and the wine.

7 ¶ And when he had opened the fourth seal, I heard the voice of the fourth beast say, Come and see.

8 And I looked, and behold a pale horse: and his name that sat on him was Death, and Hell followed with him. And the power was given unto them over the fourth part of the earth, to kill with sword, and with hunger, and with death, and with the beasts of the earth.

9 ¶ And when he had opened the fifth seal, I saw under the altar the souls of them that were slain for the word of God, and for the testimony which they held:

10 And they cried with a loud voice, saying, How long, O Lord, holy and

true, dost thou not judge and avenge our blood on them that dwell on the earth?

11 And white robes were given unto every one of them; and it was said unto them, that they should rest yet for a little season, until their fellowservants also and their brethern, that should be killed as they were, should be fulfilled.

12 ¶ And I beheld when he had opened the sixth seal, and, lo, there was a great earthquake; and the sun became black as sackcloth of hair, and the moon became as blood;

13 And the stars of heaven fell unto the earth, even as a fig tree casteth her untimely figs, when she is shaken of a mighty wind.

14 And the heaven departed as a scroll when it is rolled together; and every mountain and island were moved out of their places.

15 And the kings of the earth, and the great men, and the rich men, and the chief captains, and the mighty men, and every bondman, and every free man, hid themselves in the dens and in the rocks of the mountains;

16 And said to the mountains and rocks, Fall on us, and hide us from the face of him that sitteth on the throne, and from the wrath of the Lamb:

17 For the great day of his wrath is come; and who shall be able to stand?

Chapter 7

And after these things I saw four angels standing on the four corners of the earth, holding the four winds of the earth, that the wind should not blow on the earth, nor on the sea, nor on any tree.

2 And I saw another angel ascending from the east, having the seal of the living God: and he cried with a loud voice to the four angels, to whom it was given to hurt the earth and the sea,

3 Saying, Hurt not the earth, neither the sea, nor the trees, till we have sealed the servants of our God in their foreheads.

4 And I heard the number of them which were sealed: and there were sealed an hundred and forty and four thousand of all the tribes of the children of Israel.

5 Of the tribe of Juda were sealed twelve thousand. Of the tribe of Reuben were sealed twelve thousand. Of the tribe of Gad were sealed twelve thousand.

6 Of the tribe of Aser were sealed twelve thousand. Of the tribe of Nepthalim were sealed twelve thousand. Of the tribe of Manasses were sealed twelve thousand.

7 Of the tribe of Simeon were sealed twelve thousand. Of the tribe of Levi were sealed twelve thousand. Of the tribe of Issachar were sealed twelve thousand.

8 Of the tribe of Zabulon were sealed twelve thousand. Of the tribe of Joseph were sealed twelve thousand. Of the tribe of Benjamin were sealed twelve thousand.

9 After this I beheld, and, lo, a great multitude, which no man could number, of all nations, and kindreds, and people, and tongues, stood before the throne, and before the Lamb, clothed with white robes, and palms in their hands;

10 And cried with a loud voice, saying, Salvation to our God which sitteth upon the throne, and unto the Lamb.

11 And all the angels stood round about the throne, and about the elders and the four beasts, and fell before the throne on their faces, and worshipped God,

12 Saying, Amen: Blessing, and glory, and wisdom, and thanksgiving, and honour, and power, and might, be unto our God for ever and ever. Amen.

13 And one of the elders answered, saying unto me, What are these which are arrayed in white robes? and whence came they?

14 And I said unto him, Sir, thou knowest. And he said to me, These are they which came out of great tribulation, and have washed their robes, and made them white in the blood of the Lamb.

15 Therefore are they before the throne of God, and serve him day and night in his temple: and he that sitteth on the throne shall dwell among them.

16 They shall hunger no more, neither thirst any more; neither shall the sun light on them, nor any heat.

17 For the Lamb which is in the midst of the throne shall feed them, and shall lead them unto living fountains of waters: and God shall wipe away all tears from their eyes.

Chapter 8

And when he had opened the seventh seal, there was silence in heaven about the space of half an hour.

2 And I saw the seven angels which stood before God; and to them were given seven trumpets.

3 ¶ And another angel came and stood at the altar, having a golden censer; and there was given unto him much incense, that he should offer it with the prayers of all saints upon the golden altar which was before the throne.

4 And the smoke of the incense, which came with the prayers of the saints, ascended up before God out of the angel's hand.

5 And the angel took the censer, and filled it with fire of the altar, and cast it into the earth: and there were voices, and thunderings, and lightnings, and an earthquake.

6 And the seven angels which had the seven trumpets prepared themselves to sound.

7 ¶ The first angel sounded, and there followed hail and fire mingled with blood, and they were cast upon the earth: and the third part of trees was burnt up, and all green grass was burnt up.

8 ¶ And the second angel sounded, and as it were a great mountain burning with fire was cast into the sea: and the third part of the sea became blood;

9 And the third part of the creatures which were in the sea, and had life, died; and the third part of the ships were destroyed.

10 ¶ And the third angel sounded, and there fell a great star from heaven, burning as it were a lamp, and it fell upon the third part of the rivers, and upon the fountains of waters;

11 And the name of the star is called Wormwood: and the third part of the waters became wormwood; and many men died of the waters, because they were made bitter.

12 ¶ And the fourth angel sounded, and the third part of the sun was smitten, and the third part of the moon, and the third part of the stars; so as the third part of them was darkened, and the day shone not for a third part of it, and the night likewise.

13 ¶ And I beheld, and heard an angel flying through the midst of heaven, saying with a loud voice, Woe, woe, woe, to the inhabiters of the earth by reason of the other voices of the trumpet of the three angels, which are yet to sound!

Chapter 9

And the fifth angel sounded, and I saw a star fall from heaven unto the earth: and to him was given the key of the bottomless pit.

2 And he opened the bottomless pit; and there arose a smoke out of the pit, as the smoke of a great furnace; and the sun and the air were darkened by reason of the smoke of the pit.

3 And there came out of the smoke locusts upon the earth: and unto them was given power, as the scorpions of the earth have power.

4 And it was commanded them that they should not hurt the grass of the earth, neither any green thing, neither any tree; but only those men which have not the seal of God in their foreheads.

5 And to them it was given that they should not kill them, but that they should be tormented five months: and their torment was as the torment of a scorpion, when he striketh a man.

6 And in those days shall men seek death, and shall not find it; and shall desire to die, and death shall flee from them.

7 And the shapes of the locusts were like unto horses prepared unto battle; and on their heads were as it were crowns like gold, and their faces were as the faces of men.

8 And they had hair as the hair of women, and their teeth were as the teeth of lions.

9 And they had breastplates, as it were breastplates of iron; and the sound of their wings was as the sound of chariots of many horses running to battle.

10 And they had tails like unto scorpions, and there were stings in their tails: and their power was to hurt men five months.

11 And they had a king over them, which is the angel of the bottomless pit, whose name in the Hebrew tongue is Abaddon, but in the Greek tongue hath his name Apollyon.

12 ¶ One woe is past; and, behold, there come two woes more hereafter.

13 ¶ And the sixth angel sounded, and I heard a voice from the four horns of the golden altar which is before God,

14 Saying to the sixth angel which had the trumpet, Loose the four angels which are bound in the great river Euphrates.

15 And the four angels were loosed, which were prepared for an hour, and a day, and a month, and a year, for to slay the third part of men.

16 And the number of the army of the horsemen were two hundred thousand thousand: and I heard the number of them.

17 And thus I saw the horses in the vision, and them that sat on them, having breastplates of fire, and of jacinth, and brimstone: and the heads of the horses were as the heads of lions; and out of their mouths issued fire and smoke and brimstone.

18 By these three was the third part of men killed, by the fire, and by the smoke, and by the brimstone, which issued out of their mouths.

19 For their power is in their mouth, and in their tails: for their tails were like unto serpents, and had heads, and with them they do hurt.

20 And the rest of the men which were not killed by these plagues yet repented not of the works of their hands, that they should not worship devils, and idols of gold, and silver, and brass, and stone, and of wood: which neither can see, nor hear, nor walk:

21 Neither repented they of their murders, nor of their sorceries, nor of their fornication, nor of their thefts.

Chapter 10

And I saw another mighty angel come down from heaven, clothed with a cloud: and a rainbow was upon his head, and his face was as it were the sun, and his feet as pillars of fire:

2 And he had in his hand a little book open: and he set his right foot upon the sea, and his left foot on the earth,

3 And cried with a loud voice, as when a lion roareth: and when he had cried, seven thunders uttered their voices.

4 And when the seven thunders had uttered their voices, I was about

to write: and I heard a voice from heaven saying unto me, Seal up those things which the seven thunders uttered, and write them not.

5 And the angel which I saw stand upon the sea and upon the earth lifted up his hand to heaven,

6 And sware by him that liveth for ever and ever, who created heaven, and the things that therein are, and the earth, and the things that therein are, and the sea, and the things which are therein, that there should be time no longer:

7 But in the days of the voice of the seventh angel, when he shall begin to sound, the mystery of God should be finished, as he hath declared to his servants the prophets.

8 And the voice which I heard from heaven spake unto me again, and said, Go and take the little book which is open in the hand of the angel which standeth upon the sea and upon the earth.

9 And I went unto the angel, and said unto him, Give me the little book. And he said unto me, Take it, and eat it up; and it shall make thy belly bitter, but it shall be in thy mouth sweet as honey.

10 And I took the little book out of the angel's hand, and ate it up; and it was in my mouth sweet as honey: and as soon as I had eaten it, my belly was bitter.

11 And he said unto me, Thou must prophesy again before many peoples, and nations, and tongues, and kings.

Chapter 11

And there was given me a reed like unto a rod: and the angel stood, saying, Rise, and measure the temple of God, and the altar, and them that worship therein.

2 But the court which is without the temple leave out, and measure it not; for it is given unto the Gentiles: and the holy city shall they tread under foot forty and two months.

3 And I will give power unto my two witnesses, and they shall prophesy a thousand two hundred and threescore days, clothed in sackcloth.

4 These are the two olive trees, and the two candlesticks standing before the God of the earth.

5 And if any man will hurt them, fire proceedeth out of their mouth, and devoureth their enemies: and if any man will hurt them, he must in this manner be killed.

6 These have power to shut heaven, that it rain not in the days of their prophecy: and have power over waters to turn them to blood, and to smite the earth with all plagues, as often as they will.

7 And when they shall have finished their testimony, the beast that ascendeth out of the bottomless pit shall make war against them, and shall overcome them, and kill them.

8 And their dead bodies shall lie in the street of the great city, which

spiritually is called Sodom and Egypt, where also our Lord was crucified.

9 And they of the people and kindreds and tongues and nations shall
see their dead bodies three days and an half, and shall not suffer their
dead bodies to be put in graves.

10 And they that dwell upon the earth shall rejoice over them, and
make merry, and shall send gifts one to another; because these two
prophets tormented them that dwelt on the earth.

11 And after three days and an half the Spirit of life from God entered
into them, and they stood upon their feet; and great fear fell upon them
which saw them.

12 And they heard a great voice from heaven saying unto them, Come
up hither. And they ascended up to heaven in a cloud; and their enemies beheld them.

13 And the same hour was there a great earthquake, and the tenth
part of the city fell, and in the earthquake were slain of men seven
thousand: and the remnant were affrighted, and gave glory to the God
of heaven.

14 ¶ The second woe is past; and, behold, the third woe cometh quickly.

15 ¶ And the seventh angel sounded; and there were great voices in
heaven, saying, The kingdoms of this world are become the kingdoms
of our Lord, and of his Christ; and he shall reign for ever and ever.

16 And the four and twenty elders, which sat before God on their seats,
fell upon their faces, and worshipped God,

17 Saying, We give thee thanks, O Lord God Almighty, which art, and
wast, and art to come; because thou has taken to thee thy great power,
and hast reigned.

18 And the nations were angry, and thy wrath is come, and the time
of the dead, that they should be judged, and that thou shouldest give
reward unto thy servants the prophets, and to the saints, and them that
fear thy name, small and great; and shouldest destroy them which
destroy the earth.

19 ¶ And the temple of God was opened in heaven, and there was seen
in his temple the ark of his testament: and there were lightnings, and
voices, and thunderings, and an earthquake, and great hail.

Chapter 12

And there appeared a great wonder in heaven; a woman clothed with
the sun, and the moon under her feet, and upon her head a crown of
twelve stars:

2 And she being with child cried, travailing in birth, and pained to be
delivered.

4 And there appeared another wonder in heaven; and behold a great

red dragon, having seven heads and ten horns, and seven crowns upon his heads.

4 And his tail drew the third part of the stars of heaven, and did cast them to the earth: and the dragon stood before the woman which was ready to be delivered, for to devour her child as soon as it was born.

5 And she brought forth a man child, who was to rule all nations with a rod of iron: and her child was caught up unto God, and to his throne.

6 And the woman fled into the wilderness, where she hath a place prepared of God, that they should feed her there a thousand two hundred and threescore days.

7 ¶ And there was war in heaven: Michael and his angels fought against the dragon; and the dragon fought and his angels,

8 And prevailed not; neither was their place found any more in heaven.

9 And the great dragon was cast out, that old serpent, called the Devil, and Satan, which deceiveth the whole world: he was cast out into the earth, and his angels were cast out with him.

10 And I heard a loud voice saying in heaven, Now is come salvation, and strength, and the kingdom of our God, and the power of his Christ: for the accuser of our brethren is cast down, which accused them before our God day and night.

11 And they overcame him by the blood of the Lamb, and by the word of their testimony; and they loved not their lives unto the death.

12 Therefore rejoice, ye heavens, and ye that dwell in them. Woe to the inhabiters of the earth and of the sea! for the devil is come down unto you, having great wrath, because he knoweth that he hath but a short time.

13 ¶ And when the dragon saw that he was cast unto the earth, he persecuted the woman which brought forth the man child.

14 And to the woman were given two wings of a great eagle, that she might fly into the wilderness, into her place, where she is nourished for a time, and times, and half a time, from the face of the serpent.

15 And the serpent cast out of his mouth water as a flood after the woman, that he might cause her to be carried away of the flood.

16 And the earth helped the woman, and the earth opened her mouth, and swallowed up the flood which the dragon cast out of his mouth.

17 And the dragon was wroth with the woman, and went to make war with the remnant of her seed, which keep the commandments of God, and have the testimony of Jesus Christ.

Chapter 13

And I stood upon the sand of the sea, and saw a beast rise up out of the sea, having seven heads and ten horns, and upon his horns ten crowns, and upon his heads the name of blasphemy.

2 And the beast which I saw was like unto a leopard, and his feet were as the feet of a bear, and his mouth as the mouth of a lion: and the dragon gave him his power, and his seat, and great authority.

3 And I saw one of his heads as it were wounded to death; and his deadly wound was healed: and all the world wondered after the beast.

4 And they worshipped the dragon which gave power unto the beast: and they worshipped the beast, saying, Who is like unto the beast? who is able to make war with him?

5 And there was given unto him a mouth speaking great things and blasphemies; and power was given unto him to continue forty and two months.

6 And he opened his mouth in blasphemy against God, to blaspheme his name, and his tabernacle, and them that dwell in heaven.

7 And it was given unto him to make war with the saints, and to overcome them: and power was given him over all kindreds, and tongues, and nations.

8 And all that dwell upon the earth shall worship him, whose names are not written in the book of life of the Lamb slain from the foundation of the world.

9 If any man have an ear, let him hear.

10 He that leadeth into captivity shall go into captivity: he that killeth with the sword must be killed with the sword. Here is the patience and the faith of the saints.

11 ¶ And I beheld another beast coming up out of the earth; and he had two horns like a lamb, and he spake as a dragon.

12 And he exerciseth all the power of the first beast before him, and causeth the earth and them which dwell therein to worship the first beast, whose deadly wound was healed.

13 And he doeth great wonders, so that he maketh fire come down from heaven on the earth in the sight of men,

14 And deceiveth them that dwell on the earth by the means of those miracles which he had power to do in the sight of the beast; saying to them that dwell on the earth, that they should make an image to the beast, which had the wound by a sword, and did live.

15 And he had power to give life unto the image of the beast, that the image of the beast should both speak, and cause that as many as would not worship the image of the beast should be killed.

16 And he causeth all, both small and great, rich and poor, free and bond, to receive a mark in their right hand, or in their foreheads:

17 And that no man might buy or sell, save he that had the mark, or the name of the beast, or the number of his name.

18 Here is wisdom. Let him that hath understanding count the number of the beast: for it is the number of a man; and his number is Six hundred threescore and six.

Chapter 14

And I looked, and, lo, a Lamb stood on the mount Sion, and with him an hundred forty and four thousand, having his Father's name written in their foreheads.

2 And I heard a voice from heaven, as the voice of many waters, and as the voice of a great thunder: and I heard the voice of harpers harping with their harps:

3 And they sung as it were a new song before the throne, and before the four beasts, and the elders: and no man could learn that song but the hundred and forty and four thousand, which were redeemed from the earth.

4 These are they which were not defiled with women; for they are virgins. These are they which follow the Lamb whithersoever he goeth. These were redeemed from among men, being the firstfruits unto God and to the Lamb.

5 And in their mouth was found no guile: for they are without fault before the throne of God.

6 ¶ And I saw another angel fly in the midst of heaven, having the everlasting gospel to preach unto them that dwell on the earth, and to every nation, and kindred, and tongue, and people,

7 Saying with a loud voice, Fear God, and give glory to him; for the hour of his judgment is come: and worship him that made heaven, and earth, and the sea, and the fountains of waters.

8 ¶ And there followed another angel, saying, Babylon is fallen, is fallen, that great city, because she made all nations drink of the wine of the wrath of her fornication.

9 ¶ And the third angel followed them, saying with a loud voice, If any man worship the beast and his image, and receive his mark in his forehead, or in his hand,

10 The same shall drink of the wine of the wrath of God, which is poured out without mixture into the cup of his indignation; and he shall be tormented with fire and brimstone in the presence of the holy angels, and in the presence of the Lamb:

11 And the smoke of their torment ascendeth up for ever and ever: and they have no rest day nor night, who worship the beast and his image, and whosoever receiveth the mark of his name.

12 Here is the patience of the saints: here are they that keep the commandments of God, and the faith of Jesus.

13 ¶ And I heard a voice from heaven saying unto me, Write, Blessed are the dead which die in the Lord from henceforth: Yea, saith the Spirit, that they may rest from their labours; and their works do follow them.

14 ¶ And I looked, and behold a white cloud, and upon the cloud one

sat like unto the Son of man, having on his head a golden crown, and in his hand a sharp sickle.

15 And another angel came out of the temple, crying with a loud voice to him that sat on the cloud, Thrust in thy sickle, and reap: for the time is come for thee to reap; for the harvest of the earth is ripe.

16 And he that sat on the cloud thrust in his sickle on the earth; and the earth was reaped.

17 ¶ And another angel came out of the temple which is in heaven, he also having a sharp sickle.

18 And another angel came out from the altar, which had power over fire; and cried with a loud cry to him that had the sharp sickle, saying, Thrust in thy sharp sickle, and gather the clusters of the vine of the earth; for her grapes are fully ripe.

19 And the angel thrust in his sickle into the earth, and gathered the vine of the earth, and cast it into the great winepress of the wrath of God.

20 And the winepress was trodden without the city, and blood came out of the winepress, even unto the horse bridles, by the space of a thousand and six hundred furlongs.

Chapter 15

And I saw another sign in heaven, great and marvellous, seven angels having the seven last plagues; for in them is filled up the wrath of God.

2 ¶ And I saw as it were a sea of glass mingled with fire: and them that had gotten the victory over the beast, and over his image, and over his mark, and over the number of his name, stand on the sea of glass, having the harps of God.

3 And they sing the song of Moses the servant of God, and the song of the Lamb, saying, Great and marvellous are thy works, Lord God Almighty; just and true are thy ways, thou King of saints.

4 Who shall not fear thee, O Lord, and glorify thy name? for thou only art holy: for all nations shall come and worship before thee; for thy judgments are made manifest.

5 ¶ And after that I looked, and, behold, the temple of the tabernacle of the testimony in heaven was opened:

6 And the seven angels came out of the temple, having the seven plagues, clothed in pure and white linen, and having their breasts girded with golden girdles.

7 And one of the four beasts gave unto the seven angels seven golden vials full of the wrath of God, who liveth for ever and ever.

8 And the temple was filled with smoke from the glory of God, and from his power; and no man was able to enter into the temple, till the seven plagues of the seven angels were fulfilled.

Chapter 16

And I heard a great voice out of the temple saying to the seven angels, Go your ways, and pour out the vials of the wrath of God upon the earth.

2 ¶ And the first went, and poured out his vial upon the earth; and there fell a noisome and grievous sore upon the men which had the mark of the beast, and upon them which worshipped his image.

3 ¶ And the second angel poured out his vial upon the sea; and it became as the blood of a dead man: and every living soul died in the sea.

4 ¶ And the third angel poured out his vial upon the rivers and fountains of waters; and they became blood.

5 And I heard the angel of the waters say, Thou art righteous, O Lord, which art, and wast, and shalt be, because thou hast judged thus.

6 For they have shed the blood of saints and prophets, and thou hast given them blood to drink; for they are worthy.

7 And I heard another out of the altar say, Even so, Lord God Almighty, true and righteous are thy judgments.

8 ¶ And the fourth angel poured out his vial upon the sun; and power was given unto him to scorch men with fire.

9 And men were scorched with great heat, and blasphemed the name of God, which hath power over these plagues: and they repented not to give him glory.

10 ¶ And the fifth angel poured out his vial upon the seat of the beast; and his kingdom was full of darkness; and they gnawed their tongues for pain,

11 And blasphemed the God of heaven because of their pains and their sores, and repented not of their deeds.

12 ¶ And the sixth angel poured out his vial upon the great river Euphrates; and the water thereof was dried up, that the way of the kings of the east dried up, that the way of the kings of the east might be prepared.

13 And I saw three unclean spirits like frogs come out of the mouth of the dragon, and out of the mouth of the beast, and out of the mouth of the false prophet.

14 For they are the spirits of devils, working miracles, which go forth unto the kings of the earth and of the whole world, to gather them to the battle of that great day of God Almighty.

15 Behold, I come as a thief. Blessed is he that watcheth, and keepeth his garments, lest he walk naked, and they see his shame.

16 And he gathered them together into a place called in the Hebrew tongue Armageddon.

17 ¶ And the seventh angel poured out his vial into the air; and there came a great voice out of the temple of heaven, from the throne, saying, It is done.

18 And there were voices, and thunders, and lightnings; and there was a great earthquake, such as was not since men were upon the earth, so mighty an earthquake, and so great.

19 And the great city was divided into three parts, and the cities of the nations fell: and great Babylon came in remembrance before God, to give unto her the cup of the wine of the fierceness of his wrath.

20 And every island fled away, and the mountains were not found.

21 And there fell upon men a great hail out of heaven, every stone about the weight of a talent: and men blasphemed God because of the plague of the hail; for the plague thereof was exceeding great.

Chapter 17

And there came one of the seven angels which had the seven vials, and talked with me, saying unto me, Come hither; I will shew unto thee the judgment of the great whore that sitteth upon many waters:

2 With whom the kinds of the earth have committed fornication, and the inhabitants of the earth have been made drunk with the wine of her fornication.

3 So he carried me away in the spirit into the wilderness: and I saw a woman sit upon a scarlet coloured beast, full of names of blasphemy, having seven heads and ten horns.

4 And the woman was arrayed in purple and scarlet colour, and decked with gold and precious stones and pearls, having a golden cup in her hand full of abominations and filthiness of her fornication:

5 And upon her forehead was a name written, MYSTERY, BABYLON THE GREAT, THE MOTHER OF HARLOTS AND ABOMINATIONS OF THE EARTH.

6 And I saw the woman drunken with the blood of the saints, and with the blood of the martyrs of Jesus: and when I saw her, I wondered with great admiration.

7 And the angel said unto me, Wherefore didst thou marvel? I will tell thee the mystery of the woman, and of the beast that carrieth her, which hath the seven heads and ten horns.

8 The beast that thou sawest was, and is not; and shall ascend out of the bottomless pit; and go into perdition: and they that dwell on the earth shall wonder, whose names were not written in the book of life from the foundation of the world, when they behold the beast that was, and is not, and yet is.

9 And here is the mind which hath wisdom. The seven heads are seven mountains, on which the woman sitteth.

10 And there are seven kings: five are fallen, and one is, and the other is not yet come; and when he cometh, he must continue a short space.

11 And the beast that was, and is not, even he is the eighth, and is of the seven, and goeth into perdition.

12 And the ten horns which thou sawest are ten kings, which have

received no kingdom as yet; but receive power as kings one hour with the beast.

13 These have one mind, and shall give their power and strength unto the beast.

14 These shall make war with the Lamb, and the Lamb shall overcome them: for he is Lord of lords, and King of kings: and they that are with him are called, and chosen, and faithful.

15 And he saith unto me, The waters which thou sawest, where the whore sitteth, are peoples, and multitudes, and nations, and tongues.

16 And the ten horns which thou sawest upon the beast, these shall hate the whore, and shall make her desolate and naked, and shall eat her flesh, and burn her with fire.

17 For God hath put in their hearts to fulfil his will, and to agree, and give their kingdom unto the beast, until the words of God shall be fulfilled.

18 And the woman which thou sawest is that great city, which reigneth over the kings of the earth.

Chapter 18

And after these things I saw another angel come down from heaven, having great power; and the earth was lightened with his glory.

2 And he cried mightily with a strong voice, saying, Babylon the great is fallen, is fallen, and is become the habitation of devils, and the hold of every foul spirit, and a cage of every unclean and hateful bird.

3 For all nations have drunk of the wine of the wrath of her fornication, and the kings of the earth have committed fornication with her, and the merchants of the earth are waxed rich through the abundance of her delicacies.

4 ¶And I heard another voice from heaven, saying, Come out of her, my people, that ye be not partakers of her sins, and that ye receive not of her plagues.

5 For her sins have reached unto heaven, and God hath remembered her iniquities.

6 Reward her even as she rewarded you, and double unto her double according to her works: in the cup which she hath filled fill to her double.

7 How much she hath glorified herself, and lived deliciously, so much torment and sorrow give her: for she saith in her heart, I sit a queen, and am no widow, and shall see no sorrow.

8 Therefore shall her plagues come in one day, death, and mourning, and famine; and she shall be utterly burned with fire: for strong is the Lord God who judgeth her.

9 And the kings of the earth, who have committed fornication and

lived deliciously with her, shall bewail her, and lament for her, when they shall see the smoke of her burning,

10 Standing afar off for the fear of her torment, saying, Alas, alas, that great city Babylon, that mighty city! for in one hour is thy judgment come.

11 And the merchants of the earth shall weep and mourn over her; for no man buyeth their merchandise any more:

12 The merchandise of gold, and silver, and precious stones, and of pearls, and fine linen, and purple, and silk, and scarlet, and all thyine wood, and all manner vessels of ivory, and all manner vessels of most precious wood, and of brass, and iron, and marble.

13 And cinnamon, and odours, and ointments, and frankincense and wine, and oil, and fine flour, and wheat, and beasts, and sheep, and horses, and chariots, and slaves, and souls of men.

14 And the fruits that thy soul lusted after are departed from thee, and all things which were dainty and goodly are departed from thee, and thou shalt find them no more at all.

15 The merchants of these things, which were made rich by her, shall stand afar off for the fear of her torment, weeping and wailing.

16 And saying, Alas, alas, that great city, that was clothed in fine linen, and purple, and scarlet, and decked with gold, and precious stones, and pearls!

17 For in one hour so great riches is come to nought. And every shipmaster, and all the company in ships, and sailors, and as many as trade by sea, stood afar off,

18 And cried when they saw the smoke of her burning, saying, What city is like unto this great city!

19 And they cast dust on their heads, and cried, weeping and wailing, saying, Alas, alas, that great city, wherein were made rich all that had ships in the sea by reason of her costliness! for in one hour is she made desolate.

20 Rejoice over her, thou heaven, and ye holy apostles and prophets; for God hath avenged you on her.

21 ¶ And a mighty angel took up a stone like a great millstone, and cast it into the sea, saying, Thus with violence shall that great city Babylon be thrown down, and shall be found no more at all.

22 And the voice of harpers, and musicians, and of pipers, and trumpeters, shall be heard no more at all in thee; and no craftsman, of whatsoever craft he be, shall be found any more in thee; and the sound of a millstone shall be heard no more at all in thee;

23 And the light of a candle shall shine no more at all in thee; and the voice of the bridegroom and of the bride shall be heard no more at all in thee: for thy merchants were the great men of the earth; for by thy sorceries were all nations deceived.

24 And in her was found the blood of prophets, and of saints, and of all that were slain upon the earth.

Chapter 19

And after these things I heard a great voice of much people in heaven, saying, Alleluia; Salvation, and glory, and honour, and power, unto the Lord our God:

2 For true and righteous are his judgments: for he hath judged the great whore, which did corrupt the earth with her fornication, and hath avenged the blood of his servants at her hand.

3 And again they said, Alleluia. And her smoke rose up for ever and ever.

4 And the four and twenty elders and the four beasts fell down and worshipped God that sat on the throne, saying, Amen; Alleluia.

5 And a voice came out of the throne, saying, Praise our God, all ye his servants, and ye that fear him, both small and great.

6 And I heard as it were the voice of a great multitude, and as the voice of many waters, and as the voice of mighty thunderings, saying, Alleluia: for the Lord God omnipotent reigneth.

7 Let us be glad and rejoice, and give honour to him: for the marriage of the Lamb is come, and his wife hath made herself ready.

8 And to her was granted that she should be arrayed in fine linen, clean and white: for the fine linen is the righteousness of saints.

9 And he saith unto me, Write, Blessed are they which are called unto the marriage supper of the Lamb. And he saith unto me, These are the true sayings of God.

10 And I fell at his feet to worship him. And he said unto me, See thou do it not: I am thy fellowservant, and of thy brethren that have the testimony of Jesus: worship God: for the testimony of Jesus is the spirit of prophecy.

11 ¶ And I saw heaven opened, and behold a white horse; and he that sat upon him was called Faithful and True, and in righteousness he doth judge and make war.

12 His eyes were as flame of fire, and on his head were many crowns; and he had a name written, that no man knew, but he himself.

13 And he was clothed with a vesture dipped in blood: and his name is called The Word of God.

14 And the armies which were in heaven followed him upon white horses, clothed in fine linen, white and clean.

15 And out of his mouth goeth a sharp sword, that with it he should smite the nations: and he shall rule them with a rod of iron: and he treadeth the winepress of the fierceness and wrath of Almighty God.

16 And he hath on his vesture and on his thigh a name written, KING OF KINGS, AND LORD OF LORDS.

17 ¶ And I saw an angel standing in the sun; and he cried with a loud voice, saying to all the fowls that fly in the midst of heaven, Come and gather yourselves together unto the supper of the great God;

18 That ye may eat the flesh of kings, and the flesh of captains, and the flesh of mighty men, and the flesh of horses, and of them that sit on them, and the flesh of all men, both free and bond, both small and great.

19 ¶ And I saw the beast, and the kings of the earth, and their armies, gathered together to make war against him that sat on the horse, and against his army.

20 And the beast was taken, and with him the false prophet that wrought miracles before him, with which he deceived them that had received the mark of the beast, and them that worshipped his image. These both were cast alive into a lake of fire burning with brimstone.

21 And the remnant were slain with the sword of him that sat upon the horse, which sword proceeded out of his mouth: and all the fowls were filled with their flesh.

Chapter 20

And I saw an angel come down from heaven, having the key of the bottomless pit and a great chain in his hand.

2 And he laid hold on the dragon, that old serpent, which is the Devil, and Satan, and bound him a thousand years,

3 And cast him into the bottomless pit, and shut him up, and set a seal upon him, that he should deceive the nations no more, till the thousand years should be fulfilled: and after that he must be loosed a little season.

4 ¶ And I saw thrones, and they sat upon them, and judgment was given unto them: and I saw the souls of them that were beheaded for the witness of Jesus, and for the word of God, and which had not worshipped the beast, neither his image, neither had received his mark upon their foreheads, or in their hands; and they lived and reigned with Christ a thousand years.

5 But the rest of the dead lived not again until the thousand years were finished. This is the first resurrection.

6 Blessed and holy is he that hath part in the first resurrection: on such the second death hath no power, but they shall be priests of God and of Christ, and shall reign with him a thousand years.

7 ¶ And when the thousand years are expired, Satan shall be loosed out of his prison,

8 And shall go out to deceive the nations which are in the four quarters of the earth, Gog and Magog, to gather them together to battle: the number of whom is as the sand of the sea.

9 And they went up on the breadth of the earth, and compassed the camp of the saints about, and the beloved city: and fire came down from God out of heaven, and devoured them.

10 And the devil that deceived them was cast into the lake of fire and brimstone, where the beast and the false prophet are, and shall be tormented day and night for ever and ever.

11 ¶ And I saw a great white throne, and him that sat on it, from whose face the earth and the heaven fled away; and there was found no place for them.

12 And I saw the dead, small and great, stand before God; and the books were opened: and another book was opened, which is the book of life: and the dead were judged out of those things which were written in the books, according to their works.

13 And the sea gave up the dead which were in it; and death and hell delivered up the dead which were in them: and they were judged every man according to their works.

14 And death and hell were cast into the lake of fire. This is the second death.

15 And whosoever was not found written in the book of life was cast into the lake of fire.

Chapter 21

And I saw a new heaven and a new earth: for the first heaven and the first earth were passed away; and there was no more sea.

2 And I John saw the holy city, new Jerusalem, coming down from God out of heaven, prepared as a bride adorned for her husband.

3 And I heard a great voice out of heaven saying, Behold, the tabernacle of God is with men, and he will dwell with them, and they shall be his people, and God himself shall be with them, and be their God.

4 And God shall wipe away all tears from their eyes; and there shall be no more death, neither sorrow, nor crying, neither shall there be any more pain: for the former things are passed away.

5 And he that sat upon the throne said, Behold, I make all things new. And he said unto me, Write: for these words are true and faithful.

6 And he said unto me, It is done. I am Alpha and Omega, the beginning and the end. I will give unto him that is athirst of the fountain of the water of life freely.

7 He that overcometh shall inherit all things; and I will be his God, and he shall be my son.

8 But the fearful, and unbelieving, and the abominable, and murderers, and whoremongers, and sorcerers, and idolaters, and all liars, shall have their part in the lake which burneth with fire and brimstone: which is the second death.

9 ¶ And there came unto me one of the seven angels which had the

seven vials full of the seven last plagues, and talked with me, saying, Come hither, I will shew thee the bride, the Lamb's wife.

10 And he carried me away in the spirit to a great and high mountain, and shewed me that great city, the holy Jerusalem, descending out of heaven from God,

11 Having the glory of God: and her light was like unto a stone most precious, even like a jasper stone, clear as crystal;

12 And had a wall great and high, and had twelve gates, and at the gates twelve angels, and names written thereon, which are the names of the twelve tribes of the children of Israel:

13 On the east three gates; on the north three gates; on the south three gates; and on the west three gates.

14 And the wall of the city had twelve foundations, and in them the names of the twelve apostles of the Lamb.

15 And he that talked with me had a golden reed to measure the city, and the gates thereof, and the wall thereof.

16 And the city lieth foursquare, and the length is as large as the breadth: and he measured the city with the reed, twelve thousand furlongs. The length and the breadth and the height of it are equal.

17 And he measured the wall thereof, an hundred and forty and four cubits, according to the measure of a man, that is, of the angel.

18 And the building of the wall of it was of jasper: and the city was pure gold, like unto clear glass.

19 And the foundations of the wall of the city were garnished with all manner of precious stones. The first foundation was jasper; the second, sapphire; the third, a chalcedony; the fourth, an emerald;

20 The fifth, sardonyx; the sixth, sardius; the seventh, chrysolite; the eighth, beryl; the ninth, a topaz; the tenth, a chrysoprasus; the eleventh, a jacinth; the twelfth, an amethyst.

21 And the twelve gates were twelve pearls; every several gate was of one pearl: and the street of the city was pure gold, as it were transparent glass.

22 And I saw no temple therein: for the Lord God Almighty and the Lamb are the temple of it.

23 And the city had no need of the sun, neither of the moon, to shine in it: for the glory of God did lighten it, and the Lamb is the light thereof.

24 And the nations of them which are saved shall walk in the light of it: and the kings of the earth do bring their glory and honour into it.

25 And the gates of it shall not be shut at all by day: for there shall be no night there.

26 And they shall bring the glory and honour of the nations into it.

27 And there shall in no wise enter into it any thing that defileth, neither whatsoever worketh abomination, or maketh a lie: but they which are written in the Lamb's book of life.

Chapter 22

And he shewed me a pure river of water of life, clear as crystal, proceeding out of the throne of God and of the Lamb.

2 In the midst of the street of it, and on either side of the river, was there the tree of life, which bare twelve manner of fruits, and yielded her fruit every month: and the leaves of the tree were for the healing of the nations.

3 And there shall be no more curse: but the throne of God and of the Lamb shall be in it; and his servants shall serve him:

4 And they shall see his face; and his name shall be in their foreheads.

5 And there shall be no night there; and they need no candle, neither light of the sun; for the Lord God giveth them light: and they shall reign for ever and ever.

6 ¶ And he said unto me, These sayings are faithful and true: and the Lord God of the holy prophets sent his angel to shew unto his servants the things which must shortly be done.

7 Behold, I come quickly: blessed is he that keepeth the sayings of the prophecy of this book.

8 ¶ And I John saw these things, and heard them. And when I had heard and seen, I fell down to worship before the feet of the angel which shewed me these things.

9 Then saith he unto me, See thou do it not: for I am thy fellowservant, and of thy brethren the prophets, and of them which keep the sayings of this book: worship God.

10 ¶ And he saith unto me, Seal not the sayings of the prophecy of this book: for the time is at hand.

11 He that is unjust, let him be unjust still: and he which is filthy, let him be filthy still: and he that is righteous, let him be righteous still: and he that is holy, let him be holy still.

12 And, behold, I come quickly; and my reward is with me, to give every man according as his work shall be.

13 I am Alpha and Omega, the beginning and the end, the first and the last.

14 Blessed are they that do his commandments, that they may have right to the tree of life, and may enter in through the gates into the city.

15 For without are dogs, and sorcerers, and whoremongers, and murderers, and idolaters, and whosoever loveth and maketh a lie.

16 ¶ I Jesus have sent mine angel to testify unto you these things in the churches. I am the root and the offspring of David, and the bright and morning star.

17 ¶ And the Spirit and the bride say, Come. And let him that heareth say, Come. And let him that is athirst come. And whosoever will, let him take the water of life freely.

18 ¶ For I testify unto every man that heareth the words of the

prophecy of this book, If any man shall add unto these things, God shall add unto him the plagues that are written in this book:

19 And if any man shall take away from the words of the book of this prophecy, God shall take away his part out of the book of life, and out of the holy city, and from the things which are written in this book.

20 ¶ He which testifieth these things saith, Surely I come quickly. Amen. Even so, come, Lord Jesus.

21 ¶ The grace of our Lord Jesus Christ be with you all. Amen.

THE FATE
OF THE GODS

Snorri Sturlusson

The version of the Fate of the Gods here translated is from
the *Edda* of Snorri Sturlusson. In the first part of this work,
Gylfagynning, the Beguiling of Gylfi, Snorri tells of a Swed-
ish king, Gylfi, who sets out to find the home of the gods at
Asgard in order to find the secret of their power. He comes
upon a hall in which he meets three rulers, Har, Jafnhar,
and Thridi, who are in reality projections of Odin himself
(the names mean, literally, "The High One," "The Equally
High," "The Third"). Gylfi, who here calls himself Gangleri
(the Wayworn) inquires if there are any wise ones living in
the hall. Har and his fellows then recount to him the ancient
myths beginning with creation and ending with the following prophecy.

THEN GANGLERI SAID: "What tidings are there concerning the Fate of
the Gods? I haven't heard about that yet."

Har said: "There are great tidings and much to be said about that.
First there shall come the winter which is called Fimbulvetr—the
monstrous winter. The snow shall blow about then from all directions;
there shall be a great frost and stabbing wind. The sun won't be of any
use. Three such winters shall come together in succession without any
summer in between. But before that shall happen, three other winters
shall come in which there shall be great battles: brothers shall slay
each other for the sake of greed, and no one will spare fathers and sons
either in manslaughter or in incest. So it says in the *Voluspa:*

> Brothers will attack   and slay each other,
> sister's offspring   will commit incest;
> it will be hard for men,   a great whoredom,
> the age of the battle-ax, the age of the sword,
>   the cleaving of shields;
> the age of storm, the age of the wolf,
>   before the world falls apart.

"Then that shall come to pass which seems big news indeed: a wolf shall swallow the sun, and men shall think that a great injury. Then another wolf shall take the moon and do it likewise great harm. The stars shall disappear from heaven. Then there is the tidings that the earth shall shake and the mountains too, so that the trees shall be torn up from the earth, and the mountains fall, and all the fetters and bonds shall be broken and split apart. Then Fenris-wolf shall be loosed. The sea shall gush in on the land because the Midgard Serpent turns about in a gigantic rage and proceeds up on the land.

"After that Naglfar shall be loosed—that is a ship so-called because it is made out of the nails of dead men. (And that's a fitting lesson, that if a man die with unshorn nails, he adds much material to that ship which the gods and men wished to build slowly.) In the stormy sea Naglfar shall float along. Hrymr is the name of the giant who steers Naglfar. Then Fenris-wolf shall move along with gaping mouth, his lower jaw touching the earth and his upper one touching heaven (his mouth would gape even more if there were room for it!). Fires burn at his eyes and nose. The Midgard Serpent shall blast out poison and sprinkle all of heaven and the sea. He is the most terrible thing and he shall be along side of the wolf.

"In this din heaven shall be split apart and the sons of Muspell shall ride thence: Sutr rides first and both before and behind him is burning fire. His sword is very great and it shines brighter than the sun. When they ride over Bifrost (the Shaking Bridge), it shall collapse. Muspell's kinsmen shall push on to the plain known as Vigridr—the field of battle. Fenris-wolf shall come there too, and the Midgard Serpent. Then Loki shall come there and Hrymr accompanied by the Frost Giants; and the companions of Hel shall follow Loki, and Muspell's sons shall have their own following. It shall be bright there. The plain of Vigridr is a hundred leagues wide on each side.

"And after that happens, Heimdallr shall stand up and blast loudly into Gjallarhorn and wake up all the gods, and they shall have a thing (meeting) together. Then Odin shall ride to Mimir's Well and take counsel with Mimir for himself and his companions. Yggdrasil's ash tree shall shake and there isn't anything in heaven and earth that shall be without fear. The Æsir shall clothe themselves for war, and the heroes likewise, and they shall proceed to the field. Odin rides in front with his golden helmet and a fair byrnie and his spear which is called Gungir. He shall turn to meet Fenris-wolf in battle, and Thor shall be by his side, but he won't be much help to him because he will have his hands full fighting against the Midgard-Serpent. Freyr shall engage Surtr in battle and that shall be a hard coming together before Freyr falls: that shall be his death because he shall miss his good sword which he gave to Skirnir.

"Then Garmr, the hound of hell, shall be loosed—the one who is

bound up in front of Gnipahel; he's the greatest monster. He shall fight
against Tyr and each shall be the slayer of the other. Thor shall carry
the news of death to the Midgard Serpent and then step back nine feet;
then he shall fall down dead to the earth because of the poison the
worm blasts at him. Fenris-wolf shall gobble up Odin—and that shall
be the end of him. Right after that, Vidar, Thor's son, shall turn to the
wolf and put his foot in his lower jaw; on his foot he wears the shoe that
has been made for that purpose through all time. (The shoe is made out
of leather pieces which men cut off from the heels and toes of their
shoes, and whoever wants to consider himself an aid to the gods should
cast off these leather pieces.) With his hand he shall take the upper jaw
of the wolf and rip his mouth apart—and that shall be the death of the
wolf. Loki shall fight Heimdallr and they shall slay each other. Right
after that Surtr shall sling fire over the earth and burn up all the
regions. So it says in the *Voluspa:*

Heimdallr blasts the horn   loudly aloft,
Odin speaks with   Mimir's head;
Yggdrasil's ash,   the standing tree, shakes,
the old tree groans   when the giant is loosed.

What's with the gods,   What's with the elves?
All Jotunheim groans;   the Æsir are at the Thing,
The dwarfs moan   before the stone door,
the rock-wise ones.

Hrymr drives from the east,   hefts his shield before,
The Midgard Serpent turns about   in a giant's rage;
the worm cleaves the waves,   the eagle shall scream,
the yellow-beaked one slits corpses;   Naglfar is loosed.

The ship comes from the east;   the Muspelli shall come
over the waves of the sea,   and Loki steers.
The monstrous kin fare forth   all with the wolf:
Byleist's brother   fares with them.

Surtr fares from the south   with the bane of switches;
Off his sword shines   the sun of the battle-gods,
The rocks clash,   the trolls fall,
heroes tred hell-way,   and heaven is cloven.

Then comes to Hlinar   the second injury,
When Odin fares   in fight with the wolf;
and the bane of Belja,   the bright one, fights with Surtr;
then must Frigg's beloved   fall.

```
Odin's son goes       against the wolf in battle,
Vidar on the way       against the carrion wolf.
He lets his sword       stand by hand
in the heart of the monster's kin;       thus is a father
                                                revenged.
```

```
The mighty kin of Hlothyn       goes in
undismayed by the hostility       of the serpent;
all heroes shall empty       the homestead
As Thor, protector of Midgard,       strikes in fury.
```

```
The sun shall darken,       the earth shall fall in the sea,
the bright stars       shall fall from heaven;
smoke gushes,       fire, the nourisher of life,
the heat licks high       up to heaven itself.
```

"Here it says even so:

```
Vigrid is the plain called       where Surtr and the beloved
                                     gods
find combat with each other;
it has a hundred leagues       on each side;       for them is the
                                              field marked out."
```

Then Gangleri said: "What will happen after all heaven, earth, and the dwellings are burnt, and all the gods, heroes, and menfolk are dead? Didn't you say before that all men shall live in some home through all time?"

Then Thridi answered: "There will be many good dwellings and many evil ones. It will be best then at Gimle, in heaven, and there will be much good drink there, for those who think that pleasant, in that hall that is called Brimir; it stands at Okolni. There will also be a good hall standing at Nithafell, made out of red-gold—it will be called Sindri. In these halls good men and pure shall dwell. At Nastrand (the Strand of Corpses) shall be a great hall and an evil one; its door faces north, and it is woven out of serpent backs like a wicker house; the worm heads are turned inward into the house and they blow forth poisons so that along the hall run poisonous streams, and murderers and oath-breakers wade therein, as it is said here:

```
I know a hall to stand       far from the sun
at Nastrand;       its door faces north,
poisonous drops fall       in from the roof-hole;
that hall is wound around       with serpent backs.
There shall wade in       the heavy stream
perjured men       and murderers.
```

But in Hvergelmi it will be the worst:

> There Nidhoggr will torture   the corpses of the dead."

Then Gangleri said: "Will any of the gods live then, or will there be any earth or any heaven?"

Har said: "The earth shall rise up out of the sea and it shall be green and fair; the crops shall grow without sowing. Vidarr and Vali shall live because the sea and Surtr's flame shall not have done them injury, and they shall dwell at Idavell, there where Asgard was before; and then the sons of Thor, Modi and Magni, shall come there and they shall possess Miollni. Next, Baldr and Hodr, the sons of Hel, shall come there. They shall sit down together and talk among themselves and recall their secret lore and talk of the events which came to pass—of Midgard Serpent and of Fenris-wolf. Then they shall find there in the grass the golden playing piece which the Æsir had possessed. So it says here:

> Vidarr and Vali   dwell in the home of the gods
> when the flame of Surtr   grows black;
> Modi and Magni   shall possess Miollni
> when Ving-Thor's battle   is at an end.

"And in the place called Hoddmimi's Holt, two men, who are called Lif and Lifthrasir, will be concealed from Surtr's flame; and the morning dew shall be their food. And from these men will come a great progeny who will repopulate all the world, as it says here:

> Lif and Lifthrasir,   will be concealed
> in Hoddmimi's holt;   they shall have as food
> the dews of the morning,   and from thence come all the
> generations.

"And it will seem marvellous to you that the sun has given birth to a daughter who is not less fair than he; and she shall follow the path of her mother, as it says here:

> Alfrothul bears   a daughter
> before Fenrir   carries her off;
> she shall follow,   after the gods die,
> further along   the mother's road.

"And now, if you can ask more questions, then I don't know what comes after that, because no man has heard or says anything more about the course of the world. Now use what you have taken."

Right after that Gangleri heard a great din all around him, and he looked on each side, and when he saw more clearly about him, he was standing outside in a level valley; he could not see the hall or the castle. He then took his way back and came home to his own kingdom and told these happenings which he had seen and heard. And after him, each man told others these tales.

Translated by Martin Green.

DARKNESS

George Gordon, Lord Byron

I had a dream, which was not all a dream.
The bright sun was extinguish'd, and the stars
Did wander darkling in the eternal space,
Rayless, and pathless, and the icy earth
Swung blind and blackening in the moonless air;
Morn came and went—and came, and brought no day,
And men forgot their passions in the dread
Of this their desolation; and all hearts
Were chill'd into a selfish prayer for light:
And they did live by watchfires—and the thrones,
The palaces of crowned kings—the huts,
The habitations of all things which dwell,
Were burnt for beacons; cities were consumed,
And men were gather'd round their blazing homes
To look once more into each other's face;
Happy were those who dwelt within the eye
Of the volcanos, and their mountain-torch:
A fearful hope was all the world contain'd;
Forests were set on fire—but hour by hour
They fell and faded—and the crackling trunks
Extinguish'd with a crash—and all was black.
The brows of men by the despairing light
Wore an unearthly aspect, as by fits
The flashes fell upon them; some lay down
And hid their eyes and wept; and some did rest
Their chins upon their clenched hands, and smiled;
And others hurried to and fro, and fed
Their funeral piles with fuel, and look'd up
With mad disquietude on the dull sky,
The pall of a past world; and then again
With curses cast them down upon the dust,
And gnash'd their teeth and howl'd: the wild birds shriek'd
And, terrified, did flutter on the ground,
And flap their useless wings; the wildest brutes
Came tame and tremulous; and vipers crawl'd
And twined themselves among the multitude,
Hissing, but stingless—they were slain for food.
And War, which for a moment was no more,
Did glut himself again:—a meal was bought
With blood, and each sate sullenly apart

Gorging himself in gloom: no love was left;
All earth was but one thought—and that was death
Immediate and inglorious; and the pang
Of famine fed upon all entrails—men
Died, and their bones were tombless as their flesh;
The meagre by the meagre were devour'd,
Even dogs assail'd their masters, all save one,
And he was faithful to a corse, and kept
The birds and beasts and famish'd men at bay,
Till hunger clung them, or the dropping dead
Lured their lank jaws; himself sought out no food,
But with a piteous and perpetual moan,
And a quick desolate cry, licking the hand
Which answer'd not with a caress—he died.
The crowd was famish'd by degrees; but two
Of an enormous city did survive,
And they were enemies: they met beside
The dying embers of an altar-place
Where had been heap'd a mass of holy things
For an unholy usage; they raked up,
And shivering scraped with their cold skeleton hands
The feeble ashes, and their feeble breath
Blew for a little life, and made a flame
Which was a mockery; then they lifted up
Their eyes as it grew lighter, and beheld
Each other's aspects—saw, and shriek'd, and died—
Even of their mutual hideousness they died,
Unknowing who he was upon whose brow
Famine had written Fiend. The world was void,
The populous and the powerful was a lump,
Seasonless, herbless, treeless, manless, lifeless,
A lump of death—a chaos of hard clay.
The rivers, lakes, and ocean all stood still,
And nothing stirr'd within their silent depths;
Ships sailorless lay rotting on the sea,
And their masts fell down piecemeal: as they dropp'd
They slept on the abyss without a surge—
The waves were dead; the tides were in their grave,
The moon, their mistress, had expired before;
The winds were wither'd in the stagnant air,
And the clouds perish'd; Darkness had no need
Of aid from them—She was the Universe.

THE END OF THE WORLD

Archibald MacLeish

Quite unexpectedly as Vasserot
The armless ambidextrian was lighting
A match between his great and second toe
And Ralph the lion was engaged in biting
The neck of Madame Sossman while the drum
Pointed, and Teeny was about to cough
In waltz-time swinging Jocko by the thumb—
Quite unexpectedly the top blew off:

And there, there overhead, there, there, hung over
Those thousands of white faces, those dazed eyes,
There in the starless dark the poise, the hover,
There with vast wings across the canceled skies,
There in the sudden blackness the black pall
Of nothing, nothing, nothing—nothing at all.

THE KRAKEN

Alfred, Lord Tennyson

Below the thunders of the upper deep,
Far, far beneath in the abysmal sea,
His ancient, dreamless, uninvaded sleep
The Kraken sleepeth: faintest sunlights flee
About his shadowy sides; above him swell
Huge sponges of millennial growth and height;
And far away into the sickly light,
From many a wondrous grot and secret cell
Unnumbered and enormous polypi
Winnow with giant arms the slumbering green.
There hath he lain for ages, and will lie
Battening upon huge sea-worms in his sleep,
Until the latter fire shall heat the deep;
Then once by man and angels to be seen,
In roaring he shall rise and on the surface die.

THE SECOND COMING

William Butler Yeats

Turning and turning in the widening gyre
The falcon cannot hear the falconer;
Things fall apart; the centre cannot hold;
Mere anarchy is loosed upon the world,
The blood-dimmed tide is loosed, and everywhere
The ceremony of innocence is drowned;
The best lack all conviction, while the worst
Are full of passionate intensity.

Surely some revelation is at hand;
Surely the Second Coming is at hand.
The Second Coming! Hardly are those words out
When a vast image out of *Spiritus Mundi*
Troubles my sight: somewhere in sands of the desert
A shape with lion body and the head of a man,
A gaze blank and pitiless as the sun,
Is moving its slow thighs, while all about it
Reel shadows of the indignant desert birds.
The darkness drops again; but now I know
That twenty centuries of stony sleep
Were vexed to nightmare by a rocking cradle,
And what rough beast, its hour come round at last,
Slouches towards Bethlehem to be born?

GERMAN

William Zander

> *Every woman adores a Fascist.*
> *Sylvia Plath*

Order, I cried,
clicking my bootheels,
swishing my swagger stick, marching around the room.
O but the room wouldn't listen,
nothing would brace itself, the walls
wouldn't snap to. Pictures askew,
dishes dirty, carpet sown with crumbs and fingernails,
records scattered and jacketless, fuzzy with dust—
O dull! O heavy
sleepless torpor of amputees from the western front!
Grandfather's clock, old movies, newspapers,
Dresden china. Jews
mooing in boxcars. ORDER ORDER ORDER, I cried,
but the room soiled itself like a frightened soldier, ach!
So I kick it in,
shattering dishes, windows, skulls
of pedestrian friends with my shiny boot, break through
like a hairy giant
to Asgard, vistas, clouds, the distant Sturm und Drang—
Freude, schöner Gotterfunken,
Tochter aus Elysium!

I WAKE AND FEEL THE FELL OF DARK

Gerard Manley Hopkins

I wake and feel the fell of dark, not day.
What hours, O what black hours we have spent
This night! what sights you, heart, saw; ways you went!
And more must, in yet longer light's delay.
  With witness I speak this. But where I say
Hours I mean years, mean life. And my lament
Is cries countless, cries like dead letters sent
To dearest him that lives alas! away.
  I am gall, I am heartburn. God's most deep decree
Bitter would have me taste: my taste was me;
Bones built in me, flesh filled, blood brimmed the curse.
  Selfyeast of spirit a dull dough sours. I see
The lost are like this, and their scourge to be
As I am mine, their sweating selves; but worse.

JUDGEMENT DAY

Flannery O'Connor

TANNER WAS CONSERVING all his strength for the trip home. He meant to walk as far as he could get and trust to the Almighty to get him the rest of the way. That morning and the morning before, he had allowed his daughter to dress him and had conserved that much more energy. Now he sat in the chair by the window—his blue shirt buttoned at the collar, his coat on the back of the chair, and his hat on his head —waiting for her to leave. He couldn't escape until she got out of the way. The window looked out on a brick wall and down into an alley full of New York air, the kind fit for cats and garbage. A few snow flakes drifted past the window but they were too thin and scattered for his failing vision.

The daughter was in the kitchen washing dishes. She dawdled over everything, talking to herself. When he had first come, he had answered her, but that had not been wanted. She glowered at him as if, old fool that he was, he should still have had sense enough not to answer a woman talking to herself. She questioned herself in one voice and answered herself in another. With the energy he had conserved yesterday letting her dress him, he had written a note and pinned it in his pocket. IF FOUND DEAD SHIP EXPRESS COLLECT TO COLEMAN PARRUM, CORINTH, GEORGIA. Under this he had continued: COLEMAN SELL MY BELONGINGS AND PAY THE FREIGHT ON ME & THE UNDERTAKER. ANYTHING LEFT OVER YOU CAN KEEP. YOURS TRULY T. C. TANNER. P.S. STAY WHERE YOU ARE. DON'T LET THEM TALK YOU INTO COMING UP HERE. ITS NO KIND OF PLACE. It had taken him the better part of thirty minutes to write the paper; the script was wavery but decipherable with patience. He controlled one hand by holding the other on top of it. By the time he had got it written, she was back in the apartment from getting her groceries.

Today he was ready. All he had to do was push one foot in front of the other until he got to the door and down the steps. Once down the steps, he would get out of the neighborhood. Once out of it, he would hail a taxi cab and go to the freight yards. Some bum would help him onto a car. Once he got in the freight car, he would lie down and rest. During the night the train would start South, and the next day or the morning after, dead or alive, he would be home. Dead or alive. It was being there that mattered; the dead or alive did not.

If he had had good sense he would have gone the day after he arrived; better sense and he would not have arrived. He had not got desperate

until two days ago when he had heard his daughter and son-in-law
taking leave of each other after breakfast. They were standing in the
front door, she seeing him off for a three-day trip. He drove a long
distance moving van. She must have handed him his leather headgear.
"You ought to get you a hat," she said, "a real one."

"And sit all day in it," the son-in-law said, "like him in there. Yah!
All he does is sit all day with that hat on. Sits all day with that damn
black hat on his head. Inside!"

"Well you don't even have you a hat," she said, "Nothing but that
leather cap with flaps. People that are somebody wear hats. Other
kinds wear those leather caps like you got on."

"People that are somebody!" he cried. "People that are somebody!
That kills me! That really kills me!" The son-in-law had a stupid muscu-
lar face and a yankee voice to go with it.

"My daddy is here to stay," his daughter said. "He ain't going to last
long. He was somebody when he was somebody. He never worked for
nobody in his life but himself and had people—other people—working
for him."

"Yah? Niggers is what he had working for him," the son-in-law said.
"That's all. I've worked a nigger or two myself."

"Those were just nawthun niggers you worked," she said, her voice
suddenly going lower so that Tanner had to lean forward to catch the
words. "It takes brains to work a real nigger. You got to know how to
handle them."

"Yah so I don't have brains," the son-in-law said.

One of the sudden, very occasional, feelings of warmth for the daughter came over Tanner. Every now and then she said something that
might make you think she had a little sense stored away somewhere
for safe keeping.

"You got them," she said. "You don't always use them."

"He has a stroke when he sees a nigger in the building," the son-in-
law said, "and she tells me . . ."

"Shut up talking so loud," she said. "That's not why he had the
stroke."

There was a silence. "Where you going to bury him?" the son-in-law
asked, taking a different tack.

"Bury who?"

"Him in there."

"Right here in New York," she said. "Where do you think? We got
a lot. I'm not taking that trip down there again with nobody."

"Yah. Well I just wanted to make sure," he said.

When she returned to the room, Tanner had both hands gripped on
the chair arms. His eyes were trained on her like the eyes of an angry
corpse. "You promised you'd bury me there," he said. "Your promise
ain't any good. Your promise ain't any good. Your promise ain't any

good." His voice was so dry it was barely audible. He began to shake, his hands, his head, his feet. "Bury me here and burn in hell!" he cried and fell back into his chair.

The daughter shuddered to attention. "You ain't dead yet!" She threw out a ponderous sigh. "You got a long time to be worrying about that." She turned and began to pick up parts of the newspaper scattered on the floor. She had grey hair that hung to her shoulders and a round face, beginning to wear. "I do every last living thing for you," she muttered, "and this is the way you carry on." She stuck the papers under her arm and said, "And don't throw hell at me. I don't believe in it. That's a lot of hardshell Baptist hooey." Then she went into the kitchen.

He kept his mouth stretched taut, his top plate gripped between his tongue and the roof of his mouth. Still the tears flooded down his cheeks; he wiped each one furtively on his shoulder.

Her voice rose from the kitchen. "As bad as having a child. He wanted to come and now he's here, he don't like it."

He had not wanted to come.

"Pretended he didn't but I could tell. I said if you don't want to come I can't make you. If you don't want to live like decent people there's nothing I can do about it."

"As for me," her higher voice said, "when I die that ain't the time I'm going to start getting choosey. They can lay me in the nearest spot. When I pass from this world I'll be considerate of them that stay in it. I won't be thinking of just myself."

"Certainly not," the other voice said, "You never been that selfish. You're the kind that looks out for other people."

"Well I try," she said, "I try."

He laid his head on the back of the chair for a moment and the hat tilted down over his eyes. He had raised three boys and her. The three boys were gone, two in the war and one to the devil and there was nobody left who felt a duty toward him but her, married and childless, in New York City like Mrs. Big and ready when she came back and found him living the way he was to take him back with her. She had put her face in the door of the shack and had stared, expressionless, for a second. Then all at once she had screamed and jumped back.

"What's that on the floor?"

"Coleman," he said.

The old Negro was curled up on a pallet asleep at the foot of Tanner's bed, a stinking skin full of bones, arranged in what seemed vaguely human form. When Coleman was young, he had looked like a bear; now that he was old he looked like a monkey. With Tanner it was the opposite; when he was young he had looked like a monkey but when he got old, he looked like a bear.

The daughter stepped back onto the porch. There were the bottoms of two cane chairs tilted against the clapboard but she declined to take a seat. She stepped out about ten feet from the house as if it took that much space to clear the odor. Then she had spoken her piece.

"If you don't have any pride I have and I know my duty and I was raised to do it. My mother raised me to do it if you didn't. She was from plain people but not the kind that likes to settle in with niggers."

At that point the old Negro roused up and slid out the door, a doubled-up shadow which Tanner just caught sight of gliding away.

She had shamed him. He shouted so they both could hear. "Who you think cooks? Who you think cuts my firewood and empties my slops? He's paroled to me. That no-good scoundrel has been on my hands for thirty years. He ain't a bad nigger."

She was unimpressed. "Whose shack is this anyway?" she had asked "Yours or his?"

"Him and me built it," he said. "You go on back up there. I wouldn't come with you for no million dollars or no sack of salt."

"It looks like him and you built it. Whose land is it on?"

"Some people that live in Florida," he said evasively. He had known then that it was land up for sale but he thought it was too sorry for anyone to buy. That same afternoon he had found out different. He had found out in time to go back with her. If he had found out a day later, he might still be there, squatting on the doctor's land.

When he saw the brown porpoise-shaped figure striding across the field that afternoon, he had known at once what had happened; no one had to tell him. If that nigger had owned the whole world except for one runty rutted peafield and he acquired it, he would walk across it that way, beating the weeds aside, his thick neck swelled, his stomach a throne for his gold watch and chain. Doctor Foley. He was only part black. The rest was Indian and white.

He was everything to the niggers—druggist and undertaker and general counsel and real estate man and sometimes he got the evil eye off them and sometimes he put it on. Be prepared, he said to himself, watching him approach, to take something off him, nigger though he be. Be prepared, because you ain't got a thing to hold up to him but the skin you come in, and that's no more use to you now than what a snake would shed. You don't have a chance with the government against you.

He was sitting on the porch in the piece of straight chair tilted against the shack. "Good evening, Foley," he said and nodded as the doctor came up and stopped short at the edge of the clearing, as if he had only just that minute seen him though it was plain he had sighted him as he crossed the field.

"I be out here to look at my property," the doctor said. "Good evening." His voice was quick and high.

Ain't been your property long, he said to himself. "I seen you coming," he said.

"I acquired this here recently," the doctor said and proceeded without looking at him again to walk around to one side of the shack. In a moment he came back and stopped in front of him. Then he stepped boldly to the door of the shack and put his head in. Coleman was in there that time too, asleep. He looked for a moment and then turned aside. "I know that nigger," he said. "Coleman Parrum—how long does it take him to sleep off that stump liquor you all make?"

Tanner took hold of the knobs on the chair bottom and held them hard. "This shack ain't in your property. Only on it, by my mistake," he said.

The doctor removed his cigar momentarily from his mouth. "It ain't my mis-take," he said and smiled.

He had only sat there, looking ahead.

"It don't pay to make this kind of mis-take," the doctor said.

"I never found nothing that paid yet," he muttered.

"Everything pays," the Negro said, "if you knows how to make it," and he remained there smiling, looking the squatter up and down. Then he turned and went around the other side of the shack. There was a silence. He was looking for the still.

Then would have been the time to kill him. There was a gun inside the shack and he could have done it as easy as not, but, from childhood, he had been weakened for that kind of violence by the fear of hell. He had never killed one, he had always handled them with his wits and with luck. He was known to have a way with niggers. There was an art to handling them. The secret of handling a nigger was to show him his brains didn't have a chance against yours; then he would jump on your back and know he had a good thing there for life. He had had Coleman on his back for thirty years.

Tanner had first seen Coleman when he was working six of them at a saw mill in the middle of a pine forest fifteen miles from nowhere. They were as sorry a crew as he had worked, the kind that on Monday they didn't show up. What was in the air had reached them. They thought there was a new Lincoln elected who was going to abolish work. He managed them with a very sharp penknife. He had had something wrong with his kidney then that made his hands shake and he had taken to whittling to force that waste motion out of sight. He did not intend them to see that his hands shook of their own accord and he did not intend to see it himself or to countenance it. The knife had moved constantly, violently, in his quaking hands and here and there small crude figures—that he never looked at again and could not have said what they were If he had—dropped to the ground. The Negroes picked them up and took them home; there was not much time between them and darkest Africa. The knife glittered constantly in his hands. More than once he had stopped short and said in an off-hand voice to some half-reclining, head-averted Negro, "Nigger, this knife is in my hand now but if you don't quit wasting my time and money, it'll be in your gut shortly." And the Negro would begin to rise—slowly, but he would be in the act—before the sentence was completed.

A large black loose-jointed Negro, twice his own size, had begun hanging around the edge of the saw mill, watching the others work and when he was not watching, sleeping, in full view of them, sprawled like a gigantic bear on his back. "Who is that?" he had asked. "If he wants to work, tell him to come here. If he don't, tell him to go. No idlers are going to hang around here."

None of them knew who he was. They knew he didn't want to work. They knew nothing else, not where he had come from, nor why, though he was probably brother to one; cousin to all of them. He had ignored him for a day; against the six of them he was one yellow-faced scrawny white man with shaky hands. He was willing to wait for trouble, but not forever. The next day the stranger came again. After the six Tanner worked had seen the idler there for half the morning, they quit and began to eat, a full thirty minutes before noon. He had not risked ordering them up. He had gone to the source of the trouble.

The stranger was leaning against a tree on the edge of the clearing, watching with half-closed eyes. The insolence on his face barely covered the wariness behind it. His look said, this ain't much of a white man so why he come on so big, what he fixing to do?

He had meant to say, "Nigger, this knife is in my hand now but if you ain't out of my sight . . ." but as he drew closer he changed his mind. The Negro's eyes were small and bloodshot. Tanner supposed there was a knife on him somewhere that he would as soon use as not. His own penknife moved, directed solely by some intruding intelligence that worked in his hands. He had no idea what he was carving, but when he reached the Negro, he had already made two holes the size of half dollars in the piece of bark.

The Negro's gaze fell on his hands and was held. His jaw slackened. His eyes did not move from the knife tearing recklessly around the bark. He watched as if he saw an invisible power working on the wood.

He looked himself then and, astonished, saw the connected rims of a pair of spectacles.

He held them away from him and looked through the holes past a pile of shavings and on into the woods to the edge of the pen where they kept their mules.

"You can't see so good, can you, boy?" he said and began scraping the ground with his foot to turn up a piece of wire. He picked up a small piece of haywire; in a minute he found another, shorter piece and picked that up. He began to attach these to the bark. He was in no hurry now that he knew what he was doing. When the spectacles were finished, he handed them to the Negro. "Put these on," he said. "I hate to see anybody can't see good."

There was an instant when the Negro might have done one thing or another, might have taken the glasses and crushed them in his hand or grabbed the knife and turned it on him. He saw the exact instant in the muddy liquor-swollen eyes when the pleasure of having a knife in this white man's gut was balanced against something else, he could not tell what.

The Negro reached for the glasses. He attached the bows carefully behind his ears and looked forth. He peered this way and that with exaggerated solemnity. And then he looked directly at Tanner and grinned, or grimaced, Tanner could not tell which, but he had an instant's sensation of seeing before him a negative image of himself, as if clownishness and captivity had been their common lot. The vision failed him before he could decipher it.

"Preacher," he said, "what you hanging around here for?" He picked up another piece of bark and began, without looking at it, to carve again. "This ain't Sunday."

"This here ain't Sunday?" the Negro said.

"This is Friday," he said. "That's the way it is with you preachers—drunk all week so you don't know when Sunday is. What you see through those glasses?"

"See a man."

"What kind of a man?"

"See the man make these yer glasses."

"Is he white or black?"

"He white!" the Negro said as if only at that moment was his vision sufficiently improved to detect it. "Yessuh, he white!" he said.

"Well, you treat him like he was white," Tanner said. "What's your name?"

"Name Coleman," the Negro said.

And he had not got rid of Coleman since. You make a monkey out of one of them and he jumps on your back and stays there for life, but let one make a monkey out of you and all you can do is kill him or disappear. And he was not going to hell for killing a nigger. Behind the shack he heard the doctor kick over a bucket. He sat and waited.

In a moment the doctor appeared again, beating his way around the other side of the house, whacking at scattered clumps of Johnson grass with his cane. He stopped in the middle of the yard, about where that morning the daughter had delivered her ultimatum.

"You don't belong here," he began. "I could have you prosecuted."

Tanner remained there, dumb, staring across the field.

"Where's your still?" the doctor asked.

"If it's a still around here, it don't belong to me," he said and shut his mouth tight.

The Negro laughed softly. "Down on your luck, ain't you?" he murmured. "Didn't you used to own a little piece of land over acrost the river and lost it?"

He had continued to study the woods ahead.

"If you want to run the still for me, that's one thing," the doctor said. "If you don't, you might as well had be packing up."

"I don't have to work for you," he said. "The governmint ain't got around yet to forcing the white folks to work for the colored."

The doctor polished the stone in his ring with the ball of his thumb. "I don't like the governmint no bettern you," he said. "Where you going instead? You going to the city and get you a soot of rooms at the Biltmo' Hotel?"

Tanner said nothing.

"The day coming," the doctor said, "when the white folks IS going to be working for the colored and you mights well to git ahead of the crowd."

"That day ain't coming for me," Tanner said shortly.

"Done come for you," the doctor said. "Ain't come for the rest of them."

Tanner's gaze drove on past the farthest blue edge of the treeline into the pale empty afternoon sky. "I got a daughter in the north," he said. "I don't have to work for you."

The doctor took his watch from his watch pocket and looked at it and put it back. He gazed for a moment at the back of his hands. He appeared to have measured and to know secretly the time it would take everything to change finally upsidedown. "She don't want no old daddy like you," he said. "Maybe she say she do, but that ain't likely. Even if you rich," he said, "they don't want you. They got they own ideas. The black ones they rares and they pitches. I made mine," he said, "and I ain't done none of that." He looked again at Tanner. "I be back here next week," he said, "and if you still here, I know you going to work for me." He remained there a moment, rocking on his heels, waiting for some answer. Finally he turned and started beating his way back through the overgrown path.

Tanner had continued to look across the field as if his spirit had been sucked out of him into the woods and nothing was left on the chair but a shell. If he had known it was a question of this—sitting here looking out of this window all day in this no-place, or just running a still for a nigger, he would have run the still for the nigger. He would have been a nigger's white nigger any day. Behind him he heard the daughter come in from the kitchen. His heart accelerated but after a second he heard her plump herself down on the sofa. She was not yet ready to go. He did not turn and look at her.

She sat there silently a few moments. Then she began. "The trouble with you is," she said, "you sit in front of that window all the time where there's nothing to look out at. You need some inspiration and out-let. If you would let me pull your chair around to look at the TV, you would quit thinking about morbid stuff, death and hell and judgement. My Lord."

"The Judgement is coming," he muttered. "The sheep'll be separated from the goats. Them that kept their promises from them that didn't. Them that did the best they could with what they had from them that didn't. Them that honored their father and their mother from them that cursed them. Them that . . ."

She heaved a mammoth sigh that all but drowned him out. "What's the use in me wasting my good breath?" she asked. She rose and went back in the kitchen and began knocking things about.

She was so high and mighty! At home he had been living in a shack but there was at least air around it. He could put his feet on the ground. Here she didn't even live in a house. She lived in a pigeon-hutch of a building, with all stripes of foreigner, all of them twisted in the tongue. It was no place for a sane man. The first morning here she had taken him sight-seeing and he had seen in fifteen minutes exactly how it was. He had not been out of the apartment since. He never wanted to set foot again on the underground railroad or the steps that moved under you while you stood still or any elevator to the thirty-fourth floor. When he was safely back in the apartment again, he had imagined going over it with Coleman. He had to turn his head every few seconds to make sure Coleman was behind him. Keep to the inside or these people'll knock you down, keep right behind me or you'll get left, keep your hat on, you damn idiot, he had said, and Coleman had come on with his bent running shamble, panting and muttering, What we doing here? Where you get this fool idea coming here?

I come to show you it was no kind of place. Now you know you were well off where you were.

I knowed it before, Coleman said. Was you didn't know it.

When he had been here a week, he had got a postcard from Coleman that had been written for him by Hooten at the railroad station. It was written in green ink and said, "This is Coleman—X—howyou boss." Under it Hooten had written from himself, "Quit frequenting all those nitespots and come on home, you scoundrel, yours truly, W. P. Hooten." He had sent Coleman a card in return, care of Hooten, that said, "This place is alrite if you like it. Yours truly, W. T. Tanner." Since the daughter had to mail the card, he had not put on it that he was returning as soon as his pension check came. He had not intended to tell her but to leave her a note. When the check came, he would hire himself a taxi to the bus station and be on his way. And it would have made her as happy as it made him. She had found his company dour and her duty irksome. If he had sneaked out, she would have had the pleasure of having tried to do it and to top that off, the pleasure of his ingratitude.

As for him, he would have returned to squat on the doctor's land and to take his orders from a nigger who chewed ten-cent cigars. And to think less about it than formerly. Instead he had been done in by a nigger actor, or one who called himself an actor. He didn't believe the nigger was any actor.

There were two apartments on each floor of the building. He had been with the daughter three weeks when the people in the next hutch moved out. He had stood in the hall and watched the moving-out and the next day he had watched a moving-in. The hall was narrow and dark and he stood in the corner out of the way, offering only a suggestion every now and then to the movers that would have made their work easier for them if they had paid any attention. The furniture was new and cheap so he decided the people moving in might be a newly married couple and he would just wait around until they came and wish them well. After a while a large Negro in a light blue suit came lunging up the stairs, carrying two canvas suitcases, his head lowered against the strain. Behind him stepped a young tan-skinned woman with bright copper-colored hair. The Negro dropped the suitcases with a thud in front of the door of the next apartment.

"Be careful, Sweetie," the woman said. "My make-up is in there."

It broke upon him then just what was happening.

The Negro was grinning. He took a swipe at one of her hips.

"Quit it," she said, "there's an old guy watching."

They both turned and looked at him.

"Had-do," he said and nodded. Then he turned quickly into his own door.

His daughter was in the kitchen. "Who you think's rented that apartment over there?" he asked, his face alight.

She looked at him suspiciously. "Who?" she muttered.

"A nigger!" he said in a gleeful voice. "A South Alabama nigger if I ever saw one. And got him this high-yeller, high-stepping woman with red hair and they two are going to live next door to you!" He slapped his knee. "Yes siree!" he said. "Damn if they ain't!" It was the first time since coming up here that he had had occasion to laugh.

Her face squared up instantly. "All right now you listen to me," she said. "You keep away from them. Don't you go over there trying to get friendly with him. They ain't the same around here and I don't want any trouble with niggers, you hear me? If you have to live next to them, just you mind your business and they'll mind theirs. That's the way people were meant to get along in this world. Everybody can get along if they just mind their business. Live and let live." She began to wrinkle her nose like a rabbit, a stupid way she had. "Up here everybody minds their own business and everybody gets along. That's all you have to do."

"I was getting along with niggers before you were born," he said. He went back out into the hall and waited. He was willing to bet the nigger would like to talk to someone who understood him. Twice while he waited, he forgot and in his excitement, spit his tobacco juice against the baseboard. In about twenty minutes, the door of the apartment opened again and the Negro came out. He had put on a tie and a pair of horn-rimmed spectacles and Tanner noticed for the first time that he had a small almost invisible goatee. A real swell. He came on without appearing to see there was anyone else in the hall.

"Haddy, John," Tanner said and nodded, but the Negro brushed past without hearing and went rattling rapidly down the stairs.

Could be deaf and dumb, Tanner thought. He went back into the apartment and sat down but each time he heard noise in the hall, he got up and went to the door and stuck his head out to see if it might be the Negro. Once in the middle of the afternoon, he caught the Negro's eye just as he was rounding the bend of the stairs again but before he could get out a word, the man was in his own apartment and had slammed the door. He had never known one to move that fast unless the police were after him.

He was standing in the hall early the next morning when the woman came out of her door alone, walking on high gold-painted heels. He wished to bid her good morning or simply to nod but instinct told him to beware. She didn't look like any kind of woman, black or white, he had ever seen before and he remained pressed against the wall, frightened more than anything else, and feigning invisibility.

The woman gave him a flat stare, then turned her head away and stepped wide of him as if she were skirting an open garbage can. He held his breath until she was out of sight. Then he waited patiently for the man.

The Negro came out about eight o'clock.

This time Tanner advanced squarely in his path. "Good morning, Preacher," he said. It had been his experience that if a Negro tended to be sullen, this title usually cleared up his expression.

The Negro stopped abruptly.

"I seen you move in," Tanner said. "I ain't been up here long myself. It ain't much of a place if you ask me. I reckon you wish you were back in South Alabama."

The Negro did not take a step or answer. His eyes began to move. They moved from the top of the black hat, down to the collarless blue shirt, neatly buttoned at the neck, down the faded galluses to the grey trousers and the high-top shoes and up again, very slowly, while some unfathomable dead-cold rage seemed to stiffen and shrink him.

"I thought you might know somewhere around here we could find us a pond, Preacher," Tanner said in a voice growing thinner but still with considerable hope in it.

A seething noise came out of the Negro before he spoke. "I'm not from South Alabama," he said in a breathless wheezing voice. "I'm from New York City. And I'm not no preacher! I'm an actor."

Tanner chortled. "It's a little actor in most preachers, ain't it?" he said and winked. "I reckon you just preach on the side."

"I don't preach!" the Negro cried and rushed past him as if a swarm of bees had suddenly come down on him out of nowhere. He dashed down the stairs and was gone.

Tanner stood there for some time before he went back in the apartment. The rest of the day he sat in his chair and debated whether he would have one more try at making friends with him. Every time he heard a noise on the stairs he went to the door and looked out, but the Negro did not return until late in the afternoon. Tanner was standing in the hall waiting for him when he reached the top of the stairs. "Good evening, Preacher," he said, forgetting that the Negro called himself an actor.

The Negro stopped and gripped the banister rail. A tremor racked him from his head to his crotch. Then he began to come forward slowly. When he was close enough he lunged and grasped Tanner by both shoulders. "I don't take no crap," he whispered, "off no wool-hat redneck son-of-a-bitch peckerwood old bastard like you." He caught his breath. And then his voice came out in the sound of an exasperation so profound that it rocked on the verge of a laugh. It was high and piercing and weak. "And I'm not no preacher! I'm not even no Christian. I don't believe that crap. There ain't no Jesus and there ain't no God."

The old man felt his heart inside him hard and tough as an oak knot. "And you ain't black," he said. "And I ain't white!"

The Negro slammed him against the wall. He yanked the black hat down over his eyes. Then he grabbed his shirt front and shoved him backwards to his open door and knocked him through it. From the kitchen the daughter saw him blindly hit the edge of the inside hall door and fall reeling into the living-room.

For days his tongue appeared to be frozen in his mouth. When it unthawed it was twice its normal size and he could not make her understand him. What he wanted to know was if the government check had come because he meant to buy a bus ticket with it and go home. After a few days, he made her understand. "It came," she said, "and it'll just pay the first two weeks' doctor-bill and please tell me how you're going home when you can't talk or walk or think straight and you got one eye crossed yet? Just please tell me that?"

It had come to him then slowly just what his present situation was. At least he would have to make her understand that he must be sent home to be buried. They could have him shipped back in a refrigerated car so that he would keep for the trip. He didn't want any undertaker up here messing with him. Let them get him off at once and he would come in on the early morning train and they could wire Hooten to get Coleman and Coleman would do the rest; she would not even have to go herself. After a lot of argument, he wrung the promise from her. She would ship him back.

After that he slept peacefully and improved a little. In his dreams he could feel the cold early morning air of home coming in through the cracks of the pine box. He could see Coleman waiting, red-eyed, on the station platform and Hooten standing there with his green eyeshade and black alpaca sleeves. If the old fool had stayed at home where he belonged, Hooten would be thinking, he wouldn't be arriving on the 6:03 in no box. Coleman had turned the borrowed mule and cart so that they could slide the box off the platform onto the open end of the wagon. Everything was ready and the two of them, shut-mouthed, inched the loaded coffin toward the wagon. From inside he began to scratch on the wood. They let go as if it had caught fire.

They stood looking at each other, then at the box.

"That him," Coleman said. "He in there his self."

"Naw," Hooten said, "must be a rat got in there with him."

"That him. This here one of his tricks."

"If it's a rat he might as well stay."

"That him. Git a crowbar."

Hooten went grumbling off and got the crowbar and came back and began to pry open the lid. Even before he had the upper end pried open, Coleman was jumping up and down, wheezing and panting from excitement. Tanner gave a thrust upward with both hands and sprang up in the box. "Judgement Day! Judgement Day!" he cried. "Don't you two fools know it's Judgement Day?"

Now he knew exactly what her promises were worth. He would do as well to trust to the note pinned in his coat and to any stranger who found him dead in the street or in the boxcar or wherever. There was nothing to be looked for from her except that she would do things her way. She came out of the kitchen again, holding her hat and coat and rubber boots.

"Now listen," she said, "I have to go to the store. Don't you try to get up and walk around while I'm gone. You've been to the bathroom and you shouldn't have to go again. I don't want to find you on the floor when I get back."

You won't find me atall when you get back, he said to himself. This was the last time he would see her flat dumb face. He felt guilty. She had been good to him and he had been nothing but a nuisance to her.

"Do you want a glass of milk before I go?" she asked.

"No," he said. Then he drew breath and said, "You got a nice place here. It's a nice part of the country. I'm sorry if I've give you a lot of trouble getting sick. It was my fault trying to be friendly with that nigger." And I'm a damned liar besides, he said to himself to kill the outrageous taste such a statement made in his mouth.

For a moment she stared as if he were losing his mind. Then she seemed to think better of it. "Now don't saying something pleasant like that once in a while make you feel better?" she asked and sat down on the sofa.

His knees itched to unbend. Git on, git on, he fumed silently. Make haste and go.

"It's great to have you here," she said. "I wouldn't have you any other place. My own daddy." She gave him a big smile and hoisted her right leg up and began to pull on her boot. "I wouldn't wish a dog out on a day like this," she said, "but I got to go. You can sit here and hope I don't slip and break my neck." She stamped the booted foot on the floor and then began to tackle the other one.

He turned his eyes to the window. The snow was beginning to stick and freeze to the outside pane. When he looked at her again, she was standing there like a big doll stuffed into its hat and coat. She drew on a pair of green knitted gloves. "Okay," she said, "I'm gone. You sure you don't want anything?"

"No," he said, "go ahead on."

"Well so long then," she said.

He raised the hat enough to reveal a bald palely speckled head. The hall door closed behind her. He began to tremble with excitement. He reached behind him and drew the coat into his lap. When he got it on, he waited until he had stopped panting, then he gripped the arms of the chair and pulled himself up. His body felt like a great heavy bell whose clapper swung from side to side but made no noise. Once up, he remained standing a moment, swaying until he got his balance. A sensation of terror and defeat swept over him. He would never make it. He would never get there dead or alive. He pushed one foot forward and did not fall and his confidence returned. "The Lord is my shepherd," he muttered, "I shall not want." He began moving toward the sofa where he would have support. He reached it. He was on his way.

By the time he got to the door, she would be down the four flights of steps and out of the building. He got past the sofa and crept along by the wall, keeping his hand on it for support. Nobody was going to bury him here. He was as confident as if the woods of home lay at the bottom of the stairs. He reached the front door of the apartment and opened it and peered into the hall. This was the first time he had looked into it since the actor had knocked him down. It was dank-smelling and empty. The thin piece of linoleum stretched its moldy length to the door of the other apartment, which was closed. "Nigger actor," he said.

The head of the stairs was ten or twelve feet from where he stood and he bent his attention to getting there without creeping around the long way with a hand on the wall. He held his arms a little way out from his sides and pushed forward directly. He was half way there when all at once his legs disappeared, or felt as if they had. He looked down, bewindered, for they were still there. He fell forward and grasped the banister post with both hands. Hanging there, he gazed for what seemed the longest time he had ever looked at anything down the steep unlighted steps; then he closed his eyes and pitched forward. He landed upsidedown in the middle of the flight.

He felt presently the tilt of the box as they took it off the train and got it on the baggage wagon. He made no noise yet. The train jarred and slid away. In a moment the baggage wagon was rumbling under him, carrying him back to the station side. He heard footsteps rattling closer and closer to him and he supposed that a crowd was gathering. Wait until they see this, he thought.

"That him," Coleman said, "one of his tricks."

"It's a damn rat in there," Hooten said.

"It's him. Git the crowbar."

In a moment a shaft of greenish light fell on him. He pushed through it and cried in a weak voice, "Judgement Day! Judgement Day! You idiots didn't know it was Judgement Day, did you?

"Coleman?" he murmured.

The Negro bending over him had a large surly mouth and sullen eyes.

"Ain't any coal man, either," he said. This must be the wrong station, Tanner thought. Those fools put me off too soon. Who is this nigger? It ain't even daylight here.

At the Negro's side was another face, a woman's—pale topped with a pile of copper-glinting hair and twisted as if she had just stepped in a pile of dung.

"Oh," Tanner said, "it's you."

The actor leaned closer and grasped him by the front of his shirt. "Judgement day," he said in a mocking voice. "Ain't no judgement day, old man. Cept this. Maybe this here judgement day for you."

Tanner tried to catch hold of a banister-spoke to raise himself but his hand grasped air. The two faces, the black one and the pale one, appeared to be wavering. By an effort of will he kept them focussed before him while he lifted his hand, as light as a breath, and said in his jauntiest voice, "Hep me up, Preacher. I'm on my way home!"

His daughter found him when she came in from the grocery store. His hat had been pulled down over his face and his head and arms thrust between the spokes of the banister; his feet dangled over the stairwell like those of a man in the stocks. She tugged at him frantically and then flew for the police. They cut him out with a saw and said he had been dead about an hour.

She buried him in New York City, but after she had done it she could not sleep at night. Night after night she turned and tossed and very definite lines began to appear in her face, so she had him dug up and shipped the body to Corinth. Now she rests well at night and her good looks have mostly returned.

MY KINSMAN,
MAJOR MOLINEUX

Nathaniel Hawthorne

AFTER THE KINGS of Great Britain had assumed the right of appointing the colonial governors, the measures of the latter seldom met with the ready and generous approbation which had been paid to those of their predecessors, under the original charters. The people looked with most jealous scrutiny to the exercise of power which did not emanate from themselves, and they usually rewarded their rulers with slender gratitude for the compliances by which, in softening their instructions from beyond the sea, they had incurred the reprehension of those who gave them. The annals of Massachusetts Bay will inform us, that of six governors in the space of about forty years from the surrender of the old charter, under James II, two were imprisoned by a popular insurrection; a third, as Hutchinson inclines to believe, was driven from the province by the whizzing of a musket-ball; a fourth, in the opinion of the same historian, was hastened to his grave by continual bickerings with the House of Representatives; and the remaining two, as well as their successors, till the Revolution, were favored with few and brief intervals of peaceful sway. The inferior members of the court party, in times of high political excitement, led scarcely a more desirable life. These remarks may serve as a preface to the following adventures, which chanced upon a summer night, not far from a hundred years ago. The reader, in order to avoid a long and dry detail of colonial affairs, is requested to dispense with an account of the train of circumstances that had caused much temporary inflammation of the popular mind.

It was near nine o'clock of a moonlight evening, when a boat crossed the ferry with a single passenger, who had obtained his conveyance at that unusual hour by the promise of an extra fare. While he stood on the landing-place, searching in either pocket for the means of fulfilling his agreement, the ferryman lifted a lantern, by the aid of which, and the newly risen moon, he took a very accurate survey of the stranger's figure. He was a youth of barely eighteen years, evidently country-bred, and now, as it should seem, upon his first visit to town. He was clad in a coarse gray coat, well worn, but in excellent repair; his under garments were durably constructed of leather, and fitted tight to a pair of serviceable and well-shaped limbs; his stockings of blue yarn were the incontrovertible work of a mother or a sister; and on his head was a three-cornered hat, which in its better days had perhaps sheltered the graver brow of the lad's father. Under the left arm was a heavy cudgel formed of an oak sapling, and retaining a part of the hardened root; and his equipment was completed by a wallet, not so abundantly stocked as to incommode the vigorous shoulders on which it hung. Brown, curly hair, well-shaped features, and bright, cheerful eyes were nature's gifts, and worth all that art could have done for his adornment.

The youth, one of whose names was Robin, finally drew from his pocket the half of a little province bill of five shillings, which, in the depreciation in that sort of currency, did but satisfy the ferryman's demand, with the surplus of a sexanagular piece of parchment, valued at three pence. He then walked forward into the town, with as light a step as if his day's journey had not already exceeded thirty miles, and with as eager an eye as if he were entering London city, instead of the little metropolis of a New England colony. Before Robin had proceeded far, however, it occurred to him that he knew not whither to direct his steps; so he paused, and looked up and down the narrow street, scrutinizing the small and mean wooden buildings that were scattered on either side.

"This low hovel cannot be my kinsman's dwelling," thought he, "nor yonder old house, where the moonlight enters at the broken casement; and truly I see none hereabouts that might be worthy of him. It would have been wise to inquire my way of the ferryman, and doubtless he would have gone with me, and earned a shilling from the Major for his pains. But the next man I meet will do as well."

He resumed his walk, and was glad to perceive that the street now became wider, and the houses more respectable in their appearance. He soon discerned a figure moving on moderately in advance, and hastened his steps to overtake it. As Robin drew nigh, he saw that the passenger was a man in years, with a full periwig of gray hair, a wide-skirted coat of dark cloth, and silk stockings rolled above his knees. He carried a long and polished cane, which he struck down perpendicularly before him at every step; and at regular intervals he uttered two successive hems, of a peculiarly solemn and sepulchral intonation. Having made these observations, Robin laid hold of the skirt of the old man's coat, just when the light from the open door and windows of a barber's shop fell upon both their figures.

"Good evening to you, honored sir," said he, making a low bow, and still retaining his hold of the skirt. "I pray you tell me whereabouts is the dwelling of my kinsman, Major Molineux."

The youth's question was uttered very loudly; and one of the barbers, whose razor was descending on a well-soaped chin, and another who was dressing a Ramillies wig, left their occupations, and came to the door. The citizen, in the meantime, turned a long-favored countenance upon Robin, and answered him in a tone of excessive anger and annoyance. His two sepulchral hems, however, broke into the very center of his rebuke, with most singular effect, like a thought of the cold grace obtruding among wrathful passions.

"Let go my garment, fellow! I tell you, I know not the man you speak of. What! I have authority, I have—hem, hem—authority; and if this be the respect you show for your betters, your feet shall be brought acquainted with the stocks by daylight, tomorrow morning!"

Robin released the old man's skirt, and hastened away, pursued by an ill-mannered roar of laughter from the barber's shop. He was at first considerably surprised by the result of the question, but, being a shrewd youth, soon thought himself able to account for the mystery.

"This is some country representative," was his conclusion, "who has never seen the inside of my kinsman's door, and lacks the breeding to answer a stranger civilly. The man is old, or verily—I might be tempted to turn back and smite him on the nose. Ah, Robin, Robin! even the barber's boys laugh at you for choosing such a guide! You will be wiser in time, friend Robin."

He now became entangled in a succession of crooked and narrow streets, which crossed each other, and meandered at no great distance from the water-side. The smell of tar was obvious to his nostrils, the masts of vessels pierced the moonlight above the tops of the buildings, and the numerous signs, which Robin paused to read, informed him that he was near the center of business. But the streets were empty, the shops were closed, and lights were visible only in the second stories of a few dwelling-houses. At length, on the corner of a narrow lane, through which he was passing, he beheld the broad countenance of a British hero swinging before the door of an inn, whence proceeded the voices of many guests. The casement of one of the lower windows was thrown back, and a very thin curtain permitted Robin to distinguish a party at supper, round a well-furnished table. The fragrance of the good cheer steamed forth into the outer air, and the youth could not fail to recollect that the last remnant of his travelling stock of provision had yielded to his morning appetite and that noon had found and left him dinnerless.

"Oh, that a parchment three-penny might give me a right to sit down at yonder table!" said Robin, with a sigh. "But the Major will make me welcome to the best of his victuals so I will even step boldly in, and inquire my way to his dwelling."

He entered the tavern, and was guided by the murmur of voices and the fumes of tobacco to the public-room. It was a long and low apartment, with oaken walls, grown dark in the continual smoke, and a floor which was thickly sanded, but of no immaculate purity. A number of persons—the larger part of whom appeared to be mariners, or in some way connected with the sea—occupied the wooden benches, or leather-

bottomed chairs, conversing on various matters, and ocasionally lend-
ing their attention to some topic of general interest. Three or four little
groups were draining as many bowls of punch, which the West India
trade had long since made a familiar drink in the colony. Others, who
had the appearance of men who lived by regular and laborious handi-
craft, preferred the insulated bliss of an unshared potation, and became
more taciturn under its influence. Nearly all, in short, evinced a predi-
lection for the Good Creature in some of its various shapes, for this is
a vice to which, as Fast Day sermons of a hundred years ago will testify,
we have a long hereditary claim. The only guests to whom Robin's
sympathies inclined him were two or three sheepish countrymen, who
were using the inn somewhat after the fashion of a Turkish caravan-
sary; they had gotten themselves into the darkest corner of the room,
and heedless of the Nicotian atmosphere, were supping on the bread
of their own ovens, and the bacon cured in their own chimney-smoke.
But though Robin felt a sort of brotherhood with these strangers, his
eyes were attracted from them to a person who stood near the door,
holding whispered conversation with a group of ill-dressed associates.
His features were separately striking almost to grotesqueness, and the
whole face left a deep impression on the memory. The forehead bulged
out into a double prominence, with a vale between; the nose came
boldly forth in an irregular curve, and its bridge was of more than a
finger's breadth; the eyebrows were deep and shaggy, and the eyes
glowed beneath them like fire in a cave.

While Robin deliberated of whom to inquire respecting his kinsman's
dwelling, he was accosted by the innkeeper, a little man in a stained
white apron, who had come to pay his professional welcome to the
stranger. Being in the second generation from a French Protestant, he
seemed to have inherited the courtesy of his parent nation; but no
variety of circumstances was ever known to change his voice from the
one shrill note in which he now addressed Robin.

"From the country, I presume, sir?" said he, with a profound bow.
"Beg leave to congratulate you on your arrival, and trust you intend
a long stay with us. Fine town here, sir, beautiful buildings, and much
that may interest a stranger. May I hope for the honor of your com-
mands in respect to supper?"

"The man sees a family likeness! the rogue has guessed that I am
related to the Major!" thought Robin, who had hitherto experienced
little superfluous civility.

All eyes were now turned on the country lad, standing at the door,
in his worn three-cornered hat, gray coat, leather breeches, and blue
yarn stockings, leaning on an oaken cudgel, and bearing a wallet on his
back.

Robin replied to the courteous innkeeper, with such an assumption
of confidence as befitted the Major's relative. "My honest friend," he

said, "I shall make it a point to patronize your house on some occasion, when"—here he could not help lowering his voice—"when I may have more than a parchment three-pence in my pocket. My present business," continued he, speaking with lofty confidence, "is merely to inquire my way to the dwelling of my kinsman, Major Molineux."

There was a sudden and general movement in the room, which Robin interpreted as expressing the eagerness of each individual to become his guide. But the innkeeper turned his eyes to a written paper on the wall, which he read, or seemed to read, with occasional recurrences to the young man's figure.

"What have we here?" said he, breaking his speech into little dry fragments. " 'Left the house of the subscriber, bounden servant, Hezekiah Mudge,—had on, when he went away, gray coat, leather breeches, master's third-best hat. One pound currency reward to whosoever shall lodge him in any jail of the providence.' Better trudge, boy; better trudge!"

Robin had begun to draw his hand towards the lighter end of the oak cudgel, but a strange hostility in every countenance induced him to relinquish his purpose of breaking the courteous innkeeper's head. As he turned to leave the room, he encountered a sneering glance from the bold-featured personage whom he had before noticed; and no sooner was he beyond the door, than he heard a general laugh, in which the innkeeper's voice might be distinguished, like the dropping of small stones into a kettle.

"Now, is it not strange," thought Robin, with his usual shrewdness, —"is it not strange that the confession of an empty pocket should outweigh the name of my kinsman, Major Molineux? Oh, if I had one of those grinning rascals in the woods, where I and my oak sapling grew up together, I would teach him that my arm is heavy though my purse be light!"

On turning the corner of the narrow lane, Robin found himself in a spacious street, with an unbroken line of lofty houses on each side, and a steepled building at the upper end, whence the ringing of a bell announced the hour of nine. The light of the moon, and the lamps from the numerous shop-windows, discovered people promenading on the pavement, and amongst them Robin had hoped to recognize his hitherto inscrutable relative. The result of his former inquiries made him unwilling to hazard another, in a scene of such publicity, and he determined to walk slowly and silently up the street, thrusting his face close to that of every elderly gentleman, in search of the Major's lineaments. In his progress, Robin encountered many gay and gallant figures. Embroidered garments of showy colors, enormous periwigs, gold-laced hats, and silver-hilted swords glided past him and dazzled his optics. Travelled youths, imitators of the European fine gentlemen of the period, trod jauntily along, half dancing to the fashionable tunes which they hummed, and making poor Robin ashamed of his quiet and natural gait. At length, after many pauses to examine the gorgeous display of goods in the shop-windows, and after suffering some rebukes for the impertinence of his scrutiny into people's faces, the Major's kinsman found himself near the steepled building, still unsuccessful in his search. As yet, however, he had seen only one side of the thronged street; so Robin crossed, and continued the same sort of inquisition down the opposite pavement, with stronger hopes than the philosopher seeking an honest man, but with no better fortune. He had arrived about midway towards the lower end, from which his course began, when he overheard the approach of some one who struck down a cane on the flag-stones at every step, uttering at regular intervals, two sepulchral hems.

"Mercy on us!" quoth Robin, recognizing the sound.

Turning a corner, which chanced to be close at his right hand, he hastened to pursue his researches in some other part of the town. His patience now was wearing low, and he seemed to feel more fatigue from his rambles since he crossed the ferry, than from his journey of several days on the other side. Hunger also pleaded loudly within him, and Robin began to balance the propriety of demanding, violently, and with lifted cudgel, the necessary guidance from the first solitary passenger whom he should meet. While a resolution to this effect was gaining strength, he entered a street of mean appearance, on either side of which a row of ill-built houses was straggling towards the harbor. The moonlight fell upon no passenger along the whole extent, but in the third domicile which Robin passed there was a half-open door, and his keen glance detected a woman's garment within.

"My luck may be better here," said he to himself.

Accordingly, he approached the door, and beheld it shut closer as he did so; yet an open space remained, sufficing for the fair occupant to observe the stranger, without a corresponding displaying on her part. All that Robin could discern was a strip of scarlet petticoat, and the occasional sparkle of an eye, as if the moonbeams were trembling on some bright thing.

"Pretty mistress," for I may call her so with a good conscience, thought the shrewd youth, since I know nothing to the contrary,—"my sweet pretty mistress, will you be kind enough to tell me whereabouts I must seek the dwelling of my kinsman, Major Molineux?"

Robin's voice was plaintive and winning, and the female, seeing nothing to be shunned in the handsome country youth, thrust open the door, and came forth into the moonlight. She was a dainty little figure, with a white neck, round arms, and a slender waist, at the extremity of which her scarlet petticoat jutted out over a hoop, as if she were standing in a balloon. Moreover, her face was oval and pretty, her hair dark beneath the little cap, and her bright eyes possessed a sly freedom, which triumphed over those of Robin.

"Major Molineux dwells here," said this fair woman.

Now, her voice was the sweetest Robin had heard that night, yet he could not help doubting whether that sweet voice spoke Gospel truth. He looked up and down the mean street, and then surveyed the house before which they stood. It was a small, dark edifice of two stories, the second of which projected over the lower floor, and the front apartment had the aspect of a shop for petty commodities.

"Now, truly, I am in luck," replied Robin cunningly, "and so indeed is my kinsman, the Major, in having so pretty a housekeeper. But I prithee trouble him to step to the door; I will deliver him a message from his friends in the country, and then go back to my lodgings at the inn."

"Nay, the Major has been abed this hour or more," said the lady of the scarlet petticoat; "and it would be to little purpose to disturb him tonight, seeing his evening draught was of the strongest. But he is a kind-hearted man, and it would be as much as my life's worth to let a kinsman of his turn away from the door. You are the good old gentleman's very picture, and I could swear that was his rainy-weather hat. Also he has garments very much resembling those leather small-clothes. But come in, I pray, for I bid you hearty welcome in his name."

So saying, the fair and hospitable dame took our hero by the hand; and the touch was light, and the force was gentleness, and though Robin read in her eyes what he did not hear in her words, yet the slender-waisted woman in the scarlet petticoat proved stronger than the athletic country youth. She had drawn his half-willing footsteps nearly to the threshold, when the opening of a door in the neighborhood startled the Major's housekeeper, and, leaving the Major's kinsman, she vanished speedily into her own domicile. A heavy yawn preceded the appearance of a man, who, like the Moonshine of Pyramus and Thisbe, carried a lantern, needlessly aiding his sister luminary in the heavens. As he walked sleepily up the street, he turned his broad, dull face on Robin, and displayed a long staff, spiked at the end.

"Home, vagabond, home!" said the watchman, in accents that seemed to fall asleep as soon as they were uttered. "Home, or we'll set you in the stocks by peep of day!"

"This is the second hint of the kind," thought Robin. "I wish they would end my difficulties by setting me there to-night."

Nevertheless, the youth felt an instinctive antipathy towards the guardian of midnight order, which at first prevented him from asking his usual question. But just when the man was about to vanish behind the corner, Robin resolved not to lose the opportunity, and shouted lustily after him,—

"I say, friend! will you guide me to the house of my kinsman, Major Molineux?"

The watchman made no reply, but turned the corner and was gone; yet Robin seemed to hear the sound of drowsy laughter stealing along the solitary street. At that moment, also, a pleasant titter saluted him from the open window above his head; he looked up, and caught the sparkle of a saucy eye; a round arm beckoned to him, and next he heard light footsteps descending the staircase within. But Robin, being of the household of a New England clergyman, was a good youth, as well as a shrewd one; so he resisted temptation, and fled away.

He now roamed desperately, and at random, through the town, almost ready to believe that a spell was on him, like that by which a wizard of his country had once kept three pursuers wandering, a whole winter night, within twenty paces of the cottage which they sought. The streets lay before him, strange and desolate, and the lights were extinguished in almost every house. Twice, however, little parties of men, among whom Robin distinguished individuals in outlandish attire, came hurrying along; but, though on both occasions, they paused to address him, such intercourse did not at all enlighten his perplexity. They did but utter a few words in some langauge of which Robin knew nothing, and perceiving his inability to answer, bestowed a curse upon him in plain English and hastened away. Finally, the lad determined to knock at the door of every mansion that might appear worthy to be occupied by his kinsman, trusting that perseverance would overcome the fatality that had hitherto thwarted him. Firm in this resolve, he was passing beneath the walls of a church, which formed the corner of two streets, when, as he turned into the shade of its steeple, he encountered a bulky stranger, muffled in a cloak. The man was proceeding with the speed of earnest business, but Robin planted himself full before him, holding the oak cudgel with both hands across his body as a bar to further passage.

"Halt, honest man, and answer me a question," said he, very resolutely. "Tell me, this instant, whereabouts is the dwelling of my kinsman, Major Molineux!"

"Keep your tongue between your teeth, fool, and let me pass!" said a deep, gruff voice, which Robin partly remembered. "Let me pass, or I'll strike you to the earth!"

"No, no, neighbor!" cried Robin, flourishing his cudgel, and then thrusting its larger end close to the man's muffled face. "No, no, I'm not the fool you take me for, nor do you pass till I have an answer to my question. Whereabouts is the dwelling of my kinsman, Major Molineux?"

The stranger, instead of attempting to force his passage, stepped back into moonlight, unmuffled his face, and stared full into that of Robin.

"Watch here an hour, and Major Molineux will pass by," said he.

Robin gazed with dismay and astonishment on the unprecedented physiognomy of the speaker. The forehead with its double prominence, the broad hooked nose, the shaggy eyebrows, and fiery eyes were those which he had noticed at the inn, but the man's complexion had undergone a singular, or, more properly, a two-fold change. One side of the face blazed in intense red, while the other was black as midnight, the division line being the broad bridge of the nose; and a mouth which seemed to extend from ear to ear was black or red, in contrast to the color of the cheek. The effect was as if two individual devils, a fiend of fire and a fiend of darkness, had united themselves to form this infernal visage. The stranger grinned in Robin's face, muffled his party-colored features, and was out of sight in a moment.

"Strange things we travellers see!" ejaculated Robin.

He seated himself, however, upon the steps of the church-door, resolving to wait the appointed time for his kinsman. A few moments were consumed in philosophical speculations upon the species of man who had just left him; but having settled this point shrewdly, rationally, and satisfactorily, he was compelled to look elsewhere for his amusement. And first he threw his eyes along the street. It was of more respectable appearance than most of those into which he had wandered; and the moon, creating, like the imaginative power, a beautiful strangeness in familiar objects, gave something of romance to a scene that might not have possessed it in the light of day. The irregular and often quaint architecture of the houses, some of whose roofs were broken into numerous little peaks, while others ascended, steep and narrow, into a single point, and others again were square; the pure snow-white of some of their complexions, the aged darkness of others, and the thousand sparklings, reflected from bright substances in the walls of many; these matters engaged Robin's attention for a while, and then began to grow wearisome. Next he endeavored to define the forms of distant objects, starting away, with almost ghostly indistinctness, just as his eye appeared to grasp them; and finally he took a minute survey of an edifice which stood on the opposite side of the street, directly in front of the church-door, where he was stationed. It was a large square mansion, distinguished from its neighbors by a balcony which rested on tall pillars, and by an elaborate Gothic window, communicating therewith.

"Perhaps this is the very house I have been seeking," thought Robin.

Then he strove to speed away the time, by listening to a murmur which swept continually along the street, yet was scarcely audible, except to an unaccustomed ear like his; it was a low, dull, dreamy sound, compounded of many noises, each of which was at too great a distance to be separately heard. Robin marvelled at this snore of a sleeping town, and marvelled more whenever its continuity was broken by now and then a distant shout, apparently loud where it originated. But altogether it was a sleep-inspiring sound, and, to shake off its drowsy influence, Robin arose, and climbed a window-frame, that he might view the interior of the church. There the moonbeams came trembling in, and fell down upon the deserted pews, and extended along the quiet aisles. A fainter yet more awful radiance was hovering around the pulpit, and one solitary ray had dared to rest upon the open page of the great Bible. Had nature, in that deep hour, become a worshipper in the house which man had builded? Or was that heavenly light the visible sanctity of the place,—visible because no earthly and impure feet were within the walls? The scene made Robin's heart shiver with a sensation of loneliness stronger than he had ever felt in the remotest depths of his native woods; so he turned away and sat down again before the door. There were graves around the church, and now an uneasy thought obtruded into Robin's breast. What if the object of his search, which had been so often and so strangely thwarted, were all the time mouldering in his shroud? What if his kinsman should glide through yonder gate, and nod and smile to him in dimly passing by?

"Oh, that any breathing thing were here with me!" said Robin.

Recalling his thoughts from this uncomfortable track, he sent them over forest, hill, and stream, and attempted to imagine how that evening of ambiguity and weariness had been spent by his father's household. He pictured them assembled at the door, beneath the tree, the great old tree, which had been spared for its huge twisted trunk and venerable shade, when a thousand leafy brethren fell. There, at the going down of the summer sun, it was his father's custom to perform domestic worship, that the neighbors might come and join with him like brothers of the family, and that the wayfaring man might pause to drink at that fountain, and keep his heart pure by freshening the memory of home. Robin distinguished the seat of every individual of the little audience; he saw the good man in the midst, holding the Scriptures in the golden light that fell from the western clouds; he beheld him close the book and all rise up to pray. He heard the old thanksgivings for daily mercies, the old supplications for their continuance, to which he had so often listened in weariness, but which were now among his dear remembrances. He perceived the slight inequality of his father's voice when he came to speak of the absent one; he noted how his mother turned her face to the broad and knotted trunk; how his elder brother scorned, because the beard was rough upon his upper lip, to permit his features to be moved; how the younger sister drew down a low hanging branch before her eyes; and how the little one of all, whose sports had hitherto broken the decorum of the scene, understood the prayer for her playmate, and burst into clamorous grief. Then he saw them go in at the door; and when Robin would have entered also, the latch tinkled into its place, and he was excluded from his home.

"Am I here, or there?" cried Robin, starting; for all at once, when his thoughts had become visible and audible in a dream, the long, wide, solitary street shone out before him.

He aroused himself, and endeavored to fix his attention steadily upon the large edifice which he had surveyed before. But still his mind kept vibrating between fancy and reality; by turns, the pillars of the balcony lengthened into the tall, bare stems of pines, dwindled down to human figures, settled again into their true shape and size, and then commenced a new succession of changes. For a single moment, when he deemed himself awake, he could have sworn that a visage—one which he seemed to remember, yet could not absolutely name as his kinsman's—was looking towards him from the Gothic window. A deeper sleep wrestled with and nearly overcame him, but fled at the sound of footsteps along the opposite pavement. Robin rubbed his eyes, discerned a man passing at the foot of the balcony, and addressed him in a loud, peevish, and lamentable cry.

"Hallo, friend! must I wait here all night for my kinsman, Major Molineux?"

The sleeping echoes awoke, and answered the voice; and the passenger, barely able to discern a figure sitting in the oblique shade of the steeple, traversed the street to obtain a nearer view. He was himself a gentleman in his prime, of open, intelligent, cheerful and altogether prepossessing countenance. Perceiving a country youth, apparently homeless and without friends, he accosted him in a tone of real kindness, which had become strange to Robin's ears.

"Well, my good lad, why are you sitting here?" inquired he. "Can I be of service to you in any way?"

"I am afraid not, sir," replied Robin, despondingly; "yet I shall take it kindly, if you'll answer me a single question. I've been searching, half the night, for one Major Molineux; now, sir, is there really such a person in these parts, or am I dreaming?"

"Major Molineux! The name is not altogether strange to me," said the gentleman, smiling. "Have you any objection to telling me the nature of your business with him?"

Then Robin briefly related that his father was a clergyman, settled on a small salary, at a long distance back in the country, and that he and Major Molineux were brothers' children. The Major, having inherited riches, and acquired civil and military rank, had visited his cousin, in great pomp, a year or two before; had manifested much interest in Robin and an elder brother, and, being childless himself, had thrown out hints respecting the future establishment of one of them in life. The elder brother was destined to succeed to the farm which his father cultivated in the interval of sacred duties; it was therefore determined that Robin should profit by his kinsman's generous intentions, especially as he seemed to be rather the favorite, and was thought to possess other necessary endowments.

"For I have the name of being a shrewd youth," observed Robin, in this part of his story.

"I doubt not you deserve it," replied his new friend, good-naturedly; "but pray proceed."

"Well, sir, being nearly eighteen years old, and well grown, as you see," continued Robin, drawing himself up to his full height, "I thought it high time to begin in the world. So my mother and sister put me in handsome trim, and my father gave me half the remnant of his last year's salary, and five days ago I started for this place, to pay the Major a visit. But, would you believe it, sir! I crossed the ferry a little after dark, and have yet found nobody that would show me the way to his dwelling; only, an hour or two since, I was told to wait here, and Major Molineux would pass by."

"Can you describe the man who told you this?" inquired the gentleman.

"Oh, he was a very ill-favored fellow, sir," replied Robin, "with two great bumps on his forehead, a hook nose, fiery eyes; and what struck me as the strangest, his face was of two different colors. Do you happen to know such a man, sir?"

"Not intimately," answered the stranger, "but I chanced to meet him a little time previous to your stopping me. I believe you may trust his word, and that the Major will very shortly pass through this street in the mean time, as I have a singular curiosity to witness your meeting, I will sit down here upon the steps and bear you company."

He seated himself accordingly, and soon engaged his companion in animated discourse. It was but of brief continuance, however, for a noise of shouting, which had long been remotely audible, drew so much nearer that Robin inquired its cause.

"What may be the meaning of this uproar?" asked he. "Truly, if your town be always as noisy, I shall find little sleep while I am an inhabitant."

"Why, indeed, friend Robin, there do appear to be three or four riotous fellows abroad tonight," replied the gentleman. "You must not expect all the stillness of your native woods here in our streets. But the watch will shortly be at the heels of these lads and"—

"Ay, and set them in the stocks by peep of day,"interrupted Robin, recollecting his own encounter with the drowsy lantern-bearer. "But, dear sir, if I may trust my ears, an army of watchmen would never make head against such a multitude of rioters. There were at least a thousand voices went up to make that one shout."

"May not a man have several voices, Robin, as well as two complexions?" said his friend.

"Perhaps a man may; but Heaven forbid that a woman should!"

responded the shrewd youth, thinking of the seductive tones of the Major's housekeeper.

The sounds of a trumpet in some neighboring street now became so evident and continual, that Robin's curiosity was strongly excited. In addition to the shouts, he heard frequent bursts from many instruments of discord, and a wild and confused laughter filled up the intervals. Robin rose from the steps, and looked wistfully towards a point whither people seemed to be hastening.

"Surely some prodigious merry-making is going on," exclaimed he. "I have laughed very little since I left home, sir, and should be sorry to lose an opportunity. Shall we step round the corner by that darkish house, and take our share of the fun?"

"Sit down again, sit down, good Robin," replied the gentleman, laying his hand on the skirt of the gray coat. "You forget that we must wait here for your kinsman; and there is reason to believe that he will pass by, in the course of a very few moments."

The near approach of the uproar had now disturbed the neighborhood; windows flew open on all sides; and many heads, in the attire of the pillow, and confused by sleep suddenly broken, were protruded to the gaze of whoever had leisure to observe them. Eager voices hailed each other from house to house, all demanding the explanation, which not a soul could give. Half-dressed men hurried towards the unknown commotion, stumbling as they went over the stone steps that thrust themselves into the narrow footwalk. The shouts, the laughter, and the tuneless bray, the antipodes of music, came onwards with increasing din, till scattered individuals, and then denser bodies began to appear round a corner at the distance of a hundred yards.

"Will you recognize your kinsman, if he passes in this crowd?" inquired the gentleman.

"Indeed, I can't warrant it, sir; but I'll take my stand here, and keep a bright lookout," answered Robin, descending to the outer edge of the pavement.

A mighty stream of people now emptied into the street and came rolling slowly towards the church. A single horseman wheeled the corner in the midst of them, and close behind him came a band of fearful wind-instruments, sending forth a fresher discord now that no intervening buildings kept it from the ear. Then a redder light disturbed the moonbeams, and a dense multitude of torches shone along the street concealing, by their glare, whatever object they illuminated. The single horseman, clad in a military dress, and bearing a drawn sword, rode onward as the leader, and, by his fierce and variegated countenance, appeared like war personified; the red of one cheek was an emblem of fire and sword; the blackness of the other betokened the mourning that attends them. In his train were wild figures in the Indian dress, and many fantastic shapes without a model, giving the whole march a visionary air, as if a dream had broken forth from some feverish brain and were sweeping visibly through the midnight streets. A mass of people, inactive, except as applauding spectators, hemmed the procession in; and several women rang along the sidewalk, piercing the confusion of heavier sounds with their shrill voices of mirth or terror.

"The double-faced fellow has his eye upon me," muttered Robin, with an indefinite but an uncomfortable idea that he was himself to bear a part in the pageantry.

The leader turned himself in the saddle and fixed his glance full upon the country youth, as the steed went slowly by. When Robin had freed his eyes from those fiery ones, the musicians were passing before him, and the torches were close at hand; but the unsteady brightness of the latter formed a veil which he could not penetrate. The rattling of wheels over the stones sometimes found its way to his ear, and confused traces of a human form appeared at intervals, and then melted into the vivid light. A moment more, and the leader thundered a command to halt: the trumpets vomited a horrid breath, and then held their peace; the shouts and laughter of the people died away, and there remained only a universal hum, allied to silence. Right before Robin's eyes was an uncovered cart. There the torches blazed the brightest, there the moon shone out like day, and there, in tar-and-feathery dignity, sat his kinsman, Major Molineux.

He was an elderly man, of large and majestic person, and strong, square features, betokening a steady soul; but steady as it was, his enemies had found means to shake it. His face was pale as death, and far more ghastly; the broad forehead was contracted in his agony, so that his eyebrows formed one grizzled line; his eyes were red and wild, and the foam hung white upon his quivering lip. His whole frame was agitated by a quick and continual tremor, which his pride strove to quell, even in those circumstances of overwhelming humiliation. But perhaps the bitterest pang of all was when his eyes met those of Robin; for he evidently knew him on the instant, as the youth stood witnessing the foul disgrace of a head grown gray in honor. They stared at each other in silence, and Robin's knees shook, and his hair bristled, with a mixture of pity and terror. Soon, however, a bewildering excitement began to seize upon his mind; the preceding adventures of the night, the unexpected appearance of the crowd, the torches, the confused din and the hush that followed, the spectre of his kinsman reviled by that great multitude,—all this, and, more than all, a perception of tremendous ridicule in the whole scene, affected him with a sort of mental inebriety. At that moment a voice of sluggish merriment saluted Robin's ears; he turned instinctively, and just behind the corner of the church stood the lantern-bearer, rubbing his eyes, and drowsily enjoying the lad's amazement. Then he heard a peal of laughter like the ringing of silvery bells; a woman twitched his arm, a saucy eye met his, and he saw the lady of the scarlet petticoat. A sharp, dry cachinnation appealed to his memory, and standing on tiptoe in the crowd, with his white apron over his head, he beheld the courteous little innkeeper. And lastly, there sailed over the heads of the multitude a great, broad laugh, broken in the midst by two sepulchral hems; thus, "Haw, haw, haw,—hem, hem,—haw, haw, haw, haw!"

The sound proceeded from the balcony of the opposite edifice, and thither Robin turned his eyes. In front of the Gothic window stood the old citizen, wrapped in a wide gown, his gray periwig exchanged for a nightcap, which was thrust back from his forehead, and his silk stockings hanging about his legs. He supported himself on his polished cane in a fit of convulsive merriment, which manifested itself on his solemn old features like a funny inscription on a tombstone. Then Robin seemed to hear the voices of the barbers, of the guests of the inn, and of all who had made sport of him that night. The contagion was spreading among the multitude, when all at once, it seized upon Robin, and he sent forth a shout of laughter that echoed through the street,—every man shook his sides, every man emptied his lungs, but Robin's shout was the loudest there. The cloud-spirits peeped from their silvery islands, as the congregated mirth went roaring up the sky. The Man in the Moon heard the far bellow. "Oho," quoth he, "the old earth is frolicsome tonight!"

When there was a momentary calm in that tempestuous sea of sound, the leader gave the sign, the procession resumed its march. On they went, like fiends that throng in mockery around some dead potentate, mighty no more, but majestic still in his agony. On they went, in counterfeit pomp, in senseless uproar, in frenzied merriment, trampling all on an old man's heart. On swept the tumult, and left a silent street behind.

"Well, Robin, are you dreaming?" inquired the gentleman, laying his hand on the youth's shoulder.

Robin started, and withdrew his arm from the stone post to which he had instinctively clung, as the living stream rolled by him. His cheek was somewhat pale, and his eye not quite as lively as in the earlier part of the evening.

"Will you be kind enough to show me the way to the ferry?" said he, after a moment's pause.

"You have, then adopted a new subject of inquiry?" observed his companion, with a smile.

"Why, yes, sir," replied Robin, rather dryly. "Thanks to you, and to my other friends, I have at last met my kinsman, and he will scarce desire to see my face again. I begin to grow weary of a town life, sir. Will you show me the way to the ferry?"

"No, my good friend Robin,—not to-night, at least," said the gentle-man. "Some few days hence, if you wish it, I will speed you on your journey. Or, if you prefer to remain with us, perhaps, as you are a shrewd youth, you may rise in the world without the help of your kinsman, Major Molineux."

SELECTED
BIBLIOGRAPHY

Abrams, M. H. *The Milk of Paradise: The Effect of Opium Visions on the Works of Dequincey, Crabbe, Francis Thompson and Coleridge.* New York: Harper and Row, 1970.

Amis, Kingsley. *New Maps of Hell.* New York: Harcourt Brace, 1960.

Brown, Norman O. "Apocalypse: The Place of Mystery in the Life of the Mind," *Harper's Magazine,* May 1961, pp. 46-49.

Buchan, John, *The Novel and the Fairy Tale.* English Association Pamphlet no. 79. London, 1931.

Bush, Douglas. *Mythology and the Renaissance Tradition in English Poetry.* New revised ed. New York: Norton, 1963.

———. *Mythology and the Romantic Tradition in English Poetry.* New York: Norton, 1963.

Caligor, Leopold and Rollo May. *Dreams and Symbols: Man's Unconscious Language.* New York: Basic Books, 1968.

Campbell, Joseph. *The Flight of the Wild Gander.* New York: Viking, 1969.

———. *The Hero With a Thousand Faces.* New York: The Bollingen Foundation, 1949; rpt. New York: Meridian, 1959.

———. *The Masks of God.* 4 vols.: Vol. I, *Primitive Mythology*; Vol. II, *Oriental Mythology*; Vol. III, *Occidental Mythology*; Vol. IV, *Creative Mythology.* New York: Viking, 1970.

Cassirer, Ernst. *An Essay on Man.* New Haven: Yale University Press, 1944.

Cohn, Norman. *The Pursuit of the Millenium: Revolutionary Millenarians and Mystical Anarchists of the Middle Ages.* Revised and Expanded ed. New York: Oxford, 1970.

Cook, Elizabeth. *The Ordinary and the Fabulous.* Cambridge: The University Press, 1969.

Eliade, Mircea. *Myths, Dreams and Mysteries: The Encounter between Contemporary Faiths and Archaic Realities.* Trans. Philip Mairet. New York: Harpers, 1961.

———. *Myth and Reality.* New York: Harper, 1963.

Frankfort, H. et. al. *The Intellectual Adventure of Western Man.* Chicago: University of Chicago Press, 1946; rpt. as *Before Philosophy.* Baltimore: Penguin, 1949.

Freud, Sigmund. *The Interpretation of Dreams,* in *The Complete Psychological Works of Sigmund Freud.* Vol. 5. Trans. and ed. James

Strachey and Anna Freud. London: Hogarth Press, 1955–62. Trans.
A. A. Brill. New York: The Modern Library, 1950.

———. *On Creativity and the Unconscious.* New York: Harper and
Row, 1958.

Fromm, Erich. *The Forgotten Language.* New York: Grove Press, 1957.

Frye, Northrop. *Anatomy of Criticism; Four Essays.* Princeton, 1957;
rpt. New York: Athaneum, 1966.

Gaster, Theodor H. *The New Golden Bough: An Abridgement of the
Classic Work by Sir James Fraser.* New York, 1959; rpt. New York:
New American Library, 1964.

———. *Myth, Legend, and Custom in the Old Testament: A Comparative Study with Chapters from Sir James Fraser's Folklore in the Old
Testament.* New York: Harper and Row, 1969.

Graves, Robert. *The Greek Myths.* Baltimore: Penguin, 1955.

———. *The White Goddess: An Historical Grammar of Poetic Myth.*
Amended and enlarged ed. New York: Vintage, 1959.

Hartland, Edwin. *The Science of Fairy Tales.* London, 1891; rpt. De-
troit: The Singing Tree Press, 1968.

Heller, Erich. *The Artist's Journey into the Interior and other Essays.*
New York: Random House, 1965.

Holland, Norman. *The Dynamics of Literary Response.* New York:
Oxford, 1968.

Hoffman, Daniel G. *Form and Fable in American Fiction.* New York:
Oxford, 1961.

Hooke, S. H., ed. *Myth: A Symposium.* Bloomington: Indiana University Press, 1955.

Huxley, Aldous. *The Doors of Perception.* New York: Harper, 1963.

Jung, C. G., et. al. *Man and His Symbols.* New York: Dell, 1968.

———. *Psyche and Symbol.* Garden City, N.Y.: Doubleday, 1958.

Kermode, Frank. *The Sense of an Ending: Studies in the Theory of
Fiction.* New York: Oxford, 1967.

Kirk, G. S. *Myth: Meaning and Function.* Berkeley and Los Angeles:
University of California Press, 1971.

Laing, R. D. *The Divided Self.* Baltimore: Penguin, 1965.

———. *The Politics of Experience.* New York: Pantheon, 1967; rpt.
New York: Ballantine, 1968.

Lawrence, D. H. *Apocalypse.* New York, 1932; rpt. New York: Viking,
1966.

———. *Psychoanalysis and the Unconscious* and *Fantasia of the Unconscious.* New York: Viking, 1960.

Levi-Strauss, Claude. *The Raw and the Cooked: Introduction to a
Science of Mythology.* Trans. John and Doreen Weightman. New
York: Harper and Row, 1969.

Neumann, Erich. *Art and the Creative Unconscious.* Trans. Ralph
Manheim. New York: Pantheon, 1959.

Penzoldt, Peter. *The Supernatural in Fiction.* New York: The Humanities Press, 1965.

Raglan, Fitz Roy. *Death and Rebirth: A Study in Comparative Religion.* London: Watts, 1945.

————. *The Hero: A Study in Tradition, Myth, and Drama.* New York: Vintage, 1965.

————. *Jocasta's Crime: An Anthropological Study.*

Raine, Kathleen. *Defending Ancient Springs.* New York: Oxford, 1967.

Rank, Otto. Beyond Psychology. Camden, N.J.: Haddon, 1941. (private printing)

————. *The Myth of the Birth of the Hero.* New York: Knopf, 1959.

Riceour, Paul. *The Symbolism of Evil.* New York: Harper and Row, 1967.

Roheim, Geza. *The Eternal Ones of the Dream.* New York: International Universities Press, 1945.

————. *The Gates of the Dream.* New York: International Universities Press, 1969.

Roszak, Theodore. *The Making of a Counter-Culture.* Garden City, N.Y.: Doubleday, 1969.

Scarborough, Dorothy. *The Supernatural in Modern English Fiction.* New York: Octagon, 1967.

Senior, John. *The Way Down and Out: The Occult in Symbolist Literature.* New York: Greenwood Press, 1968.

Sewell, Elizabeth. *The Orphic Voice.* New Haven: Yale, 1960.

Shumaker, Wayne. *Literature and the Irrational.* Englewood Cliffs, N.J.: Prentice-Hall, 1960.

Thomson, William Irwin. *At the Edge of History: Speculations on the Transformation of Culture.* New York: Harper and Row, 1971.

Tolkien, J. R. R. *Tree and Leaf.* Boston: Houghton Mifflin, 1964.

Ussher, A. and C. von Metzradt. *Enter These Enchanted Woods: An Interpretation of Grimm's Fairy Tales.* Chester Springs, Pa.: Dufour Press, 1966.

Van Gennep, Arnold. *The Rites-of-Passage.* Chicago: University of Chicago Press, 1960.

Vickery, John B. *Myth and Literature: Contemporary Theory and Practice.* Lincoln: The University of Nebraska Press, 1966.

Weisinger, Herbert. *The Agony and the Triumph: Papers on the Use and Abuse of Myth.* East Lansing: Michigan State University Press, 1964.

Weston, Jessie L. *From Ritual to Romance.* Cambridge, 1920; rpt. Garden City, N.Y.: Doubleday, 1952.

Wheelwright, Philip. *The Burning Fountain: A Study in the Language of Symbolism.* Bloomington: Indiana University Press, 1954.

————. *Metaphor and Reality.* Bloomington: Indiana University Press, 1962.

Wilson, Colin. *The Strength to Dream: Literature and the Imagination.* Boston: Houghton Mifflin, 1962.

Zaehner, R. C. *Mysticism: Sacred and Profane.* Oxford: Clarendon Press, 1957.

Zimmern, Heinrich. *The King and the Corpse.* Princeton: Princeton University Press, 1956.